MW00527494

# Praise for
# THE AGE OF REVOLUTIONS

"Between 1760 and 1825, two generations of revolutionaries challenged old inequalities in Europe and the Americas. A fascinating book about the individual trajectories and the generational divides that contributed to this decisive era in the history of equality."

—Thomas Piketty, *New York Times*–bestselling author of *Capital in the Twenty-First Century*

"*The Age of Revolutions* offers a vivid and insightful account of an era that did much to create the world we live in today. Drawing on a remarkable range of historical sources, Nathan Perl-Rosenthal carefully traces how radical ideas, political movements, and counter-revolutionary reactions flourished within and between societies. He makes clear the ambiguity of historical outcomes. Even as mass activism emerged on the world stage, setting the stage for revolutions to come, elements of old regimes—notably slavery—survived, mocking the new language of equal rights. As a result, Perl-Rosenthal shows, subsequent generations throughout the Atlantic world had to continue the revolutionary project."

—Eric Foner, author of *The Second Founding*

"In this magisterial survey of the Age of Revolutions, Perl-Rosenthal ranges boldly across time and space, exploring familiar sites like Philadelphia and Paris alongside others less known, like Indigenous Peru or Hasidic Poland. Grounded in archives in multiple languages on three continents, this extraordinarily ambitious book challenges traditional ways of thinking about revolutionary change. An impressive accomplishment."

—François Furstenberg, author of *When the United States Spoke French*

"Perl-Rosenthal delivers a beautifully written and deeply considered account of the Atlantic Age of Revolutions. His stands with the best new work on this key era, highlighting the long fights that give rise to political change, the ironies and illiberalism that characterize such fights, and the legacies they bequeath. Both panoramic and granular, *The Age of Revolutions* makes one really feel and experience the fraught changes seen by the many ages and stages, and most especially the diverse people, that made revolution."

—Sujit Sivasundaram, author of
*Waves Across the South*

"Perl-Rosenthal's book is a tour de force of originality and erudition. A vivid new interpretation, in elegant prose, of the generations who transformed the Atlantic world and founded new nations on the American continent. From the independence of the United States to the emancipation of Haiti and Peru, without omitting the political eruptions in Europe, the book synthesizes the latest research and develops new interpretations in accessible, elegant prose. Weaving together famous episodes and little-known characters and events, *The Age of Revolutions* makes an argument about the limits of the revolutions' emancipatory and egalitarian character. Vividly describing individual trajectories, with an extraordinary mastery of facts and historiography, Perl-Rosenthal draws a new map of the revolutionary Atlantic, stretching from the Netherlands to the Andes, via Paris, Saint-Domingue, and Philadelphia."

—Clément Thibaud, School for Advanced
Studies in the Social Sciences

# THE AGE OF REVOLUTIONS

**Also by Nathan Perl-Rosenthal**

*Citizen Sailors:*
*Becoming American in the Age of Revolution*

# THE AGE OF REVOLUTIONS

## AND THE GENERATIONS WHO MADE IT

NATHAN PERL-ROSENTHAL

BASIC BOOKS
New York

*For my parents*

---



Cover design by Emmily O'Connor
Cover images © Bridgeman Images; © MM_Photos / Shutterstock.com


Basic Books
Hachette Book Group
1290 Avenue of the Americas, New York, NY 10104
www.basicbooks.com

Printed in the United States of America

First Edition: February 2024

Published by Basic Books, an imprint of Hachette Book Group, Inc. The Basic Books name and logo is a registered trademark of the Hachette Book Group.



Print book interior design by Bart Dawson.

Library of Congress Cataloging-in-Publication Data

Names: Perl-Rosenthal, Nathan, 1982– author.
Title: The age of revolutions : and the generations who made it / Nathan Perl-Rosenthal.
Description: First edition. | New York : Basic Books, 2024. | Includes bibliographical references and index.
Identifiers: LCCN 2023028253 | ISBN 9781541603196 (hardcover) | ISBN 9781541603202 (ebook)
Subjects: LCSH: Revolutions—History—18th century. | History, Modern—18th century. | Revolutions—History—19th century. | United States—History—Revolution, 1775–1783. | France—History—Revolution, 1789–1799. | Haiti—History—Revolution, 1791–1804.
Classification: LCC D295 .P47 2024 | DDC 303.6/4090333—dc23/eng/20230812
LC record available at https://lccn.loc.gov/2023028253

ISBNs: 9781541603196 (hardcover), 9781541603202 (ebook)

LSC-C

Printing 1, 2023

# CONTENTS

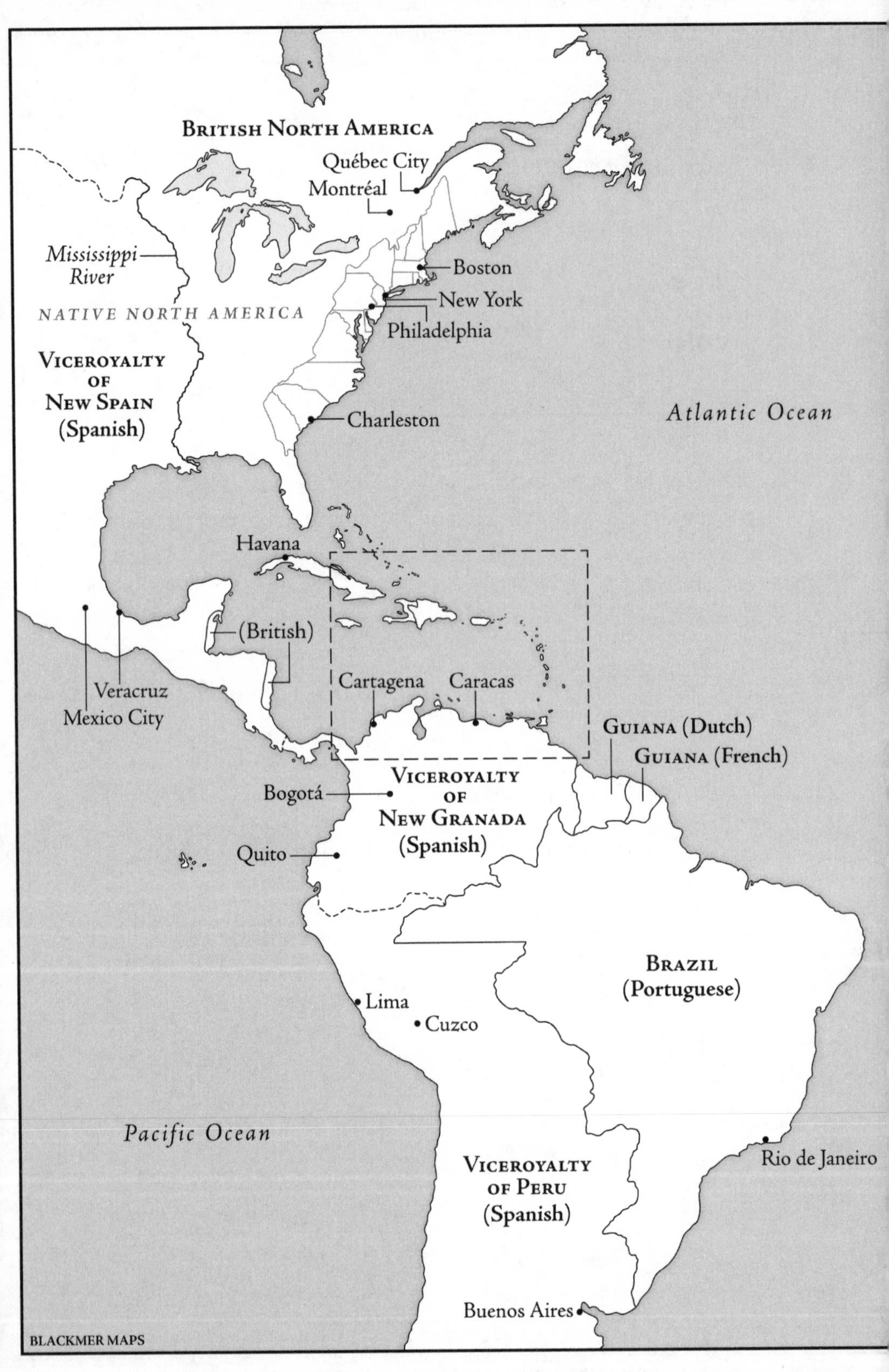
British North America
Québec City
Montréal
Mississippi River
Boston
New York
Native North America
Philadelphia
Viceroyalty of New Spain (Spanish)
Charleston
Atlantic Ocean
Havana
(British)
Veracruz
Mexico City
Cartagena
Caracas
Guiana (Dutch)
Guiana (French)
Viceroyalty of New Granada (Spanish)
Bogotá
Quito
Brazil (Portuguese)
Lima
Cuzco
Pacific Ocean
Rio de Janeiro
Viceroyalty of Peru (Spanish)
Buenos Aires
BLACKMER MAPS

ATLANTIC WORLD, ca. 1760

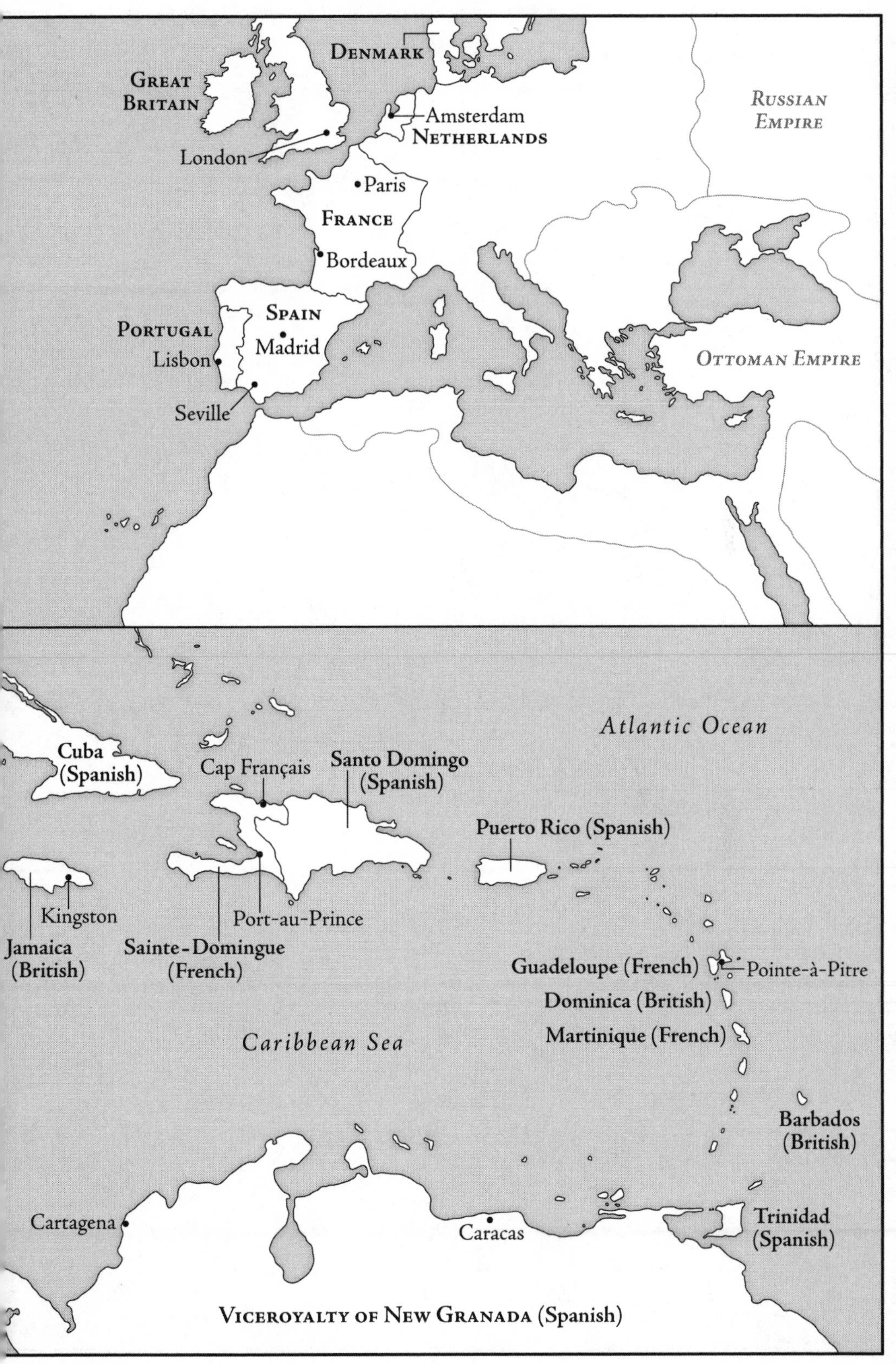

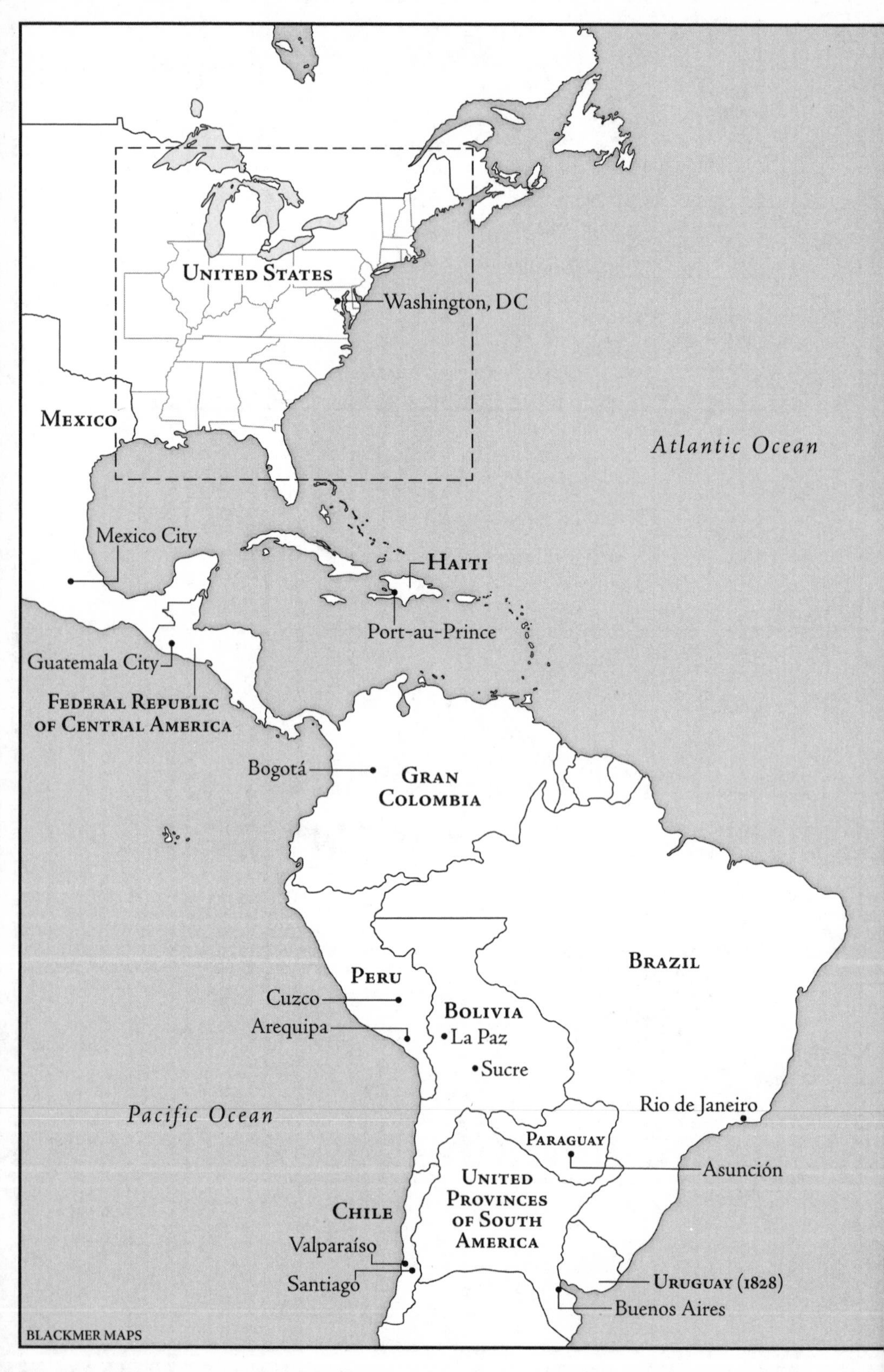

United States
Washington, DC
Mexico
Atlantic Ocean
Mexico City
Haiti
Port-au-Prince
Guatemala City
Federal Republic
of Central America
Bogotá
Gran
Colombia
Brazil
Peru
Cuzco
Bolivia
Arequipa
La Paz
Sucre
Pacific Ocean
Rio de Janeiro
Paraguay
Asunción
United
Provinces
of South
America
Chile
Valparaíso
Santiago
Uruguay (1828)
Buenos Aires
BLACKMER MAPS

ATLANTIC WORLD, ca. 1825

# INTRODUCTION

JOHN ADAMS'S LONG LIFE BEGAN IN ONE WORLD AND ENDED IN another. The year he was born, 1737, a handful of kings ruled over most of Europe and a good part of the American landmass. He grew up in a world of empires built around political and social hierarchies that set the rulers apart from the ruled. By the time Adams died in 1826, a series of revolutions on both sides of the Atlantic had swept away much of this old regime: the American, French, and Haitian Revolutions; the Spanish American independence movements; and a host of smaller uprisings. The world they made was one in which republics and individual rights, though not necessarily equality, were in the ascendant. They varied in their scope and aims, but contemporaries saw unity in their diversity: Thomas Paine, writer and legislator, spoke for many when he anointed the period a single "age of revolutions."[1]

The era's revolutions were a work of both light and shade. They shattered the empires that had bracketed the Atlantic Ocean, creating dozens of new states, but did so in part through a series of destructive wars. Kings in France, North America, Spain, and much of western and central Europe were overthrown, at least temporarily, and republican regimes rose in their place. These governments, based on the sovereignty of the people, gave the populace a new voice in politics, yet most excluded women and non-white people from full citizenship. The new nations' leaders not infrequently used elections to win and retain dictatorial power. And though some revolutionaries challenged the institution of slavery, enslavement persisted and grew in many jurisdictions.

An archipelago of paper spread across three continents documents the lives of the revolutions' protagonists. Take Louis-Augustin Bosc, born in France when Adams was twenty-two. His journals and letters, held in two high-ceilinged Paris libraries, tell the story of a deep friendship with leaders of the French Revolution and a decades-long struggle to find his way after they were murdered during the Terror. Or Maria Rivadeneyra, the wellborn prioress of a convent in Peru. Her story is written in fat bundles in Spain's General Archive of the Indies and slim dossiers in one-room archives in Cuzco. In 1780, as Adams traveled in Europe as an emissary of the revolutionary United States, Madre Maria was weighing whether to support a massive Native-led rebellion. Three decades later, her nephew took part in some of the early movements toward Spanish American independence. A box of neatly organized business papers, tucked inside another family's collection in a Philadelphia archive, is what survives of Marie Bunel. Born into slavery in the French island colony of Saint-Domingue, she became a successful trader under the old regime and a confidant of Toussaint Louverture, the Haitian Revolution's preeminent leader.

How these individuals and other revolutionaries transformed the political world is the subject of this book: the first history of the age of revolutions to encompass the entire period from the 1760s to the 1820s on both sides of the Atlantic Ocean. While no history can claim to be comprehensive, I aim to understand the age of revolutions as a whole, both geographically and temporally. This was the challenge laid down more than six decades ago by two great historians of the era, R. R. Palmer and Eric Hobsbawm. They showed that to understand the period's role in larger historical processes, from the rise of democracy to the emergence of capitalism, one had to look beyond any single revolution. But their books, though foundational, are not the final word. An enormous amount of new knowledge has accumulated about the revolutionary era since Palmer's second volume appeared in 1964, especially about ordinary people and revolutionary culture. Both historians also slighted two regions, the Caribbean and Spanish America, that played a crucial part in how the revolutionary era unfolded. I follow the trail that Palmer and Hobsbawm mapped out but did not quite travel themselves: a history that traverses the entire sixty-year period, on both sides of the Atlantic, across social classes.[2]

Showing how revolutionaries organized and mobilized politically is at the center of the story that I tell. Political revolutions have multiple causes: new ideas, political and social tensions, a leadership ready to take the reins. But what makes a revolution happen, in the most immediate sense, is political organizing and political mobilization. Revolutionaries organize by making connections with one another and creating the means, informal or institutional, to work together toward common goals. Mobilization means that revolutionaries recruit a significant segment of the population to their cause—which is essential for major and lasting changes in a political system to occur. I argue that it took two generations for durable mass political movements to emerge in the age of Atlantic revolutions. The first generation, which dominated revolutions before 1800, largely failed to create such movements; the second generation, rising in the early nineteenth century, succeeded. The slow development of mass politics across two generations had profound political consequences, shaping each of the era's revolutions and leaving an imprint on the political cultures and institutions that the era created.[3]

During the first three decades of unrest in the Atlantic world, circa 1765 to 1799, patriots struggled to organize political movements that could bridge classes and racial groups. The revolutions during these decades began in North America, where British colonists rose against imperial taxes and reforms, and in Spanish South America, where armed rebellions pitted colonists, Natives, and the imperial government against one another. Smaller revolts followed during the 1780s in the Netherlands, the Swiss Confederation, and Belgium (then part of the Habsburg empire). In 1789, the Kingdom of France broke out into a revolution that would, in less than four years, transform the continent's most powerful country into a republic. In 1791, enslaved people in France's preeminent Caribbean colony, Saint-Domingue, began a decade-long revolutionary struggle for emancipation. After 1795, French armies spurred the overthrow of governments in the Low Countries, Switzerland, and parts of Italy and Germany. France itself experienced a further series of abrupt political changes during the middle years of the 1790s, culminating in the seizure of power by Napoleon Bonaparte in 1799.

The actors in this first wave of revolutions had worldviews that were shaped by their upbringing in the hierarchical world of the mid-eighteenth-century Atlantic empires. A worldview, or what the social scientist Pierre Bourdieu called a "habitus," is a mental matrix or set of principles for navigating the world. Each person's habitus is formed in early life by the kind of society in which the young person grows up. Early experiences become an inner template, a set of expectations about how the world works, which influences how the individual behaves throughout later life. All the members of the first revolutionary generation, from the enslaved person to the prince, had been reared in a world in which largely fixed social statuses were an inescapable "social fact," a lived reality that pervaded their societies. Their early lives had been an education in living with hierarchy, teaching them to stand, speak, and act in ways that protected their status while grasping for whatever advantages might be winnable. Social structures and stratification were not the same in every part of the Atlantic world, to be sure. But the variations were differences of degree, not of kind. Even in regions with strong egalitarian traditions, social and political hierarchy was a fact of life.[4]

The hierarchical reflexes of the first-generation revolutionaries, acting as so many barriers between class and racial groups, made it difficult for them to form sustained political movements. The problem was already apparent during the political crises in British North America and Spanish Peru that inaugurated the age of revolutions. The North American patriot movement was divided between elite and working-class wings: both wings largely excluded Black Americans and they pursued distinct strategies of resistance to the British government. Riven by internal divisions, the patriot movement teetered repeatedly on the edge of collapse between 1765 and 1775; it owed most of its victories to the imperial government's missteps. Politics in the United States remained quite status bound after the colonies declared their independence in 1776. Similar divisions undercut the revolutionary movement in Spanish Peru. A powerful Native-led revolt in 1780 was crushed by the government with the help of American-born colonists. A prolonged conflict over local governance then ensued between the imperial authorities and those same colonists, which ended in the colonists' defeat.

Revolutionaries in Europe during the 1780s and early 1790s had if anything even more trouble uniting populations with divergent worldviews. The 1787 collapse of an initially powerful patriot movement in the Netherlands came about in good part because its elite and working-class arms could not agree on how to collaborate. The French Revolution, beginning in 1789, had greater success and a wider impact. Yet at its center, in Paris, it was perpetually unstable: the revolution went through half a dozen distinct political regimes between 1789 and 1799 and experienced repeated bloody purges of its leadership. This instability had multiple causes, but a crucial part of the story was that revolutionary elites and working-class patriots had sharply different approaches to organizing and ideas about who should lead. This pattern of damaging internal division was repeated, with some variations, in the many client states that revolutionary France created after 1794, the so-called sister republics.

Saint-Domingue, where the first modern antislavery revolution began in 1791, experienced another version of this early revolutionary pattern. The island was more riven by structures of domination than any place in the Atlantic world: a slave society, it was ruled by a small population of free people who held 90 percent of the island's inhabitants in permanent bondage. A host of fine gradations existed within these categories, with major differences between wealthy white planters and other white people, and a substantial population of free people of color who held a middle space between the free and the enslaved. The revolution took shape in and around these complex divisions. The initial revolt of the enslaved had been preceded by an unsuccessful revolt led by wealthy free people of color. Once the revolution had begun, many of the caste and class groupings developed their own military forces and sought to defend their prerogatives against the others. When collaborations did develop across lines of caste and class, they were always shadowed by suspicion.

By 1799, patriots' inability to sustain large-scale political mobilizations had left many of their revolutions looking distinctly wobbly. France's republican government, along with those of many of its sister states, was teetering on the edge of collapse by 1799. Formerly enslaved people had gained control of Saint-Domingue, but their freedom remained under severe threat. Spanish America was back under the thumb of its imperial government. Even the United States, which had a relatively stable republican government, was bitterly divided internally and at risk of being drawn into wars it could not win. The fate of the first wave of revolutions appeared very uncertain. Their various promises, including independence, republican government, local autonomy, and great social equality, were nowhere firmly established.

The first wave of revolutions nonetheless succeeded in disrupting the social, economic, and political structures of the eighteenth-century Atlantic empires. Purposeful political changes eroded some of the foundations of the old regime, including monarchies, legal privileges, and a variety of aristocratic ruling bodies. Just as important were the indirect effects of political change, especially the havoc wrought by revolution-sparked wars. These wars swept up tens of thousands in a whirlwind of destruction. Fortunes were made and lost, injecting significant mobility—both upward and downward—into Atlantic societies.

The Atlantic-wide crisis of the late eighteenth century was an incubator in which the second revolutionary generation was born, grew up, and came to maturity. Those born after 1760 in most regions of the Atlantic world experienced firsthand the disruptions that the revolutions caused. Napoleon Bonaparte, born in 1769, is a good example: he was a child during the American Revolution and just twenty when the Bastille fell. These younger revolutionaries' upbringing in a world set in motion—a chaotic, exciting, frightening world—shaped their worldviews in ways that were quite different from those of their elders. The members of this second revolutionary generation took for granted that social status was changeable and not fixed. (Naturally, there were outliers in both directions; generational shifts always occur along a spectrum.)[5]

As they came to maturity around 1800, members of this generation became the engines of a major cultural shift. Theaters, dance halls, and other public spaces proliferated in which members of different classes and castes were present on terms of relative equality. Gentlemen in places as different as Washington, DC, and Cuzco began to socialize on terms of relative equality with the lower orders. Younger members of the elite were also far more accepting of significant social mobility than their parents had been. A different social imaginary accompanied these changes in practice. Playwrights and visual artists found ready audiences for stories about mobility between and among castes and classes. Religious movements flourished on both sides of the Atlantic, Jewish as well as Christian, that reimagined spiritual success as within the reach of all believers rather than just a small elite.

These younger people became the main protagonists of a second wave of revolutions, which included continuations of prior revolutionary movements and extensions of political agitation into new areas. In 1804, Haiti declared its independence and solidified a national government. In 1808, under now emperor Napoleon Bonaparte, France invaded Spain and effectively toppled the Spanish monarchy. This sparked a political crisis in Spanish America that would last most of two decades. Spanish Americans innovated new forms of government, seized control of state power, and declared their independence. Between 1806 and 1814, French arms and diplomacy pushed major political change throughout Europe, reaching as far as Poland. The restoration of the French monarchy in 1815, after Napoleon's fall, ushered in a broad return to kingly government in Europe, though hardly a return to the old regime. In the Americas, the hemisphere's independent states continued to change rapidly, including radical expansions of the franchise, strikes against the institution of slavery, and the creation of new political institutions. These transformations culminated in the early 1820s, when nearly all of Spanish America secured its independence.

Having grown accustomed to sharing social and cultural spaces, elite and working-class revolutionaries after 1800 were far more comfortable than their forebears had been taking part in mixed-class political movements. Where elite patriots in 1780 might have considered it dishonorable or disreputable to associate too closely with working-class patriots, by 1820 this stigma had substantially diminished. Acceptance of social mobility made it possible for activists from the lower orders to rise to leadership positions and for elites to accept or co-opt them. Lowborn leaders became more numerous and more prominent after 1800. Mobility also forced elites to pay closer attention to demands "from below." Elite leaders, recognizing that their positions were not immutable, took active measures to manage their coalitions. All of this helped to foster political mobilizations that were, on the whole, much more durable and at a larger scale than those before 1800.

Sustained, large-scale mobilizations, like a more advanced plow, could furrow the political soil more deeply. The post-1800 mobilizations could accomplish changes that had not been possible before. This was plainly visible in the durable new forms of political life that emerged. Political parties stabilized in the United States, and both Saint-Domingue and western Europe gained their first stable political regimes since 1789. In Spanish America, where revolution had previously been impeded, new political units erupted into existence with unprecedented speed after 1808. These new regimes successfully pushed through far-reaching political reforms, including a number that had failed before, such as expansions of suffrage, reforms of administration and the law, and the abolition or limitation of slavery.

The powerful political mobilization that took place after 1800 could turn in a number of directions. Alexis de Tocqueville, the great nineteenth-century French political observer and theorist, suggested as much in a passage in *Democracy in America*. There were two ways that "equality" could be reflected in politics, he wrote: "Rights must either be given to each citizen or given to no one." Peoples "must choose . . . between the sovereignty of the people and the absolute power of a king." Tocqueville oversimplified the matter when he suggested that there were only two options. In practice, every revolutionary state opted to grant rights to some and not to others. But his intuition that mass politics built on ideas of equality could go in multiple directions is spot on. Mass mobilization could lead to democratic outcomes, in which everyone was endowed with a piece of the sovereignty. Or it could become the foundation for tyranny and one-man rule.[6]

During the quarter century after 1800, many of the revolutionary movements in the Atlantic world took an illiberal turn. New monarchies and empires developed, first in France under Napoleon and then in the rest of Europe. These monarchies, though formally conservative, had revolutionary projects of their own. The Dutch monarchy created in 1814–1815, for instance, modernized the Netherlands' political and economic systems. On Saint-Domingue, in the United States, and in Spanish America, political movements strengthened equality for the majority at the expense of minorities. The enslaved, free people of color, and Native peoples were pushed out of the charmed circle of the polity in order to permit equality to reign within. Progress that had been made on the rights of women was reversed in a number of regions, including the loss of rights to vote and divorce that had been acquired earlier. The mass movements that took off after 1800, in sum, fulfilled some of the greatest dreams of the early revolutionary era but only by dint of abandoning or betraying others.

In order to tell the story of the Atlantic revolutions over six decades, I have adopted a structure that brings key regions, events, and groups of revolutionary actors into focus sequentially. The book begins in the prerevolutionary period and goes through the 1820s, moving around the Atlantic world as it moves forward in time. In each chapter, I have made choices about which revolution to spotlight, which episodes within it to consider at length, and which actors should have pride of place. These decisions are based on my sense of which moments are most necessary and illuminating for understanding the revolutionary era. Some will be unsurprising: the American, French, Haitian, and Spanish American revolutions each get extended treatment. Other choices, including my attention to the republican movement in Genoa, to Hasidism and Protestantism, or to monarchic revolutions after 1800, may be unexpected. These more offbeat movements illuminate larger phenomena and offer "limit cases" that reveal the outer boundaries of widespread revolutionary processes.[7]

The focus throughout these chapters, even as they move from place to place, remains squarely on how revolutionaries organized political movements, especially across class and caste divides. This means devoting special attention to the mechanics of political organizing while putting other elements of revolutionary politics in the background. In the case of the French Revolution, for instance, I spend more time teasing out how revolutionary crowds came together, and how they worked with or against political clubs run by gentlemen, than discussing the intricacies of constitutional texts or the revolutionary French state's fiscal strategies. In general, constitutions and constitution making, which were most often the product of political organizing rather than the cause, remain in the background. And while warfare is an important element of the story, the details of grand strategy and individual battles remain largely off in the distance.

There are also limits to the book's geographic scope. It encompasses North and South America, the Caribbean, and Europe. It does not deal in depth with either Africa or Native America, the large swath of the American continent that remained under effective Native rule during this period. Excellent recent scholarship has shown the distinctiveness of these regions' political and cultural development during this period. They cannot and ought not be folded unceremoniously into the Atlantic revolutions framework that emerged out of European and Euro-American empires and nations. Similarly, the book learns from and complements new work on the age of revolutions in the Pacific and Indian Ocean regions without presuming to include them.[8]

Throughout the book, I combine three distinct methodologies that historians have developed for studying worldviews and practices in the past. One approach is biographical. I have selected a small group of individuals whose political lives and worlds I study in detail. Four of them—John Adams, Louis-Augustin Bosc, Marie Bunel, and Maria Rivadeneyra—have already been introduced. John Quincy Adams, John Adams's son; Eudora Roland, the daughter of Bosc's friends; and Joseph Bunel, Marie's husband, each get shorter biographical treatment. These seven lives, though not representative in any strict sense, offer a way into the politics of the revolutionary era from the broad middle of the social spectrum. I chose individuals who inhabited different regions and somewhat different social strata: they include three women and four men, two North Americans, two born in the Caribbean or South America, and three born in Europe. Several were people of color or had intimate ties to communities of color. This diversity makes these individuals good entry points into distinct corners of the revolutionary world inhabited by people of different races, ethnicities, sexes, and homelands. Most of these individuals are relatively unknown, even to historians, and though all were deeply involved in revolutionary politics, none except for the Adamses held major political office.[9]

A second approach to studying the revolutionary world involves examining the practices of sociable and collective life: from crowds in the streets to coffee shops, theaters, and clubs to networks of letter writers or religious communities. These communities and collectives were central to the process of political organizing. Several of them, such as the coffeehouse, the political club, and the urban crowd, have long been recognized by historians as crucial to the formation of revolutionary movements. By looking at how these communities functioned, at the mostly unwritten rules by which they constituted and governed themselves, we can catch glimpses of shared worldviews and see how they changed over time. Noting the local variations that were visible in widely shared practices—a crowd in Boston or Cuzco, for instance, looked different from one in Paris—makes possible comparisons and contrasts around the Atlantic.

I use literary, visual, musical, and material cultures as a third way to observe social and political change. The arts were engines of revolutionary politics in the eighteenth and nineteenth centuries: patriots churned out prints, songs, clothing and accessories, and furnishings stamped with political messages. Artistic productions without an obvious political agenda can be even more revealing. Artists and craftspeople are close observers of changes in the world around them and skillful generalizers. The arts refract the world through the conventions of a medium, so a straight line cannot be drawn from artistic object to lived reality. But when read with due attention to their formal properties and social contexts, artists' creations are among the most sensitive instruments available for detecting the vibrations of a seismic political or social transformation in progress.[10]

Three main insights flow from this generational history of the Atlantic revolutions, which may hold lessons for the present day as well. One is, simply, that we should not expect radical political change to happen quickly. There has long been a tendency, in speaking of revolution, to focus on supposedly sharp turning points and dramatic transformations. The instinct to dwell on inflection points has only deepened with the digital conquest of the past thirty years, which has made attention spans grow shorter and given credence to the utopian idea that technology can change "everything" virtually overnight. Buying into this fantasy of instantaneous revolution has significant consequences—most damagingly, a potential loss of faith in the possibility of change if the transformation fails to arrive as quickly as expected.

The history of the Atlantic revolutionary era, as I tell it here, suggests quite a different way of looking at revolutionary change. To be sure, the revolutions of the eighteenth and early nineteenth centuries did sometimes bring about rapid, even abrupt political change. The abolition of legal privilege on the night of August 4, 1789, in the French Revolution and the US Declaration of Independence of July 4, 1776, are classic examples. But it usually took time for deep and enduring change—the kind of change that made the age of Atlantic revolution so important—to occur. North Americans decided during six months in early 1776 to quit the British empire. But it took seven years for Britain to recognize the split and decades longer before the new nation felt secure. For all the sweep of the French National Assembly's August 4 declaration, the full effects of the end of "feudalism" were not felt until years later.[11]

A second implication of this book's argument is that scholars need to rethink the special place that we accord to the American and French Revolutions in the history of modern politics. These revolutions are often celebrated for having invented the model of the stable, democratic-republican nation-state that dominates our world. In this interpretation, Spanish American independence and the Haitian Revolution were part of a "South Atlantic" second wave of revolutions, more autocratic and less stable.[12] This argument is hard to sustain within the wider, generational frame for the revolutionary era that I propose in this book. There were certainly important differences between the revolutions in the South and North Atlantic. But the pattern of change over time, common to the two regions, is more striking. Revolutions before 1800 were radical in vision but limited by the weight of old-regime cultures. Revolutionary coalitions in this period, including those in France and North America, were fragile and unstable. It was the post-1800 revolutionary movements, propelled by a new generation with a more socially flexible vision, that consolidated the revolutionary accomplishments of the first phase—albeit with a significant illiberal slant.

Third, this book offers up an anti-exceptionalist history of the age of revolution. "Exceptionalism," the idea that one of the period's revolutions was uniquely important or singularly transformative, has been a constant companion of revolutionary history since its early days. From the nineteenth century through the late twentieth century, such exceptionalist claims were usually positive. Historians of the French Revolution asserted that "their" revolution was, in the words of one of its preeminent historians, the only "real" revolution in the eighteenth century. Historians of the American Revolution have been no less prone to asserting the centrality of their revolution in "the long sweep of world history" and arguing that it had made "America into the most liberal, democratic, and modern nation in the world." In recent years, there has been a surprising spread of negative exceptionalist views of the American Revolution. These accounts, which are an important correction to the hagiographic histories that circulated unquestioned for far too long, view the American founding as unique in a negative sense, distinctively tainted by the patriot movement's imbrication with slavery and racism.[13]

A generational perspective should have us questioning any exceptionalist version of the revolutionary era. The revolutionaries of the late eighteenth and early nineteenth centuries were certainly fighting to create a new world. But to make revolutionary ideas concrete, to give them reality, they had to work through everyday practices: marching, writing, praying, eating. The inevitable interlocking of theory and practice, vision and reality, meant that everywhere revolution took hold during these sixty years, the ghostly forms of old practices persisted within the body of the new politics. The American Revolution was haunted, to be sure, by the specters of slavery and racial prejudice. Each of the era's revolutions was shadowed by its own old regime, by its protagonists' habits and ways of seeing the world. That tension remains tangible and probably irresolvable—an enduring fissure in the bedrock the Atlantic revolutions lay down, on which our modern political world is built.

# PART I

# THE WEIGHT OF THE OLD REGIME, 1760–1783

# 1
# A HIERARCHICAL WORLD

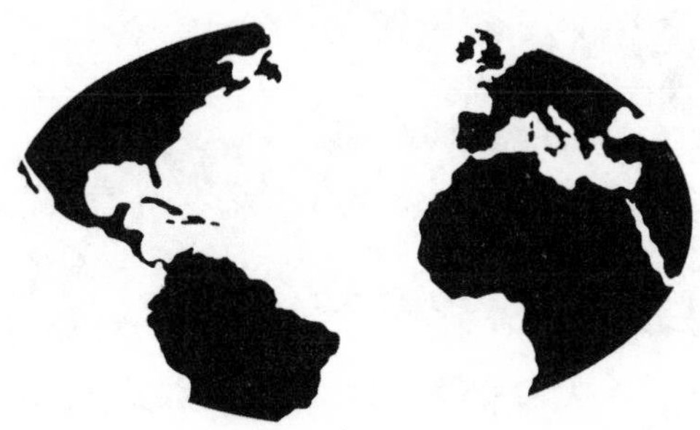

TUESDAY, MARCH 12, 1776. THE PRESIDENTS AND COUNSELORS of the Parlement of Paris, dressed in their scarlet formal robes, filed into one of the great chambers of the palace at Versailles. In the corner rose a high seat, specially constructed for the occasion, covered with a fleur-de-lis tapestry. The counselors and presidents took their seats on benches that extended out from the throne, filling the floor of the large room.[1]

When the time came, the presidents of the *parlement* rose and went to the door, accompanied by bailiffs and heralds, to meet the king. He came surrounded by an entourage of princes, trailing a procession of provincial governors, lieutenants, and knights. In the center of the room, two bailiffs and six heralds went down on their knees, holding ceremonial staffs. Last came the keeper of the seals, the king's chief judicial officer.[2]

A *lit de justice* in the 1780s; print by Abraham Girardet. Courtesy of Musée Carnavalet, Paris.

The grand display, ceremonious even by the standards of the time, staged the performance of a supposedly timeless political order. In this idealized version of the French monarchy, everyone and everything existed permanently in its assigned place in the political cosmos. The exquisitely fine gradations of status conveyed by the ceremonial—who entered when, who sat where—acted out a political order in which each person was fixed in his position circling the center: the king himself.

The king, once seated, spoke only a handful of words. "I have assembled you here to make known my desires," he announced. "My Keeper of Seals will explain them to you."[3] It was the keeper who announced the dramatic commands that the king was making on this day. Having examined the lamentable state of the poor in his kingdom, he had decided to issue a series of edicts that would reform virtually every corner of French society: abolish forced labor service for peasants, allow the free circulation of grains, and dissolve corporate bodies such as guilds.

The men of the *parlement*, one of the kingdom's powerful sovereign courts, objected to the king's commands. The First President gave a biting discourse that criticized the king for forcing the reforms through. His colleague Antoine-Louis Séguier applauded the king for responding to the "frightful situation" in which many poor French people found themselves, unable to "earn their subsistence." Yet he pleaded with the king to not force "property owners" to shoulder the cost of helping them. The *parlementaires* recognized the misery of the peasantry. Great men themselves, they did not want to bear the financial burden of solving the problem.[4]

But the king had come not to listen but to require. The point of the *lit de justice* ("seat [literally: bed] of justice") was to invoke the king as the font of justice and allow him to override the will of his subjects, even the stubborn noblemen of the *parlement*, who had no choice but to "register" (ratify) these edicts. When it was over, when they had done it, the king spoke again, three short sentences: I expect you to conform to my wishes; I wish to rule only by justice and the law; if problems arise, I will solve them. Then he rose and "departed in the same order in which he has entered."[5] The *lit de justice* was over.

The reforms that the king pushed through the *parlement* in 1776 were forward looking. Their goal was to spur economic and social change in the kingdom, leveling some long-standing inequalities. But the *lit de justice* ritual itself, the means by which these reforms were enacted, was anything but modern. The ritual invoked a world fixed in place. The jarring contrast between the program of social reform that the king advanced and the way he forced it onto his recalcitrant subjects reflected the era's larger paradox: the age of revolutions took shape in a distinctively hierarchical world.

Evidence of social and economic stratification in human societies stretches back to well before the earliest recorded history. In the early modern era, roughly 1500 to 1800, inequality remained the norm, and its many forms overlapped and mutually reinforced one another. Foundational to all European societies were a series of supposedly natural hierarchies determined by birth: between nobles and commoners, between men and women, and among members of different racial or ethnic castes. Caste underpinned the social order in Europe's American colonies. Europeans during these centuries gradually came to believe that Native Americans and people of African descent formed separate populations marked by bodily differences. Both groups, by the eighteenth century, were treated as subordinate castes whose status passed from one generation to the next.[6]

Other forms of inequality reinforced the hierarchies of birth. Inherited wealth lay largely though not exclusively in the hands of nobles. Laws sanctioned and sharpened social divisions. Legal privileges granted to guilds and corporations, as well as to established churches, allowed them to avoid taxation and police themselves. In Spanish America, Native communities were laden with burdensome fiscal obligations. The institution of slavery rendered most Black people in the Americas mere chattels in the eyes of the law.[7]

During the seventeenth century, which scholars have called Europe's "century of crisis," a modest softening of some of these hierarchies took place. The 1600s saw unusually destructive warfare and civil unrest across Europe. Crisis conditions made life difficult, but they could have the effect of reducing inequality—or, at least, rendering the power of the dominant classes less secure. Both England's civil war (1630s and 1640s) and Germany's destructive Thirty Years' War (1618 to 1648) may have led to some leveling of economic inequality. Egalitarian political theories certainly flourished: in England, "Levellers" called for the redistribution of the nation's wealth to benefit the poor.[8]

In the late seventeenth century, the trend line began to reverse. Inequality rose again and social stratification was reinforced. In the Americas, this change was driven by a deepening and hardening of the lines separating racial caste groups. The promulgation of the *code noir* (Black code) in French colonies severely limited the rights of enslaved people and curtailed the liberties of free people of color. In Virginia and the Carolinas, newly written slave codes conferred absolute legal power on enslavers and codified the perpetual character of enslavement. Legislators in these and other colonies also limited the avenues for manumission and curbed the rights of free people of color. By the middle of the eighteenth century, those who were descended from Africans, whether free or enslaved, were legally and socially subordinate to white colonists, with little hope of bettering their condition. In Spanish America, Natives had long been considered members of a separate but formally equal "republic of the Indians." During the eighteenth century, the Spanish Crown systematically eroded the autonomy and the limited privileges of this "republic."[9]

Prodigious economic growth powered the eighteenth century's rising tide of inequality on both sides of the Atlantic. Britain, France, and the Netherlands all experienced significant growth throughout the century, driven in good part by their colonial empires. The colonies themselves grew fast. The economic output of British North America increased sevenfold between 1700 and 1774. Parts of Spanish America experienced veritable economic booms. This was particularly the case in regions, such as the Plate River estuary (present-day Buenos Aires), that had been relatively underdeveloped before. Most of this growth was fueled by the labor of the enslaved. It was their work and suffering that brought commodities like sugar, coffee, and tobacco within reach of even the humblest households of free people elsewhere in the Atlantic.[10]

The eighteenth-century economic boom distributed its benefits in a very unequal fashion. White workers, from the cobbler to the skilled weaver, experienced some improvements in their standard of living. As manufacturing and trade increased, what had formerly been luxury goods became more widely and cheaply available. But the gains of these workers were far smaller than those that accrued to the holders of capital: the owners of valuable land in Europe, the owners of land and enslaved people in the Americas, and the owners of productive capital goods such as ships, factories, and the like. The lion's share of the financial benefits of expanding plantations, trade, and manufacturing went to those who were already rich. Precise figures on wealth distribution are limited for the early modern era, but the extant evidence is revealing. In France, the nobility probably accrued an increasing share of national wealth during the eighteenth century, in good measure by absorbing the fortunes non-noble families made in industry, trade, and plantation agriculture.[11]

Conversely, the bottom 90 percent of the Euro-American population probably held a shrinking share of the society's total wealth from the beginning of the eighteenth century to the 1770s. Even relatively egalitarian societies, like Massachusetts, became "more stratified and unequal." The slave societies of the Atlantic world—the Caribbean, the southern coast of North America, and parts of continental Spanish America—exemplified this eighteenth-century drama most sharply. In French Saint-Domingue, nearly 90 percent of the population consisted of enslaved people of African descent. They were, at least as far as the law was concerned, property themselves and thus could own nothing of their own. The remaining 10 percent, plus absentee landlords, held all the island's property. It was the "most extreme case of inequality" for which we have evidence in world history.[12]

Inequality reshaped the cultural fabric of eighteenth-century societies. Rich and poor in Europe had always had different ways of living, from how their homes were organized to their ways of speaking. The eighteenth-century economic divergence heightened and simplified the cultural divide. The elite across the Euro-American world, from the wealthier artisans through the nobility, converged on a culture of gentility whose forms were similar from South America to central Europe. Among its most visible features were a code of civility, restrained elegance in dress, and the habit of socializing in spaces out of the public eye. Differences persisted within this shared elite culture, of course, corresponding to gradations of wealth and regional traditions. But these differences were small by comparison to the growing gulf that separated elite gentility from the cultures of the working classes. Working-class cultures remained more varied from region to region. In one important respect, though, they converged: as elite men and women partly withdrew from public spaces in the eighteenth century, working-class people took them over. In places as different as the streets of Paris and Boston, the plantation fields of Saint-Domingue, and the market squares of Charleston, the lower sorts gained an unexpected measure of dominance.[13]

EVEN FOR THE BEST POSITIONED AND MOST TALENTED, THE ROAD to success in the stratified world of the mid-eighteenth century was long and uncertain. Louis-Augustin Bosc, born in 1759 to a moderately well-off family, was about seventeen when the *lit de justice* of 1776 took place. The first decades of his life illustrate the steep challenges that his family and millions of others like it encountered as they tried to rise in the unequal societies of the late old regime.

Bosc's father, Paul, had the energy of a man on the make. Before Louis-Augustin was born, Paul had already become a minor figure in Paris savant circles, publishing regularly with scientific academies and societies. The recognition he gained came slowly and in insufficient quantity; he felt his essays and experiments were ignored or slighted. In 1769, perhaps tiring of his fruitless efforts to enter the inner circles of Paris science, he accepted an offer to helm a new glass manufacturer near Saint-Flour, in south-central France.[14]

While his father fought to advance, young Louis-Augustin ran "wild" at the home of his maternal grandmother. At the age of ten, he was sent to a boarding school in Dijon. Though the school was run by monks, his teachers did not insist that he appear at mass, and they allowed him—perhaps even encouraged him—to read books by deists and skeptics. The school, too, was an element of the elder Bosc's strategy to rise above his station. Because his maternal grandfather had been an artillery officer, the young Bosc had a leg up on entry into the artillery corps. This called for a scientific and practical education focused on mathematics. Latin and Greek might be fine for poets, but geometry and chemistry were what made the cannons fire right. This did not keep Bosc from imbibing great draughts of eighteenth-century polite culture anyway, lessons in how to carry himself and converse.

Just as Louis-Augustin was reaching the point at which his father hoped to vault him into the French elite, disaster struck. The glass manufacturer into which the elder Bosc had invested both his reputation and his money collapsed in acrimony. There were no longer means for his son to enter the army. Paul sought out another position for Louis-Augustin within the royal administration, a newly created commission on royal lands. Decades later, Louis-Augustin still remembered the exact day that his father had called him back to Paris to take up his post: February 28, 1777. This was a momentous turning point, the end of his formal education and the beginning of a new life of service to the French state.[15]

Louis-Augustin Bosc's new position was intimately connected to the *lit de justice* that had taken place a year earlier. In 1774, a new king had come to the throne, the sixteenth French king named Louis. He had taken over upon the death of his grandfather, King Louis XV—better known as Louis le Bien Aimé, "the beloved." Unlike his grandfather and his predecessor (the Sun King, Louis XIV), the new king was a true product of the eighteenth century. The youthful monarch, though serious and reform minded, was terribly inexperienced. In the space of his first five years on the throne, he whipsawed among advisors who held very different ideas about how to reorganize and restructure the institutions of the monarchy and the state. The *lit de justice* had been part of an effort by one of them, Anne-Robert Turgot, controller-general of finances from 1774 to 1776, to reform the French economy.[16]

Bosc found himself caught up in the accelerating pace of change. The commission to which his father had gotten him appointed was created in 1776 or 1777 by Turgot's successors, Louis-Gabriel Taboureau and the Protestant financier and fiscal reformer Jacques Necker. A year later, in one of the period's abrupt changes of direction, they abolished the commission and with it Bosc's sinecure. Bosc was hardly the only person to find his dreams of glory thwarted by the rapid-fire reforms of Louis XVI's early reign. The marquis de Lafayette, a prominent liberal aristocrat later known for his involvement in the American war, found himself similarly stymied in his military career. He had just managed to get himself appointed to a promising post in a mounted regiment in 1773 when it was rendered superfluous by the new minister of war's plans to reform the army. Lafayette could fall back on his wealthy, powerful family's resources and connections. For Bosc, the loss of his foothold in government was potentially disastrous.[17]

Salvation came along in the form of another government position, this one in the post office. The offer came from Claude-Jean Rigoley d'Ogny, a prominent aristocrat whose son had until recently served in the royal artillery. Rigoley held the powerful position of intendant general of the mails. The position's power came not just from the many opportunities for patronage that it offered, nor from the rich pension that the king bestowed on its holder. As the head of the kingdom's mail and courier services, Rigoley was in a position to receive information before nearly anyone else. Mastery of the mails, in this era before telecommunications, put a kingdom's secrets in one's hands.[18]

A glamorous vision of the mail was hardly in the forefront of Bosc's mind as he began his new job. The early modern mail services were intensely tangible and material. Each letter was written by hand, each envelope hand folded and addressed, closed with sealing wax marked by a thumb or a nub or a recognizable insignia. There were no mechanical sorting machines and few house numbers to which letters could be delivered. Postal workers had to sort the mail by hand, scrutinizing hastily written addresses. The carriers who brought letters to their destination had to navigate the bewildering heterogeneity of addresses anew: some letters came with just a name and a neighborhood, others were sent care of tavern keepers. Bosc's days were filled with utterly mundane matters. Did he wonder what had become of his dreamed-of career as he sat on the administrative council of the postal service, gravely considering the waterproofing of mail carriers' uniforms in Paris?[19]

The young postal employee gamely tried to turn his new position, however uninteresting in itself, into a gateway to some intellectual relevance. One of the fringe benefits of working for the post office was that Bosc could send mail free of charge. Since in this era recipients usually paid for postage, each of his letters represented a small gift to its recipient. The privilege also made him a useful conduit for others' mail. Before long, he claimed in a memoir with some bombast, he had "become the center of the correspondence of all of the naturalists of Europe" and a "friend to thousands of people whom I obliged, though always with moderation."[20]

His boasting aside, the young Bosc at the start of his career faced the same kind of social limitations that had bedeviled his father. From a family with little fortune, which lacked a distinguished military or ecclesiastical record, Bosc had little chance of rising through the traditional ranks of old-regime French society. If he played his cards right and was diligent, he could expect a certain level of comfort and security. By the late 1770s he had already achieved that, with his post bringing in around three thousand livres per year, a small but respectable living for a young gentleman. But the kind of grand destiny to which both he and his father seem to have aspired, one that would touch the upper echelons of French government or science, remained permanently out of reach.

Bosc's experience was echoed in lives all around the Atlantic world. For a child growing up in the mid-eighteenth century, birth was usually destiny. Fixity rather than mobility was what one could expect out of the course of one's life. Even in regions that have often been imagined as more egalitarian, such as British North America, the possibilities for social and economic mobility were limited and dwindling over the course of the eighteenth century.[21]

Fixity was the rule in Massachusetts, one of the economic and cultural centers of Britain's North American colonies. Boston's elite formed a virtual closed corporation. Thomas Hutchinson, lieutenant governor and then governor of the colony during its last years under British rule, was the scion of a family that was already producing colonial leaders in the 1630s. John Hancock, who became one of Hutchinson's principal antagonists as a financier and leader of the American patriot movement, had inherited most of his wealth. Hancock began his life at the top of the social ladder and he ended it there as well. For those who began farther down, the chances of rising were slim. John Adams Sr., the father of the American revolutionary and future US president John Adams, illustrates the point. Born in 1691 into a family of locally prosperous farmers, the elder John Adams enjoyed a respectable position. He farmed and worked as a shoemaker in the colder seasons. Like his ancestors, he took on a role in town government and was prominent in his local church. Yet John Adams Sr. ended his life in almost exactly the same station in which he had begun it: as a small-town notable.

The southern colonies of British North America were more socially rigid than the northern colonies. Arthur Lee, an American revolutionary who served as a diplomat alongside John Adams in the late 1770s, was one of the members of the generational gentry that ruled the southern colonies. His ancestors had come to Virginia during the seventeenth century and amassed a considerable fortune in land. From the 1640s onward, the Lees had served in leadership roles in the colony. Lee's father was himself the inheritor of power: an enslaver of hundreds and one of the colony's most prominent citizens.[22]

The experiences of enslaved people formed a mirror image to those of this permanent southern elite. Take Lizette, an "old Negro Wench" who surfaces briefly in the historical record in Charleston, South Carolina, during the years before the American Revolution. She was a marketer—one of the enslaved women who bought and sold produce, much of it grown by enslaved people in their own gardens. Lizette may have been a relatively prosperous enslaved person: she appeared in the historical record because she was accused of having taken part in a "Robbery," suggesting that she was involved in larger commercial circuits.[23] Yet whatever profits she accrued, Lizette almost certainly was born, lived, and died as an enslaved person. There was no possibility of significant status mobility in her world.

More and more people were being enslaved during these years, crossing the often fatal threshold between freedom and unfreedom. Between 1700 and 1775, the transatlantic slave trade doubled in volume, from a million people every twenty-five years to two million. Those who were enslaved faced the near certitude of a lifetime of bondage as avenues to freedom closed off for enslaved people in much of the Atlantic world.[24]

Fixity was the rule in Spanish America too. A wellborn woman like Maria Rivadeneyra could expect a life of leisure and power. Buoyed by the income from her family's lands and mines, as a young woman she found a prominent place in a Cuzco convent. She remained there, a leading member of the city's female religious hierarchy, until near the end of her life. Manuela Gonsales, a servant in the convent, lived an entirely different kind of life under the same roof. After decades of service to one of the other nuns, she inherited a small cell as a reward for her loyalty to her mistress. Yet she could never hope to find her way to the heights of power and wealth that she saw daily incarnated by Rivadeneyra.

The reality of the eighteenth-century economy and society was inescapably hierarchical. But in a number of this world's corners, dreams of change and ideas of equality were beginning to percolate.

The eighteenth century marked the apogee of the enlightenment, a diffuse and "polyphonic intellectual movement" that ranged over many domains, from philosophy to politics and political economy to social and cultural criticism. Its participants were intellectually diverse but shared some common touch points. Among the most important was a belief that all human beings had a common origin and nature and were on some fundamental level equal. This led many of them to advocate for significant changes to the existing social and political order. Thinkers from many of the enlightenment's disparate strands favored lifting legally mandated or culturally prescribed forms of inequality. Legal barriers to commerce and professions, discrimination against members of minority religions, and luxury were frequent targets of their ire. A small number took up the banner of antislavery and anti-imperialism, though far more found slavery and empire compatible with their concepts of natural (in)equality.[25]

Few of the enlightenment's prominent thinkers dared to challenge monarchy or absolutism. On the contrary, many enlightened writers and projects found a home in the halls of power. Voltaire, one of the most celebrated figures of the French enlightenment, spent years corresponding with Frederick the Great of Prussia and took up residence at his court briefly during the early 1750s. Over the course of the century, some of the most energetic critiques of contemporary society and politics came from within governments. Political economists, lawyers, and government officials had an up-close view of the problems caused by persistent and deepening inequality. When they wrote and spoke about these issues, their arguments spread to wider publics—sometimes by accident, but often quite deliberately.[26]

Older intellectual currents, long circulating around the Atlantic, thrummed with notions of equality. A venerable English radical tradition, originating in the ferment of the English civil war of the previous century, had remained a subterranean stream in the Anglo-American world, kept alive by artisans and working-class radicals. It celebrated republicanism and the leveling of social and economic difference. Similarly republican traditions radiated out from the Netherlands, more or less effectively suppressed by governments. Less radical but more widespread around the Atlantic world were traditions of local autonomy and self-government, often built on ideas of civic or urban equality. In a limited and local fashion, these could provide a foundation for opposition to certain forms of inequality. Enslaved people also fought the ultimate inequality of slavery. Though the mid-eighteenth century saw few large-scale revolts of the enslaved, there is incontrovertible evidence that enslaved people were consistently advocating for themselves and seeking freedom.[27]

New religious movements in the eighteenth century, arising in many faiths and in multiple locations, spoke another kind of challenge to the hierarchical eighteenth-century order. In the Protestant world, the Methodist and Baptist movements took the lead. Methodism developed within the Anglican Church, in opposition to what its founders considered a spiritually bankrupt religious establishment closely tied to state religion. Methodists were firm believers in the ability of all Christians to experience forgiveness of sin and attain salvation. Baptists, whose congregations spread rapidly in North America during the decades before the American Revolution, based their faith on a radical belief in the fellowship of all believers. In their religious life, at least, they lived on a "footing of equality" with one another.[28]

Similar radical religious movements were taking shape around this time even in the most far-flung corners of the European world. In present-day Ukraine during the mid-eighteenth century, Jewish pietists led by a charismatic rabbi, Israel ben Eliezer (the "Besht"), lay the foundation for a revolutionary mass spiritual movement, Hasidism. Followers of the Besht rejected the ordinary religiosity of their age, seeking to achieve what they called *devekut*: a higher attachment to or communion with the divine. They believed that most Jews could achieve this with the help of tzaddikim, leaders with a unique spiritual endowment (and often a prominent rabbinic lineage) who acted as conductors of divine connection. Though spiritual hierarchy was integral to their belief system, the Hasidim were genuinely radical in their belief that all Jews, not just a spiritual elite, should pursue *devekut*.[29]

Spiritual and religious radicalism in the eighteenth century spilled over into political protest and challenges to the established order. In New England, Christian millennialism merged into and amplified political protests. The Methodists' belief in the possibility of salvation for all made them political outcasts in many of the regions where the movement put down deep roots. In Britain and North America, members of the established church and the political elite regarded Methodists with suspicion if not outright dislike. Baptists, whose beliefs were widely consider heterodox in the period, were harassed and even prosecuted. One influential scholar argued that their spiritual beliefs played an important role in the coming of the American Revolution. The Hasidim in eastern Europe engaged in similar confrontations with the established Jewish communal leadership, both secular and religious. As the Hasidic "conquest" unfolded, it brought with it fierce battles over money, religious authority, and communal power.[30]

By the eve of the revolutionary era, visions of change were widespread across the European and American worlds. Many of these ideas remained marginal or unrealized. But their power and appeal were already unmistakable.

The revolutions that began in the 1760s set their sights on breaking the Atlantic world's stagnant political and social order. Over and over, revolutionaries denounced inherited statuses, proclaimed equality, and called for a loosening of the economic and social bonds that held down the people. They knew the task of reforming or even overturning the old regime would not be easy. They knew that there would be many obstacles to overcome on the way to making their visions into reality. Yet few of the revolutionaries could imagine how deeply their own worldviews implicated them in the hierarchical world that they denounced.

# 2

# THE FIRST IMPERIAL CRISIS

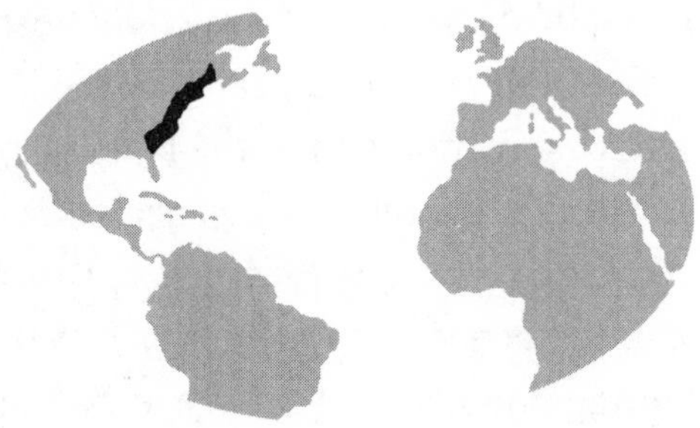

North America was the first part of the Atlantic imperial world to burst open in a major uprising. During the seventeenth and eighteenth centuries, the British Crown had founded or conquered colonies that stretched along the North American coastline. They reached from the plains and barrier islands of Georgia in the south to stony New England and the vastness of Canada's Hudson Bay in the north. The North American empire led Britain into a global war with France in the mid-eighteenth century. When it ended in 1763, the British government set out to rebuild its eroded finances. Among the measures that Parliament adopted were modest new taxes on its American colonists and enhanced enforcement of existing revenue laws.

A sizeable and politically potent segment of North American colonists took umbrage at these imperial reforms. Between 1765 and 1770, colonists in thirteen of Britain's North American provinces began to build a political movement. They organized resistance committees, nullified imperial authority on the ground, and secured the repeal of several acts of Parliament. But the patriot movement was far from an unstoppable force. Their cause advanced haltingly, with periods of intense activity giving way to quiescence. Even the most fervent devotees of the cause were divided among themselves and struggled to mount sustained campaigns. Much of the population remained indifferent or outright hostile.

The eighteenth century's hierarchical social order lay at the root of the discord and dysfunction within the North American patriot movement. John Adams, the future US president and an early participant in the movement, was an eyewitness to the social world out of which this divided patriot party grew. As a gifted striver born in 1737 into a middling household, Adams had had to push his way into the elite during the middle decades of the century. He struggled to rise against a constant current of opposition, straining to gain his footing without the hidden ropes of wealth and status to guide him. He finally gained acceptance in elite circles around 1765, just as the imperial crisis began. He went on to play a central role in organizing the opposition to the imperial government in Boston and then across the colonies. But the memory of his painful ascent, and his enduring sense that he did not belong, never left him.

The hierarchical world of the colonies spawned a divided patriot movement in the cities and towns along the coast after 1765, split between groups drawn from different social strata. Gentleman patriots in New York and Boston clubbed and communicated with other gentlemen while working-class urban men formed parallel movements from below. The two groups frequently worked at cross-purposes. When they did manage to march together, it was usually a haphazard and disjointed collaboration. The patriot movement was even more sharply divided along lines of caste. Black men and women, enslaved and free, found little place for themselves within the movement against the imperial government. The patriots' decision to organize along lines of caste meant that at least a fifth of the colonies' population had little if any incentive to join with them.

John Adams's early life foreshadowed the possibilities and the challenges the American patriot movement would face. He came from a farming family in Braintree, a quiet and undistinguished town just south of Boston. His parents' household was comfortable but hardly on an upward trajectory. His father, John Adams Sr., hoped fervently that his son would rise above his own station. He despaired that John seemed to like nothing better than to spend his days in play: "Driving hoops, playing marbles, playing Quoits, Wrestling, Swimming, Skaiting and above all . . . shooting." School, when John paid attention at all, did not excite him.[1]

Had the Adamses been well-off, secure, and confident in their social position, Deacon Adams might have let John enjoy his carefree days. In a 1693 pamphlet entitled *Some Thoughts Concerning Education*, the bible of eighteenth-century genteel child-rearing, the philosopher John Locke advised the parents of young gentlemen to leave their boys "perfectly free and unrestrained" in "all their innocent folly, playing, and childish actions." "A child will learn three times as much," he opined, "when he is in tune, as he will with double the time and pains, when he . . . is dragged unwillingly to it."[2] This laissez-faire approach assumed that young gentlemen, no matter how little they learned in school, would be floated along into prosperous adulthood by their families' wealth and prestige.

The Adamses did not have the luxury of such dynastic good fortune. John Adams would have to work for it. In school, he learned the basics of mathematics and science, and learned to read classical authors in Greek and Latin. Just as important, he began to acquire the skills of genteel behavior that he would need in order to fit into the upper classes. He learned how to enter a room and carry on a conversation according to the ritualized, unwritten rules of the fashionable eighteenth century. His schoolmaster showed him how to write elegant letters addressing people of different stations, each with its distinct tone and phrasing. He eventually matriculated at Harvard at the age of fifteen, roughly the average for freshmen at the time. There, in nights spent in intense discussions with other men his age, or drinking together with them in clubs, he practiced comporting himself as a young gentleman was supposed to among his peers.[3]

A year after finishing college, Adams decided to become a lawyer. The law appealed to him intellectually. Just as important—for he had learned the lesson his father had tried so hard to teach him—the law provided a well-trodden path to respectability without the need for money or family connections. Becoming a merchant, storekeeper, or manufacturer could all provide paths to potentially great wealth. But each required substantial investments of capital to begin, and they entailed significant ongoing risk. Lawyering, though less likely to make one rich, was respectable and relatively cheap to get started. It was also becoming, in the eighteenth century, a skilled profession whose practitioners had created a closed guild that protected them from competition.[4]

It did not take long for Adams to discover that his success in the law might still be stunted by the constricting social forces of the mid-eighteenth century. Though it was relatively easy to enter the law, mobility within the profession was as limited as it was elsewhere in his society. The leaders of the Boston bar mostly came from prominent families who by this time had many generations of distinguished ancestors behind them. When he completed his legal apprenticeship in the fall of 1758, Adams found that there were "dozens of young barristers" in Boston in a similar situation to him and felt that he was "in a poor position to compete with most of them." He did not have to wait long for confirmation of his worries. Shortly after he moved to Boston, Adams went to meet one of the leading lawyers in town, Benjamin Prat. Prat bluntly told the young attorney that "no Body in this Country knows any Thing about you. So no Body can say any Thing in your favour, but by hearsay."[5]

Having come this far, Adams refused to accept the second-class role he was being offered by Prat and his ilk. He went to meet with the other leading light of the Boston bar, Jeremiah Gridley, to seek his blessing. That meeting went considerably better than the one with Prat. True, Gridley offered him patronizing advice—including counseling him to avoid an "early Marriage," which would be undesirable for his career. But he offered an embrace as well. "I will recommend you to the Court," he assured Adams, a promise that he fulfilled a little more than a week later.[6]

Over the next two years, with the help of Gridley's sponsorship and a great deal of hard work, Adams slowly made a place for himself in the Boston legal community. It was a slog: he built his practice by making the rounds of the local courts, taking on small-time property cases involving debts and inheritances. The work was dull and his progress frustratingly slow. Adams dealt with the irritation he experienced by criticizing himself. I am "grop[ing] in dark Obscurity," he griped about his inability to land any of the larger cases that would earn him more money and allow him to make his mark. Two years later, he was still excoriating himself for his self-perceived failures. In spite of often waking up near dawn, he wrote, "I have not improved my Time, properly. I have dozed and sauntered away much of my Time."[7] The feeling of failure Adams expressed was exaggerated, but it did reflect the very real obstacles he encountered as he tried to advance professionally.

Adams's path during these years was made more difficult by the colony's precarious military situation. Britain and France had been at war since 1756—their fourth major conflict since the 1680s.

During the initial years of the war, in 1757 and 1758, British forces had fallen back on nearly every front, from India to the Caribbean to continental Europe. In North America, French forces allied to Native nations threatened New England and the western borders of the colonies to the south. New England troops and British regulars went on the offensive in 1759 and, in 1760, as the tide of the war began to turn around the globe, conquered French Canada. All of this, in addition to creating political instability and anxiety, was fantastically expensive; the war drained the treasuries of both the British government and its colonies. When the two powers concluded the Treaty of Paris in 1763, ending the war, Britain had gained colonies and bragging rights but was looking financial disaster in the face.[8]

As Britain's fortunes improved in the war, Adams's personal life began to look up as well. In 1761, he started courting a well-educated woman, ten years his junior, named Abigail Smith. Their relationship was lighthearted and sweet. "Miss Adorable," he addressed Abigail with mock ceremony in October 1762, "I hereby order you to give him, as many Kisses, and as many Hours of your Company after 9 O'Clock as he shall please to Demand." Money, the means to support a new household, was never far from the young couple's minds. "I presume I have good Right to draw upon you for the Kisses," John joked in one letter to Abigail, likening her to a delinquent business partner, "as I have given two or three Millions at least, when one has been received." The two married in late 1764, and within a few months Abigail was pregnant.[9] She gave birth to their first child, a girl whom they named Abigail (Nabby), in July 1765.

Nabby's arrival coincided with the start of a new phase in the empire's politics. With the war over, the new prime minister, George Grenville, decided to try to revive the empire's finances by raising revenue in the North American colonies. He proposed a modest stamp tax, which would have required all printed documents—everything from shipping forms to newspapers and legal documents—to be produced on special stamped paper sent over to the colonies from England. The Stamp Act would have been the first tax levied directly on the colonies by Parliament, but it was otherwise unremarkable; similar stamp taxes had long been levied in Britain itself. So Grenville was somewhat surprised when news of the act, arriving in North America in June 1765, generated an enormous outcry. Merchants, lawyers, and printers worried that the stamps would impose new costs on their businesses. Other colonists feared that the direct imposition of taxes on the colonies signaled the beginning of a shift toward more hands-on governance from the imperial center, with a corresponding loss of local autonomy and power. Pamphlets and newspapers blared out "Defiance" to the "Tyranny" of the government and its "deliberate, cruel" attack on the rights of the North American colonists.[10]

---

THE CRISIS THAT DEVELOPED OVER THE STAMP ACT IN 1765 AND 1766 marked the first time that Britain's North American colonists, famous for their internecine squabbling, made common cause against the imperial center. How to organize a political movement across the colonies, with their varied societies, was a new problem. The movement, centered in the coastal cities and towns, included both working people and genteel colonists. Drawing on their mid-century upbringings, the two wings took substantially different approaches to organizing against the act. Artisans and laborers, channeling traditions of popular protest, organized riots and targeted violence to prevent the Stamp Act from going into effect. Gentlemen created an intercolonial conversation through polite letters. These exchanges allowed them to affirm their shared political beliefs without committing to any specific action or assuming much personal risk.

The American opposition to the Stamp Act crystallized around self-appointed groups calling themselves the Sons of Liberty. The New York Sons were the first to organize in November 1765, and similar groups popped up in towns across New England and upstate New York. By early 1766, they were present in all of the colonies' major towns. The vast majority of the participants in these groups were members of the lower orders. In maritime Boston and New York, which lived from their overseas trade and fisheries, sailors formed the largest part of the crowds. In Philadelphia and Charleston, artisans who worked in the less skilled and more precarious trades—shoemakers, candlemakers, ropewalk workers—appeared most frequently.[11]

All of the Sons groups also included at least a sprinkling of genteel members, with larger numbers joining in the cities. These genteel Sons for the most part had close ties to commerce. Many, especially in New England and the Middle Colonies (New York, New Jersey, Pennsylvania), were merchants or merchant captains. Boston's Sons included John Hancock, a wealthy merchant and smuggler, and Samuel Adams, son of another of the town's leading merchants. In the South, the leading patriots were almost all planters and traders who enjoyed some form of dynastic wealth: Randolphs and Lees in Virginia, Laurenses in South Carolina, Pacas and Chases in Maryland. Lawyers played a prominent role—among them John Adams, a relative newcomer enlisted in the cause by his onetime patron Jeremiah Gridley.[12]

Working-class patriots did the physically hard and often dirty labor of nullifying the Stamp Act on the ground. Starting in the summer of 1765, they attacked the individuals who were charged with distributing stamped paper. In Boston and Annapolis, crowds pulled down homes and warehouses belonging to stamp distributors. They did not hesitate to rough up merchants or officials who dared to disobey their orders. When the first shipments of stamped paper from England arrived in the colonies in each of the major port towns, from Boston in the North to Charleston in the South, the same patriots organized to prevent the paper from being landed, to seize and destroy it once it had reached land, and to prevent it from being used. These crowd actions were simultaneous but not coordinated. In the early fall of 1765, a number of such actions took place across the colonies, far enough apart that news of one action could not have reached the others beforehand.[13]

In February 1766, within a few days of each other, New York City and Philadelphia crowds independently torched piles of the "infernal" stamped paper. The sooty smoke that the burning papers gave off, coating the faces and hands of the men who tended the bonfires, hung in the sharp winter air, a reminder of the tangible quality of the crowds' resistance.[14]

The more genteel members of the Sons groups involved themselves only peripherally in these local forms of direct action. They focused their attention outward, toward their peers in other towns and colonies. The idea of such intercolonial exchanges had already been broached at the so-called Stamp Act Congress held in New York City in October 1765. The meeting had produced a forceful declaration of colonial rights but little in the way of practical plans for coordination among the colonies. As the crisis deepened, merchant-patriots began to slip passages about politics into letters with their commercial correspondents in other colonies. In late 1765, William Holt of Virginia dropped an aside about politics into the end of one of his commercial letters to William Palfrey, John Hancock's right-hand man. "We are as violent opposers of ye Stamp Act here as you in N England," he wrote, "& we will never submit to ye chains." Exploiting business letters in this way was risky, however, since it violated the cardinal rule of eighteenth-century polite correspondence. Gentlemen avoided off-topic or potentially controversial subjects to keep their correspondents from finding them "disagreeable."[15]

Gentlemen Sons of Liberty soon created a new model of correspondence for their intercolonial exchanges that co-opted the form of the polite letter to purely political ends. Scores of these letters, stuffed with political platitudes, flowed in and out of the hands of Sons groups, helping to create an easy sense of solidarity among them. The Baltimore Sons assured their correspondents in New York City in early 1766 that "we firmly unite with you for the preservation of our constitutional rights, and liberties." The New York Sons, in turn, praised their counterparts in Fairfield, Connecticut, for "firmly . . . uniting with the sons of liberty throughout the colonies." And writing to other counterpart groups in Connecticut, they congratulated them on their "spirit of liberty and union." The letter writers were fond of reiterating their "highest detestation" of the Stamp Act to one another. These statements offered nothing that was new from an ideological point of view; they merely conveyed empathy and agreement. The Sons' correspondence practices gave them a sense of common purpose while avoiding the knotty questions that the intercolonial opposition raised, from stark differences between more urban and more rural areas to huge differences in population and power among colonies.[16]

Yet the Sons increasingly recognized that this low-risk approach to politics brought correspondingly few rewards. The Sons' resistance had prevented the Stamp Act from going into effect, but Parliament seemed unwilling to repeal the offending legislation. A stalemate appeared to be forming. In March 1766, the genteel and working-class Sons belatedly began to contemplate practical coordination across the colonies. In a circular letter to other Sons groups, the Providence Sons suggested that an interruption of "commercial intercourse" with Britain might be an effective pressure tactic against Parliament. The New York Sons agreed but stressed that "if that is the case, we conceive a personal interview (previous to it) indispensable." Other groups agreed that the only way to move toward fuller coordination across the colonies would be to hold an in-person meeting: their existing epistolary arrangements simply would not permit the creation of such a coordinated, governance-like body. The New Yorkers wrote in similar terms to the Boston Sons: before a "general plan to be pursued" by all the colonies could be developed, they insisted, it had to be discussed at a "Congress of the sons of liberty" first.[17]

Before the Sons could call another face-to-face meeting, though, the British government blinked. Later in March 1766, reports began to filter back to America that Parliament had repealed the Stamp Act. In point of fact, the British government had decided to stage a tactical retreat: Parliament repealed the act while declaring (in another act, passed simultaneously) that it had a perfect right to tax the American colonies. The news of repeal was nonetheless greeted with elation by the North American resistance. The Sons began to disband almost as soon as the news arrived. The New York Sons, who had been the first to organize, were the first to dissolve themselves. They were followed, in quick succession, by the groups in Boston, Philadelphia, Charleston, and smaller towns and cities.[18]

The Sons' pride in having helped secure the Stamp Act's repeal could not hide the weaknesses that the immediate crisis had revealed. The Sons of Liberty had recognized from the outset that they could only hope to turn back the power of the British empire by working together across colonies and classes. An improvised collaboration along these lines, thrown together by local groups and loose intercolonial coordination, had been enough to jockey the empire into a temporary retreat in 1766. But as the conflict deepened and grew more complex in the subsequent years, the gaps and fissures that the Sons had overlooked in 1765 and early 1766 would only became more apparent and more difficult to manage.

One of the American movement's weaknesses in 1765–1766 and after, was that it shut its doors to the Black people who made up nearly a quarter of the colonial population. Most of these half a million people of African descent lived, enslaved, in the southern colonies. Tens of thousands lived in colonies farther to the north, especially New York and Pennsylvania. Philadelphia, New York, and several smaller cities were home to substantial communities of free Black people. These were not small or inconsequential populations. Yet the organized patriot movement made virtually no effort to enlist them in the cause. Indeed, some patriots tried to use fears of slave revolt to push white colonists into greater solidarity, suggesting darkly that the imperial government might try to enlist the enslaved on their side of the conflict.[19]

For the vast majority of enslaved people in North America, who lived and labored on plantations, the first years of the British imperial crisis were little more than a distant rumble. Direct action against the Stamp Act was concentrated in cities and towns that received the shipments of the paper. The agitation against the Stamp Act brought almost no visible disruption to daily life on the large plantations in the Virginia tidewater or the South Carolina low country. It had even less impact in the smaller plantations that predominated farther west and in the hilly country of North Carolina. But the lack of action did not mean an absence of information. Letters, newspapers, pamphlets, and proclamations about the Stamp Act circulated through plantation households. Enslaved people were surely aware that a political crisis was brewing. The language that the patriot press used to talk about the act would also have grabbed their attention: denunciations of the Stamp Act as an instrument of "Slavery" aimed at the "liberty" of American colonists.[20]

In a few instances, particularly near towns in turmoil, the crisis may have aided enslaved people as they sought to escape from bondage. For as long as slavery had existed in North America, enslaved people had sought to flee. Marronage, as scholars call flight from slavery, was a fundamental part of every slave society, and North America was no exception. Marronage could take many forms and had a variety of purposes, from a form of protest to a strategy for self-emancipation. Sometimes enslaved people would escape from their enslavers for a short time, seeking to avoid violence or a specific harm, such as a potential sale. At other times, marronage was intended as a permanent escape from bondage. By the 1760s, advertisements for enslaved people who had fled were present in almost every issue of every North American newspaper.[21]

Enslaved and free people of color who lived in cities and towns witnessed and participated in the early imperial crisis more directly. Many of the Black men and women who lived in urban settings were in domestic service or had skilled professions, such as carpenter or metalworker (for men) or seamstress (among women). In port cities such as Philadelphia or Charleston, South Carolina, another large group would have been involved in the maritime trades: sailors, stevedores and porters, and innkeepers. So-called market women, free and enslaved women who operated the public markets, played a crucial role in the provisioning of towns and cities.[22]

Like their white working-class counterparts, some Black urban dwellers took part in direct action against the British empire. The composition of revolutionary-era crowds is notoriously hard to pin down, but there were certainly Black participants in some of them. Crispus Attucks, a free Black man who was killed during the Boston Massacre in 1770, is just the best known. There is evidence that Black sailors participated in crowd actions in New York and Philadelphia. Yet the patriot leadership, far from encouraging the participation of Black colonists in the unrest, did what it could to conceal it. Black people did not appear in patriot-produced propaganda images, and they were systematically erased from published descriptions of the crowds written by patriot authors.[23]

Some Black Americans in the northern and middle colonies took the conflict as a promising opportunity to demand their freedom. In Massachusetts in 1773, an enslaved man named Felix Holbrook led a campaign on behalf of a group of enslaved people, asking the colony's government to grant them their freedom. In a series of petitions delivered in 1773 and 1774, he and others adopted the language of liberty employed by the patriot movement and deployed it against the institution of slavery. The petitioners received favorable notice from a handful of prominent white patriots but no immediate action on their demands from the government. Petitions in Connecticut, including one addressed to the Sons of Liberty, picked up the language of the Massachusetts petitions, suggesting that the rhetoric of collective liberty was circulating widely and finding a ready audience.[24]

Market women were the most visible and arguably the most important group of Black people in the towns of the southern colonies. Their role in the early resistance movement is revealing as well. Market women served as essential links between enslaved people who produced food and urban consumers, both white and Black. Theirs was a world of predictable routines and the most regular habits. Their day began early, with the first light of dawn or even before, when farmers came into town with their wares from the country. The women intercepted the producers at the entrance to the town and bought their goods for resale. They then took up station in their usual spots in the market area, much as the stalls at present-day farmers' markets tend to be in the same place each market day. The women had regular customers and acquaintances, who were well-known in the community.[25]

The market women's work brought small but steady profits that enabled them to secure a degree of economic freedom that could lead in time to other forms of freedom—up to and including emancipation for themselves and their kin. We know an unusual amount about their lives because markets were very visible to the white population. The markets were always centrally located, and townspeople circulated through them. The forces of order watched over them closely. White observers' complaints reveal the dominance of Black women in the markets. One newspaper charged market women with being "loose, idle, and disorderly" and "bay[ing]" like animals. Other white observers claimed the women were rough or rude: a Charleston grand jury complained of the "Negroes and other Slaves . . . cussing and talking obscenely" in the market.[26]

The markets could act, in a limited way, as a refuge from slavery. As the scholar Shauna Sweeney has observed, many enslaved women in the Caribbean escaped from slavery *to* markets. As market women, they could hope to have a degree of autonomy that was denied them and their fellow enslaved people on the plantation. The market also brought them into contact with many free people of color. The Charleston grand jury complained in the early 1770s of the many "Negroes" who were "selling Rice and other Victuals . . . about the Markets and Streets," which they suspected was providing sustenance for "Run-away Slaves." Sweeney has called this pattern, which she dubs "market marronage," its own kind of political act: a "bold, public political gesture."[27] But market marronage was not a frontal challenge to the slave system. The market women could even be said to be participating in its perpetuation by supplying provisions and maintaining the circulation of goods.

Market women took advantage of the developing British imperial crisis after their own fashion, to advance and shore up their position in hostile slave societies. There are hints that they became bolder, at least in the eyes of white observers, in asserting their primacy within the space of the market. In 1772, a Charleston observer complained of the "insolent" enslaved women who would "even . . . wrest things out of the hands of white people, pretending they had been bought before." The image of a Black woman, whether enslaved or not, taking something out of the hands of white people clearly shocked the author's sense of racial hierarchy. A few years later, the "Commissioners of the Markets" published an announcement that they believed the "good People of this State" were being "greatly imposed on by the Free Negroes, who usually attend the Market." They put in place a series of safeguards intended to keep enslaved and free Black marketers from acting as "Extortioners."[28]

The North American patriot movement, during its initial phases in the mid-1760s, remained indifferent at best and hostile at worst to Black American women and men. Even in cities with substantial Black populations, the movement did not address itself to their needs or interests. Indeed, to the contrary, leaders tried to obscure even limited involvement by Black patriots in crowd actions. Shut out of the organized movement, enslaved and free people of color nonetheless followed the events of the crisis and sought to turn them to their advantage. Urban workers, male and female, found opportunities amid political upheaval to advance their economic and social standing. Enslaved people heard the language of liberty and found in the political conflict some slim chances to gain their freedom. These fissures in the system of North American slavery, though as yet modest, were forerunners of much larger cracks that would open in the armor of slavery after 1770.

The triumphant Sons of Liberty, who imagined in 1766 that the imperial crisis was over, did not get much time to enjoy their victory. The British government still had the hunger for revenue that had led it to impose the Stamp Act in the first place. The imperial government soon started to lay plans for raising new revenue in the colonies. Three years of on-and-off political conflict ensued. The American opposition movement evolved during these years, changing form to counter the new initiatives from Britain and adapting its strategies and tactics. But the division between its elite and popular wings remained a constant.

In the early months of 1767, the chancellor of the exchequer, Charles Townshend, crafted a proposal for a portfolio of new duties on imports to the colonies. The new taxes, unlike the Stamp Act, were directed squarely at American merchants: they would pay the duties, and many of the specific taxed items, such as building materials for ships and warehouses, were primarily consumed by merchants. (A duty on tea was one of the few provisions targeted at consumers.) Parliament deliberated on the acts in the spring of 1767 and passed them in June, and by the late fall the texts were circulating among colonists across North America.[29]

From an ideological standpoint, there was no good reason why someone who had opposed the Stamp Act would not find the Townshend Acts offensive. In spite of differences in how they were constructed, both were measures enacted by Parliament to raise revenue from the colonists. But as Townshend had intended, the two sets of acts looked quite different to colonists depending on their social and economic situation. Where the Stamp Act had been universal in its application, the Townshend Acts were aimed primarily at merchants—and their effects would fall most heavily on the richest among them. It was the largest importers of British goods, among the very wealthiest members of colonial society, who would end up paying the bulk of the Townshend duties. So it was natural that this small merchant elite and its political allies took the greatest umbrage at the new acts.[30]

The merchant elite decided that the best way to respond to the new acts would be to stop the importation of British goods. A boycott would have the felicitous double effect of denying the government revenue from the duties while putting pressure on it to repeal the acts via the British merchants who would suddenly find themselves without access to an important market. For nonimportation to be a successful strategy, however, merchants in all the major port towns would have to join in. Without such agreement, British goods could simply flow in through one American port and be reshipped to the others, rendering nonimportation completely ineffective.

Prominent merchants in each of the major port cities organized associations, modeled on genteel clubs and societies, to create and enforce the nonimportation agreements. In Boston, John Hancock and his man William Palfrey took the lead in mustering most of the town's wealthiest merchants behind the agreement. The Philadelphia merchants' committee produced an elaborate set of rules for their own government. In Charleston, the first general meeting of merchants consented to nonimportation and then appointed "a Committee of thirteen Gentlemen, for the particular Purpose of concerting and doing whatever might be farther necessary to give Force to the new Association." There was hardly a pretense that the merchants who constituted these bodies were anything but a self-selected leadership group. Even with this robust organization, agreement did not come easily. The committees spent nearly a year trying to secure the consent of all the ports' merchant associations to a nonimportation resolution. The last holdouts, the merchants of Philadelphia, only agreed to join in March 1769, at which point the resolutions went into effect.[31]

The merchant committees had such difficulty securing agreement, their considerable prestige and power notwithstanding, because nonimportation was not very popular with the majority of the population. British goods were cheaper than American manufactures. Some finished goods, which were not produced in North America, could only be acquired from Britain. Shutting off the flow of imports from Britain would surely raise the prices of many goods and make others unavailable or hard to find. Colonial consumers were aware that they were being asked to make significant sacrifices. Many were not eager to do so. And it was not only consumers who were leery. Small-time merchants, who lacked the resources of the merchant princes, knew that they would bear the brunt of the losses if they were forced to stop importing British goods.[32]

As with the decision to adopt nonimportation, the committees dominated by wealthy merchants regarded it as their prerogative to enforce the agreements on everyone else. They created committees of inspection charged with policing the nonimportation agreements, to which they granted coercive powers. The committees took their charge very seriously. In October 1769, the Boston Committee of Inspection made "strict Enquiry after such Persons, as may hereafter purchase Goods of those who continue to import from Great Britain, contrary to the Agreement of the Merchants, and publish their Names in the News Papers." In addition to public shaming, the committees of inspection assumed the right to ban merchants from participation in commerce. At the end of 1769, another committee of inspection set out to "discover the owner or owners of such Goods [illicitly imported] upon their Arrival" so that the importers could be shunned for "the space of two Years." The committees were so sure of their authority that they found it (as one committee put it in April 1770) "unaccountable and extraordinary" that some merchants continued to disobey their orders.[33]

Predictably, given the divide between the leading merchants and the rest of the population, the nonimportation movement proved to be a rickety and leaky vessel. Though British imports to North America dropped significantly in 1769 and 1770, it was not enough to significantly dent British revenues or hurt British merchants. British goods continued to trickle into North American ports. Efforts to tighten the blockade brought strife, with pro- and anti-nonimportation crowds taking turns demonstrating in the streets of Boston, Philadelphia, and New York. By the spring of 1770, the nonimportation agreements had begun to unravel as New York merchants and then merchants in the other ports reopened trade with Britain.[34]

Once again, just as the divisions within the patriot movement seemed on the verge of causing its collapse, the resistance got a stroke of good luck. In January 1770, the prime minister who had been in power since 1767, the Duke of Grafton, resigned. He was replaced by Frederick, Lord North. North would eventually prove quite hostile toward the American colonists. But in 1770, he took their side of the argument against his political opponents in the previous ministry. In Parliament in March, he denounced the Townshend duties as "preposterous" and called for their repeal. Only the duty on tea should remain in place, he argued, to assert Parliament's right to tax the colonies. The repeal quickly passed, the king gave him assent as expected, and by April the news had reached the colonies. The protesting colonists had scored another victory over the British imperial government.[35]

THE FIRST FIVE YEARS OF THE CONFLICT BETWEEN THE BRITISH empire and its North American colonies, from 1765 to 1770, showcased the early revolutionary era's fragmented character. There was strong opposition in the colonial port cities and towns to new British taxes and other measures in the aftermath of the Seven Years' War. As the resistance movement developed during these years, it took on the shape of the deep social divisions that existed within the colonies—and their attendant attitudes. Working-class and elite patriots differed profoundly on strategies and tactics. During the fight against the Stamp Act, the two factions used radically different techniques to different ends. Fighting the Townshend Acts, merchant supporters of the boycotts found themselves at odds with much of the rest of the population. There was coordination among the groups, but it was intermittent, informal, and often unsuccessful.

More insidious and just as consequential was the colonial resistance's caste bias. The patriot movement largely excluded the Black

Americans who made up at least a fifth of the colonial population. Elite white patriots did their best to erase from the public story the Black men who did take part in crowd actions in the cities. At the same time, they floated the specter of racial violence and servile insurrection to enlist white people in the patriot cause. Black men and women, enslaved as well as free, nonetheless found avenues to freedom in the interstices of the developing transatlantic political conflict. They heard and interpreted according to their own lights the rhetoric of slavery and freedom that patriot leaders deployed in print and correspondence. Political turbulence opened up fissures in the slave system, providing opportunities to seek greater autonomy and perhaps even escape from bondage.

The early North American resistance's socially narrow, internally divided, caste-based organization undermined its effectiveness as a budding political movement. The patriots won two signal victories during the first five years of the crisis: the repeal of the Stamp Act and of most of the Townshend Acts. The opposition to the Stamp Act succeeded because the act's wide-ranging effects rallied patriots across the social spectrum, each using their own distinctive tactics. Yet the Sons of Liberty disbanded as soon as they thought they had achieved victory. The opposition to the Townshend Acts, which depended on a higher degree of coordination and agreement, proved much more difficult to carry off. The movement was slow to organize and nonimportation was quick to unravel. The repeal of the acts in 1770 resulted as much from a lucky break in British politics as it did from the effectiveness of a fractured American opposition.

# 3

# THE AMERICAN REVOLUTION

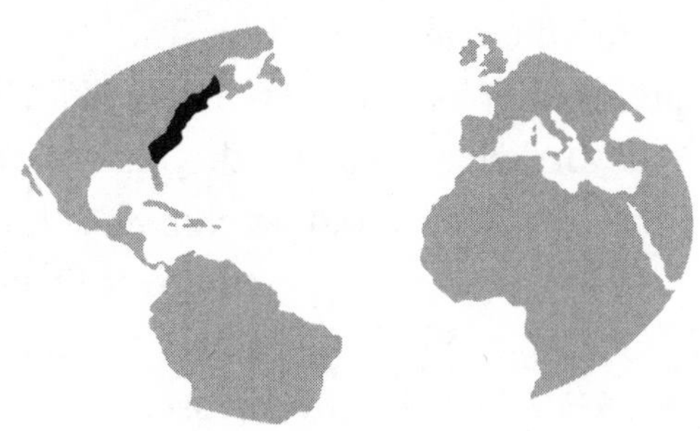

FIVE YEARS OF DEEPENING CONFLICT IN BRITISH NORTH AMERica followed the partial repeal of the Townshend Acts in 1770. The British government and its agents were the principal authors of this escalating crisis. In March 1770, British soldiers stationed in Boston fired on a rowdy crowd, killing five. The so-called Boston Massacre became a media sensation, sparking outrage across the colonies, which was kept alive by a steady drumbeat of smaller conflicts over smuggling. Then, in late 1772, the ministry began work on legislation to shore up the nearly bankrupt East India Company (EIC) by granting its tea an effective monopoly in the American colonies. The 1773 Tea Act reignited resistance across the colonies. Events now began to move quickly. In the last days of 1773, Boston patriots destroyed cargoes of tea on board ships sitting in the harbor. Parliament passed the Coercive Acts in 1774 to punish Boston in particular and the colony of Massachusetts that it led. In late 1774 and early 1775, the British government made moves to bring the colonists back in line with military force. By the spring of 1775, open warfare had begun in New England. A matter of months later, the British government declared the colonies in a state of rebellion.

The patriot movement responded to the growing pressures from the British government by starting to form institutions and developing a more cohesive leadership. The Tea Act sparked a revival of the quiescent Sons of Liberty movement. The passage of the Coercive Acts further galvanized the resistance. Most of the colonies answered the call for an intercolonial congress to meet in the fall of 1774, choosing their representatives through extralegal conventions. The First and Second Continental Congresses, which met in 1774 and 1775, slowly began the process of institutionalizing an intercolonial leadership. In 1775, the Second Continental Congress directed colonists to seize the reins of government and formed the Continental Army. By the end of that year, the conversation about independence had begun, though it would be six months—and require another assist from the British ministry—before the Congress voted unanimously to declare thirteen North American colonies independent. As late as the beginning of 1776, deep disagreements persisted in the patriot party about the fundamental question of whether to break from Britain.[1]

As American resistance hardened, the fissures within the patriot movement came under increasing pressure. For John Adams, still struggling to move up into the Bay Colony elite, his successes came with the temptation to turn against his erstwhile patriot allies. The emergencies of the Tea and Coercive Acts called for an unprecedented degree of coordination within and among colonies. The patriot elite struggled to deliver this in 1773 and 1774. Divisions between the wealthy and the working class, and between the wealthy and the very wealthy, bedeviled organizing in the colonies and in Congress. In 1774 and 1775, efforts by patriots both male and female to organize across class lines faced significant hurdles. The exclusion of Black Americans from most corners of the patriot movement became an increasingly serious problem as the conflict became militarized. It was, in point of fact, a weak and divided patriot movement that limped toward independence in the first months of 1776.

THE YEARS OF CONFLICT OVER THE TOWNSHEND ACTS, 1767–1770, had given John Adams, at last, a way to break into the Boston establishment. Positioning himself as one of the leading lawyers for the patriot cause in Massachusetts, Adams used the conflict as a ladder, moving up rapidly in the political pecking order. Yet even as he became an increasingly prominent figure, Adams could never escape the sense of not belonging—of being on the outside, looking in at the tight-knit, hereditary Boston elite. An ambivalence settled in his mind about this privileged club, a desire at once to join it and to spurn it, which accurately reflected the deep social and cultural divide he was traversing within the maturing movement.

By 1768, the Adams family had grown to four: a son, John Quincy, had been born to John and Abigail in 1767. But John Adams was still hunting for his big break. Over the course of the previous decade, he had managed to move from the outskirts of Massachusetts legal society to the inner circle. His patron Gridley had marked this transition by ceremoniously inviting Adams in 1765 to join a private "Law Clubb" with a select group of other prominent lawyers. But Adams still craved a more secure position, and his need for income was only growing along with his family.[2]

It was John Hancock who unwittingly provided Adams with the opportunity for which he had been waiting. Hancock, a longtime smuggler and prolific violator of the revenue laws, was among the first to face prosecution under the Townshend Acts. In 1768, the Crown brought a case against him, charging that Hancock and a number of others had smuggled Madeira wine from Hancock's sloop *Liberty* into the province without paying duties. The new revenue laws that were part of the Townshend Acts provided that Hancock and any others involved could be sued as individuals for three times the value of the smuggled goods.[3]

Hancock asked Adams to represent him personally in the *Liberty* case. The offer was enticing for Adams. He would gain a steady stream of income thanks to Hancock's deep pockets. It would also bring him greater prominence. Hancock, of course, was universally known and recognized as a leader of the Boston patriot party. What's more, the prosecuting attorney in the case, Jonathan Sewall, was the newly appointed attorney general of the province. Adams would get the chance to face off with him, head-to-head. He did not delay in accepting the case.[4]

Adams took a two-track approach in developing his defense of Hancock. One side was to adopt the high-toned rhetoric of the patriot movement to attack the legitimacy and fairness of the law in question. What proof was there, Adams asked—straining credulity, it must be admitted—that Hancock had even known about the acts in question? "If he neither consented to it, nor knew of it, how can he be lyable to the Penalty?" This argument opened out into a broader attack on the new revenue acts. Adams expatiated on how they had been "made without our Consent" and abrogated the normal rule of jury trial. Invoking the Magna Carta and the principle of the consent of the governed, Adams asserted in the strongest possible terms the patriot leaders' view of the illegitimacy of British regulation of American trade and the heady constitutional questions that increasingly divided Britain and many of its North American colonists.[5]

At the same time, Adams set up a more conventional defense, which centered on convincing the court to exclude the Crown's key evidence. In the end, it was this slow slog, not the flamboyant intellectual argument, that won the day. Over the course of nearly five months, Adams examined witnesses, weighed testimony, looked for gaps and holes through which he could inject doubt and uncertainty. Adams fought hard, albeit unsuccessfully, to convince the court that it should hew to the rules of the civil law regarding witnesses, which would have helped his client. He found more success in impeaching the credibility of the government's star witness, one Joseph Maysel. He finally broke the government's case by showing convincingly that Maysel was a wanted criminal and thus unreliable. Faced with prosecuting a hollowed-out case, the Crown withdrew its pleading in late March 1769.[6]

Winning the case of the *Liberty* for Hancock gave Adams the entry, at last, that he had long sought to the upper echelons of the Massachusetts political and legal elite. The proof of his new status came in the form of a job offer. Jonathan Sewall, his opposing counsel, came to dinner one evening. After some small talk, Sewall confided to Adams that he had been sent by the governor, Francis Bernard, to offer him the position of advocate general in the Court of Admiralty. This was the position that Sewall himself had held until recently. The position not only paid well; it also represented a mark of the governor's trust in Adams. (Or, as Adams interpreted it, a desire to corrupt him.)[7]

Though pleased by the offer, which indicated that his "Reputation" had grown, Adams refused it on the spot. He explained his decision in his usual high-minded terms, invoking his political opposition to the governor and his party. Their "System," he told Sewall, was "inconsistent with all my Ideas of Right, Justice and Policy."[8] Yet in this refusal there was also more than a dash of an arriviste's ambivalence about his social rise. Adams had spent years struggling to get noticed by the Boston elite. Now that they had deigned to notice him—and even to offer him an entry-level position within the hierarchy—he recoiled from it.

Less than a year later, Adams gave a far more public demonstration of his continuing ambivalence about his social ascent. On March 5, 1770, British soldiers killed five Bostonians in the course of a confrontation in the streets. The "Horrid Massacre," as patriots led by Samuel Adams instantly christened it, had probably been a terrible mistake. But the patriot leadership would not miss a chance to press its case that the British government was the enemy of the people. A Boston grand jury indicted the soldiers who had fired on the crowd and their commanding officer, Captain Thomas Preston, for murder. In a town in which there was little love for British regulars, the men could find no lawyer willing to defend them.[9]

Sensing another cause that would elevate his profile—this time, men accused of a crime and unable to gain representation—John Adams took the case. He knew perfectly well that in doing so he was taking the opposite side from his erstwhile allies in the patriot leadership, especially his distant cousin Samuel Adams. Cousin Adams had been the moving spirit behind the drive to prosecute the men, and he pushed hard for a conviction. He was even present every day during the trial. From the gallery, over the next few weeks, he watched John Adams mount a brilliant and devastating defense, arguing persuasively that the captain had not given the order to fire and that the soldiers had acted in self-defense against the unruly crowd. The jury of Bostonians, to Samuel Adams's disgust, acquitted the captain and nearly all the soldiers.[10]

Adams's ambivalence about his station shone through this latest legal victory. Happy to have won the case, he was concerned that his defense of Preston had permanently damaged his relationship with the patriot movement. But it soon became clear that he needn't have worried. The respect that he earned for standing on principle more than offset the opprobrium he had attracted for defending Preston. Adams's reputation as an eloquent and effective defender of the colonists' rights was beyond doubt. But his own doubts about his status, poised as he was between the patriot movement's two social spheres, were far from over.[11]

For nearly two years after the Boston Massacre trials and the repeal of the Townshend Acts, the British imperial conflict went largely quiet. Small incidents continued to occur in the port cities, including further chapters in the long-running cat-and-mouse game between imperial revenue officers and smugglers. This relative quiet owed mostly to the inaction of the British government, which was temporarily preoccupied with other matters. Even Samuel Adams, enthusiast that he was for confrontation, recognized that he could do no more than watch and wait for the government to act again.[12]

The quiet came to an abrupt end during the first months of 1773. Britain's East India Company, which had governed the empire in South Asia since the late seventeenth century, was facing interlocking crises in the early 1770s. The company was massively indebted and could not sell the tea it imported at a profit. The British ministry reckoned that they could down two birds with one stone by granting the company a monopoly on the tea trade to North America, creating a captive market for its product. To sweeten the deal for the Americans, Parliament lowered the duties on tea imports, thus actually making EIC tea cheaper even than the smuggled Dutch tea to which the colonists were already addicted.

Remarkably, in spite of the fact that the Tea Act would probably have *lowered* costs for most American consumers, patriot leaders in the colonies managed to find reasons to oppose it. They denounced it as a stalking horse for future taxes, a harbinger of "Tyranny." They fulminated that the creation of a tea monopoly would make Americans dependent on the EIC. In the future, they would be unable to resist price increases and the imposition of higher import duties. Pamphleteers urged resistance in the most overblown terms. "Will you my Countrymen," one asked in October 1773, "suffer these Miscreants . . . to rivet the Chains their Wickedness has . . . forged for you?"[13]

Whatever ideological confidence the patriot leadership might project about the evils of the Tea Act, their actions sent a different message. They knew, as did the ministry, that most American consumers would have a hard time resisting cheaper tea. If the experience of the nonimportation acts had taught the leaders anything, it was that American consumers could not necessarily be counted on to make their choices in the marketplace on the basis of their political leanings. The patriot leadership had the ability and willingness to pay higher prices for goods in order to make a political point. But they could not count on others to do the same.[14]

The well-known result of the Tea Act, the so-called Boston Tea Party—in which disguised patriots destroyed the EIC tea that had been shipped to Boston—was a product of the patriot leadership's justifiable anxiousness about whether they could actually hold together a broad-based coalition against cheap tea. Once it became clear that the act would go into force, patriot leaders in the major ports decided to keep the tea from being landed. This would prevent the general public from even being tempted to purchase the cheaper tea. When the tea ships began to arrive in the last months of 1773, local patriot committees, helped in some cases by complaisant officials, forced the tea ships to return to England or got the tea landed under lock and key.[15]

Boston, however, posed a unique problem for the patriots. The governor, Thomas Hutchinson, had committed to landing the tea and ensuring that it was put on the market. When the first ship carrying the tea arrived in Boston on November 28, 1773, a high-stakes chess match began. The patriots tried to get the shipment sent back, and Hutchinson and his allies tried to get it officially landed and sold. All the participants in this struggle knew that if and when the tea was landed, it would find buyers. But Hutchinson had a trump card. Boston port regulations dictated that if duties were not paid on imports within twenty days of a ship's arrival, the contents would be seized and sold at auction. This would happen to the EIC tea on December 17, bringing it to the market. The patriot leaders were checkmated.[16]

Destruction of the tea was the Boston patriot leadership's messy way to undo their loss. Running out of time, they decided to eliminate the problem at the source. On the night of December 16, men costumed as Native Americans boarded the three tea ships, ordered the hatches opened, and dumped the tea into the harbor. The destruction of the tea was an awkward move for the patriot leaders. They had spent much of the previous several years harping on the sanctity of property. Yet the limits of their movement, their recognition that it could not command anything close to a majority of the population, forced their hand. Their discomfort was quite obvious. The tea destroyers disguised themselves because they recognized that their actions were flagrantly illegal and would probably elicit hostility from a good part of the public. They were right. Though committed patriots in Boston and other urban centers praised the activists, other colonists were less charitable. Residents of one Massachusetts town called the destruction of the tea "unnecessary" and destructive of "all good order."

The British government's response to the destruction of the EIC tea was swift and harsh. Parliament passed a set of four Coercive Acts intended to single out Boston for exemplary punishment. The Boston Port Act closed the port of Boston to all trade until the town reimbursed the East India Company for the destroyed tea. The Massachusetts Government Act significantly altered the colony's governance, granting expanded powers to the governor and other royally appointed officials, while also abolishing elections for key posts including the governor's council. Other acts ordered troops housed in Boston and created a mechanism for trying offenders against the Navigation Acts, which governed trade and customs, in England.[17]

The goal of the Coercive Acts had been to divide Boston from the other American colonies, by tarring it as uniquely rebellious, and to put pressure on the fragile alliances between the parts of the patriot movement. When news of the acts arrived in North America, it quickly became clear that Parliament and the ministry had overreached. The acts were so extreme that they had the opposite of the desired effect. Instead of dividing the Bostonians, they gave them a common cause. Even many Bostonians who had previously opposed the patriot movement found themselves agreeing with fiery Samuel Adams that these "cruel" acts were nothing more than "vengeance." Instead of making Boston a pariah, the acts excited sympathy for its plight from the residents of other colonies. Expressions of support and material aid flowed up the coast from as far away as the Carolinas.[18]

The British ministry's attack on colonial autonomy and self-governance sparked a call to convene a general congress of the colonies, which could deliberate on how to respond to this new challenge. The proposal for a congress was initially put forward by a rump group of delegates to Virginia's House of Burgesses, the colony's elected assembly, in late May 1774. The proposal first made the rounds of the southern colonies. During the summer, voters in Virginia, Maryland, and both North and South Carolina elected delegates to colonial conventions. These conventions selected delegates to send to the proposed congress. They each also adopted proposals to begin a new round of nonimportation and non-exportation to put pressure on the British government. Many of the conventions also began to take on wider responsibilities, especially establishing durable communication networks with other colonial conventions.[19]

A few weeks after North Carolina's Provincial Congress met in August 1774, a group of women in Edenton, one of North Carolina's larger towns, convened to express their support for the proposed boycott of British trade. Fifty-one women signed on to a text supporting the Provincial Congress and expressing a willingness to do "every Thing as far as lies in our Power to testify our sincere Adherence" to nonimportation and non-exportation. The resolves appeared in a number of colonial newspapers and in the London press. They are often cited as the first organized political action by women in the American Revolution.[20]

The Edenton women, like the genteel Sons of Liberty in the 1760s, envisioned their political statement as a collective effort firmly guided by their leaders. The first fourteen signatories of the resolves were members or friends of one of the town's most prominent families, who included a daughter of a former governor of the colony and the mother of an English baronet. These powerful women probably authored the resolves and were the first to sign them. After they had shaped and authorized the resolves, they set about securing the signatures of a cross section of the town's white female population. It is likely that they did so in the living, sitting, and drawing rooms that had become common in eighteenth-century genteel homes. Some of the subsequent signers were from distinctly lower-status families: Teresia Cunningham, for instance, was the wife of a shipmaster. Others were wives of artisans, widows, or married to tavern owners, and three were unable to write their own names. Their names, added later, gave a veneer of cross-class support to the resolves.[21]

On September 5, just as the Edenton women were soliciting signatures for their resolves, the First Continental Congress convened in Philadelphia. With the creation of this initial forum for discussion among the colonial patriot leadership, the focus of resistance shifted, becoming more continental in scope. Yet the divisions within the movement did not diminish as its geography widened. Where previously the separate trajectories of wealthy and working people in individual colonies had posed the greatest difficulties, now divisions among the men who served in the Congress took center stage. To be sure, the men elected to Congress were more or less well-off. There were no paupers. But the delegates' levels of wealth and power, and the expectations that they had of one another, were still quite varied. On the whole, the planters from the southern colonies were the wealthiest and from the grandest families, and the delegates from the middle and northern colonies had more modest origins. (John Hancock, one of the delegates and the wealthiest man in Massachusetts, was the exception that proves the rule.)[22]

Lines of division quickly emerged in the first Congress about how to respond to the Coercive Acts. Wealth and the prerogatives of gentlemen were never far below the surface in these discussions. The very first debate in the new Congress was over representation: Would each colony have an equal vote, or would there be some kind of proportional representation? Thomas Lynch of South Carolina called for both wealth and population to be counted for representation. This method would have added weight to the South Carolina delegation's voice: they had a small free white population and many enslaved people. But it also reflected the South Carolina patricians' sense that they were among the natural leaders of the colonies; they deserved to have a loud voice in the colonies' councils. The fact that the Congress lacked information about the colonies' relative wealth and population made any kind of proportional representation impractical, but the principle would reappear a decade later in the debates over the US Constitution.[23]

The colonial leaders' economic interests created further divisions when the Congress debated a program of nonimportation and non-exportation. Thomas Mifflin, a Pennsylvania delegate, proposed a nonimportation agreement to begin on November 1, 1774, a date convenient for Philadelphia merchants. Richard Henry Lee, speaking for the Virginia planters, countered with a proposal for delaying nonimportation and non-exportation to some point in 1775. The Massachusetts delegation, desperate to get the port of Boston reopened, demanded an immediate cessation of imports and exports. The final compromise measure, called the Association, created a lumpy phase-in of boycotts that would stretch over more than a year. Almost the only thing most of the delegates could agree on was a general declaration of rights, whose main plank was the anodyne claim that colonists ought to enjoy all the "rights, liberties, and immunities of free and natural-born" Englishmen. With this facade of unity in place, the Congress adjourned on October 22, 1774, with plans to reconvene the following spring.[24]

That winter of 1774–1775 could be considered the nadir of the entire American patriot movement. After the closing of the First Continental Congress, North Americans "turned upon one another as never before." The colonists had never had a single view of Britain or how to respond to the measures it was trying to impose on the American colonies. But until this point, strong public dissent to patriot measures had come largely from members of the colonial governments and their close allies. The steps taken by the first Congress—especially the proposed Association—cracked this fragile unity. Strong polemics against further resistance to the British government spouted from printing presses across the colonies. A gulf emerged between those who favored conciliation with the British government and the patriot movement. To make matters worse, the Association revealed deep fractures over strategy and tactics within the patriot camp.[25]

Simultaneously, the British public began to bestir itself against the expansive liberty claims of the American patriots. The events of 1773 and 1774, particularly the Tea Party and the Coercive Acts, had pushed American patriots closer to one another. But they had had just the opposite effect in England: British individuals and groups that had been supportive of the colonists turned against them. As the American patriots seemed to be refusing all forms of imperial authority, it became increasingly difficult for British politicians to sympathize with them. In January 1775, the celebrated author Samuel Johnson published a pamphlet with the blunt title *Taxation No Tyranny* in "answer" to the "American Congress." Johnson fiercely denounced the American colonists as "rebels" engaged in sedition and called for imposing Parliament's authority and sovereignty "by force" if needed.[26]

The patriot women of Edenton found themselves pulled into the growing transatlantic polemic and their efforts to build a coalition fiercely denounced. Shortly after their resolves were published in the London press, a cartoon appeared in several magazines satirizing them—and, by extension, the American patriot movement as a whole. Captioned "A Society of Patriotic Ladies," the cartoon showed a motley group of women and a few men in an elegant salon. The choice of setting in the cartoon is remarkable. Nowhere in the resolves themselves, as printed and reported on in the London newspapers, was there an explicit indication that they had been composed or signed in living rooms or similar private spaces.[27] The cartoonist, looking at the resolves themselves, was clearly able to put them in the appropriate setting. The cultural strategy to which the Edenton women had turned was all too visible to those across the ocean.

Once the anonymous cartoonist had set the resolves in a salon, he could readily draw on an extensive visual vocabulary, developed over the previous century, that dismissed these spaces as potentially louche and uncouth. For a British cartoonist, the obvious master was William Hogarth, whose disordered interiors often featured domestic animals and children in various states of undress and degrees of disobedience. His images called back, in turn, to

*A Society of Patriotic Ladies* (1774). Courtesy of the Metropolitan Museum of Art.

the works of Jan Steen, a seventeenth-century Dutch painter whose chaotic (though mostly happy) domestic scenes are still proverbial in the Netherlands as the epitome of household mess, what they call a *huishouden van Jan Steen.*[28]

Echoing the visual language of those artists, the cartoonist of *A Society of Patriotic Ladies* suggested that the resolves had been created and signed under conditions that veered far from the high-minded tone of the document. Signs of disorder are everywhere. A child, sitting on the floor under the table, is playing with food or a tea tray. A dog licks the child while raising a leg and releasing a copious stream of urine onto a disorderly pile of tea boxes that have been left on the floor. Behind the table on which the resolves are being signed—the word "solemnly" is clearly visible—a man kisses and embraces a woman holding a quill. Such images of affection were highly unusual, if not entirely absent, in non-pornographic visual art of the eighteenth century. One of the central group of female figures is also depicted with distinctly mannish features.

The cartoonist took care to indicate that the disorder of this salon was social as well as physical in nature. One way that he gestured at this was by including a remarkably wide range of women in the picture. The women in the main group, as well as some of the others in the back, are fashionably dressed in the latest styles. Their piled-up hair, beribboned dresses, and chic bonnets mark them out as ladies of distinction. But the figures in the background, who are depicted drinking tea, perhaps as guests or as interlopers, are far less fashionably dressed. They wear an older style of clothing, from previous decades. Their lack of ornamentation completes the suggestion of lower social status.[29]

The cartoonist also certainly knew something about North America, because he included a particularly needling gesture against the patriot party: between two heads of the main group stands an enslaved woman. The woman's head, wrapped in a cloth, is rendered with unusual precision and expressiveness for this artist; only the other two main figures, both elite white women, are depicted with similar care. Her attentive, alert gaze seems to be directed at the manuscript of the resolves lying on the table. In her hand, she holds a quill and ink. She seems to be proffering them to the signers, but the tray on which they rest is distinctly in her hands.

Inserting an enslaved woman so prominently into the picture was nothing short of incendiary. In slave societies, respectability of social spaces depended on the exclusion of non-white women. By including an enslaved woman in the image, and one holding the instruments of literacy at that, the cartoonist suggested that the elite women of Edenton had breached one of the basic boundaries of polite sociability, in the process calling into question the respectability of their entire political endeavor.[30]

The cartoonist seems to have had two targets in mind with this harsh denunciation. One was the Edenton women themselves. This cartoon was part of a much broader effort by many patriots and their opponents to discourage female participation in politics. By charging women with being masculine, ridiculous, or disreputable, political actors sought to shame them into abandoning the political sphere.[31] In a wider sense, though, the cartoonist was indicting the entire American resistance: the implication was that the whole movement, not merely a small group of North Carolina women, were disreputable and politically untrustworthy. The culture of eighteenth-century genteel sociability, which had provided the women with the ability to create their political statement, had become the way to undermine it.

The disagreements within the American patriot movement, combined with the withering scorn from across the Atlantic, created a grim and sour mood. Abigail Adams, writing to her friend Mercy Otis Warren in February 1775, reflected something of the atmosphere. Her "Heart" was "tremblingly anxious," she wrote. The colonies were plunged into a "palpable darkness" that "threatned [*sic*] to overwhelm us in one common ruin." She feared that North Americans had no recourse left to them but the "Sword."[32] The situation, in short, did not look promising for the patriots as the Second Continental Congress got underway in Philadelphia in the last days of April 1775.

ONCE AGAIN, THE BRITISH IMPERIAL GOVERNMENT CAME TO THE rescue of the patriots. This time, providence arrived in the person of General Thomas Gage, who had been appointed governor of

Massachusetts in 1774. Gage's authority had been effectively confined to the city of Boston by a slow-rolling rebellion that began when the Coercive Acts came into force. Across the colony, significant segments of the population refused to cooperate with the existing government, shutting down the courts and electing representatives to the patriot Provincial Congress. Gage had let this collapse of royal authority continue largely unchecked, awaiting firm instructions from London about how to proceed.

In early April 1775, he received word from the ministry that he was to take a more active role in putting down the rebellion. A few days later, he put in motion a plan to seize a cache of arms and gunpower that the Provincial Congress had stashed in the town of Concord, just outside Boston. A column of British regulars departed Boston on the evening of April 18. Men from the surrounding towns, well warned by messengers, mustered to oppose them. On the town green of Lexington, on the road to Concord, some seventy colonial militiamen squared off against the regulars. Shots were fired and, minutes later, eight American militiamen were dead. News of these "barbarous murders," as the patriots dubbed them, spread rapidly in New England and across the colonies.[33]

Similar scenes unfolded elsewhere across the colonies during the spring. In Virginia, the royal governor, John Murray, Earl of Dunmore, escalated his conflict with the colony's patriot leadership. In April, just days after the confrontation in Lexington, Lord Dunmore had sent troops to seize the Provincial Congress's gunpowder stores. In New York City, patriot-affiliated crowds took the initiative: they attacked the local armory, took the weapons and powder they found there, and distributed them among the public. In Philadelphia, militia groups began forming and drilling; the Pennsylvania Assembly reluctantly allocated funds to buy military stores. In a telegraphic, triumphant letter sent to Abigail Adams on the last day of April, John Adams reported that the fighting had quickly shifted opinion in the patriots' favor across the colonies.

"Lord North is ensuring us success," he wrote, referring to the prime minister who had appointed Gage and whom he considered the ultimate author of the Lexington massacre.[34]

When the Second Continental Congress convened on May 10, it moved quickly to organize a unified armed force for the colonies. Congress recommended to Provincial Congresses that they recruit militiamen, allegedly for defensive purposes. The Continental Congress itself formed a committee tasked with securing military supplies. On June 15, the Congress appointed George Washington, a Virginia delegate and former colonel in that colony's militia, as commander in chief of the Continental forces. Washington rode north and in early July 1775 took command of the still embryonic army outside Boston. Though as yet not much of a fighting force by European standards, its mere existence marked a major step in the direction of autonomy from Britain.[35]

Black Americans began to publicly choose a side in the conflict once the fighting began. Most Black Americans lived in the southern colonies—from Virginia to South Carolina and Georgia—and most of them chose the side of the empire. The patriot movement, after all, had consistently excluded Black Americans from its ranks. Patriot leaders had made considerable efforts to convince themselves and observers on the other side of the Atlantic that they had no intention of challenging the firm lines of caste. The enslaved communities on plantations and farms, who had been following the imperial crisis for years, would have been well aware of this. Planters were perpetually fretting during the early years of the 1770s about how much enslaved people knew about the transatlantic conflict, and as early as 1773 and 1774, there were strong hints that some enslaved people were well-informed. Some even thought that it was creating possibilities for them to seek their own freedom. James Madison, Virginia planter and future president, let a correspondent know quietly about an alleged plot by enslaved Virginians to welcome British troops.[36]

The start of the war in 1775 provided enslaved people with new opportunities to gain their freedom. The British government, aware of the American patriot movement's racially restrictive character, saw a chance to recruit an important constituency to their side. Embattled British colonial governments turned to enslaved people as potential allies in their struggle against patriot planters. In Virginia, the royal governor, Lord Dunmore, considered the idea of recruiting enslaved people to his side in exchange for their freedom. In November 1775, he issued a proclamation offering freedom to enslaved people and indentured servants who would serve the British Crown. Thousands of enslaved people answered his call, fleeing to British lines. Dunmore formed some of them into a celebrated and feared "Ethiopian Regiment," which fought in a number of battles in and around Virginia in 1775 and 1776. Overall, it is likely that four times as many Black Americans joined the empire's armies as enlisted in the patriot forces.[37]

Dunmore and other British commanders, though content to have the help of formerly enslaved people in their military effort, ultimately shared the patriots' prejudices. Service to the empire could not, in their eyes, overcome the stark lines drawn by caste. The British commanders did not give the formerly enslaved people the protection and aid that many of them expected—and that had been promised to them. British commanders repeatedly abandoned Black men and women who had fled to join their ranks.[38]

FROM THE TIME THAT THE CONTINENTAL CONGRESS RECONVENED in Philadelphia in September 1775, the crisis spiraled continually into greater escalation. In August, King George issued a proclamation officially declaring the colonies in a state of rebellion. Shortly thereafter, he and the ministry rejected out of hand a last-ditch attempt by Congress to appeal for peace, the so-called Olive Branch

Petition. Not long after, Parliament passed the Prohibitory Act, imposing a trade blockade on the rebellious American colonies. The ministry was in advanced discussions to dispatch twenty thousand additional troops to North America to put down the rebellion. Congress and the provincial assemblies matched the British government point for point. In October and November, Congress advised several colonies to establish governments on their own authority. Congressional committees began to act with increasing confidence as governing bodies and put out feelers to potential foreign allies.[39]

By December 1775, it was already clear to most of the American patriot leaders that a permanent break with Britain was in the offing. To all intents and purposes, the American colonies were already acting as independent states. In the first weeks of January 1776, Thomas Paine's *Common Sense* appeared in print. Its urgently reasoned pages laid out the reasons to formalize the colonies' separation from Britain. Paine offered a fierce denunciation of monarchy in general and of the British monarchy in particular. Moreover, he tried to make his readers see the end of British rule in the colonies as inevitable. "There is something absurd," he mused, "in supposing a Continent to be perpetually governed by an island." "The authority of Great Britain over this continent," he affirmed, must come to an end "sooner or later."[40]

Declaring independence was at best a step into the unknown for the American colonists. At worst, it might prove to be a leap into the void, which would end in disaster for all concerned. The well-off patriot leaders in Congress, who had a great deal to lose if the movement were to fail, took their time deliberating about it. In private meetings and public forums, they searched for a way to present a united front in spite of their home colonies' different economies and social structures. The inevitability that Paine had felt, the sense of a foregone conclusion, pushed them onward. In early June, Virginia delegate Richard Henry Lee, an older brother of Arthur Lee, proposed a resolution for independence to Congress. The delegates postponed consideration but formed a committee to draft a statement. The result, the Declaration of Independence, passed Congress on July 2, 1776. Two days later, on July 4, American independence was publicly proclaimed in Philadelphia.

# 4
# THE REVOLUTIONS IN THE ANDES

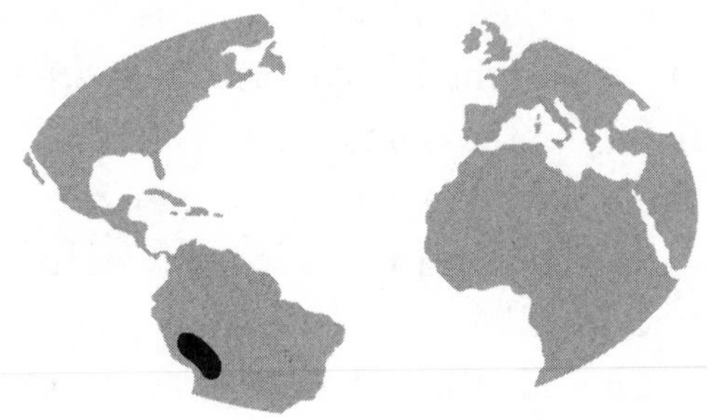

WHILE CONGRESS DEBATED INDEPENDENCE AT ITS SEAT IN Philadelphia, another imperial crisis was starting to simmer in the high mountains of Peru. The Viceroyalty of Peru was the heartland of Spain's empire in South America, its most populous kingdom and a main source of the empire's wealth. In the eighteenth century, it covered much of the territory of present-day Peru and Bolivia. By 1776, imperial reforms and local rivalries had turned this vast, central kingdom into a powder keg attached to a short fuse. In 1780, the Peruvian highlands exploded into a two-part imperial crisis that continued for most of the decade. Its protagonists faced similar challenges to those their North American counterparts had encountered, especially the task of working across the deeply incised lines of social division. But with less good fortune and an environment in which class divisions overlapped substantially with caste, the Spanish American rebels proved less successful. The Andean crisis of the 1780s ended with a temporary victory for the empire.

The match was first set to the Peruvian tinderbox in 1780 by José Gabriel Condorcanqui (or Túpac Amaru), a descendant of the Native nobility, and his wife, Micaela Bastidas. In November 1780, they unleashed a well-organized revolt that drew in large segments of the region's Native population. It became one of the largest colonial rebellions in the eighteenth century. The bloody conflict raged for six months in the highlands in and around Cuzco, the former Inca capital and the economic and administrative center of the empire in the Andes. The battle mostly pitted Native Andeans against "Spaniards." Túpac Amaru and Bastidas tried, with limited success, to attract criollos (American-born colonists of Spanish descent) to their cause. In the end, though, most criollos sided with the imperial government. Royal troops, with the aid of criollo-led forces, defeated the main insurgent army in 1781. Most of its leaders were tried and executed. Armed groups carried on the struggle for several more years in remoter regions but without seriously threatening the government's stability.

The crisis's second phase, a confrontation between leading criollos and imperial officials, came to a boil after the Native-led rebellion had been suppressed and lasted deep into the 1780s. Criollos had long contested the authority of the central government. Reforms by the government in the 1770s, aimed at strengthening its grip on the empire, had put criollos on edge. In the tense aftermath of the Great Rebellion, these conflicts erupted into the open in Cuzco, with each side seeking to control the reins of one of the kingdom's most important cities. Madre Maria de la Concepción Rivadeneyra, a Dominican nun from a prominent criollo family, was one of the most unlikely protagonists of this struggle. From inside the walls of the convent of Santa Catalina, where she was prioress from 1780 to 1783, Madre Maria became a key figure in the political struggle. In 1787, the viceroy of Peru himself declared, in frustration, that Madre Maria had had "a principal role in all of the riots and scandals that . . . occurred in the City of Cuzco" during these years.[1]

The uprisings of the 1780s in the Andes had important differences from the North American resistance movement. Both the leadership and the foot soldiers of Túpac Amaru's rebellion, unlike those in the North American movement, belonged to a subaltern caste. Women, among them Bastidas and Madre Maria, played a direct role in revolutionary politics that had no exact analogy in North America. Armed conflict developed more quickly in Peru than in North America, but the Andean movements of the 1780s seem always to have aimed for autonomy, not independence.[2]

The similarities between the revolts in Peru and North America were substantial as well. In both regions, they were sparked by new imperial policies and reforms coming from Europe during the 1760s and 1770s. Both reflected the desire for self-governance by members of an American-born elite. And both rebellions faced the same fundamental problem: the steep challenge of building cohesive and broadly based political movements in societies in which profound inequality structured and shaped the inhabitants' worldviews. The refusal of criollos to make common cause with the Native revolt was part of what doomed the Great Rebellion. But the criollos' rejection of an alliance with the Native majority had dire consequences for them as well. Like patriot leaders in the southern colonies of North America, Spanish America's criollos had a fundamentally precarious position: sandwiched between the imperial government above and a large Native population below. When Madre Maria and the criollo community confronted the empire in the 1780s, they found themselves rather alone in the struggle—and soon faltered in the face of imperial repression.

The highlands of Peru, where the dramas of both Túpac Amaru and Madre Maria unfolded, were an ancient imperial landscape. Fanning out from the vertebral column of the Andes Mountains, the highlands had been the heartland of the pre-European Inca empire. In this terrain of rocky peaks interspersed with lush valleys and fertile, steep hillsides, the Incas had engineered a highly productive agricultural economy. Inca peasants squeezed enough grains, tubers, meat, and wool from this difficult land to supply an expanding empire and its armies for over a century before the Spanish arrived. The peasants' surplus fed a massive royal court and priestly and noble castes, who ruled over the empire from growing cities. The Inca capital, Cuzco, sat perched atop a stony ridge near one of the region's major river valleys.[3]

After the Spanish conquest in the 1530s, the political and economic life of the region changed significantly, but its fundamental social structure persisted. The Spanish built the coastal city of Lima as capital of the viceroyalty, displacing Cuzco from its position of political preeminence. But Cuzco remained very important as the central node in the silver trade. It linked together Lima, the Andean highlands that grew foodstuffs, and the mining regions of the high plateau—especially the great silver mine at Potosí, a mountain in present-day Bolivia marbled with silver ore. The highlands provided labor to the mines and fed and clothed the miners and ancillary workers. Most of the silver that they extracted from this mine on the top of the world was supposed to make its way back to Lima, where it was shipped to Spain.[4]

The Spanish layered a caste structure atop the existing social hierarchy. The Spanish Crown granted Indian labor service to the conquistadors and to many of the Spanish colonists who came to Peru subsequently. The American-born Spaniards, the criollos, formed local dynasties. They dominated the economic life of the region and took a commanding role in its culture and politics. Their scions filled the benches of the sovereign courts and monopolized the upper ranks of the clerical establishment. They had a mostly rivalrous, occasionally collaborative relationship with more recent arrivals from Spain, whom they called *peninsulares*. Criollos competed fiercely with the *peninsulares* for royal and ecclesiastical offices, but they also regularly went into business and intermarried with them.[5]

As elsewhere across the Atlantic empires, the inequities of Peru's colonial society deepened during the eighteenth century. The decades after the 1720s had brought a gradual increase in Peruvian trade, especially cheaper imports. While this benefited the urban middle and even lower classes, it was disastrous for the rural majority, who had long depended on their role as the manufacturers of textiles for the region. Inequality was hardened by the increasing weight of the impositions that the Spanish government placed on rural communities beginning in the 1760s. In the wake of the Seven Years' War, the Spanish government had seen the need to strengthen its imperial administration and increase its revenues, so as not to fall further behind the French and the British. The result was what historians call the "Bourbon reforms," after the royal dynasty that put them in place. The reforms sought to streamline and centralize colonial governance, shifting power to officials dispatched from Spain. The reforms were also intended to more efficiently extract income for the Crown from the empire. They increased the fiscal pressure on the entire society, but most of the burden was borne by those at the bottom.[6]

These eighteenth-century political and economic changes pressed Native-descended Peruvians more and more firmly into a single, subordinate caste. In earlier centuries, the Native elite had enjoyed legal privileges and status that put them in an intermediate position between the castes of colonial Spanish American society. They were exempt from labor duties and tribute, and they held hereditary positions of authority over Native communities. The Bourbon reforms curbed this long-standing autonomy.

Many of the Native elite's fiscal privileges were either abolished or severely curtailed. The colonial government even interfered with their hereditary authority over Native communities, a core principle of the separate "republic of the Indians."[7] As a result of these changes, the gap between elite and non-elite Native people narrowed, and the caste line separating them from "Spaniards" grew sharper.

Native Andeans, especially members of the elite, responded to the hardening of the caste line by embracing ideologies that valorized the Native past and communities. The most powerful tradition along these lines in the Andes was a utopian vision that revolved around an imagined reconstituted Inca empire. This utopian dream had first emerged in the wake of the Inca empire's defeat in the 1530s. It had been developed and then extended in the seventeenth and eighteenth centuries, first by the Andean chronicler Garcilaso de la Vega and then by the mid-eighteenth-century rebel Juan Santos Atahualpa. The heart of this "neo-Inca" ideology was the notion that the descendants of the Native Andean elite were still, in some fashion, the direct and legitimate heirs of the rightful rulers of the former Inca domain. They envisioned the return of the Incas, in the form of a "singular" figure who would effect a "messianic" revival of their kingdom and restore them to their rightful place.[8]

José Gabriel Condorcanqui, born in 1738, was one of the members of the Inca-descended elite who had experienced downward mobility over the course of the eighteenth century. He had inherited a position as a Native noble from his father, along with lands and other valuable properties. His family even claimed descent from the last Inca rulers of Peru. The 1770s saw him increasingly indebted and with his economic horizons closing. His authority was contested by newly appointed Spanish officials. He found himself locked in prolonged litigation with another family, the Betancur or Betancourt, over who was the rightful heir to a rich marquessate. The colonial courts dragged out the litigation, refusing—in Condorcanqui's view—to vindicate his rights. In April 1777, he went to Lima to plead his case before the highest tribunal in the viceroyalty. Even this aggressive step, however, did not speed up the case. By the end of the 1770s, Condorcanqui had grown angry about his mistreatment at the hands of royal officials. In secret, along with his wife, Micaela Bastidas, he began to plan a major uprising.[9]

In the first days of November 1780, Condorcanqui set his plan in motion. Fittingly, he began the revolt by imprisoning and executing a royal official, Antonio de Arriaga, who was responsible for the collection of taxes in Condorcanqui's home region. Using a name, Túpac Amaru, that invoked his connection to the last Inca emperor, he declared he was taking action in the name of the king of Spain against a nebulous array of bad actors in the viceroyalty. The carefully plotted uprising caught fire. Using a combination of persuasion and trickery, Túpac Amaru in a matter of weeks had rallied thousands of peasants to his banner from across the region. The rebels gathered in the town of Tungasuca, where Túpac Amaru and his lieutenants formed them into an army. Within weeks, they had become masters of a large part of the countryside in the Peruvian highlands and threatened Cuzco from the south.[10]

Women occupied major leadership roles in the rebellion. This reflected long-standing practices in the Andes. Noble women in Inca and other pre-Columbian Native societies had held important ceremonial and political roles. The Spanish conquerors reaffirmed this tradition of female leadership: women held hereditary chiefdoms in the republic of the Indians throughout the colonial period. These positions, which passed through the female line, conferred both prestige and significant legal authority over Native communities. What's more, Spanish law did not have the doctrine of coverture, which subsumed the legal personality of married women under that of their husbands. This meant that Spanish American women could inherit significant sums of property, which remained under their ownership and (at least in a limited fashion) their control. Elite Spanish American women were thus not only conduits for significant wealth but economic actors in their own right.[11]

A number of female *kurakas* (hereditary Native leaders) declared for Túpac Amaru and Bastidas in 1780. Doubly imbued with authority by the colonial government and their own lineages, the *kurakas* could bring with them significant resources: land, supplies, and men to bear arms. The role played by these female leaders was all the more notable given that many of the hereditary male *kurakas* of the Cuzco region opposed the rebels. Female *kurakas* may have decided to participate in the rebellion in larger numbers because they received relatively less of the Spanish authority and largesse, and thus had more to gain from rebellion. They were crucial in the recruitment of soldiers and allies, many of whom joined at the behest of family members.[12]

Bastidas herself was the most remarkable of the movement's female leaders. Just thirty-five at the time of the revolt, she served as a de facto coleader of the movement. Her responsibilities were broad. During a feverish week in the middle of December, Bastidas was active in every possible arm of the rebellion. On December 10, she wrote to Condorcanqui with news of military movements from the loyalist city of Cuzco. Two days later, she received a note from Angela Pacuri, who sought aid to exonerate her husband, who she claimed had been falsely accused of opposition to the movement. The following day, the thirteenth, Bastidas received and responded to letters about the theft of 160 sheep from the hacienda of Gabriel Ugarte, a leading Cuzco criollo, and received reports from several of her agents letting her know that her orders to subordinates had been followed exactly. Also on the thirteenth, Bastidas issued a proclamation calling on the populace to obey her appointees, to avoid committing any injuries to the peasantry, and to respect priests and the Catholic faith. Later the same day, an agent of Bastidas's named Diego Visa reported to her on his mission to carry her letters to nearby villages and secure a supply of coca.[13]

Bastidas's correspondence shows a woman clearly in command of those around her. Allies and subordinates addressed her as *gobernadora* and she exercised an expansive power. In a letter sent in February, Bastidas appointed Antonio de Chavez y Mendoza to be parish priest of the town of Sicuani—a type of appointment usually made by a bishop. The closing formula conveyed her sense of her authority and the respect that was due: "The said Dr. Chavez will give me notice by correspondence subsequent to this determination, without any excuse or protest." Her exchanges with Condorcanqui reveal a partnership of equals. The spouses' letters in both directions were equally filled with information and advice. In a couple of celebrated letters, Bastidas even chewed out Condorcanqui for not acting decisively enough.[14]

The scale of female leadership in the Túpac Amaru revolt is striking within the context of the early age of revolutions. Women were certainly involved in the other revolutionary movements of the era, but in few of them did they occupy such a clear set of leadership roles, or in such unambiguous fashion, as they did in the highlands of Peru. Equally remarkable was the conservatism of this female revolutionary leadership. In their correspondence during the revolt and in the justifications they gave of their conduct in its aftermath, female leaders of the revolt emphasized that they did not seek to overturn the social order. Their aim, as they often reiterated, was to create a society in which they occupied the dominant place to which their birth entitled them.[15]

From the start of the revolt, Túpac Amaru and some of his leading lieutenants tried to persuade the criollo community to join their side. They were well aware that the criollos held significant power in the region. The success of the revolt would depend, in some measure, on whether Túpac Amaru and his allies could breach the caste line and form a movement that included both Natives and criollos.

The idea of a cross-caste alliance was far from implausible. Criollos and Indians had some common grievances: both were unhappy with the growing influence of Spanish-born colonists who were being favored by the government in Madrid. And there was a long history of intermarriage and collaboration between the two groups. Túpac Amaru presented his movement in the most favorable light to them, as a struggle against "evil government" embodied by the *peninsulares* or "*chapetones*" (European-born Spaniards). In early proclamations, he called on Native peasants to make common cause with the criollos against these *peninsulares*, whom the imperial government had placed in positions of authority in Peru in growing numbers. "Let us live like brothers, gathered in one body," he wrote in an address to the people of the province of Lampa in November, "and destroy the European-born colonists."[16]

Some of Cuzco's leading criollos seriously considered collaborating with him and his forces. The prospect of colonial autonomy appealed to this group, which saw itself as the natural ruler of the region. When the first news of the revolt arrived, Juan Manuel Moscoso—the wily bishop of Cuzco, who came from a prominent criollo family in the nearby city of Arequipa—adopted a studied neutrality. He declined to either endorse or condemn Túpac Amaru and the rebels. The Ugartes, a powerful criollo clan based in Cuzco and led by three brothers, received a letter from Túpac Amaru during the earliest days of the revolt asking for their support. They seem to have carefully weighed the pros and cons of throwing in with the rebels.[17]

The Ugartes surely discussed the rebellion with Maria Rivadeneyra, who had just been elected prioress of Santa Catalina. Maria Rivadeneyra was, in many respects, the epitome of the criollo elite. Her ancestors had come to Peru during the 1520s, in the entourage of Francisco Pizarro, and occupied a place among Cuzco's leading families ever since. Maria's sister, Josefa, was married to the eldest Ugarte. As a privileged young woman in Cuzco, she had her pick of the finer things Peru could offer. She enjoyed ballads, suitable for a lover to sing from a balcony, and short comic plays, called farces, that would be performed to round out an evening party. Her wardrobe held skirts with mother-of-pearl medallions and pairs of embroidered white shoes. She liked to drink chocolate in the mornings.[18]

Her stylish facade concealed a hard and calculating political mind. In the 1770s, probably in her twenties, Rivadeneyra had joined in the family's pursuit of power after her own fashion, when she took holy vows as a nun in Cuzco's convent of Santa Catalina. The venerable institution was an economic and political powerhouse as much as a spiritual center. Its properties and financial interests reached into every corner of the region. Rising rapidly into the convent's leadership, the newly minted Madre Maria was ideally positioned to advance her family's interests in Cuzco and across the region.[19]

People who knew Madre Maria in Cuzco thought that she, like her brothers-in-law, was sympathetic to the rebels. A few years after the rebellion, a royal official charged that she had led an uprising in the convent intended to aid the rebels in their efforts to conquer Cuzco. Another person charged that she had tried to hide the Ugarte brothers in the convent at a moment when Túpac Amaru's forces seemed likely to overrun the city. More a commentary on the Ugartes than on Madre Maria, the charge nonetheless suggested that the nun believed the rebels were likely to be successful and was taking active steps to protect herself and her family from an impending invasion. The implication, too, was that the convent under Madre Maria's governance would not be harmed by the rebels.[20]

Most old criollo families, like the Rivadeneyras, had intimate connections to the Native world: Native ancestry, in many cases, and certainly Native servants and nursemaids. An archival document, unknown until now, gives a surprising hint about Madre Maria's relationship to the Native community. In the early 1780s, she wrote a letter to a close friend (possibly a lover) in Quechua, the main Native language of the Cuzco region. She wrote, "Munacuicani Guaguachaita, sinchita soncai ucupi hapicauscaiqui" (I love you very much, my son/darling, and I hold you strongly/dearly in my heart). We have it on good authority that she wrote the letter herself. While many criollos probably spoke some Quechua, Madre Maria's ability to write in the language and her use of it as a language of the heart point to an uncommonly strong connection with Native Andeans.[21] Could it be that this attachment helped her see the rebellion, at least in some measure, as a chance to right some of the injustices that she knew the Indians of the Peruvian highlands had suffered?

Whatever affection she had for Native Andeans, however, Madre Maria never lost sight of the interests of her caste. As the revolt gathered strength and Túpac Amaru's forces crept closer to Cuzco, the city's criollos as a group decided that the rebels' threat to their property and persons outweighed any autonomy that they stood to gain from Spain by working with them. Túpac Amaru continued declaring his solidarity with them and calling for them to make common cause. But his forces' actions, in the criollos' eyes, spoke louder. By the time the rebel forces arrived at the gates of Cuzco in December 1780, they had killed a number of criollos in the countryside and destroyed or appropriated a great deal of property that belonged to them.[22]

At this point, the community of wealthy urban criollos sided decisively with the Spanish government against the revolt from below. Bishop Moscoso, Madre Maria's superior in the ecclesiastical hierarchy, publicly excommunicated Túpac Amaru and ordered priests under his authority not to cooperate with him or his forces. (Local priests in some country parishes were known to have supported the rebels.) The actions of Madre Maria's family were equally swift and decisive. The Ugartes took concrete steps to show that they were siding with the government and contributing to the repression of the rebellion. Gabriel Ugarte served as a lieutenant colonel in the reserve forces responsible for the defense of Cuzco. Over the next month, he and his brothers helped to raise and train a loyalist army in the city. They were instrumental in the successful repression of the revolt over the next few months, providing crucial support to the professional soldiers whom the viceroy sent into the highlands.[23]

Their combined armies first forced the rebels to withdraw from their siege of Cuzco on January 10, 1781. By February, royal forces began a concerted push out of Cuzco that sent the rebels retreating south toward the town of Tinta. As royal troops recaptured rebel-held territory, they massacred hundreds of Indians. By March, the rebel army was nearing collapse. Túpac Amaru and his forces were defeated decisively in the field. In April 1781, he and most of the other leaders were captured by royal forces. After Túpac Amaru, members of his family, and his leading lieutenants were captured, the Crown put dozens of them through show trials whose outcome was never in doubt.[24]

The Túpac Amaru rebellion trials put women in the docket in numbers that would be unequaled during the remainder of the age of revolutions. Of the eighty individuals who were convicted or executed at the show trials in Cuzco, twenty-five were women. In the course of their prosecutions, many of the women defendants tried to exculpate themselves by claiming that they had merely been following the direction of their husbands. The prosecutors and courts systematically refused to accept these defenses. The evidence that the women were entirely in command of their own actions was incontrovertible.[25]

Criollos had front-row seats to the heavy hand of royal retribution against the rebels. Some came to witness the brutal executions of the rebellion's leaders, including Túpac Amaru and Micaela Bastidas, in the Plaza de Armas. But the screams of the tortured and dying were easily audible from the criollos' city mansions and from the convent courtyard that lay just down an alley from the plaza. Only a handful of those who had been close to the revolution's leadership were left alive. Túpac Amaru's brother, Juan Bautista, was among the lucky ones. He was sent into exile in North Africa, where he would remain for almost forty years.[26]

BY THE TIME TÚPAC AMARU'S REBELLION ENDED, MADRE MARIA and her brothers-in-law were already deeply enmeshed in the next phase of the Andean imperial crisis. This was the conflict that pitted leading criollos against the royal government and *peninsulares*. This phase of the Spanish imperial crisis mirrored earlier phases of the North American revolution of the previous decades. The essential object at stake, in both regions, was which group would enjoy the functional power to rule in the colonies: long-standing local elites or a reinvigorated imperial bureaucracy. Like the North American crisis, too, the second Andean phase unfolded on both very large and very small scales. The underlying conflict was empire-wide. But it played out through intensely local disputes. In Cuzco, the wealthy convent of Santa Catalina became a focal point for the larger conflict. The competing groups sought control over the convent's resources, and they saw it as a field of battle on which to wage their struggle over the region's governance.

Santa Catalina was a considerable prize in conflicts over resources and power in the Andean highlands. Religious foundations like the convent were a bit like black holes for property: they constantly acquired it, through donations and the "dowries" of new entrants, and almost never alienated it. By the eighteenth century, after two centuries of acquisition, major convents like Santa Catalina held immense resources. The convents had been the largest institutional investors in Cuzco during the late seventeenth century. They remained wealthy even through decades of relative decline thereafter. All this wealth was effectively controlled by a handful of the convent's religious and lay leaders. The prioress ruled over the convent as a near despot, exercising minute control over her sisters' lives, from granting permission to speak with outsiders to deciding how well they were fed. She managed the financial affairs of the convent with a small council of other sisters. Just as important, the prioress appointed the lay administrator of the convent's finances. He enjoyed wide latitude to manage these resources, usually with only loose supervision by the ecclesiastical authorities.[27]

During the years leading up to the explosion of Túpac Amaru's rebellion, Madre Maria and her family had worked tirelessly to gain control of Santa Catalina. The main obstacle they faced was another nun, Madre Francisca del Trancito. Madre Trancito, born Francisca Valdez, was from a respectable Cuzco family with "no inheritance and no patrimony." Having served three years as the convent's secretary, she was elected in 1777 to a three-year term as prioress. Allegations of financial impropriety swirled around her. She purchased a larger living space, and there were "suspicions" that some seventy thousand pesos had disappeared from the convent's coffers. The charges of financial misconduct gave Madre Maria the opening she needed to mount a campaign for prioress in the 1780 convent election. Drawing on her "alliances [*amistades*] with laypeople" outside the convent and support from the clerical hierarchy, including the powerful Bishop Moscoso, Madre Maria won election to the priorate on June 13, 1780, by a slim margin. Reflecting the high stakes of the election, Madre Trancito and her party made a very public protest, marching noisily out to the courtyard and loudly proclaiming that they would leave the convent. Madre Trancito herself, playing the tragic heroine and declaring that she would be "in prison" under Madre Maria's rule, formally requested to be moved to another convent in Cuzco, the house of Santa Teresa.[28]

The new prioress of Santa Catalina took command of the convent with her characteristic confidence and set to work to make it a center of aristocratic criollo life. She immediately engineered the appointment of her brother-in-law, Antonio Ugarte, as lay administrator of the convent. This position gave him authority over the convent's rents and properties, putting Madre Maria's family firmly in charge of the institution's resources. Ugarte himself became a constant presence in the convent. He came nearly every day to eat meals or take a siesta in Madre Maria's apartments. He even spent the night there when his wife was out of town. (His presence gave rise to ugly rumors that he and Maria Rivadeneyra had been "lovers" before "he married her sister.")[29]

Within the warren of floors and rooms that made up the convent, Madre Maria used her control over everyday life to bend the nuns to her will. Food was an instrument for rewarding those who were loyal and punishing her opponents. She held back the best supplies for those of her "party." They dined "splendidly" multiple times a day, starting with "punch, chocolate, and tea" in the morning. The prioress's opponents found their food much "reduced." On days when meat was permitted, they might only get *lagua*, a corn-based soup. On Fridays, they found themselves with nothing but ill-cooked greens or a thin *locro*, a sad preparation of "three or four potatoes swimming in water." Madre Maria presented these changes as necessary to preserve the convent's resources. But it escaped nobody's notice that only the prioress's enemies seemed to be suffering.[30]

Santa Catalina became a meeting place for members of Cuzco's criollo upper crust. Madre Maria organized lavish meals complete with "loud music" and productions of "farces" and "plays" (*teatros*). "Laypeople," including the cream of criollo society, moved more or less freely in and out of the convent on a daily basis. Santa Catalina's conversion into a space of sociability for the city's elite, open to both men and women, had some earlier precedent. From the days of their seventeenth-century origins, the prestigious urban convents had functioned as places apart, by and for the community's wealthy women. They were already spaces that worked to concentrate power and maintain the social order. It was only a short step from there to transform the convent into the kind of aristocratic gathering place for men and women that had become common elsewhere in the eighteenth-century Atlantic world.

Wholeheartedly embracing the role of the great aristocratic lady, Madre Maria took a lover—or something quite like it. Around 1781, she began a relationship with Fray Juan Medina, prior of the Dominican monastery down the street. There was a long tradition of close relationships and alliances between the Dominican nuns of Santa Catalina and the Dominicans of Santo Domingo. But the relationship between Madre Maria and Fray Medina, by all accounts, was something new. They were not just colleagues. Fray Medina was captivated by Maria, so much so that her fellow nuns took to calling her *facinerosa*—enchantress.[31]

In spite of the rumors, the relationship, though certainly romantic, was not obviously sexual in nature. Fray Medina did often come around to the convent, and he was known to enter through the back entrance, the so-called trash gate. But his presence in the convent was "open and notorious," as one witness put it, hardly the stuff of illicit romance. Most of the relationship seems to have consisted of a constant exchange of intimate notes. The two religious were supposed to have corresponded almost every day. Fray Medina wrote to Madre Maria "every night." One witness claimed that they "infallibly" wrote to each other three times a day. But these notes were carried by their servants in an elaborate system that seems to have been intended, at least in part, to insulate the principals from any suspicion of physical intimacy.[32]

New decor for the convent's vaulted chapter house (*sala capitular*) summed up the transformation of the convent that Madre Maria tried to bring about during her priorate. The chapter house was the heart of the convent: the room where the nuns met to carry out the sacred duty of electing their prioresses. How they chose to adorn this space, like their choices about the adjoining church in which they prayed, held a mirror up to their notions of themselves. The nuns chose a program of frescoes, in three parts, that covered the walls and the ceiling. The top half of all the walls were devoted to large, rather wooden images of saints and martyrs. A middle tier of decoration, depicting scenes from an idealized aristocratic world, ran around the room at roughly eye level. Men on horseback chase a deer over wooded hills. Two heralds arrive in a formal garden, surprising a lady and gentleman out for a stroll. Two of the scenes depict couples at alfresco meals accompanied by music; in one, the couple is enjoying a serenade on the lute. Beneath the rows of images, the artist added a band of floral and geometric designs common in the hybrid baroque idiom of Andean frescoes.[33]

The decorative program of the *sala capitular* reflects Madre Maria's vision for the convent when she was at the height of her powers. Standing in the room, the larger-than-life bodies of the saints loom over the viewer. They convey the gravity and importance of the place. But it is the images of aristocratic leisure that

Mural painting (details), Chapter House of Convent of Santa Catalina, Cuzco. Photos by author.

draw the viewer's eye. Visitors and nuns alike were meant to see these genteel men and women, relaxing in walled gardens or sitting astride their horses, and to admire their elegance and polish. Every time the nuns came into that room, they had before their eyes, unavoidable, a reminder of the wealth and power from which some of them had come. And they might find a reminder, too, of the way their own convent was lending its veneer of authority—maybe even an aura of the sacred—to the Rivadeneyra and Ugarte clans who claimed to have the right to rule over them.

Madre Maria's conduct and her family's all-too-obvious exploitation of the convent's resources began to alienate some of their erstwhile allies. The most important of these was Bishop Moscoso. Moscoso, a political animal to the core, was plainly concerned that Madre Maria had accumulated too much power in her fortress. In a blistering letter addressed to another nun in the convent, Moscoso called Madre Maria a "Lucifer," the "fanatic" head of a "party," who was engaged in the "rough business of the secular world." By 1783, he was using every resource at his disposal to ensure that Madre Maria did not secure another term as prioress. He launched investigations into her conduct, reported her alleged misdeeds to the royal audiencia (superior court) in Cuzco, and lobbied the other nuns.[34]

Two months before the scheduled election for the new prioress, Moscoso took drastic action that thrust the conflict into public view. Skirting the outer edges of his authority, he issued an order deposing Rivadeneyra from the priorate and named a president in her stead, one Madre Maria de la O. Madre Maria Rivadeneyra's partisans protested her removal by dressing the convent's tower, church, and steeple in mourning and ringing the convent's bells "incessantly . . . to move the people." In reply, Moscoso called out troops to surround the convent. Madre Maria then petitioned the royal audiencia in Lima for assistance. The audiencia, which knew Madre Maria from prior litigation, speedily granted a *recurso de fuerza*, a writ permitting members of the clergy to have their disputes heard by regular tribunals. The audiencia ordered the bishop to reinstate Madre Maria, remove the troops, and set a date for a new election. At the convent's election in September 1783, probably with Madre Maria's tacit blessing, the nuns chose Madre Cecilia de San Sebastian as their new prioress.[35]

THE SQUABBLING AMONG THE CRIOLLOS OPENED THE WAY FOR A much more serious threat to the fortunes of Madre Maria and her family. Since 1780, royal officials in Cuzco, most of them *peninsulares*, had harbored suspicions about the loyalties of Maria Rivadeneyra and the Ugartes. Much of the officials' time in 1782 had been taken up with prosecuting Túpac Amaru and his immediate family. Given the prominence of the Ugarte-Rivadeneyra clan and their deep pockets, the bureaucrats were no doubt cognizant that mounting a successful legal case against them would be far more difficult than punishing the defeated Túpac Amaru and his allies.[36] So it was not until early 1783 that royal officials began to move against these leading criollos, slowly at first and then with increasing speed and force.

The spearhead of the campaign against Madre Maria and the Ugartes was the new Spanish-born intendant (royal administrator) of Cuzco, Don Benito de la Mata Linares. He had been dispatched to the Andes in 1780, during the Túpac Amaru revolt, to investigate its roots and stamp out any remaining embers of rebellion. A tenacious and stubborn man, prone to self-righteousness and hyperbole, he proved to be all too zealous in executing these tasks. From 1780 until 1786, when he was replaced as intendant, Mata Linares undertook an implacable effort to root out anyone in the city who might have supported or even sympathized with the Túpac Amaru rebels. The city's powerful criollo elite became one of his main targets.[37]

The initial case against the Ugartes and Madre Maria came together during the winter and spring months of 1783 (June to September). It began with the dispatch to the Lima audiencia of information casting doubt on the Ugartes' loyalty. This sparked a full-scale investigation, managed by Mata Linares, which by September 1783 had congealed into a set of formal charges against the Ugartes. The marquee allegations were that they had collaborated with, or at least been sympathizers of, Túpac Amaru. (The prosecutors tried to root this in an alleged long history of disloyalty.) Other charges focused on their public conduct: They were accused of fomenting unrest and dissention in Cuzco. There were also several specific charges against individual brothers. The allegations against Antonio included accusations of financial and personal impropriety related to his stewardship of the convent's finances and his relationship with Madre Maria.[38]

The legal process against the Ugartes dragged on for years. They were called to Lima in person in 1783 to answer the charges—a typical move in serious cases. But it was not until 1785 that the audiencia issued its findings. Though they were favorable to the Ugartes, by this point the brothers had suffered considerable losses as a result of their presence in Lima—away from their properties in the highlands—and from the costs of the litigation itself. But worse was to come. In late 1786, the ministry ordered that the Ugarte brothers be sent to Spain. The government simply no longer trusted them and doubted that the viceroyalty's courts, stacked with criollos, would hold them to account. The Ugartes departed in December 1786. At almost the same time, Bishop Moscoso was also ordered to Spain. The assault on criollos, spreading like a slow-moving lava flow, had caught up to him as well.[39]

At precisely this vulnerable moment for Cuzco's criollos, the time arrived for a new election in Santa Catalina. Madre Maria made it known that she would try to recapture the office, and Mata Linares lost no time in making his opposition known. He claimed that he objected to her return because she had abused her power as prioress. Yet Mata Linares seemed most disturbed by Madre Maria's success in projecting her power beyond the convent. Over the previous six years, he complained to his superiors, she had repeatedly and successfully enlisted the highest political authorities in the viceroyalty in her cause. These included the audiencia of Lima, to which she had appealed multiple times in 1783 alone, and the viceroy himself. She had seeded "disunion" in Cuzco, he wrote in one particularly embittered letter, threatening the stability of the state and the royal government's ability to enforce its will on criollos and Natives alike.[40]

The imperial government in Peru came to share Mata Linares's view of Madre Maria as a central figure in an ongoing challenge to imperial authority. In 1787, the viceroy wrote a long letter to the king reporting on the history of the Rivadeneyra affair. After noting that Madre Maria was the "cause" of many disturbances in Cuzco, including ones associated with the Túpac Amaru revolt, he connected her story explicitly to the uprising. Her case, he wrote, had a "precise link, and connection" with the "general rebellion of the kingdom" (i.e., the Túpac Amaru revolt). Though Madre Maria and the Ugartes had all publicly taken the side of the government against the *amarista* rebels, from the point of view of the government, what they shared was more important than their differences. Both sought to claim authority that the imperial government intended to keep for itself.[41]

The election in Santa Catalina went forward on June 14, 1786, in spite of Mata Linares's opposition, and Madre Maria won election as prioress. Don Josef Pérez, the bishop's second-in-command, certified her election, and once again she took possession of the keys to the convent and the book containing its constitutions.[42] That Maria Rivadeneyra was able to reclaim this prominent role during the early winter of 1786, near the nadir of the criollos' power, was a notable accomplishment in itself. Her in-laws were in the process of being expelled from Peru. The powerful Bishop Moscoso was facing down a not-so-subtle threat of exile. But within the convent, Madre Maria still stood tall. Santa Catalina had become one of the last redoubts of criollo power in Cuzco, still resisting the heavy hand of the empire.

Mata Linares took Madre Maria's reelection as an almost personal affront and immediately tried to overturn the vote. The nuns got wind of his plan even before he had committed anything to paper and swung into action to thwart his "design." In a matter of days, they wrote three petitions to the viceroy demanding that he grant them a *recurso de fuerza* to appeal to the audiencia for assistance. The request was granted, and in short order the audiencia in Lima heard their plea and issued a decree affirming Madre Maria's election. "We believed," the nuns wrote in a letter a few months later to the king himself, "that by means of this . . . we were protected from all insult, and welcomed in the protection . . . of Your Majesty."[43]

Madre Maria's triumph was short-lived. On September 30, 1786, just before midnight, the nuns of Santa Catalina were awakened by loud knocks on the convent's heavy outer door. The knocking became battering—the main door was broken through—and a small group of men entered the convent: seven soldiers, two clergymen, and a notary. The armed party made a beeline for Madre Maria's apartments. When they arrived, they announced that they had an order from the viceroy to remove her from the convent. Unwilling and feeling ill, she nonetheless followed the men out of her cell and toward the entrance.[44] After a short walk across the Plaza de Armas and a little ways up the hill on its far side, they arrived at the small portal of the convent of Santa Teresa. This would be her new home: she had been sentenced to an indefinite exile in another convent, where she had no rights and no voice. She would not leave Santa Teresa again for five years. Her reign in Santa Catalina was definitively over.

DURING THE FIRST HALF OF THE 1780S, THE VICEROYALTY OF PERU experienced an imperial crisis that was every bit as wide and deep as the upheaval that had taken place in Britain's North American empire a decade earlier. Significant changes in imperial policy starting in the 1760s had proven disruptive to both societies. The empires, aiming to impose new costs and controls on their colonial subjects, inadvertently gave a powerful jolt to their colonies' unstable social equilibrium. Significant numbers of colonists rose in opposition to the empire's projects and their messengers. The conflicts that ensued lasted for years and became military as well as political confrontations. In both British North America and Spanish Peru, the crises caused significant and enduring damage: tens of thousands of lives were lost, an enormous amount of property was stolen or destroyed, and warfare left enduring scars on both regions.[45]

For patriots in both places, how to build political movements that bridged the eighteenth century's deeply incised social divisions was a central problem—arguably their most important problem. The empires that colonial subjects faced were powerful entities, and they knew it. The empires had money, an administrative apparatus, and armies and navies at their disposal. Unity among the opposition was the only way to imagine triumphing against these long odds. For North American patriots, the idea of a common cause was a sacred fiction, invoked over and over again in letters and proclamations to rally the colonies and their inhabitants behind the common banner. Túpac Amaru, even more explicitly than his North American counterparts, made a concerted effort to forge an alliance across the hard lines of caste and class in the Andes. He found some success in this, managing to enlist both Native leaders and peasants in large numbers and even convincing some criollos to join with him.

In Peru in the 1780s, as in North America during the 1770s, elites made only limited progress in building movements across lines of caste and class. Guided by worldviews formed in the highly hierarchical eighteenth-century world, they found it all but impossible to set social distinctions aside in order to advance a joint cause. Túpac Amaru and his allies failed to recruit the bulk of the region's criollos to their cause. Cuzco criollos, like Madre Maria and her family, were unwilling to make common cause with a Native-led political movement. North American patriot leaders could not agree among themselves, let alone work closely with working-class or Black patriots. Slowed by these enduring divisions, patriot movements in both regions struggled to maintain their momentum and to hold off imperial counterattacks. Indeed, these divisions continued to bedevil the United States long after independence.

Yet the two imperial crises in the Americas during the 1770s and early 1780s did have different outcomes. The North Americans gained their independence in 1783 while Peru came more firmly under the empire's thumb, remaining a bastion of Spanish colonialism into the early nineteenth century. The different paths that the two movements took owed something to luck. It was fortunate for white North American patriots that the imperial crisis in which they were embroiled did not bring about a revolt of the enslaved. They were fortunate, too, that the British government proved to be a much more hesitant opponent than the Spanish Crown: American patriots benefited, more than once, from well-timed retreats by the British ministry. In the final equation, though, the Cuzco criollos owned their fate. Having chosen the empire's side in the Great Rebellion, they were then left to confront it alone. First the Ugartes, then Bishop Moscoso, and at last Madre Maria were swept away by the forces of an empire intent on reasserting its hegemony over rebellious subjects. The Cuzco criollos had wanted to stand alone. The price of that lonely preeminence had now come due.

# PART II

# REVOLUTIONS, LIMITED, 1778–1798

# 5
# THE NEWS OF WAR

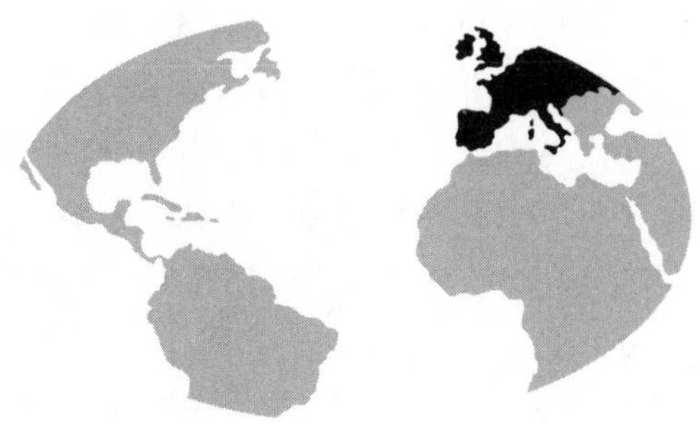

EUROPE VIBRATED IN THE 1770S AND 1780S TO THE RHYTHM OF American rebellions. Europeans had been following events in North America with avid attention since well before the United States declared its independence. The events of 1776 made the subject inescapable. Newspapers reported breathlessly on the progress of military events. Then one by one, the major European powers joined the fight. After providing secret aid to the North Americans for nearly two years, France declared war on Britain in 1778, becoming the United States' first avowed ally. Spain came in the following year, and in 1780 the Netherlands entered the war. By the middle of 1780, the colonial dispute on the North American coast had become yet another global confrontation among Europe's imperial behemoths.[1]

As the European empires mobilized for war, they brought the American Revolution home to their subjects on both sides of the Atlantic and around the world. The war's effects reverberated throughout European society in ways that reflected its hierarchical character. Merchants and landowners saw opportunities for profit from wartime supply contracts, increases in the prices of certain commodities, and commerce raiding. For working people, the effects were far more mixed. In Bordeaux, one of the European cities most exposed to the Atlantic world, the war brought hard times for many of the working-class people who made the city run. They suffered from competition from soldiers and sailors passing through the town and hardships related to the interruption of trade. Some found opportunities for profit too. But never on the scale of the grandees.

The war years brought the first sustained encounters between American patriot leaders and their European counterparts. A handful of US diplomatic representatives, among them Benjamin Franklin and John Adams, made their way across the Atlantic to rally support for the war with Britain. The envoys slid into the well-worn grooves of eighteenth-century European gentry life, which helped them persuade their allies to provide the money, arms, and military support the nascent American republic so desperately needed.[2] The envoys' success reveals just how much the new republican government was cut from the same kind of hierarchical cloth out of which the European courts were formed. The friction that became apparent in some of these diplomatic interactions is telling in another way. Misunderstandings and disagreements among the envoys, and between them and European ministers, laid bare subtle but consequential differences of worldview. Even the genteel leaders of the two hemispheres, it seemed, did not find it so easy to slough off the social habits and prejudices that divided them.

News of the American crises flowed into Europe through a latticework of intersecting channels. Merchants' letters were probably the first and most constant source of information that Europeans had about events on the other side of the Atlantic. The letters that early modern merchants wrote were perfect vehicles for news. The rules of commercial letter writing commanded writers to be concise and focus on practical and actionable items. They wrote missives filled above all with the movements of ships, with how many hogsheads they might carry, with how cargoes were to be sold or distributed. But in wartime, merchants took it upon themselves to share information about any political or military matters that might have an influence on trade. Merchants prized accuracy, and they expected their correspondents to convey this information, as far as possible, untainted by their personal views.[3]

Commercial letters passed through multiple hands, bringing disparate streams of information together and creating new ones. Coffeehouses were one of the most important places for these exchanges of news. By the 1770s, coffeehouses were thick on the ground in Paris, London, and Amsterdam, not to mention Madrid, Porto, and the main cities and towns of the Americas. Proprietors made newspapers available to attract customers; some even produced their own in-house newsletters. The coffeehouse occupied a prominent place in the daily rounds of businessmen, politicians, and many others. In larger cities, some coffeehouses were highly specialized. One late eighteenth-century visitor to Lloyd's, one of the most prominent mercantile coffeehouses in London, remarked that its regulars were "almost entirely . . . rich merchants." They collected information and shipping news from around the world, shared it with one another in a systematic fashion, and used the resulting evidence to set insurance rates.[4]

Coffeehouses were also one of the places where eighteenth-century newspapers were made. Much of the content of newspapers in the eighteenth century was composed from the primary material of letters in one way or another. Though it was thought impolite to republish a received letter in extenso, the anonymous publication of extracts from letters was expected and sometimes even desired by correspondents. Every newspaper in the late eighteenth century filled its pages with these printed clippings, either taken directly from correspondence or acquired secondhand from other newspapers. News writers, who assembled these fragments and supplied them to the publishers, were one of the stock figures in descriptions of coffeehouses. Their professional hunger for information did not endear them to many observers. One writer compared news writers to "House-breakers." He charged that they listened in on conversations in the coffeehouses and cozied up to "the Footmen and other Servants" in order to discover secrets. Another critic painted a caricature of a hopeless hack who had been reduced to inventing news items from whole cloth and selling these "scraps" to publishers to make ends meet.[5]

Whatever the source, Europeans eagerly followed news about North America. The vast majority of what they consumed concerned the military aspects of the war. The newspapers, in particular, were full of information about the dispatch of troops, military strategies, and descriptions of engagements. News about major battlefield commanders was especially valued. American general-in-chief George Washington was a particular favorite of the news writers. Any news of his doings was faithfully reprinted. This avid interest could also result in the rapid and uncontrolled spread of false news. The European press, for instance, repeatedly printed reports of Washington's death over the course of the war. News about individual battles could be equally hard to parse, with even basic questions—such as who had won and who had lost—becoming the subject of heated disagreement.[6]

The transmission of news from North America made it out to be a rather ordinary, even run-of-the-mill affair to European governments and subjects. The American crisis, at least as far as French officials perceived it before 1776, had fit comfortably within a familiar mold: this was a colonial revolt centered on disputed taxation. Every European empire had experienced these types of conflicts, and with almost no exceptions they had ended with some kind of negotiated settlement. Independence had been, in some respects, a surprising outcome. But once the United States had become an independent nation, the conflict quickly reverted to familiar dimensions. From the point of view of many Europeans, it was now just one more war in a long century of warfare in Europe, the Americas, and, increasingly, the globe.[7]

This is not to say that there was no discussion of the ideological content of the American Revolution in Europe—including the notes of representation and republican governance that the American resistance movement had hit hard and often during the early 1770s. In intellectual circles and fashionable salons, a lively debate was brewing about the newly created republic. One key text early on in this conversation was the *History of the Two Indies*, a multivolume work that became one of the period's bestsellers. Written by Guillaume-Thomas-François Raynal with contributions by others, including the prolific enlightenment writer Denis Diderot, the book offered a history and critique of European empire around the globe. Raynal and his collaborators devoted hundreds of pages to a damning account of the destruction wrought by European explorers and colonists in the New and Old Worlds. A radical critique of slavery filled an entire two-hundred-page chapter, its contents easily summed up by the eloquent title of a single section: "Slavery is entirely contrary to humanity, reason and justice."[8]

Raynal's message echoed in distorted fashion within Bordeaux and the French empire, favoring the independence of the American colonists. France, and Bordeaux in particular, profited enormously from overseas colonies and the labor of enslaved people. Raynal's attack on slavery was certainly taken to heart by some intellectuals. But for the political elite, and for the social elite of an Atlantic port city like Bordeaux, Raynal's explosive attack on the realities of the colonial system was to be heard selectively. They could take on board Raynal's arguments as far as they justified American independence—and leave it at that.[9]

The British imperial crisis and American independence also fed an ongoing enlightenment debate about how to reform European politics. Starting in 1770, Benjamin Franklin, tireless advocate for American causes, began quietly pushing the publication of some persuasive tracts by American patriots in Europe. The first one that made it into French was John Dickinson's *Letters from a Farmer in Pennsylvania* (1768), which took the dramatic position that Britain's Parliament had no power to levy taxes on the American colonies. Shortly thereafter, Franklin published French translations of several of his scientific publications, which served to draw favorable attention to the accomplishments of the rebellious American colonists. Publications of the colonies' "petitions and resolutions" followed in the French-language press. North America came to be increasingly associated, at least in the minds of some influential editors, with the idea of "liberty" and the pursuit of political reform.[10]

Beginning in 1776, translations of American constitutions and legislation began to appear across Europe. These included renderings in French and other languages of the Declaration of Independence, of course, but also of state constitutions, the Articles of Confederation, and state-level revolutionary legislation. For enlightenment critics of tyranny and absolutism, these documents became a source of practical evidence that another form of politics was possible. French observers extolled the North Americans for having created ideal governments—the "purest democracy that ever existed," as the editor of one collection of state constitutions put it. The American documents were particularly important for closet republicans and democrats, who could not safely or legally express anti-monarchical views.[11]

Yet these publications cannot be said to have significantly altered the political discourse in Europe. By the 1770s, enlightened European thinkers were already decades into a critique of absolutism and tyranny. They had been extolling republics and popular sovereignty—albeit usually in strictly abstract terms to avoid crossing their own governments—since at least the seventeenth century. The American republic represented an actualization or enactment of a political model that many enlightened thinkers held dear. They were perhaps, because of that, inclined to take too rosy a view of American society, to exaggerate the ways in which it was a fulfillment of their long-held dreams. But to them, it was not much more than that—the realization of a dream.[12]

THE AMERICAN WAR HAD A SIGNIFICANT BUT NOT ESPECIALLY DISruptive effect on the lives of European working people. This was powerfully in evidence in Bordeaux, eighteenth-century France's third or fourth largest city. Though it lies some 3,500 miles east of the American coast, Bordeaux was intimately enmeshed in the Atlantic society and culture that enfolded the cities of Anglo-America as well. Over the course of the early eighteenth century, like many other cities of the Atlantic world, it had become in effect two superimposed metropolises. One was the city of the elite, who lived increasingly in a circuit of privileged and prettified spaces; the other was a spread-out city of workers and itinerants, who lived and breathed the air of the streets and squares.

Bordeaux in those days hugged one side of the river Garonne some miles above its opening into the Bay of Biscay. The eighteenth century had brought an economic boom as Bordelais merchants became dominant in the French sugar, rum, and colonial commodity trades. A frenzy of construction ensued, transforming the city. The powerful midcentury intendant Louis-Urbain Aubert de Tourny had made it his mission to turn Bordeaux into a miniature Paris. He straightened the streets, put in place lighting and gutters. Tourny's greatest project was the improvement of the Chartrons, a new working suburb built just downriver from the old medieval center with its narrow streets and forest of steeples. The Chartrons had taken shape as a collaboration between the government and the local merchant elite. The government cleared land, and merchants financed the construction of new buildings along the neat streets of the suburb. Along the waterfront, the largest merchant houses built the facades of their warehouses looking directly onto the port.

The well-off and the working class led increasingly separate lives in this changing city. For the well-to-do, a circuit developed that led them from spacious home to place of business to genteel entertainment. The Chartrons were linked to the medieval city by a new planted promenade, the Cours Saint André, which abutted the Jardin Royal, a park constructed at Tourny's behest. Modeled on the royal parks of Paris, the *jardin*'s tree-lined walks, flowerbeds, and artificial lake were protected by guards who kept out ordinary Bordelais. As the elite came to live exclusively in these spaces created for their use, a curious kind of social distance developed in the street. Genteel Bordelais continued to pass through the city, moving from one privileged space to another, but they interacted less and less with Bordeaux's working-class denizens. There were, as one scholar has said of Paris during these years, "two cities" layered on top of each other.[13]

Working-class people took possession of the streets. Their numbers grew rapidly in the eighteenth century, as migrants, transients, and young people were drawn to Bordeaux in droves. (The population doubled, from about fifty thousand to more than one hundred thousand, between 1715 and 1789.) Men and women sat outside on stoops and benches in the narrow streets. Workshops opened onto squares and passageways, allowing artisans and laborers to interrupt their work to exchange a word of gossip or a joke. Peddlers traversed the city carrying bundles of goods for sale. Then there were those who lived outside: itinerants, migrants looking for work, those who could not afford a lodging from one day to another.[14]

The Bordeaux of the ordinary folk had the peculiarity of being a city of women. Many cities and towns that lived from the sea had an important female presence. With husbands and sons away at sea or working elsewhere in the region, the streetscape had a distinctly feminine cast. It was women who made swaths of the economy function: they kept the inns and taverns, traded with one another, and provided their families with a subsistence.[15]

In many neighborhoods of Bordeaux, in the absence of men, women ruled the streets, setting the social tone and policing the presence of strangers. Late on a New Year's Day during the American war, Bernarde Faucon, a *caffetière* (coffeehouse keeper), found her premises invaded by a pair of unfamiliar soldiers. The men burst in, demanding wine. The main room was occupied by two neighborhood girls having a dancing lesson. The men brusquely inserted themselves into the café and began dancing with the girls. When the girls tried to leave the room, declaring themselves tired and ill, the unnamed soldiers became violent, grabbing and hitting them to the point of drawing blood. By this time, attracted by the cries from inside, a crowd had gathered. The men fled shortly before the city watch arrived.[16] The next day, Faucon brought the case before the city magistrates, who conducted a thorough investigation.

Women in Bordeaux did not merely defend their homes and places of business. They could also have a powerful voice in the streets. In May 1779, officers of the city guard were called out by the owner of a cabaret because a man in her establishment, in the heart of the old city, was refusing to pay what he owed and becoming violent. When they tried to arrest the suspect, they were set upon by a mob led by a young woman of the neighborhood who went by the name Rey. Yelling and insulting the officers, Rey brought a crowd of workers into the streets and told the guardsmen proudly that she would be applauded in the neighborhood for the "good work that she had done." The police noted that she had gone so far as to say that she believed she did not "owe obedience to the police."[17]

The working people of the city took an interest in the American war. The evidence suggests that they saw it through the lens of the military conflicts and imperial competition with which they were already familiar. In March 1779, the police arrested a peddler named Pierre Sicot who was hawking printed copies of the French and British fleet lists. The government considered this information to be a state secret: on the relative strength of the French fleet depended the likely success of French arms in this new conflict.[18] Memories of the bad days of the Seven Years' War just over a decade earlier, during which Bordeaux had suffered profound economic losses, were no doubt still fresh in the minds of the populace. Sicot had hoped to profit off these worries, until the police put an end to his little business venture.

Many among the Bordeaux working classes likely welcomed the war for the jobs and income that it promised. The influx of sailors and soldiers meant higher prices for food, lodging, and sex. For innkeepers, women in the provisioning trades, and sex workers, these customers represented a potential windfall. Young men, and mariners who were able to avoid enlistment in the navy, found new employment opportunities and could expect higher wages. Bordeaux merchants fitted out dozens of privateers after 1778. These private ships of war, which sailed under commissions from the king and targeted enemy vessels and cargo, employed thousands of young men. While the work was dangerous, it came with the chance of a rich payout: privateersmen were rewarded with a portion of the value of any enemy property their ship captured. Even so, wartime could be difficult for working people. Soldiers, sailors, and other transients competed with locals for jobs, resources, and sexual partners. The city magistrates were kept busy addressing complaints brought by aggrieved citizens against these interlopers. In January 1781 alone, they heard dozens of cases, including accusations against four sailors from Périgord who had beaten up a local ship captain.[19]

The biggest winners in wartime were not the workers but those who were already wealthy, the holders of capital. In Bordeaux, that meant the great merchant houses, and none more so than Abraham Gradis and Company. Built over generations by a family of Sephardic Jews, Gradis & Co. by the late eighteenth century was one of the largest and most powerful merchant firms in Bordeaux. Its activities during the American war were on a correspondingly stupendous scale. Gradis entered into contracts with the French government to supply specie to its Caribbean colonies—essentially, a high-interest loan to the state. In late 1777, he was sending over one hundred thousand livres in cash every month to Martinique and Guadeloupe, two of France's possessions. In 1779, he signed an agreement to send over half a million livres per month to Saint-Domingue, the largest of France's island territories in the Caribbean. At a time when five livres represented a week's wages for an ordinary artisan, these were truly staggering loans—with correspondingly massive returns for the company.[20]

For working people in Bordeaux and similar European cities, the American Revolution brought a familiar mix of ordeals and rewards. The eighteenth-century war machine created a great deal of work for European laborers. Those who avoided being thrown into combat might find the wartime economy rewarding. But strains were inevitable as empires mobilized armies and navies. Tensions rose as governments went scrounging for the manpower and money to fight. And even the most disciplined fighting forces produced a degree of disruption wherever they went. When the

American war began, the working people of Bordeaux were already prepared for it by long experience—ready to profit from the opportunities war offered while mitigating its dangers.

It was in Bordeaux that John Adams arrived in April 1778 on his very first journey overseas. The US Congress had chosen him as one of the emissaries to the Kingdom of France. Congress had been contemplating how to seek the help of foreign powers in the fight with Britain since the United States had declared its independence. From a strategic and military perspective, France was the obvious partner. The French monarchy had been fighting the British empire, on and off, for decades. It had by far the most powerful army and navy in continental Europe, certainly the only one that could hope to match or overmaster the British armed forces. And France's humiliating defeat in the Seven Years' War, less than fifteen years earlier, had left the French public and government eager for an opportunity to get their revenge on Britain.[21]

Adams was a natural choice for the role of emissary to France. He had distinguished himself as one of the most active and useful members of Congress. For two years, he had been serving in a highly visible position as a member of the Board of War, the committee responsible for supervising the war effort. His qualities, including his sharp tongue and inability to suffer fools, did not necessarily endear him to others. But his tireless work ethic earned their respect. Adams, characteristically, was somewhat ambivalent about being charged with the mission to France. The journey would be long, the mission's success far from assured, and Abigail was not eager to see him go. But his sense of duty, perhaps aided a bit by his vanity, resolved him to say yes. He departed, with John Quincy, his eldest son, in tow, on a blustery New England day in February, aboard the *Boston* with Captain Samuel Tucker.[22] They arrived at the Garonne about six weeks later.

In a superficial sense, Bordeaux was terra incognita for Adams. Perhaps most peculiar for him, as for many of the *Boston's* New England–bred seamen, was the city's overt Catholicism. Like all of France, Bordeaux had been vigorously re-evangelized by the Catholic Church over the course of the eighteenth century. The American emissary had remarked on the array of steeples as the ship passed by Spain earlier in the voyage. Now he found himself in a city profoundly imprinted by the nation's official Catholic faith. Sharpening the impact was the fact that the *Boston* had arrived in Bordeaux during the Easter season, a time when the city saw a spate of public processions and rituals.[23]

The common language of gentility helped to ease Adams's way into this unfamiliar world. Like Boston, Bordeaux was a commercial city dominated by merchants. Even before he had officially landed in Bordeaux, Adams was invited aboard an outbound merchantman, the *Julie*, for dinner. He enthused about his first French meal for an entire page of his diary. They began with a "fine french Soup" followed by "the Lights of a Calf, dressed one Way and the Liver another." All of this was accompanied by "very fine" bread "baked on board" and a string of excellent desserts and drinks. "Every Thing was as clean as in any Gentlemans House," he raved. In the afternoon, the officers of another French ship visited the *Boston*. Though Adams spoke no more than the few words of French he had learned on his passage over, the officers' bearing and manners conveyed all that was necessary. Adams deemed them "very genteel" and considered himself well greeted.[24]

Adams was thrilled as the rapturous reception continued for days. (He may or may not have realized that many of these enthusiastic locals were confusing him with his distant cousin, Samuel, who at this juncture was far better known internationally.) The *Boston* was so mobbed by well-wishers that its captain marveled in his logbook that "one would think they never saw a ship before." After another lavish dinner, Adams reported back in a letter to his colleague Patrick Henry that "high eulogiums . . . are everywhere bestowed by learned and ingenious men upon our constitutions, our laws, our wisdom, valor and universal virtue." He did not forget his habitual dose of arsenic either: they "do us rather more honor than we deserve."[25]

But Bordeaux and its modest pleasures were not the aim of Adams's voyage. He had to continue on to Paris. On April 4, Adams stepped into a coach with John Quincy, crossing France to take up his position as one of the three American commissioners to the French court.[26]

Adams quickly discovered that the commission he was joining was a snake pit. Until very recently, it had been composed of Connecticut merchant Silas Deane, accomplished Virginia gentleman Arthur Lee, and the famous Dr. Benjamin Franklin. Adams replaced Deane, who had been unceremoniously recalled by Congress. But though Adams was the new arrival, he could not avoid entering a complex situation. The commissioners had been at one another's throats for a year or more already. Their disagreements had become so severe that Deane and Lee were barely on speaking terms. News of these arguments circulated openly in Paris, in Europe, and back to the United States.[27]

Ostensibly, the arguments among the commissioners were about how they were executing their diplomatic mission. Franklin and Deane accused Lee (and another southerner, Ralph Izard) of being intemperate, overly easy to anger, and generally unsuited to diplomacy. Lee charged that Franklin and Deane were living beyond their means and that they had excluded him from important decisions. But the vitriol sprang from differences in the worldviews of these men who were having to work together closely under high pressure. Lee, from a prominent Virginia family, had grown up amid one of the most rigid social hierarchies in North America. He was proud of the power he held as a white man, viciously deriding Black people as "stubborn, base, and wicked." But he also bent to hierarchical rule himself. After his father died, he had been his eldest brother's ward. The brother sent him to England, against his will, and forced him into an education for which he was ill-suited. Franklin and Deane came from middling families in colonies with relatively greater social mobility. For both of them, social flexibility greased by gifts and friendship held the promise of political and personal advancement.[28]

Adams found himself thrust into the role of mediator between these men. Franklin, who shared his up-and-comer background, was clearly the one with whom he had more sympathy and understanding. Still, Adams tried his level best to smooth over the differences, to accomplish the business of the revolution in spite of the divisions. He had done so before in the Massachusetts patriot movement during the 1760s and in Congress earlier in the decade. But this particular conflict proved intractable. The three commissioners could not agree on anything. They could hardly get anything done at all. Even drafting a letter that could go out under their collective signature was usually more than could be hoped for.[29]

In September, mere months after Adams arrived in Paris, Congress dissolved the three-man commission. Franklin was named sole minister plenipotentiary in France, and Arthur Lee was sent to the Spanish court in Madrid. Nobody said it outright, because everybody involved already knew: even in a foreign land, the self-made Philadelphian revolutionary and his born-to-the-manor Virginian counterpart held worldviews that could hardly, if ever, be reconciled.

AS IF THE FIERCE CONFLICT BETWEEN HIS FELLOW COMMISSIONERS was not reminder enough of the heavy hand of the prerevolutionary past, Adams found himself constantly reminded in France of just how modest his upbringing had been. Paris and the society of the court came as a shock to him, especially after he had tasted the relatively easy familiarity of genteel life in Bordeaux. Few American revolutionaries could claim to have the self-awareness and sharp social eye of John Adams. Within days of his arrival in Paris, he had become acutely conscious of the gap between himself and his hosts. It was made all the more visible to him by the smooth ease of Benjamin Franklin, who seemed somehow to have slipped into the life of the French aristocracy without the slightest trouble. (Franklin's years living in London before the revolution had given him a significant head start in figuring out how to emulate the manners of a European court.)[30]

The homes and palaces of the high nobility and the royal family overwhelmed Adams. He described Versailles as "sublime," which is hardly a surprise. But he quickly found that he was exhausting the range of available superlatives to describe buildings and furnishings. The duc d'Ayen's home was "in the highest Style of magnificence," he wrote. He even admitted several times—as he rarely did, wordsmith that he was—that some of these scenes were "beyond my Talent at Description." A certain discomfort seemed to take hold of him when he had to think about these scenes. The day that he was called to meet the king for the first time, May 8, his daily diary slipped into the third person: "This Morning Dr. Franklin, Mr. Lee, and Mr. Adams, went to Versailles, in Order that Mr. Adams might be presented to the King."[31] It was as if another person were inhabiting his body.

Most discomfiting to Adams seemed to be his relative lack of facility with the language of the court. His French was poor, and he repeatedly expressed his frustration with his inability to make himself understood in even the simplest conversation. Yet this was a time when knowing where to put one's hands and feet—as much as mastery of words—was a key measure of one's social quality. Adams had been relatively at home with the physical language of the merchant gentry in Bordeaux: the bows and the little courtesies and the gestures on which to hang a phrase. Yet he was perceptibly ill at ease with the courtly culture he encountered in Paris. When he first met the king, Adams recorded his discomfort with the alien movements of his body. He was brought into the royal "Bed Chamber" and positioned behind the king. The monarch then "turned about" and "smiled." A few moments later, Adams was "conducted . . . to the Door of another Room." The king passed by him as he made his way through. A month later, Adams was present at another royal ceremony, at which he remarked on the "Kneelings, the Bows, and the Curtesies" of the participants: "Every Muscle, Nerve and Fibre . . . seemed perfectly disciplined to perform its function."[32]

Like his third-person narration of his May encounter with the king, Adams's remarks on the gracefulness of the court nobles in June marked out a moment of failure for him. The rules of bodily comportment were supposed to be learned in childhood, to become all but second nature to the genteel individual. To remark on them so insistently, as Adams did, showed that one had not properly internalized them. He was studying the nobles, not being one of them. He had come exceedingly far since his youth on the farm in Braintree. The shoemaker's boy, who had liked nothing more than to shoot and ramble in the fields, was now treating with kings. But his humble origins continued to tell; he could not escape them. In this stratified society, the ingrained habits of his youth anchored him to the place from which he had come.

# 6
# THE TOP-DOWN REVOLUTIONS

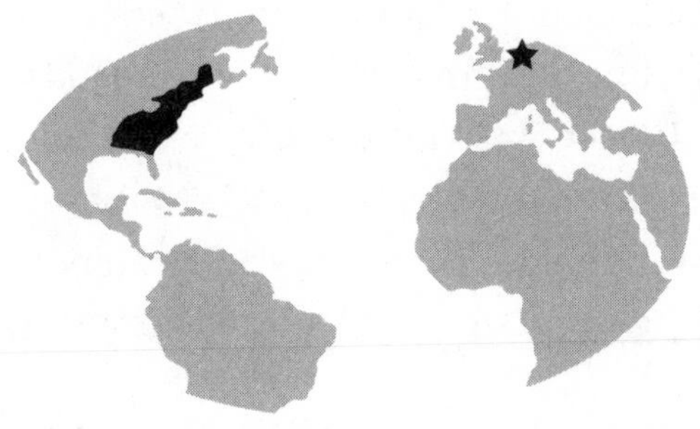

JOHN ADAMS DID NOT REMAIN LONG IN PARIS. IN JUNE 1780, Congress appointed him to a new post as the republic's ambassador to the Netherlands. Adams left for Amsterdam without knowing that he had been appointed, arriving in early August with a double mission to gain official recognition of his country from the Dutch government and to raise funds for the American war from Amsterdam bankers. The work proved exhausting and, for nearly two years, almost entirely unsuccessful. Adams struggled to gain any traction with the Dutch, who feared British retaliation if they made any public acknowledgment of the North American rebels.

A slow-moving revolution in the Netherlands, which had begun about the time that Adams arrived, eventually tipped the Dutch Republic over to the North Americans' side. Dutch aid helped the United States gain its independence in 1783. Over the next four years, the two republics, one brand-new and the other in its dotage, experienced intense political unrest.

In both the Dutch Republic and the United States during the 1780s, there was a powerful appetite for significant political change. In both, internal divisions—as much about different habits and expectations as about divergent interests—made such change hard to achieve. The Dutch patriots, a loose federation of opponents of the existing political regime in the Netherlands, first began to organize in 1780. The patriot revolt spread gradually, eventually forcing the Prince of Orange, the quasi-royal head of state, to flee his palace in The Hague. The revolt was brought to an abrupt end in 1787 when the prince returned with Prussian troops and reconquered the country.

Across the Atlantic in the United States, the middle years of the 1780s brought a deep economic depression and fierce political infighting among the now victorious patriots. In almost every state, political coalitions powered by the less well-off tried to gain control of the government and enact debt relief. Where they could not control the government, as in Massachusetts, they resorted to direct action. The weak national government could do little to constrain these state-level efforts. So in 1786 and 1787, a group of gentlemen from across the colonies decided to convene in Philadelphia and frame a stronger national government. The result was the US Constitution, written in 1787 and ratified during 1788 after a difficult campaign.

The struggles of the 1780s had different outcomes in the two republics. The Dutch patriot movement was defeated while the North Americans succeeded in establishing a national government that continues to exist to this day. But in both republics, the gap between elite and working-class revolutionaries was key to the political outcome and left a lasting mark. In the Netherlands, the dynastic elite patriots assumed that it was their role to lead their fellow citizens. They established an exclusive political network, built around closed correspondences limited to men like themselves, to organize a nationwide movement. Working-class patriots organized primarily at the local level, through existing militia institutions. As the patriot movement grew, the two wings remained largely detached. This divided movement proved unable to mount serious resistance when foreign troops finally intervened in 1787.[1]

In North America, the social distance separating elites from the working classes was smaller than in the Netherlands. Political leaders in the United States were also the lucky beneficiaries of more favorable circumstances: they did not have to contend with large, heavily armed states on their borders. But North American elites had no less a sense of their leadership role than their Dutch counterparts. It was precisely this powerful sense that they were the natural leaders of the country that led them to create the US Constitution. In key respects, the Constitution was the product of a successful revolution from above. The Constitutional Convention itself was a virtual coup by the elite against the existing government. The Constitution, once ratified, enhanced the power of the national political leadership at the expense of more working-class politicians primarily operating at the state level.

The patriot revolt of the 1780s in the Netherlands was a new chapter in a long and baroque history of political conflict in the Dutch Republic. The Netherlands in the eighteenth century occupied much the same wedge of territory between the French- and German-speaking lands of northern Europe as it does today. The republic originated in the late 1500s as a federation of provinces and towns that revolted against their sovereign, Philip II of

Spain, of the House of Habsburg. During the 1570s and 1580s, seven primarily Protestant and Dutch-speaking provinces formed themselves into a de facto federal republic. Its structure was complex: cities and provinces retained their own governments, with multiple levels of authority, in which both townspeople (burghers) and noblemen played a role. Each province sent delegates to a joint parliament, the States General, but according to most observers the provinces retained much of their sovereign power.[2]

During the early years of the struggle with the Habsburgs, the provinces had pressed an old institution, the stadtholderate, into service as a kind of executive office. The stadtholder had been an official appointed as chief magistrate in the Netherlands by the king when he was absent. The Dutch rebels kept the office but gave each provincial parliament the right to elect its own stadtholder. The stadtholder served as the head of the armed forces and had significant patronage at his disposal. In theory, he remained subordinate to the provincial parliament and the States General. There was also no requirement that a province choose a stadtholder, and the provincial parliament could remove or replace him. Though the office was elective, the stadtholders were always members of the House of Orange, a high-ranking princely family. (William I of Orange had been the leader of the revolt against the Habsburgs until his assassination in 1584.) One member of the family was usually chosen as stadtholder of all the provinces, though there were periods when the provinces chose different ones.[3]

The republic flourished during the seventeenth century, and a potent merchant elite and political class took shape in its leading cities. The provinces of Holland, Utrecht, and Zeeland, clustered in the west of the country along the North Sea, experienced rapid growth and urbanization. Amsterdam in Holland, the city of Utrecht in its namesake province, and Middelburg in Zeeland all became major hubs of international trade. The four provinces to the east and north—Gelderland, Overijssel, Drenthe, and Friesland—remained more rural. The long war with the Habsburgs turned the republic into a major military power, produced tremendous economic growth and allowed the Dutch to establish a colonial empire that spanned the globe. The rising tide lifted all boats: consumption and the standard of living, especially in the cities of the populous province of Holland, soared. Yet social stratification remained strong. By the early seventeenth century, a largely hereditary political class known as the regents (*regenten*) had coalesced across the republic, who combined political power with dynastic wealth. They dominated city and provincial governments as well as powerful public entities such as water boards and trading companies.[4]

The regents, especially those from the most wealthy and urbanized provinces, Holland and Utrecht, competed fiercely with the stadtholders for the upper hand in the republic. Throughout the seventeenth and eighteenth centuries, the regents (sometimes called the States Party) consistently sought to expand their power at the stadtholders' expense. For several decade-long periods, they even succeeded in preventing the appointment of a stadtholder altogether. The stadtholders, for their part, could generally count on the support of the more rural provinces and a portion of the urban working classes in these struggles. (The working classes' Orangist sympathies were certainly connected to the resentment that many of them felt toward the urban regents.) The two sides were generally fairly evenly matched during the seventeenth century. This did not prevent the struggle from becoming ferocious at times. In 1672, Johan de Witt, the head of the States Party, was murdered along with his brother by an Orangist mob. Their bodies were mutilated and partially cannibalized.[5]

In the eighteenth century, the republic experienced a relative decline. Economic growth and the republic's military position peaked in the middle of the seventeenth century and began to erode seriously by the end of the century. The republic remained a wealthy state, but the rapid ascent came to an end. This decline chilled the political and economic system, fixing the regents more firmly in place while the majority of the population experienced stagnation of their social and economic situation. The regents' confidence in the security of their position affected their attitudes and ways of life. The vestiges of the modesty and simplicity of Dutch burgher culture that had survived into the later seventeenth century gradually disappeared. The regents increasingly lived a faithful imitation of the elite lifestyle of the French court.[6]

The stadtholders, always looking for opportunities to strengthen their position against the States Party, took advantage of the regents' decadence to consolidate their power. For much of the first half of the century, the regents had prevented the election of a stadtholder. In 1747, a major Orangist uprising took place across the Dutch provinces. Sparked by French military action but propelled by popular anger against the regents, the revolt had as its main demand the appointment of a new stadtholder. The regents were forced to acquiesce, appointing William IV of Orange as stadtholder. Over the next thirty years, he and his successor, William V, systematically expanded the stadtholder's power in the republic. They accumulated ever-increasing amounts of patronage and took direct control of a growing number of the republic's political institutions. For the first time, the republic had something that resembled a royal court.[7]

The American revolutionary war sparked a new challenge to this ossified political scene. The Dutch Republic had remained neutral during the Seven Years' War, which had pitted France and Britain against each other during the 1750s and early 1760s. At the beginning of the American war, the British government had called on its longtime Dutch allies to provide troops and financial support for their war with the rebellious colonists. This demand quickly aroused opposition from some of the regents. Some, especially in Holland, sympathized with the American rebels. Others both sympathized with the rebels and feared that supporting the

British would strengthen the long-standing alliance with Britain that they despised.[8]

The most prominent and outspoken opponent of aiding Britain in the American war was Baron Joan Derk van der Capellen. Born in 1741, Van der Capellen was the scion of a noble family in the rural province of Overijssel, which lay hard up against the German border to the east of Holland. By virtue of his status, he was able to secure a seat in the governing Estates of Overijssel. In 1775, when the British Crown asked the Dutch government to provide military aid, in the form of a brigade of troops, to help suppress the American rebellion, Van der Capellen spoke out forcefully against it. His intervention, though not decisive on its own in preventing the dispatch of the troops, significantly increased the political cost of doing so. The stadtholder abandoned the plan of offering direct military aid to Britain shortly thereafter. Van der Capellen soon became an active advocate for the North American rebels' cause, corresponding with US political leaders and even providing a personal loan to the American war effort.[9]

In 1781, clearly inspired in part by the intellectual ferment around the American war, Van der Capellen turned his critical eye on the political situation of the republic. He secretly wrote a pamphlet, *Aan het volk van Nederland* (*To the People of the Netherlands*), which he had printed and distributed to most of the country in a single night in September. The pamphlet offered a powerful indictment of the stadtholderate and what Van der Capellen depicted as an emergent tyrannical regime. He asserted the Lockean principle that "all men are born free"—they are "equal by nature . . . and one is not subject to another." The Netherlands, he wrote, was a "great society [or company]," and the people were its rightful rulers. "You," he wrote, addressing the people of the Netherlands, "are the members, the owners, and masters of the national society." The "great ones" were merely "directors and treasurers": they are "your servants; they are accountable to [you], and bound to obey your orders."[10] It was up to the people of the Netherlands to reclaim their rightful commanding role in politics.

*Aan het volk* ended with a rousing call for a popular movement to reclaim power from the stadtholder and his allies. Van der Capellen called on ordinary people to form popular assemblies in the centers of their cities and towns and choose individuals to represent them. They should elect, he wrote, "good, cautious, pious men; choose good patriots whom you can trust." These representatives should then be sent to the meeting places of the various provincial estates, where they were to demand immediate reforms "in the name . . . of the nation." Van der Capellen also urged that these representatives should have to keep their constituents apprised of what they were doing "from time to time by means of the press in a public and open accounting." Last, but hardly least, he urged citizens to "arm themselves" in defense of their liberties.[11]

UNDER THE IMPULSION OF VAN DER CAPELLEN'S FORCEFUL CALL to arms, the patriot movement began to spread across the republic. Yet as the political movement grew, it found itself enmeshed in the powerful reflexes of a divided society. The political and cultural habits of both regents and commoners proved to be ill-suited to making durable political alliances across the incised lines of class in the late eighteenth-century Netherlands.

Efforts to organize a more broadly based patriot movement from below began across the Netherlands during the first months of 1783. Not coincidentally, this occurred shortly after the Netherlands signed a treaty with the United States in October 1782, marking a significant victory for the patriot party in government and its pro-American agenda. In January 1783, with the encouragement of patriot regent Cornelis de Gijselaar, a group of burghers in the Holland town of Dordrecht formed a paramilitary political society open to all who wished to take part, which they called the

Free Corps. Other towns soon followed their lead: by the middle of the year, similar societies, variously called *exercitiegenootschappen* (literally "exercise societies") or Free Corps, had been formed in important towns across the provinces, including Rotterdam, Utrecht, Deventer, Zwolle, and Kampen.[12]

The Free Corps drew on a combination of old and new ideas and practices. A very old precedent existed for the Free Corps in the form of the urban militia or *schutterij*. These institutions of medieval foundation had played a crucial role during the revolt against Spain, helping to organize urban defense and maintain order in the absence of regular troops. They had undergone a steep decline since the revolt's end, so that by the early 1780s, the *schutterij* were little more than a color guard for annual urban rituals. Nonetheless, the simple existence of these militias—and the powerful myth of burgher military self-sufficiency that they embodied—served to legitimize the creation of the new militia groups in the 1780s. Once formed, the Free Corps in every town asked the local government for recognition and, in many cases, to be allowed to take the place of the *schutterij*.[13]

Though they invoked centuries-old practices and ideals to legitimize their formation, the Free Corps departed in at least two important ways from those traditions. While the traditional *schutterij* had been limited to those with property, and in some cases even just to those who enjoyed the freedom of the city, membership in most Free Corps was open to all individuals, even those who had little or no property. This relative social openness made the Free Corps far more representative of the full range of urban society than their predecessors had been. The backbone of the movement was artisans, shopkeepers, and professionals, the middling sorts of Dutch urban life. The Free Corps also developed a leadership structure that was markedly more democratic than that of the *schutterij*. Though the *schutterij* held elections, they had become entirely pro forma by the end of the eighteenth century, invariably resulting in the choice of a select group of regents. The Free Corps instituted a practice of electing their leadership from within their own ranks. Reflecting long-standing habits of social deference, the members for the most part chose well-off individuals to be their leaders; yet the simple fact of choosing non-regents for leadership positions was a significant change.[14]

Once they had formed, the patriot militias sought to build links with like-minded groups elsewhere in their provinces and across the Netherlands. Yet unlike the patriots from the regent class, many of whom had long-standing connections with one another across provincial boundaries, the Free Corps and reformed *schutterij* did not have preexisting networks. Even where the Free Corps took over an existing *schutterij* infrastructure, such as in Utrecht, they had to start from scratch because the militia company was fundamentally a single-city institution; there was no tradition of interurban (let alone interprovincial) contact among companies. Ironically, the process of creating links with other towns was made more difficult by the democratic practices of the new militia companies: their leaders, specifically not drawn from the local regent elite, lacked the experience in provincial and interprovincial politics for which a role in urban politics was a prerequisite.

At the same time as the rank-and-file patriots were organizing through the militia movement, patriot regents were beginning to think about creating a national structure themselves. In 1783, a group of leading patriot regents from across the republic decided to create a formal interprovincial correspondence network. At the first meeting where this was discussed, in August 1783, the main proposal was put forward by Robert Jasper van der Capellen, Joan Derk's younger cousin, and himself a leading nobleman in the province of Gelderland. The younger Van der Capellen proposed the creation of a formal system of interprovincial patriot correspondences. Nothing could be more important, he wrote in his draft plan, than forming "a greater and more intimate correspondence among the representatives, the governments of the seven provinces."

The system that Van der Capellen and his collaborators envisioned would be both secretive and hierarchical. The system he wished to create would be federal, like the republic itself, but designed to channel information via "men of proven loyalty." The basic structure would be a correspondence among the "well-intentioned patriots," who would then choose "a representative to correspond with the representatives of the other provinces." He would first correspond with the members from one or two other provinces and then they would coordinate with the other departments. In times of need, the members would meet in person in Amsterdam, "in order to avoid any offense," and communicate their decisions back to their respective provinces to be diffused throughout the network.[15]

During the discussion of the plan, Jacob Nanning du Tour, an official from the province of Holland, raised a number of questions. Would the position of corresponding member be a temporary or a lifetime appointment? How would they be chosen? What procedures would they follow in case of disagreement? The most telling question he raised, however, was "What security is there for the papers of the correspondents in case of death?" Evidently, he expected that the letters would be the personal property of the members. If one of them died, they could pass to politically unsympathetic heirs. On the recommendation of F. G. Blok of Leiden, a correspondent of both Van der Capellen cousins, the meeting also decided to limit the scope of the correspondence to ordinary business, leaving any larger debates over the movement's strategy either to local initiative or to the face-to-face meetings. The largely informational purpose of the correspondence union was reiterated and its specific duties enumerated during the next meeting of the patriot regents in October 1783.[16]

Van der Capellen's proposal and the discussion around it offer a striking contrast to the proposals for intercolonial systems of correspondence made by American patriots in the early 1770s. Americans like Arthur Lee and Samuel Adams had also planned to restrict active participation in their networks to politically reliable gentlemen. Yet even they had not envisioned a closed, elite network like the one the Dutch patriots sought to create. The Boston Committee of Correspondence did more than facilitate communication among patriot leaders; it also claimed to speak for the "people" of Boston (and in some cases Massachusetts), and its correspondence incited other localities to form committees that made similar claims. The American committees of correspondence system was also thoroughly decentralized: every community could have one, and they expected to correspond on more or less equal terms. The Van der Capellen plan envisioned a relatively small group of patriot leaders directing the network from the center, deliberating among themselves and distributing information outward to satellite clubs and eventually the populace. It was a hierarchical model of formal interprovincial communication, tightly governed by the patriot elite.

Between 1784 and 1786, the Dutch patriot militia movement spread and became increasingly well organized. With its relatively wide social reach, it became a vehicle for political mobilization by members of the working classes. Even as this was happening, the division between the militias and the patriot regents grew sharper. In 1786, militia companies, presenting themselves as the voice of a popular movement, demanded a more prominent role in the formal governance of the republic. Patriot regents in the province of Holland and elsewhere, protective of their prerogatives, balked at these demands. By early 1787, some had become disenchanted enough with the pressure from below that they were beginning to tilt back politically toward the stadtholder and the status quo from before 1780.

The rapid growth of the Free Corps gave them a growing aura of authority as a voice for a popular movement. The militia in Overijssel, Joan Derk van der Capellen's home base, counted some two thousand members across the province's towns by the end of 1784. A June 1785 meeting of the Free Corps in the city of Utrecht brought together thousands of militiamen from across the republic. A subsequent mass gathering in August 1786, also held in Utrecht, brought out over thirteen thousand militiamen from across the republic's provinces. Not unlike the American committees of correspondence and safety, patriot militias connected with groups in neighboring towns and across their provinces. In Overijssel, the groups went as far as to organize a series of meetings among the province's militias, though these did not meet regularly until 1786.[17]

As the patriot militia movement expanded, its leaders sought to give it a more robust national organization. In early 1784, the Utrecht Free Corps groups called for a national meeting of representatives from Free Corps across the nation. Patriot regents were not invited. Though mostly ceremonial, the meeting was fruitful enough that the Free Corps leaders began to meet on a regular basis. At their third meeting, the Free Corps leaders drafted an act of association (*Acte van verbintenis*) for the patriot militias. This document was a "program of democratic patriotism," which called for a radical expansion of popular participation in the governance of the republic and an end to the domination of both the regents and the stadtholder. This was followed a few months later by a manifesto with even more radical elements, the Leiden Draft (*Leidse ontwerp*), which used powerful natural-rights language to argue for a radical reshaping of the Dutch polity.[18]

The militia movement's relations with the regent patriot leaders remained highly hierarchical; the social gulf between them yawned wide. High-ranking regent patriots, including De Gijselaar and the Van der Capellen cousins, regularly received letters from patriot clubs and militia companies across the Netherlands. The societies wrote to offer congratulations on specific achievements or to invite the nationally known figures to join their society as honorary members. The surviving letters are almost embarrassingly obsequious. The Utrecht *exercitiegenootschap* Pro Patria et Libertate, for instance, greeted Joan Derk van der Capellen in rapturous terms in 1783: "It is in your footsteps, o hero! that we are so willingly following! In order to show that we will willingly be your sons! O loving father! . . . See how living fire sparkles from our eyes! O freedom's lover!"[19]

After Joan Derk's death in 1784, many of the militias redirected their attention toward Robert Jasper van der Capellen. He received a large number of letters from militia companies in 1786. Most were written on extra-large sheets of heavy paper with the opening and closing formulas carefully calligraphed—marks of respect and deference. The Leiden *schutterij*, asking for Robert Jasper's help in 1786, addressed him as "great man!" and "brave defender of the people's legal rights!" They asked him to bring his authority and reputation to bear in favor of a new constitution for the Netherlands. The Delft *schutterij* sent him a long poem, elegantly calligraphed, which praised him immoderately. It was his "virtue," they wrote, that had protected the Netherlands from "tyrants": "We [and] the Netherlands, do offer you tribute!" The poem from Delft was signed by Gerrit Paape, who had a reputation as one of the most democratically inclined leaders of the patriot party.[20]

Whatever genuflections they performed toward the national regent leadership, the Free Corps on the local level made an increasingly aggressive push for greater power. In Utrecht, for instance, the militia repeatedly pressured the regents to dismiss Orangist members of the urban government and (in 1785) to incorporate Free Corps candidates. They succeeded in taking over the Utrecht city government in early 1786. The story was similar in Deventer, where the regents at first sought to keep the Free Corps at arm's length, only to have the militia force them to incorporate its leaders into the city government in 1784. In a few cases where the conflict between the militia and the town government became serious enough, as in Rotterdam in 1784, the provincial government stepped in and took the patriots' side. But these moments of solidarity between the local militia and regent patriot leaders were rare.[21]

For much of 1786, the patriot movement, in spite of its internal divisions, managed to hold its own against the Prince of Orange and his supporters. A military and political stalemate prevailed between the forces of the patriot movement and those of the stadtholder, with neither side strong enough to vanquish the other. The patriot party seemed to be holding strong in the cities of Holland and Utrecht, the wealthiest and most populous of the republic's provinces. The movement also had support in a crucial handful of towns in the eastern and northern provinces. Yet underneath this veneer of strength, the foundation of the movement was weakening. Dissention between the Free Corps and the patriot regents continued to grow in many of these towns. Neither wing had the organizational heft or the incentive to force a reckoning, but the two sides of the movement were far apart by the middle of 1787. The movement was held tensely together by fear of its opponents.

In the end, the arrest of a single woman—though, admittedly, a princess—set in motion the collapse of the patriots' house of cards. In June 1787, Wilhelmina, wife of William V and sister of the new king of Prussia, Frederick William II, set out on a journey to The Hague. The goal of the trip was political, to encourage the Orangists in the province of Holland. Instead, she was unexpectedly stopped and briefly detained by members of the Gouda Free Corps. Though she was released unharmed, the stadtholder and his brother-in-law considered the arrest of one of their own to be an intolerable insult. Frederick William II sent his army into the Netherlands. The divided and weakened patriot movement proved unable to offer much resistance. The Netherlands was overrun in a few weeks. Members of the Free Corps melted back into civilian life and patriot regents made little effort to prevent the troops from taking back their towns and cities. William V returned to The Hague, the seat of government, and initiated a massive purge of the government at all levels, removing virtually everyone with patriot sympathies from positions of authority.[22]

On October 9, 1787, a matter of weeks before the Prussian troops entered the Netherlands, John Adams lamented in a letter to John Jay that the "Affairs [of] Holland" were "too dismal, to be repeated." The situation of the Dutch Republic was a "living Warning to our United States." He diagnosed the problem with the patriot movement in simple terms: The "Plebians" were closely allied to the "Monarch." The "Patrician Aristocracy," that is to say the patriot regents, could not "overcome" this affiliation. Having failed to gain the collaboration of the bulk of the population in their quest for a reformed republic, their revolution was doomed.[23]

Adams was well aware, when he wrote this letter, that his colleagues back in the United States were engaged in a similar enterprise. Less than a month before he wrote to Jay, a closed meeting of eminent gentlemen, held at the former Pennsylvania State House in Philadelphia, had concluded its business and proposed a new constitution for the United States. The meeting, later branded the Constitutional Convention, was seemingly worlds away from the ignominious public collapse of the Dutch patriot movement. As Adams suggested in calling the Dutch situation a "living Warning," however, the delegates to the Philadelphia convention had similar problems on their minds to those that animated their Dutch counterparts. Foremost among them: how to create a strong state in a dangerous world while fostering order at home. But it was not just the problems that they had in common. The solutions the men of the convention proposed, in both substance and style, drew from the same well of hierarchical ideas and attitudes that they shared with the Dutch patriot leaders on the other side of the Atlantic.

The previous four years, since the peace treaty that ended the American revolutionary war in 1783, had been difficult ones for the United States. Economic challenges came from three directions. Debts from the war weighed heavy on the newly independent country. Most of the debt had been incurred by the states and had been sold to individuals. Servicing it became a conundrum. The states needed to raise revenue to pay for it, but higher taxes were both unpopular and strained the economy. Either the states' creditors or their taxpayers were left unsatisfied. A steep drop-off in demand with the end of the war added to the economic pressure on many Americans, from artisans to farmers. The formal separation from Britain exacerbated these pressures by forcing a significant rejiggering of trading relationships around the Atlantic, affecting both the export of American crops and products and the importation of manufactured goods.[24]

Political unrest accompanied the economic troubles of the 1780s. Fierce conflicts arose in many of the states over the issue of paper money: in general, debtors wanted their states to issue paper money, which would make it easier for them to pay their debts, while creditors opposed it. State and local governments became battlegrounds over all kinds of political and economic issues during the 1780s. Disputes about tax rates, the role of courts in collecting debts or foreclosing on debtors who were in arrears, and tariffs on foreign goods roiled the states. The tone of these conflicts, even in the statehouses, was acrimonious. In many states, particularly in the more rural western reaches of larger states like Massachusetts and Pennsylvania, desperate farmers turned to direct action against what they perceived as overbearing state governments. The agitation in western Massachusetts culminated in 1786–1787, when farmers in the region around Amherst and Northampton rose in revolt against the government in Boston. They closed down the local courts to prevent the collection of debts and threatened representatives of the state. The state government responded with an armed expedition from Boston, which forced the rebels into surrender. But the government, aware of the fragility of its position, avoided meting out harsh punishments.[25]

The economic and political difficulties were compounded, in the eyes of political leaders across the states, by the weakness of the US government. The Articles of Confederation, passed by Congress in 1777 and finally ratified in 1781, had put in place a deliberately weak government for the new nation. The Articles in fact specified that each individual state retained its full "sovereignty." The government the Articles formalized consisted of a Congress in which each state had a single vote and in which most important decisions required consensus. Such agreement was very hard to achieve, given the widely varying needs and desires of the states. The national government had no executive officer and it did not have the power to levy taxes. Its role was limited to foreign policy (including declaring war, making peace, and conducting diplomacy) and to acting as a forum for adjudicating disputes among the states. Congress had no power to help resolve the political crises in the states, nor did it have any authority to shape economic policy. Indeed, by 1785, the Congress had been so starved of money by the states that it had become virtually impotent.[26]

Leaders in a number of states saw a reinvention of the national government as crucial to addressing the postwar crisis. In January 1786, the Virginia House of Delegates, possibly at the behest of one of its members, a thirty-four-year-old James Madison, voted to call a convention of states to reexamine aspects of the national compact. The meeting, held in September in Annapolis, Maryland, attracted delegates from only five states. With such limited attendance, it was not possible to propose serious revisions to the frame of government. The delegates to the Annapolis convention, not unlike their predecessors in the First Continental Congress, settled for calling a second convention. They sent a letter to their respective state legislatures, "beg[ging] leave" with "the most respectful deference" to "suggest" that delegates from all the states meet in Philadelphia in May 1787. Congress offered its qualified support for the plan, the states chose delegates, and on May 5, 1787, James Madison was the first to arrive in Philadelphia.[27]

There were no poor men among the delegates to the convention in Philadelphia. The representatives from the southern states consisted entirely of planters and planter-lawyers, among them some of the wealthiest and most prominent men in Virginia and South Carolina. The delegations from Pennsylvania, New Jersey, and New York included figures like Alexander Hamilton (married to an heiress), financier Robert Morris, Benjamin Franklin, and scions of some of the region's largest landholding families, the Livingstons and the Lansings. The delegates from New England included a few men of more modest means: Nathaniel Gorham of Massachusetts, for instance, won and lost several fortunes during his life. But a handful of exceptions aside, even these New England men were the sons of moderately well-off and genteel fathers. Most were well educated and unmistakably part of the gentry. The delegates chose George Washington, former commander in chief of the Continental Army and one of the richest men in America, to preside.[28]

It has long been a vexed question whether and how the convention delegates' wealth and position shaped the Constitution. The Progressive-era historian Charles Beard influentially argued that the Constitution was an instrument of class domination. He believed that the delegates had written it primarily to protect their considerable investments in revolutionary-era debt. Scholarship over the past hundred years has shown that this thesis was overly simplistic. Many of the delegates did not have major investments in revolutionary debt or western lands. What's more, their personal economic interests were not the sole factor driving their decision-making. Each of the delegates spoke for states with distinct interests that flowed from their populations, geographies, economies, and political complexions. Even if the delegates did have some shared economic interests, they could not have pursued them single-mindedly, given the crosscutting interests of their states. Scholars who have closely examined the records of the convention have shown beyond a doubt that a crude mapping of economic interests onto the Constitution is an error.[29]

The delegates to the convention did, however, follow the well-established model of American political leaders claiming sweeping authority to direct the path that revolutionary change would take. The delegates' choices about how the convention would operate, implicit as well as explicit, signaled this attitude. One of the first decisions the delegates took was to close the convention's doors to the public and put a seal of secrecy on their deliberations. There were practical reasons for both choices. They also sent the unmistakable message to the public that the gentlemen who formed the convention, like their Dutch counterparts, believed it was their prerogative to work out solutions to the nation's problems in private. The form the debate took sent an equally strong signal that constitution making was best left to the cream of society. Speeches were dense and lasted many hours—even, in some cases, stretching over more than one day. Such speeches were difficult to deliver and challenging for their listeners to follow; they called for training in rhetoric. In this way, too, the delegates made clear to one another that they and only they had the legitimate authority to shape the new Constitution.[30]

This tendency to favor elite control of politics ran through the convention's substantive decisions. The constitutional structure that the convention arrived at is well known: a national government composed of three coequal branches (legislative, executive, judicial), drawing its authority from the people, and endowed with a limited but still impressive range of powers, including regulating interstate and foreign commerce. Three of the most difficult problems the delegates faced in creating this structure were the composition of the upper house of the legislature (the Senate), the nature of the presidency and selection of the president, and how property in persons would be represented in the new government. On each of these subjects, the delegates gave the most serious consideration to options that empowered people like themselves. From the outset, most of them envisioned the Senate as a check on the popular will. They rapidly decided on long terms for the senators and a form of indirect election that would ensure that only "better men" were selected for the role. They created a presidency that was as powerful as any state chief executive. They again opted for indirect election, this time going so far as to create a new body, the Electoral College, to choose the president. After a somewhat difficult debate, the convention also decided to have enslaved people count toward three-fifths of a person for the purpose of apportioning House seats. This amounted to a major boost to the political power of the southern planter class.[31]

Deliberations and drafting occupied the entirety of the hot Philadelphia summer. On September 17, 1787, the convention sent the proposed Constitution to Congress for ratification. The covering letter that George Washington sent, drafted by the Pennsylvania delegate Gouverneur Morris, eloquently expressed the sense of noblesse oblige that pervaded the entire constitution-writing exercise. "We have now the Honor to submit . . . the Constitution which has appeared to us the most advisable," the letter began. Even for the eighteenth century, the wording was arch, verging on haughty; the genteel "we" of the delegates clearly expected their sense of what was "most advisable" to prevail. Morris and Washington described the convention in rather Olympian terms:

"The Constitution which we now present is the Result of a Spirit of Amity," they wrote, and of "mutual Deference & Concession." They closed the short letter with another self-assured gesture. Though the Constitution would not meet with "the full and entire Approbation of every State," they wrote, the delegates were confident that it was the best that could "reasonably have been expected."[32]

The ratification of the new Constitution followed the by now well-established pattern of elite control. The Constitution's text itself declared that it would enter into force when ratified by "the Conventions of nine States." The word "Conventions" was key: it meant that the framers intended for ad hoc bodies, not state legislatures or the people at large, to decide on ratification. In state after state, the conventions that convened to consider whether to ratify the Constitution were stocked with prominent political leaders. It would be going too far to say that the state conventions were exclusively elite bodies. Each one included some individuals who had origins in the lower orders. William Findley, a leading opponent of the Constitution in the Pennsylvania convention, was one such member: an Irish immigrant who made his living as a farmer. Yet his case confirms rather than disproves the elitist tendency of the state conventions. Though Findley was already politically prominent when he was elected, the more genteel members of the Pennsylvania ratifying convention looked down on him as a hick.[33]

As the ratification process proceeded, leading figures made efforts to stage-manage it, trying to shape the order in which states considered the Constitution, the types of arguments that were available, and who was elected to the conventions. The proponents of the Constitution called themselves "Federalists"—a bit of a willful misnomer, since they were advocating for a more centralized (in other words, less federal) republic. *The Federalist Papers*, a series of newspaper essays published anonymously by James Madison, Alexander Hamilton, and John Jay as contributions to the New

York ratification debate, are just one of the most durable pieces of the sprawling effort under this name. The opponents of the Constitution found themselves labeled "Anti-Federalists," a moniker they resisted. The opponents were a varied bunch, whose arguments against the Constitution ranged from claims that it deprived states of their sovereignty to claims that it would infringe on individual liberty.[34]

The efforts of the Philadelphia convention's delegates and their allies bore fruit. After Pennsylvania ratified the Constitution, four more states (Delaware, New Jersey, Georgia, and Connecticut) ratified in quick succession, three of them by unanimous votes of their conventions. Massachusetts made six by early February 1788. Maryland and South Carolina ratified in the spring, making eight, one shy of the number required for the Constitution to come into effect. It fell to Virginia, whose convention was stocked as usual with planters and gentlemen, to ratify at the end of June, bringing the Constitution into effect. New Hampshire and New York followed shortly thereafter, albeit in close votes. The gentleman revolutionaries had won another battle in their long struggle to create a republican nation conceived in their image.[35]

The Dutch and American republics in the 1780s had a good deal in common. Revolutionary change was an ongoing fact of life in both regions. Much remained unsettled about the political situation of the United States after it gained independence in 1783. The pressures of economic crisis heightened and sharpened the conflicts that were bubbling under the surface. As in the Netherlands, the genteel wing of the revolutionary party saw an opportunity and even an obligation in this moment of crisis.

Gentlemen revolutionaries in both the Netherlands and the United States genuinely believed that their positions gave them a vocation to steer the ongoing political transformations. They each adopted, seemingly unselfconsciously, modes of private, closed political organizing as a way to direct the revolutionary movement into what they regarded as appropriate channels. This approach put patriot elites at odds with political mobilizations from below, whether spearheaded by farmers in western Massachusetts or by artisans and shopkeepers in Utrecht and Amsterdam. The class-divided, hierarchical habitus of the mid-eighteenth-century Atlantic world still loomed large, shaping the political instincts of leaders in the republics on both continents.

The revolution from above succeeded in the United States during the 1780s while in the Netherlands it went down to defeat. American observers of the Dutch Republic were at no loss to explain the republic's fate. Writing to John Adams as Prussian troops were marching through the Netherlands, Thomas Jefferson saw a "lesson" for the United States in the "present miseries of Holland": republics, he warned, must "never . . . call in foreign nations to settle domestic differences." It went without saying that such a mistake was easy to make in the Netherlands, where well-trained armies stood just over the borders in every direction. In his acerbic reply, Adams doubted whether Americans would really learn from the patriot movement's failure: "Lessons . . . have little Effect upon Nations when they contradict a present Passion." But even Adams had to admit that a military intervention of this sort in the United States was not likely to occur for some time—not until the "next Generation" at the earliest.[36]

# 7
# THE REVOLUTION BEGINS IN PARIS

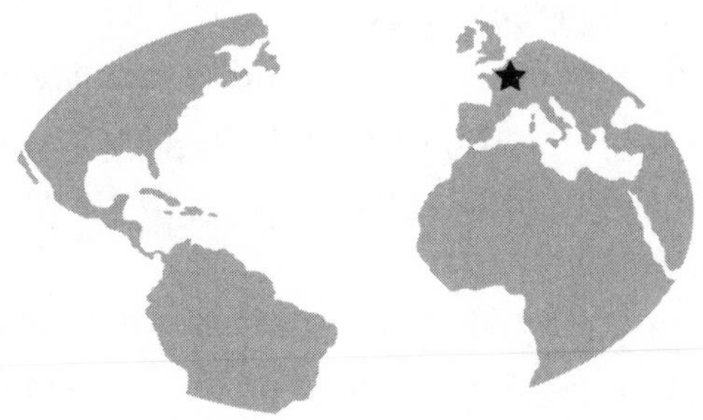

THE DEFEAT OF THE DUTCH PATRIOT MOVEMENT SENT ITS FERvent supporters fleeing to safety across the republic's borders. Some fled to France, which had favored the patriots out of a common distaste for the Orangist party, and went to Paris, where they settled in for what seemed likely to be a long exile. The Dutch refugees clustered around the Palais Royal, an elegant complex of homes and businesses built on a plot of land in the center of the city that belonged to the French king's cousin, the duc d'Orléans. The Palais Royal and its gardens made an island of green in the midst of the hurly-burly French capital. It had become, by the 1780s, a main gathering place for genteel Parisians and visitors to the capital.[1]

The Palais Royal occupied a central role in the unrest that was brewing in the French monarchy during the second half of the 1780s. The proximate cause was the parlous state of the French government's finances, burdened by large debts that France had incurred during the American revolutionary war. Successive ministries tried a variety of strategies to raise more money and cut expenditures. These efforts succeeded mostly in alienating or offending many of the kingdom's vested interests, from court nobles to financiers to urban artisans. As the government flailed, public criticism of the ministry became harsh. The Palais Royal, which was outside the jurisdiction of the Paris police by virtue of its owner's royal blood, became a kind of free-speech zone in the heart of the kingdom. Pamphlets attacking the ministry circulated more or less freely in its cafés while the gardens became a meeting place for the government's critics.

In the summer of 1789, the political storm finally broke over France. The initial stages of the French Revolution, from June through October 1789, implicated virtually every corner of the kingdom. Elections for a long-dormant political assembly, the Estates General, galvanized public interest in political and financial affairs in the most distant corners of the country. Once the Estates General began to meet near Paris in May, the delegates kept their constituents informed of what was happening with a steady stream of letters, newspapers, and government publications. In June, the Estates General reconstituted itself as the National Assembly, laying claim to speak for the nation and setting the stage for a dramatic expansion of its authority.

By virtue of their proximity to the seat of power, the people of Paris had a unique influence on the National Assembly and the unfolding revolution. Though the early French Revolution cannot by any means be reduced to events in Paris, how the revolution took shape in the city had a profound influence on the larger story. At several key junctures during the first months of the revolution, events in Paris decisively shifted its course. The most celebrated episode of this kind was the seizure by Parisians of the Bastille, a fortress on the eastern edge of the city, on July 14. This brought about a major shift in the balance of power away from the king and toward the National Assembly. In early October, crowds of Parisians came to Versailles and forced the king to relocate to Paris. The National Assembly followed suit. This change of location placed the government and the revolution even more firmly within the Parisians' orbit.

The revolution in Paris in 1789—like the revolutions in the United States, Peru, and the Netherlands—was powered by several socially distinct political movements. The elite and working-class wings of the movement each had their own organization, and they worked toward somewhat different ends. As in the earlier movements, these divisions created significant political challenges. Indeed, the divisions in Paris were among the more extreme. Paris was a far larger city than any in either the Netherlands or the United States. And the gap in status between the Parisian elite and the working classes was more akin to that in Peru than to what one might find in Dutch or North American cities. All of this contributed to making the 1789 revolution in Paris, for all of its undoubted energy and influence, a troubled movement. And as yet, the Parisian revolutionaries seemed to have little understanding of the problem, let alone of its scope.

Before the Palais Royal was a cradle of revolution, it was an exclusive space for the Paris gentry. Since the seventeenth century, the Palais Royal's gardens had been enclosed by elegant townhomes owned for the most part by wealthy, well-connected aristocrats. The long promenade down the center of the garden became their private playground. It was not uncommon for the proprietors of the houses surrounding it to walk out in the garden at night in their bedclothes. A 1760 perspectival view of the garden shows a few dozen well-dressed members of the elite. Most of the figures are in pairs, with a handful of triads and individuals. They appear to be in conversation; in one of the central groupings, a blue-clad gentleman is bowing to a woman in a rose-colored dress.[2]

The gardens were open intermittently to those lower down the social ladder. They came to use its amenities but never to stay. On any given day, one could find financial speculators and con-men wandering among the trees. By both day and night, the gardens were a site for erotic rendezvous. This could take the form of encounters between respectable young men and women. More often, however, it took the form of prostitution. A common sight in the gardens was two women walking together, one young and one old; the older one sold the sexual services of the younger. But with no place to sit, no spot for a person to set up a boutique or even have someone sign a piece of paper, the gardens were a temporary refuge. In periods of bad weather—and in Paris, that was half the year—the gardens were well-nigh unusable because they lacked any kind of shelter from the elements.[3]

The duc d'Orléans had transformed the gardens in the early 1780s into one of the characteristic genteel spaces of the eighteenth century, one dominated by the elite but open in a limited way to the wider public. Orléans brought in one of the leading architects of eighteenth-century France, Victor Louis, to guide the transformation. He had just completed construction, in 1780, of the massive new theater in Bordeaux. The heart of the Louis plan was an arcaded gallery filled with commercial spaces that would run the length of the garden on both sides. When it was completed in 1784, the arcade turned the Palais Royal garden into a true commercial center. There were proper storefronts and lighting to illuminate the spaces on evenings and dark days.[4]

The duc created a new set of popular entertainments. At the north end of the garden, in what had been a somewhat neglected

Entertainments in the Palais Royal gardens, ca. 1785. Courtesy of Musée Carnavalet, Paris.

corner of the complex, the duc had a 750-seat theater built. A bit later came a massive "circus," a hippodrome-shaped building set in the middle of the garden, and several smaller round pavilions. Marvels were the stuff of the new garden: A giant Prussian girl, over six feet tall, who could be viewed at number thirty-three in the arcades. Ventriloquists and illusionists were on view just a few minutes' walk away. There was a mechanized café, in which patrons placed orders through a speaking tube and comestibles ascended through openings in the table. There were exhibitors who displayed the bodies of natives of Africa and Asia, a wax museum, and other so-called amusements. Leisure was mixed with much that was more serious. Coffeehouses, of which there were many nestled in the arcades, each with its own character and public, were centers of discussion. The circus was sometimes rented out for scientific meetings. By the mid-1780s, the Palais Royal garden had become one of the main centers of Parisian polite sociability.[5]

*Miss La Pierre, Young Giantess.* Courtesy of Musée Carnavalet, Paris.

The Palais Royal became an important political space during the 1780s. Because the complex was the personal property of a royal prince, it was officially out of the jurisdiction of the Paris police. This made it a haven for free thought and illicit publishing—and a favorite hunting ground for police informants. The informants, colloquially known as "flies," buzzed around the gardens disguised as "honest fellows," gathering up tidbits of conversation.

In 1786, the *jardin* figured prominently in a tawdry political crisis, the so-called Affair of the Diamond Necklace. The affair, which involved a desperate high-end jeweler, a noble-born cardinal, and a penniless aristocrat, revolved around the alleged sale of a fabulous diamond necklace to the widely disliked Austrian-born queen, Marie-Antoinette. The mastermind of the affair, Jeanne de Valois, had forged letters from the queen purporting to be interested in purchasing the necklace. She found a prostitute who frequented the garden of the Palais Royal to impersonate Marie-Antoinette. With her assistance, Valois maneuvered the cardinal de Rohan into acquiring the necklace and turning it over to her—after which it disappeared. Five months later, when the scheme unraveled, both Rohan and Valois were put on trial. The queen was not involved, except as a victim of a stolen identity. But the breathless coverage of the affair in the press and in the rumor mill further blackened her reputation and left a taint of scandal on the entire royal family.[6]

The flashy discussions of the affair in 1786 served as a distraction from much more serious problems that were facing the French monarchy. The financial state of the French government, which had long been questionable, took a turn for the worse during the mid-1780s. The immediate cause of the problem was the enormous debt that the Crown had racked up in joining the American revolutionary war. This included both the direct costs of the war against Britain and the additional burden of massive loans that the French government had made to the American rebels starting in 1776. The Crown's revenues had failed to keep pace with the growing cost of servicing this debt. By the later summer of 1786, the king was being told that, absent some immediate action, the Crown would have to declare bankruptcy. This would be catastrophic both to the state's credit and to France's international standing, which depended on its ability to muster substantial resources in order to make war.[7]

To address the debt crisis, the king and his ministers convened a meeting of a select group of the kingdom's noblemen to consider proposals for fiscal reform and additional taxation. Charles-Alexandre de Calonne, the minister who masterminded this unorthodox plan, dubbed it an Assembly of Notables. The duc d'Orléans, as one of the kingdom's leading princes, served in a prominent role. Officially, he headed one of the working groups (known as *bureaux*) of the Assembly of Notables, though in practice he was usually absent. The assembly gave lengthy consideration to the Crown's proposals. Ultimately, however, it declared itself unable to act on them. New taxation, the assembly's *bureaux* found, required the assent of the "nation," which they were not able to give. Some *bureaux* questioned whether there was any need for new taxes at all.[8]

The French ministry began making increasingly desperate maneuvers to secure new revenues. Ministers first tried to get the *parlements*, the same bodies the king had forced to register reforms in 1776, to approve new taxes. When the *parlements* refused, the ministry tried to abolish them to impose new taxes directly. Large protests, some violent, greeted this measure, and again the ministry retreated. Now out of options, the government decided in July 1788 to call an Estates General. This body, which had last been convened more than a century before, brought together members of the three "orders" of the realm: clergy, nobility, commons. There was little doubt about this body's power to grant new revenue to the Crown. Its power also made it hard to predict what would happen once it convened: like the Assembly of Notables, it might refuse to follow the ministry's directions. But the monarchy had little choice. The process of calling the Estates General began in earnest in January 1789, when the king invited his subjects to form electoral assemblies that would choose representatives to send. The process would be consultative, producing *cahiers de doléances* (statements of grievances) from every town and corporate body in the country. Even the Jews were invited to produce their own *mémoires*—though as non-Christians they were not permitted to elect representatives to the Estates.[9]

The Estates first met on May 5, 1789, accompanied by a grand ceremony that recalled that of the *lit de justice*. Within a matter of weeks, it had become clear that there was significant resistance within the Estates General to the king's program. Disputes also swirled about how to organize the body. These centered on the key question of whether each member would have a vote or if each order would have just one vote among them. Members of the commons, or Third Estate, refused to accept the vote by order. On June 17, after a month of fruitless debates, the Third Estate voted by a large majority to unilaterally declare itself a "National Assembly" that represented the whole "people." Three days later, fearing that the ministry might try to break their newfound resolve, the men of the Third Estate and some members of the two other orders gathered at a nearby indoor tennis court and swore to remain together until their work was complete and the nation's "constitution" had been "regenerated." The Tennis Court Oath, as it soon came to be known, marked a major turning point, signaling that a revolution in the political constitution of the monarchy was underway.[10]

June 1789 birthed a new political language as well as new structures of power. Members of the National Assembly, drawing on discussions that had already begun in 1788, spoke openly of "regenerating" France, restoring its constitution to what they imagined as a happier and better earlier state. They spoke fervently of reestablishing the "liberty" of the French "nation," including freedoms of association, religion, and speech that had long been limited to the well-off and powerful, if they were allowed at all.[11]

The creation of the National Assembly took place alongside parallel mobilizations in the city of Paris. One was an unofficial but quiet activation of the capital's local elite: the minor noblemen and wealthy businessmen who had long controlled the city government.

The city council met in a continuous session. Meanwhile, a much larger mobilization swelled from below. Discontent was already swirling in the city as a result of the rising price of bread: bad harvests and mismanagement since 1788 had made this staple of the urban diet increasingly unaffordable, and the price was still rising in June. In the poorer and heavily populated quarters of the city—the insalubrious center and the recently constructed suburbs sprawling away from it—artisans, factory workers, and peddlers gathered together to talk and to plan, hoping that the new National Assembly would find a way to address the dire situation. Proclamations by the National Assembly, even those unrelated to subsistence, were often greeted with fireworks and huzzahs by the working-class public.[12]

The Palais Royal gardens became one of the meeting places for these two mobilizations in June and July 1789. In late June, a group of soldiers from a regiment with close ties to Paris, who had manifested strong sympathies for the National Assembly, was arrested and held in the prison of the Abbaye Saint-Germain. A crowd gathered at the Palais Royal gardens to protest their detention, went to the prison to liberate the soldiers, then brought them back to the gardens for a celebration—of which a print was created. The central figure is a seated soldier, legs splayed wide apart, one foot next to a basket of wine bottles and his arm upraised, cup in hand, to be filled with wine from a waiting bottle. To one side (left in some states, right in others), a *limonadier* is in the process of broaching another bottle of wine. On the opposite side, an aristocratic man reaches out for a baby held by another well-dressed man.[13]

Nowhere in the image of the June 30 celebration is there any sign of ordinary people: all of the visible figures are genteelly dressed. Even those wearing caps are sporting smart, fashion-forward coats. Among the ghostly crowd that forms the background, there is no sign of anyone from the lower classes; every head seems bewigged and every well-turned leg is wrapped in breeches. The public mobilization has been socially elevated and cleaned up, bringing the depiction of the crowds in line with the social image of the Palais Royal gardens. What is happening here, moreover, is a scene of entertainment—a happy or comedic resolution to a crisis. The contrast with the accompanying image of the actual jailbreak is illuminating. That image, set at the door of the prison, explains in its caption that it represents "a crowd of workers led by respectable individuals" taking the prison. At the right of the frame, bending forward with activity, are three members of the lower orders: a

Crowd gathered in the Palais Royal gardens, night of June 30, 1789. Courtesy of Musée Carnavalet, Paris.

woman in a mobcap and two men, one of whom wears pants rather than breeches (a sans-culotte, in other words).[14]

THE POPULAR MOBILIZATIONS THAT TOOK PLACE AROUND THE SEIzure of the Bastille fortress, on July 14, starkly illuminated both the power and the limits of working-class organizing in early revolutionary Paris. The working classes in Paris, conditioned by decades of increasingly separate living, had a remarkable capacity for self-organization. Yet the same social realities that had made them effective self-organizers also defined the horizon of their political vision. The Paris crowds' tactics, during the crucial months of 1789, were fundamentally different from those of the revolutionary leadership in Versailles and Paris.

The Bastille sat at one end of the rue Saint-Antoine, the central artery of Paris's premier neighborhood for artisans. Somewhere north of fifteen thousand workers lived there, including many cabinet and furniture makers, metalworkers, glaziers, builders, and representatives of dozens of other trades. The faubourg Saint-Antoine, as the neighborhood was known, formed a shabby but tightly knit community. The Bastille's stony bulk loomed over them, governing the approach to Paris. But its stern appearance was deceptive: the old fortress held only a small garrison and hardly any weapons or ammunition. Since the mid-seventeenth century it had served primarily as a state prison.[15]

The faubourg was restless in the spring of 1789. The political ferment of the Estates General had stirred it up just as it had the rest of France. The artisans had their ears to the ground; rumors about what was happening in the halls of power coursed through their communities. They had grievances of their own as well. Rising prices and stagnant wages were long-standing concerns. In late April, in response to some incautious words from Jean-Baptiste Réveillon about a possible decrease in salaries, large crowds formed outside his wallpaper factory in the faubourg. Over three days, forming and then dispersing at the sight of the forces of repression, the crowds grew increasingly restive. On April 28, they managed to gain entry to Réveillon's house, which they sacked before being bloodily driven off by a fusillade from a detachment of troops.[16]

The Réveillon riots showed the Paris crowds' capacity for self-government. We do not have much direct evidence about the mechanisms of organization, which were undoubtedly face-to-face and left few archival traces. But the evidence of direction and structure is clear enough. The crowds dissolved and reformed repeatedly. The restraint they showed when they entered Réveillon's home, destroying property but not committing bodily harm, like the Boston crowd that destroyed Lieutenant Governor Thomas Hutchinson's home in 1765, points to a degree of direction. In the case of the Réveillon crowds, common life and work experiences may have played a role in this cohesion. Most of those identified as participants in the riots were younger men, mostly twenty- and thirtysomethings born between the mid-1750s and the mid-1760s. These young artisans were at a shared, critical juncture in their lives: twenty-five was the rough average age at marriage for men and also when artisans typically entered their professions as full-fledged journeymen.[17]

Many subsequent Paris crowds showed a similar aptitude for self-organization, and this general ability was sturdily rooted in the broader experience of social division in prerevolutionary Paris. Eighteenth-century Atlantic societies in general were characterized by a widening gulf between the well-off and the working class. Paris, a large, dense city that was the capital of a powerful empire, experienced one of the starkest social separations of any place at the time. Scholars of eighteenth-century Paris have emphasized the "growing alienation of the urban elites" from the working-class city. The working classes' relative social isolation dovetailed with a robust associational life, which provided a thorough apprenticeship in the practice of self-government. Some of these organizations, such as religious confraternities (lay religious brotherhoods), had a formal institutional apparatus. Others, such as journeymen's associations and associations for gaming or conducting illicit business, existed in the shadows. How these organizations "from below" functioned is difficult to know, but they helped to order working-class communities and strengthened their internal networks and leadership.[18]

In the weeks after the National Assembly proclaimed itself on June 20, the court sought to regain the initiative. On June 27, the king gave his imprimatur to the National Assembly, ordering the nobility and the clergy to officially join together with the commons. On June 30, the Paris crowds stormed the Abbaye Saint-Germain prison. During these weeks, the king had quietly called several regiments of troops to the Paris region. He seemed to be laying the groundwork for regaining control of the situation by force, if necessary. Popular suspicions that a coup against the National Assembly was imminent reached a fever pitch on July 11 and 12. The king abruptly dismissed several popular ministers, who had been important mediators between the National Assembly and the court, and replaced them with individuals who were perceived as hard-liners. On the afternoon of the twelfth, cavalry attacked Parisians gathered in the Tuileries gardens near the Louvre palace. It seemed to many in the city that the court was preparing to put in motion the plan, which they assumed was in contemplation, to end the revolution almost as soon as it had begun.[19]

Paris spent the night of the twelfth and the thirteenth in a state of extreme tension. Wild rumors circulated about possible movements of the troops stationed just outside the city. Faced with what they assumed was an imminent military intervention, crowds of Parisians embarked on a search for weapons with which they could defend themselves and their neighborhoods. The search, conducted across the city, was remarkably well organized and thorough.

Between the night of the twelfth and the evening of the thirteenth, crowds searched private businesses and lightly guarded public buildings: the Hôtel de Ville (city hall), boats transporting military supplies on the Seine, the stores of individual arms dealers, and the monastery of Saint-Lazare, among others. These searches produced some powder, which was brought to the city hall, but not many weapons. The crowds then turned their attention to the more ample but better-protected royal stores. The most important of these was known to be in the Hôtel des Invalides, the military hospital. On the morning of the fourteenth, a large crowd assembled with the arms they had already acquired and marched to the Invalides. Brushing past the commander and his troops, who offered no resistance, they took the cannon and guns held in its vaults.

Once the crowds had armed themselves, they turned their attention to the Bastille. They had several reasons for deciding to target the fortress in spite of its seemingly impressive defenses. Rumors were coursing through the city that some of the cannons on the fortress's battlements might be prepared to fire onto the adjacent neighborhoods. The public had learned, too, that some of the powder previously kept at the Invalides had been moved to the Bastille for safekeeping. And the fortress-prison had acquired an evil reputation over the previous century, depicted in popular books as a vast, grotesque torture chamber. By early afternoon on the fourteenth, a crowd numbering in the thousands had gathered before the gate to the Bastille. They forced their way into the outer courtyard with the help of a cannon. Around five o'clock, faced with a crowd that threatened to fight its way into the fortress proper, likely with significant loss of life on both sides, the commanding officer opted for surrender.[20]

One of the most remarkable sources for understanding what the Bastille's captors envisioned, and how it was understood by observers, is the large number of prints that depicted the attack and seizure of the fortress. Well over a hundred individual prints were produced in 1789 and 1790 depicting the events of July 14. They offer a contemporary view of the scene that day, which in some cases reflected firsthand knowledge of the crowd and shaped how it would be remembered. These images are not a pure transcription or reflection of the scene as it occurred. The artists who created them drew on a preexisting visual vocabulary and imitated, echoed, and elaborated on one another's depictions.[21] Yet for all of their limitations as testimony, the images offer a unique window onto the attack on the Bastille and answers to the crucial question of what the attackers understood themselves to be doing.

Most of the images of the assault have a consistent visual grammar. On the left side, dominating the background, looms the bulk of the Bastille fortress itself, easily recognizable by its outsize scale and its multiple rounded towers. On the right side is a large arched door or gate topped by a triangular Grecian pediment; it dominates the middle ground of the image. This was the *pont-levis de l'avancé*, the drawbridge that led into the main courtyard of the fortress, where the commander's lodgings and outbuilding were located. The viewer in almost every one of these prints stands in the rue Saint-Antoine, looking west toward the fortress.[22] He or she, in other words, is part of the crowd coming down from the faubourg.

The drawbridge marked the transition from the public space of the street to the closed-off domain of the fortress complex. The viewer stands, as it were, on the threshold between these two zones. This mode of representing the capture of the Bastille is remarkably consistent in the contemporary imagery. Even in a highly stylized image that represents the fortress schematically, with soldiers who are half the height of its walls, a figure in the center foreground stands on the drawbridge with the broken chains behind him. Almost unanimously, the images focused on the comportment of the people of Paris in and around this borderline between the city's public spaces and the king's domain. Some artists put the

Top: Capture of the Bastille, July 14, 1789, by Dupin. Courtesy of Musée Carnavalet, Paris.

Bottom: Capture of the Bastille, July 14, 1789, by Couché. Courtesy of Musée Carnavalet, Paris.

emphasis heavily on the preparing and firing of the cannon. Other images prioritized the capture and assassination of the chevalier de Launay, the commandant of the fortress. Yet others focused on the casualties. A number of the images stressed the friendly mixing of soldiers and civilians in the street, signaling a departure from the usually tense relations that prevailed between them.[23]

The central story in all of the prints, though, was what they had in common: the stage of the street and the mass of people extending their power from the street into the fortress. It is down in the street where the soldiers and citizens are marching, the dead are being carried away and the wounded tended, and (in many of the images) de Launay is being held by the crowd. In one image, by Jean-Louis Prieur and Pierre-Gabriel Berthault, the foreground is so dense with bodies that only a strip of the cobblestoned ground is visible. The visual focus of the image is a vast crowd, shoulder to shoulder, seemingly more than five people deep in most places; there are at least two hundred and perhaps as many as three hundred figures individually depicted.[24]

In the visual retellings of the assault on the Bastille and its capture, the story is one of a rather familiar sort for the mid-eighteenth century. The people were extending their authority within and over the streets into a new domain. The focal point of all these images is the breaching of the barrier between the public space of the streets, dominated for at least two generations by the common people, and the private space controlled by the monarch. This undoubtedly had revolutionary implications: it marked the monarchy's inability to maintain its power and sovereignty. But what the people were doing, at least in the visual depictions, was far from unprecedented. Just as they had in the case of Réveillon, they were incorporating a piece of private, enclosed space into the public space that they controlled.

This passion for turning the private public extended well beyond the moment of the Bastille's capture. In the immediate aftermath of the fall of the fortress, the captors seized its sizeable archive and dumped the papers out in the courtyard. These included recent police reports as well as documents related directly to the administration of the Bastille and its prisoners. For all of its imprudence, this was no act of vandalism. Read within the context of the habitus of the citizens acting in the streets, it was another manifestation of their desire to reduce what had been private, what had remained hidden away, to the same kind of openness that the street provides. The physical destruction of the fortress complex—which began with fires and ended in its complete demolition under the orders of the builder Pierre-François Palloy—symbolically reduced it back to the level of the street. By taking down the Bastille, the patriots of Paris literally transformed a royal fortress into part of the domain of the people.[25]

Though the seizure of the Bastille was a symbolic victory, the crowd's ideas about the hierarchical division of the city's spaces were self-limiting if not actually self-defeating. They spurred action against places and people who did not in fact have much power to meet their demands. "The people, always free with their blood, give it without any profit," one observer complained as he watched the events of mid-July unfold. This was the case of the Bastille itself, which was neither a royal residence nor a meeting place of the government. By the late eighteenth century, the fortress was no longer either a political or a military nerve center, containing neither weapons nor prisoners. It was the story of the Bastille's archives as well. After they were strewn in the street, the municipality of Paris, unwilling to let such valuable information be destroyed, gathered up the scattered documents the following day and took them to the Hôtel de Ville.[26]

The crowd's ideas about whom to target sealed the fate of the chevalier de Launay, the military governor of the Bastille. In the heat of the fight, the minor functionary de Launay became the face of the enemy to those down in the streets: it was he, allegedly, who ordered the soldiers to forcibly resist the attackers. Once it became impossible for his soldiers to hold out any longer, de Launay reluctantly surrendered the fortress. In a number of the images of the seizure of the Bastille, including many that follow the same basic visual template set before the *premier pont-levis*, de Launay is shown being escorted from the complex. He faces the viewer, emerging from the space of the fortress into the space of the street, surrounded by members of the conquering force.[27]

Not long after his capture, de Launay was murdered by members of the crowd. His head was put on a pike and displayed in the Place de Grève, one of the main squares before the city hall. A cycle of images depict this moment as well. Their visual grammar rests on the counterpoint between the single head, suspended from a lamppost, and the unnumberable crowd in the plaza below. Here, again, was an image of "the people" dominating the public spaces of the city—in this case, a plaza—and the transformation of the very body of a royal officer into a kind of public property. Yet however satisfying this was symbolically, it was a small victory in practical terms. De Launay no more had the power to meet the wider demands of the Paris crowd than did any other low-level army officer.

The two main wings of the revolutionary movement remained highly active from mid-July through September 1789, crucial months that consolidated the revolution within the kingdom. The two wings did not work at cross-purposes, exactly. But neither were they operating in anything like close coordination. During these months, indeed, the various groups of genteel leaders were repeatedly surprised by sudden political eruptions from below that had their own agendas.

Elite revolutionaries in Paris seized the opportunity that the tumult of mid-July and the seizure of the Bastille offered to rapidly expand and solidify their political position. On July 13, as the city convulsed, the electors whom the city had elected to choose their representatives to the Estates General convened at the Hôtel de Ville. The electors, having long since completed their task, had no formal political role, but they had been meeting intermittently ever since. They now declared themselves the municipal council and began functioning as a city government. One of their first orders of business was to create a city militia, which was folded shortly afterward into the newly created National Guard. A few days later, after the Bastille had fallen, Paris got its first mayor, the elegant and erudite scientist Jean Sylvain Bailly. The marquis de Lafayette, a young nobleman who had fought in the American revolutionary war and who was extremely well-connected at the highest levels of the court, was named commander of the National Guard. These developments gave institutional form to the elite revolutionary leadership and created settings through which it could organize and mobilize in Paris.[28]

The strengthened elite leadership soon faced a severe test from a burst of political fear and violence that swept across the French countryside and provincial France. The movement, which became known as the Great Fear, had a variety of causes. There were the habitual late-summer worries about the harvest and the food supply. They flowed together with growing expectations that the National Assembly would radically improve the living conditions of the peasantry. The mood among rural people was further soured by rumors about mysterious "brigands" roaming the countryside and attacking defenseless villagers. During the last two weeks of July, thousands of peasants armed themselves, ostensibly to defend their homes and property against the phantasmagorical "brigands." In many regions across France, the armed peasantry turned on the local lords and their estates, taking aim at the institutions that maintained the social and economic position of the nobility. Attacking primarily property rather than persons, they destroyed seigneurial records, rolls of tax payments, and monopolistic institutions such as grain mills. The National Assembly and court received a wave of panicky letters from officials and private individuals worried that the social and political fabric of the kingdom was coming apart.[29]

The National Assembly responded to the crisis during the first weeks of August with one of the most sweeping gestures of the entire revolutionary era: the abolition of "feudalism." A group in the Assembly called the Breton Club, which held some of the most radical views among the deputies, set the event in motion. They planned to have a liberal nobleman take the floor on the evening of August 4 and propose the abolition of legal privilege. The move sparked an impassioned all-night session during which member after member stood up to renounce their privileges and call for the repeal of others. When August 5 dawned, it was not entirely clear what the deputies had actually agreed upon. Over the next week, a committee gave legislative form to these gestures. The proposal they drafted was radical in some respects but quite conservative in others. It did away with the power, including judicial power, that attached to privilege. But it also characterized feudal privileges as property. Privileges would have to be "redeemed" by being purchased back from those who held them. Privilege was not so much abolished as put up for sale. The National Assembly adopted the proposal on August 11.[30]

For the remainder of August and September, the National Assembly settled into a steadier rhythm of legislating. In late August, it approved a draft of the Declaration of the Rights of Man and of the Citizen. The declaration, which became one of the most hallowed texts of the French Revolution, was supposed to be a draft. In seventeen articles, it outlined the principle of legal equality among Frenchmen—the gendered language was no accident—based on the idea of natural rights, the by then widespread notion that all human beings had a basic set of rights by virtue of their humanity. The Assembly also continued work on what it saw as its main task: writing a constitution for France. During the first weeks of September, the Assembly took a series of difficult votes on aspects of the constitution, including the vexed issue of whether the king would have a veto over legislation.[31]

The king, who in mid-July had seemed ready to conciliate the National Assembly and the Paris crowds, became more recalcitrant in September. He repeatedly put off giving his assent to the decree of August 11. He remained laconic about the discussions of the constitution, giving credence to those who thought that he might be at best a reluctant participant in the constitutional process. Most threatening, the court had again, as it had during the very early days of the revolution, begun to call troops to Paris. Patriot observers were particularly alarmed by the arrival in the Paris region of the Flanders Regiment, a well-disciplined unit known to be highly loyal to the court. By early October, the National Assembly and the court had reached an uneasy impasse. Neither side seemed eager to provoke a crisis, but progress on the major political issues had stalled.

Once again, the autonomous action of crowds in Paris intervened and jarred both the monarchy and the National Assembly out of their entrenched positions. The morning of October 5, a Monday, bells rang out across Paris. Crowds, this time composed mostly of women, gathered in the faubourg Saint-Antoine and near the central food markets. As they had in mid-July, the members of the crowds had both high political and pragmatic concerns on their minds. A new shortage of bread in Paris had spurred grumbling and protests against bakers over the previous weeks. Members of the crowds were also evidently well-informed about the political situation in Versailles. The crowds gathered near the city hall, where less than three months earlier the head of the chevalier de Launay had been hung, armed with a motley array of weapons. From there—at whose initiative, we do not know—they set out on a twelve-odd-mile march to Versailles.[32]

Arriving in Versailles in the evening, the crowd went straight to the National Assembly. The deputies were taken aback by their arrival. Several deputies gave speeches to try to calm and reassure the crowd. The speakers included Maximilien Robespierre, a well-turned-out deputy from the northern town of Arras who was gaining influence in spite of his weak voice. Encouraged by the deputies, the crowd selected six of their number to seek an audience with the king. In the meantime, the women moved from the Assembly chamber to the gates of the royal palace. Later that night, the Paris National Guard, under the personal command of Lafayette, arrived in force. The following morning, there were skirmishes between members of the crowds and the palace guards, which resulted in the deaths of both demonstrators and guards.

As the crowd waited outside the palace on the morning of the sixth, word circulated with growing insistence that the king and the royal family should come back to Paris with them. Who initiated this demand remains obscure. But the notion was clearly appealing, since in short order it became the common cry of the crowd. When the king and queen eventually appeared in the afternoon, along with Lafayette, the king acceded to this, by then the crowd's main demand. Escorted by the now immense armed crowd, the royal family slowly made its way from Versailles to Paris. The royals set up in the Louvre palace, which had been largely abandoned by the kings generations earlier.

The march on Versailles and the king's forced move to Paris brought about a series of further political changes. The National Assembly, though not under similar pressure from the crowd, followed the king to Paris less than two weeks later. It set up new quarters in an indoor riding rink adjacent to the palace. The move to Paris also ended the monarch's recalcitrance about both the

August 11 decree and the Declaration of Rights. Shortly after the crowd escorted him to Paris, he accepted both, albeit without much enthusiasm. One of the revolution's celebrated historians, Alphonse Aulard, described this as a "victory" for the Assembly, aided by the people of Paris. Yet it would be more accurate to say that the people of Paris forced the hands of both the Assembly and the king.[33]

The early French Revolution, like the revolutions of the previous two decades, began under the sign of the mid-eighteenth century's divided social world and the worldviews that went with it. Paris, which was by far the largest and wealthiest city to experience revolutionary activity thus far, was riven by even more extreme divisions than the ones that existed in North America or the Netherlands. This led to the creation of a sharply bifurcated patriot movement, in which elite and working-class patriots formed their own, largely autonomous political organizations.

The members of the Paris crowds had goals and tactics shaped by a habitus drawn from their midcentury upbringing. The world they knew was one in which the well-off and powerful held the reins of politics and in which it was hardly imaginable that they would give them up. When the artisan families of the faubourg Saint-Antoine wished to make their voices heard, they did so by flexing their power over the public spaces of the city, bringing one of the king's sanctums under their control, and eventually bringing the king himself, bodily, into their domain. These were powerful-seeming acts, richly laden with symbolism. But the crowds' habits also led them to target individuals and spaces that, while symbolically important, were unlikely to advance their concrete political goals. The murder of de Launay and indeed the seizure of the Bastille itself were prime examples of this tendency.

The sharply different worldviews of the elite and non-elite wings of the patriot movement also meant that their political agendas and tactics were often at odds. The National Assembly no more directed the crowds of Paris than the crowds of Paris directed the Assembly. The mismatch between the goals and strategies of the two wings put them frequently out of sync. In June, when the Assembly seemed to be under dire threat from the court, the crowds of Paris did not directly intervene to defend it. In August, the Assembly took some of its most dramatic action to date without giving much apparent thought to how the Paris crowds might react. Conversely, in July and again in October, the actions of the Paris crowds dragged a visibly uncomfortable National Assembly along with their plans. As had happened during the early phases of the American Revolution, this largely uncoordinated double action from above and below succeeded in achieving many of the movement's goals in the short term. Yet the gap between the two wings of the movement remained a weakness, which was likely to grow along with the movement. French revolutionaries needed to look no further than the Dutch border to be reminded of the mortal danger that faced a patriot movement that failed to bridge the divisions within its ranks.

# 8

# THE POLITICS OF CROWDS AND CLUBS

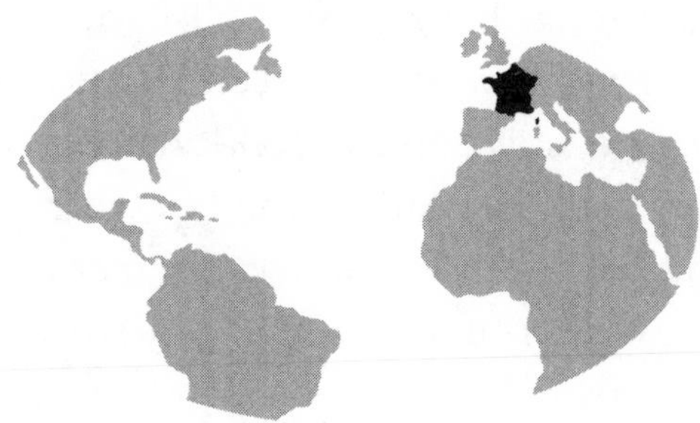

LOUIS-AUGUSTIN BOSC'S CLOSE FRIEND FRANÇOIS LANTHENAS hardly slept the night of July 13. There was gunfire in the streets. Grim-faced men who seemed to have been fighting all night passed by his door, bound (so they said) for the Palais Royal. He heard "workers talking amongst themselves" about "the Building"—perhaps a reference to the Bastille. The following morning, he told Bosc and a group of their mutual friends that he had been "unable" to get to the city hall. Whether he was prevented from venturing forth by the density of the crowds, or was too frightened by the armed people in the street, he did not say.[1]

Over the next five years, complex relationships between the working people of Paris and the political leadership, to which Bosc and Lanthenas belonged, shaped the course of the French Revolution. As they had in the revolutions of the previous two decades, revolutionary elites rapidly organized themselves and gave institutional form to their political movement. The Jacobin Clubs, a network of independent political clubs headquartered in Paris, were the most important of these new bodies. The Jacobins were numerically dominated and led by men of some means. These clubs competed and occasionally collaborated with several other clubs and club networks, notably the Paris-based Cordeliers Club. The working people of Paris developed their own political organizations, centered on the "sections" (districts) into which Paris was divided starting in 1789. The sections became increasingly well organized and active on the political scene over the course of the first years of the revolution. Unlike earlier political organizations from below in the Atlantic world, the sections remained continuously in existence over a span of years and developed a homegrown leadership.

The interactions among these socially distinct political organizations and the National Assembly played an outsize role in determining how the revolution unfolded between the fall of 1789 and the summer of 1794. The various patriot clubs and political organizations were in broad political alignment. In 1790 and 1791, they worked together to reshape the role of the Catholic Church and eliminate legal privilege and inequality, all while making common cause against the court and more conservative revolutionaries who wanted to slow or reverse the political changes that had already taken place. In 1792, with the Jacobins and sections playing key roles, the monarchy fell and France became a republic. Over the next two years, the sections and the Jacobins helped to push a dramatic program of political change, including the sale of church lands, the creation of one of the modern world's first citizen armies, and drastic (albeit mostly ephemeral) changes to everything from the names of the months to forms of address.

Yet the collaboration between the more elite and the more grassroots political organizations, however effective it could be, was always unstable. The Jacobins and the Paris sections remained distinct, even at the moments of greatest political pressure and peril, with their own political agendas and strategies. The collaboration between them, and their interactions with the revolutionary legislatures, contributed to instability and rapid oscillations in the political system. Just as it had in the summer and fall of 1789, the popular wing of the revolutionary movement regularly surprised the more elite leaders and their organizations. The elite, just as they had in earlier revolutions, sought control over the working-class patriots. This dynamic was not limited to Paris: similar divisions between elite and working-class movements took shape throughout France.[2]

This unstable collaboration between working-class and elite revolutionaries during the first years of the French Revolution is one of the most thoroughly studied subjects in the entire history of the Atlantic revolutionary era. There are any number of angles from which to see this dynamic at work. Bosc and a group of his close friends who became prominent members of the Jacobin Club offer one way to chart its vectors. Bosc and his circle flew near the center of this stormy collaboration in the years between 1789 and 1793—so close, indeed, that the political hurricane ended up hurling several of them into the grave.

THE *CLUB DES JACOBINS*, OR JACOBIN CLUB, COULD TRACE ITS ORIGINS to the earliest days of the revolution. On April 30, 1789, a group of deputies to the Estates General from the then province of Brittany had begun to meet informally to discuss the body's work and coordinate strategy. This so-called Breton Club played a prominent role in some of the early revolution's most important episodes. After the National Assembly moved to Paris in October

1789, the Breton Club dissolved. But some of its former members got together and created a new club to carry on its work. Within a few months, growing interest in the club's activities led them to rent space at the former monastery of the Jacobins, located on the fashionable rue Saint-Honoré. By this time, requests to affiliate with the club were already beginning to come in from the provinces. In February 1790, the Jacobins approved a constitution, which among other things formally invited patriots throughout France to join a national network of affiliates.[3]

The Jacobins drew their repertoire of revolutionary practices principally from the canon of eighteenth-century elite sociability—just as the people of Paris drew theirs from the domination of the streets that they had achieved. The gentility of the Jacobin Club has been obscured over the years by hostile contemporary caricaturists, who enjoyed portraying it as chaotic and anarchic, and historians who have been eager to stress the club's populist bona fides. Yet in most respects, from how it recruited to whom it admitted to how it functioned, the Jacobin Club belonged to eighteenth-century genteel society. Even the word "club," borrowed from English, evoked the politeness and respectability of the eighteenth-century club movement in England.[4]

The membership of the Jacobins skewed heavily toward men of means. Its ranks were stocked with those from professional families in Paris and the provinces who either had achieved or were seeking entry into the interlocking higher echelons of society, government service, and patronage. Maximilien Robespierre, who would become the central leader of the Jacobins and the revolution more generally in 1793–1794, was in many ways a typical member. Born in 1758 and trained as a lawyer, he spent much of the 1780s writing for the prize competitions of local learned academies. He became president of the academy in his hometown of Arras in 1786. Like the Paris club, the membership of the provincial affiliated clubs also skewed toward the wealthy. For most of their existence, all of the Jacobin Clubs, including the central one in Paris, charged significant membership fees, a powerful deterrent to prospective working-class members.[5]

Bosc's circle, all of whom participated in meetings of the Jacobin Clubs during the revolution's early years, match the general profile. The group included François Lanthenas, the younger son of a well-off artisan; Jean-Marie Roland, an inspector of manufactures; Roland's brilliant and literary wife, Marie-Jeanne Roland, the only surviving child of a skilled artisan; and Henri Bancal, a Paris notary's son. Perhaps the most important member of the circle, though he was not part of the closely knit core, was Jacques-Pierre Brissot. A writer and publicist, he would become a prominent national leader and one of Robespierre's fiercest antagonists. These five had become close in the decade before 1789—starting with Lanthenas, who met the Rolands in Italy in 1777, and Bosc, who bonded with the couple at a botany class in 1780.[6]

As had been the case in the elite-dominated political clubs of North America and the Netherlands, the way the Jacobins recruited their members and conducted their business made their culture forbidding to those who were not well-off and well educated. Correspondence lay at the heart of how the Jacobin Club functioned. Most clubs had a special corresponding committee—the Paris committee had over twenty members—charged with receiving the club's mail, responding to everyday matters, and bringing other letters to the full club's attention. These committees tended to be composed of the more socially prominent members. Important incoming letters would be read aloud and discussed at a meeting. If appropriate, the club would then commission the corresponding committee to draft a response, which would also be read aloud to the club before being sent off. It was no coincidence that all the members of Bosc's circle were involved in the Jacobins: membership in the early Jacobin Clubs often followed the lines of preexisting friendship groups and professional ties.[7]

The Jacobin Clubs interfaced not just with one another but with an array of other formal and informal groups. The organs of the government had multiplied rapidly after the formation of the National Assembly. Particularly important were the new municipal governments—such as the Paris municipality that Bancal had helped to create in 1789—and the National Guard. The Paris municipality was further divided between the overall city government and the sections, each of which had an elected body of its own. The Jacobins heard from and interacted with many unofficial players as well, from newspaper editors and publishers to business groups to deputations of citizens.[8]

A separate movement of "popular societies" developed in parallel to the Jacobin Clubs in Paris and, to a lesser extent, in the provinces. In Paris, the popular societies originated in the division of the city into electoral circumscriptions in the spring of 1789. Each of the divisions or "sections" was to hold an electoral assembly as part of the process for choosing representatives to the Estates General. But after the elections, the sections continued to meet. The arrangement was eventually formalized, with each section having its own assembly, as a kind of ultra-local deliberative body under the aegis of the Paris municipal government. Alongside these official bodies, unofficial political clubs began to meet in a number of the sections. Their existence remains somewhat shadowy and hard to trace during their early years. By 1791, many of them had become more or less formally organized societies with regular meeting times, operating procedures, and membership.

The membership of the popular societies differed from that of the Jacobins. Where the Jacobins were dominated by the well-off and professionals, the popular societies were composed primarily of poorer artisans, manual laborers, and small-time traders and peddlers. The neighborhood "fruit and vegetable seller" was one of the societies' stock figures. (Though there was overlap: Brissot and other members of the Roland circle attended meetings of the popular societies in 1791 and 1792.) Most of the popular societies did not have regular dues or even a regular membership list. Individuals who wished to participate in a club's meetings might be asked to make a small contribution. But even this could usually be waived if it would pose a hardship. More remarkable still, a number of the popular societies opened their doors to women, who were excluded from membership and active participation in the Jacobins. The numbers the popular societies brought together could be large: hundreds of participants showed up for sectional club meetings with some regularity. The societies remained in close touch with one another, though not primarily via correspondence. The popular societies were more apt to send in-person deputations to convey news or rally allies. This practice fit well with the in-the-streets habitus of the Paris working class.[9]

The most important of the popular societies was the Cordeliers Club, so named for the chapel in which it met. The Cordeliers had begun as a sectional popular society and then evolved, in 1790, into a more general club that drew members and participants from across Paris. Though it had grown into a stature similar to that of the Jacobins, the Cordeliers remained faithful to their roots as a popular society: membership continued to be inexpensive, the club welcomed all comers, and the tone of the discussions could be more violent than in the Jacobins. What made the Cordeliers particularly important as a node of political organizing was that two popular political leaders, Jean-Paul Marat and Georges Danton, made the club their main oratorical platform and political vehicle. Marat gained renown through his newspaper, *L'Ami du peuple* (The people's friend); Danton had been part of the initial Paris municipality and was renowned as a highly effective orator. He was also a regular presence in the Jacobins, another key point of connection between the rival societies.[10]

Differences of political orientation and ideology separated the Cordeliers and the popular societies on the one hand from the Jacobins on the other. All these societies were in support of the revolution and committed to defending it. But the two kinds of societies tended to favor different ways of achieving their aims. The Jacobins, as befit a club that had been started by deputies to the Estates General, focused on influencing the government through petitions, publications, and direct persuasion of legislators. The approach to change that predominated in the Jacobins, at least during the early years of the revolution, tended to be legalistic. The popular societies, including the Cordeliers, were far more likely to call for direct action. They were also much more attentive to issues of subsistence and the problems of daily life that faced the poor, who were after all an important part of their constituency.[11]

THE CIRCLE AROUND BOSC AND THE ROLANDS TOOK AN EARLY part in revolutionary political organizing in Paris and beyond. Bosc and his friends were not elected to positions of national leadership during the revolution's first year, but they were still all eager to participate in the political process. As the members of the circle entered the political arena, they became embroiled in the conflicts among the various revolutionary bodies, each with its distinct social base and vision of how to effect political change.

During the first two years of the revolution, from mid-1789 to mid-1791, the circle was split between Paris and the provinces. Bosc and Brissot were consistently in Paris, which both had made their permanent home for more than a decade. The Rolands spent most of their time in the environs of Lyon, France's second-largest city. They had inherited a rambling country estate nearby and went back and forth between it and the city. Lanthenas split his time between Paris and his hometown of Le Puy-en-Velay, in a region just to the west of the Lyonnais.[12]

The Rolands involved themselves most directly with local politics in the Lyonnais during these early years. Already in late 1789, they were engaged in regular correspondence with leading local patriots and were supplying information to newspapers. In February 1790, the first elections were held for the Lyon city government under a new electoral system the Assembly had adopted in 1789. Only "active" citizens—men who met certain residency and tax-paying requirements—could participate in these elections. In cities and towns across France, the initial elections in 1790 and 1791 produced low turnout, averaging under 30 percent in the largest cities. During the first elections in the cities, most of those who were chosen were "recruited from the social elite." Jean-Marie Roland was one: he was chosen as a "notable" in the first Lyon municipal elections. Once in office, he and a handful of like-minded patriot "notables" sought to push the newly elected government, still dominated by a conservative faction, to take action on popular grievances, including curbing the overwhelming power of local merchants and manufacturers, ameliorating workers' conditions, and reducing the tax burden on artisans.[13]

Even as they pushed for significant reforms, the Rolands and their allies remained ambivalent about direct action by the populace. In July 1790, a dispute over the abolition of the octroi, a duty levied on goods coming into the city, put Roland in an uncomfortable position. After patriots in the municipal government proposed abolishing the octroi, large popular assemblies met and demanded its immediate abolition. When the municipality resisted, the popular assemblies took matters into their own hands: they formed crowds who went and opened the city gates themselves, nullifying the duties. Roland distanced himself from this extralegal behavior, protesting publicly that he had been out of town at the time of the crowd actions and implicitly refusing to endorse their direct-action remedy. He wanted change but not through extralegal means.[14]

Bosc and Brissot, the two most active members of the circle in Paris, became members of the main Jacobin Club virtually from its inception. Bosc soon found a role for himself in a familiar spot. He was chosen to serve on the club's all-important committee of correspondence. Brissot began publishing a daily newspaper, *Le Patriote français*, in late July 1789. Though shaped by his idiosyncratic political vision—including a fascination with the United States and uncommonly strong antislavery views—the paper functioned as something of a house organ for the Paris Jacobin Club. Like most eighteenth-century newspapermen, Brissot assembled his issues largely from three sources: paragraphs of news copied from other newspapers, passages of letters and essays provided to him by friends and allies, and essays and commentary of his own composition. The blistering pace of publication meant that Brissot was exceptionally dependent on information that came from his reliable correspondents. The Rolands became important interlocutors, particularly for anything having to do with Lyon.[15]

The members of the circle avidly followed the National Assembly's steady progress on the projects of reform it had begun in 1789. In January and February 1790, the deputies passed a sweeping spatial reorganization, dividing France into eighty-three administrative regions called *départements*. During the summer and fall, the Assembly created a new judicial system built around a newly created corps of justices of the peace. These changes were felt everywhere across the national territory; they created winners and losers, which inevitably provoked complaints. More controversial were the far-reaching reforms that the deputies imposed on the Catholic Church. Church property was one target. The Assembly in 1790 organized the sale of the church's vast holdings, which it had declared in late 1789 rightfully belonged to the nation. A February decree abolished some monastic orders and made significant changes to others. The most far-reaching decree concerning the church was the Civil Constitution of the Clergy, adopted in July 1790 after months of deliberations: it reorganized the Catholic Church in France administratively, modified parish boundaries, made priests and bishops subject to election by voters, and prescribed an oath of loyalty for all clerics. Though initially received with a degree of equanimity, as the government implemented its provisions, they would encounter rising resistance.[16]

By the beginning of 1791, as this initial wave of reforms culminated, Bosc and his friends had become minor but familiar figures in France's revolutionary politics. None of the circle yet exercised any significant national political power; only Brissot was even moderately well-known. But the members of the group had transformed the friendship networks they had created in the old regime, which had been mainly a means to strengthen their bonds with one another, into a solid foundation for political activism in the new landscape the revolution had created.

The strength of the political network that Bosc, the Rolands, and their friends built on their old-regime relationships revealed itself during the summer of 1791. Acting on their growing discontent with the direction that the Assembly was taking—and dissatisfaction with the implementation of the Civil Constitution—the king and his immediate family decided in the spring of 1791 to flee the country. The plan had been in preparation for months. On June 20, the king and his family were smuggled out of the palace in Paris and a letter was left behind indicating their intention to defect. In an unadorned carriage, accompanied only by a small detachment of troops, the royal party rode toward the present-day Belgian border. Everything seemed to be going according to plan until they reached the small town of Varennes, where they were stopped by an enterprising group of national guardsmen. A short while later, a local official was brought to see the refugees and recognized the king. The jig was up.[17]

The king's attempted flight sent the revolutionary government into a panic—and it ripped open the Jacobin Clubs. After the royal family was captured at Varennes, the Jacobins found themselves deeply divided over how to respond. Some felt that it was time to do away with the monarchy. Others hoped to salvage it by allowing the king to save face, pretending that he had merely been traveling to the border to negotiate with France's enemies. Dissatisfied with the radical course that some Jacobins were advocating, a large majority of the members, led by several powerful deputies, seceded from the club on July 16 and formed a new club, which came to be known as the Feuillants. The next day, in the wake of a bloody massacre carried out by troops on the Champ de Mars, the city parade ground, the Paris municipality declared martial law and began to repress the radical patriot movement. The Jacobin rump suddenly found itself under siege from all sides.[18]

For the remaining Jacobins, the most dangerous aspect of the crisis was the threat the Feuillants posed to the national network from which the Jacobin Club drew much of its strength. Within days of the split, the Feuillants had mounted a campaign to persuade provincial patriots and their clubs to abandon their Jacobin affiliation and join with the new club.[19] The Rolands and their circle played an important and until now only dimly perceived role in the Jacobins' ultimate success in the struggle for the allegiance of the provincial clubs.

Members of the Roland circle began to contact one another as soon as the split in the Paris club occurred and crafted plans to keep the Jacobin network together using both private and public channels of communication. On the seventeenth, just a day after the founding of the Feuillants, Madame Roland wrote to inform Henri Bancal about the new club and warned him that they were planning to "detach" the affiliated societies from the Paris Jacobin

Club. She urged Bancal to write "privately" to like-minded patriots and inform them about what was happening. "Do nothing except privately, that is to say, from one private citizen to another," she reiterated. In this tense moment, she warned him, the club's opponents would be "very quick to seize on [any] pretext for persecuting a vigorous society." Acting on a similar impulse, Bosc's friend Gilbert Romme, based in the *département* of Puy-de-Dôme in central France, got in touch with Bosc on July 23 to pass along an address from the Jacobin Club in his hometown of Riom. Over the next two weeks, Romme passed information in both directions, helping to ensure that the Riom club remained aligned with the Paris Jacobins.[20]

The speed with which Romme, Bosc, and Madame Roland could mobilize their private correspondence networks made them decisive in sustaining the Jacobin Club's public network. The Paris Jacobins did not publicly take their fight against the Feuillants to the provinces until after August 1, when Robespierre read out a draft of an address to the provincial clubs. And it was several more weeks before the Jacobins began actively soliciting affiliations. It was cumbersome to mobilize the official correspondence practices of the clubs, with their collective authorship and layers of transparency. Private networks, which could react faster and in a more tightly focused fashion, became the spearhead of the national effort against the Feuillants.[21]

The Roland circle's most important contribution to the Jacobin network after the Feuillant schism was keeping Lyon, France's second city and the Rolands' home base, in the Paris Jacobin Club's corner. In late July, Roland learned from his friend Luc-Antoine Champagneux, a Lyon publisher and close political ally, that the city's Jacobin affiliate, the Club du Concert, had cut ties with the "impure fraction" that remained with the Jacobins and switched its allegiance to the Feuillants. Roland was distressed but not surprised; the Club du Concert had long had a conservative bent. He, Madame Roland, and the other members of the circle also saw an opportunity. Lyon had another large club, the Club Central, which was a federation of smaller popular societies organized in the city's local districts. The Club Central's politics were more in line with the Roland circle's. Because the Paris Jacobins had a rule that they would only affiliate with one club per town, the Club Central had never been formally connected to the Jacobin network. The Rolands and their allies immediately began a multipronged campaign—including private letters, newspaper articles, and public appeals—to ensure that the Club Central became the Paris Jacobins' Lyon affiliate.[22]

By the end of August, the Roland circle had persuaded the Club Central to throw its lot in with the Jacobins. The club entrusted the well-off Richard brothers, friends of Lanthenas, with their petition for an affiliation. The brothers, in a manner very much like the Sons of Liberty two decades earlier, channeled the official petition through their private friendship. They sent the petition to Lanthenas personally, with a plea that he be the Lyon club's "interpreter . . . before the Jacobin Club and . . . leave nothing undone so that its request . . . might be favorably received." It was an effective strategy. Lanthenas brought the request to the August 28 meeting of the Paris Jacobins, and the assembly immediately granted the Club Central an affiliation. Of the seven societies that requested an affiliation at that meeting, Lyon was one of only three that gained it immediately. The news arrived back in Lyon a few days later in yet another private letter, this time from Lanthenas to the Richards.[23]

The Club Central's affiliation proved to be an indication of how other provincial Jacobin affiliates would act. Over the next two months, provincial clubs gradually turned away from the Feuillants and expressed their loyalty to the Jacobins. By November 1791, the Feuillants had been reduced to a fifth (at most) of the size of the reinvigorated Jacobin network. As the Feuillants' stable of affiliates diminished, moreover, the club itself went into a decline. More and more members defected back to the Jacobins. By January 1792, the Feuillants had become a rump with almost no political influence; the Jacobins had won the struggle for control of the elite patriot movement.[24]

In the months after it played its triumphant role in rescuing key Jacobins and the Jacobin Club from destruction, the Roland circle reached the apogee of its influence. Elections were held for a new Legislative Assembly in September 1791. Members of the outgoing Assembly were not permitted to stand for election to the new one, so Robespierre (among many others) was excluded. Brissot, buoyed by his reputation as a publicist for the Jacobins, was elected as a deputy from Paris. He and others of his persuasion formed a loud and influential bloc in the Assembly.[25]

France faced growing challenges as the Legislative Assembly convened. Domestically, the two most daunting issues were resistance to the Civil Constitution of the Clergy and individuals who left the country and declared their opposition to the revolutionary government (dubbed émigrés). Deputies who were affiliated with the Jacobin Club, especially Brissot, took a prominent role in guiding the Assembly's response to emigration. In November, it adopted a decree on émigrés, proposed by Brissot, which castigated and punished émigré princes. In subsequent months, he and his allies continued as prominent advocates of a hard line on the issue. The Assembly tried to act as well against the mounting numbers of priests (called nonjurors) who were refusing to swear the oath required of them by the Civil Constitution. The deputies voted for laws that aimed to make the nonjurors submit through financial and other penalties. All these efforts to address the conflict with the church, however, were thwarted by the king, who vetoed all the Assembly's measures.[26]

The Legislative Assembly brought the Rolands to national prominence as well. In early 1792, with Brissot's support, Roland was called to be the interior minister, one of the most powerful executive positions in the government. He worked quickly to put a Jacobin stamp on the ministry, including creating a propaganda bureau directed by his Lyon friend Champagneux. Yet once they had gained control over some of the levers of national power, Brissot and the Rolands found that their habitual way of doing politics, built on close-knit, genteel friendships, was an unstable foundation for power. This weakness became apparent first within the Jacobin Club. In 1792 and 1793, political alliances within the Jacobins based on networks of friendship hardened into entrenched, opposed factions. The enduring gap between the political strategies of the gentlemanly Jacobins and the more working-class patriot movement, represented by the sections and the Cordeliers, presented an equally grave problem. During the two years following Roland's ascent to the ministry in March 1792, successive Jacobin leaders clashed with the more working-class patriot organizations. These conflicts, internal and external, split the Jacobins, crushed the Legislative Assembly, and ultimately led the radical patriot party to turn on itself with fatal results.[27]

The first major blow to the position of Bosc's friends was a bitter split that developed within the Jacobin Club in the spring and summer of 1792. The ostensible subject of the split was a serious disagreement about foreign policy. Brissot and his allies, including Roland, had begun at the end of 1791 to urge the Assembly to declare war on the states that were sheltering and abetting armed French émigrés. Robespierre was firmly opposed to the idea, regarding it as foolish and likely to empower the revolution's enemies at home. Since Robespierre was not a member of the Legislative Assembly, he and Brissot debated the question in the Jacobin Club. Over the course of several months, from December 1791 into March 1792, the two men and their allies traded barbed speeches. Brissot easily got the better side of the argument: by the time France declared war on the Austrian emperor in April 1792, Robespierre was one of the few remaining public voices strongly opposed to the war.[28]

The debate over the war drove a permanent wedge between Brissot and Robespierre, seeming to cleave the Jacobin Club into two camps. That the disagreement over the war prompted strong feelings was not surprising. Nor was it unusual for the members to air arguments publicly: part of the club's strength was that it provided a space for fairly open and explicit debate among patriot leaders. The trouble was that members of the club increasingly suspected that their opponents were not just disagreeing openly but plotting secretly—indeed, forming cabals and conspiring with the enemies of the revolution. The habit among the Jacobins of overlapping friendship and political networks made it easy to imagine such conspiracies. It was an article of faith among Jacobins that friendship was a powerful and double-edged political tool, which could solidify virtuous alliances or cement dangerous cabals. The very real intimate bonds among Jacobin factions lent a certain plausibility to these charges. Many of Robespierre's closest allies were men he had known for years, and he socialized with them almost exclusively and hardly ever with the Roland circle. The same charge could be lobbed in both directions. In 1793, Robespierre's friend Armand-Joseph Guffroy painted a detailed (if embellished) picture of the meetings among "close friend[s]" and "dinner[s]" at which the Rolands and their allies had supposedly plotted their political conspiracies. The very old-regime habits that had helped to make the Jacobins such powerful political players had begun to destroy them from within.[29]

As the habits of the Jacobins set them against one another, the friction between their approach to politics and the ones prevalent among the lower orders was becoming more pronounced. Over the course of 1791, the popular mobilization in Paris had grown more organized. The Paris sections, which had started out as improvised stopgap measures in the early days of the revolution, had gained a formal structure and considerable powers. In addition to administrative authority, they had grown to have de facto police power: in practice, they could arrest those whom they suspected of engaging in counterrevolutionary activity. They were not shy about using this authority. They had also developed their own expanding network of popular societies. During the spring of 1792, the sections and the Paris commune to which they responded demanded that they be allowed to meet in continuous session—effectively making them into miniature legislatures.[30]

Brissot's triumph on the war question proved to be short-lived. After war was declared, the military situation for France quickly deteriorated. French forces, which had earlier entered the Austrian Netherlands, were routed by the Austrians in May near Tournai. By August, Austrian troops had entered France and captured major fortresses along the border, including Longwy and Verdun. Robespierre, his anti-war position vindicated, regained much of the authority he had held in the Jacobins, at Brissot's expense. In early August, the sections and the Paris commune both lost patience with the conduct of the war and the Assembly that had begun it. In loose cooperation with the Jacobins, the more radical sections denounced the ministry and the king, declaring that they were guilty of anti-revolutionary activities. Some sections specifically singled out the Roland circle and its allies in the Assembly.[31]

Matters came to a head on August 10 when a large crowd of national guardsmen and section members lay siege to the Tuileries, the king's palace. The king and queen fled to the Assembly, which offered them asylum. But a pitched battle took place for the palace itself. The king's personal guard, barring the gates and firing from windows, succeeded in holding off the much larger attacking force. After a few hours of combat, the king ordered his men to cease fire and yield. Hundreds were dead on both sides. The sections seized the building and, shortly thereafter, the royal family itself, imprisoning them in the Temple, a fortress in the east of Paris. The capture of the Tuileries and the royal family marked a watershed in the political consciousness of the Paris popular movement. Until this point, the people of Paris had remained largely out of doors, operating within the constraints of their prerevolutionary compass. Now the popular movement turned its attention to the seat of power. By seizing the royal residence and then the royal family, they asserted themselves as the masters not merely of the streets but of the political leadership itself. After three years of revolutionary agitation and rapid transformation, the popular movement was finally beginning to move out of the habits bred in the old regime.[32]

Almost as soon as the royal family had been imprisoned, the Legislative Assembly set in motion elections for a new National Convention. This body would exercise temporary power and write a new constitution for France. The hastily organized elections took place starting on September 2. The Assembly, the Jacobin Clubs, and local administrators all exerted their influence in favor of candidates who were known to be strong patriots or who had publicly opposed the court in previous legislatures. Their efforts were well rewarded: at least half of the more than seven hundred deputies chosen were strong patriots or political radicals. Brissot and Robespierre, though not Roland, were among those elected. The Convention opened on September 20 and the next day, September 21, abolished the French monarchy. The following day, after slight hesitations, it declared France a republic. Over the next months, the Convention tried the former king and condemned him to death.[33]

The inauguration of the Convention marked the start of a consequential but ultimately short-lived alliance between the Jacobins led by Robespierre and the sections of Paris. Robespierre built on the considerable renown he had already gained in the Jacobins to become one of the dominant voices in the Convention. After Brissot and his friends formed a loose alliance with a group of deputies from around Bordeaux (capital of the Gironde *département*), Robespierre and his allies dubbed them the Girondins. On October 10, 1792, the Jacobins expelled Brissot from the club. During the months that followed, Robespierre and his allies in the Paris sections waged an increasingly open battle against Brissot and the so-called Girondins. Riots in February and March, propelled in part by an ongoing subsistence crisis in the city, turned into public attacks on the Girondins. The final straw was probably the April 1793 defection of a leading general, Charles-François Dumouriez. Dumouriez had been closely associated in the public mind with the Girondin group, and his betrayal reflected very badly on Brissot and his allies.[34]

On May 31, 1793, a small army of national guardsmen, under the command of section leader François Hanriot, lay siege to the Convention, demanding that it surrender the Girondins. The Convention at first refused to go along with the demand. Now that the sections had extended their out-of-doors agitation to the revolutionary assembly itself, the Jacobins—even Robespierre, who certainly had no love lost with the Rolands, Brissot, and their allies—resisted. But the Convention, in spite of its self-proclaimed power, could hardly resist the direct military pressure being brought to bear on it by the people in the streets. On June 2, the Convention proscribed the twenty-two deputies whom the sections had demanded be expelled and turned them over to the National Guard.[35] If the seizure of the Tuileries had signaled that the popular movement had finally learned how to play the enemy's game, the siege of the National Convention in May and June 1793 demonstrated how volatile the enemy's tools could be. It had taken less than a year for the revolutionaries in the street to begin turning against their erstwhile patriot allies.

At the same time that they besieged the Convention, the sections moved against the private sphere of the Girondin deputies. They recognized the post office—Bosc's bureau in particular—as a key site of their power. The sections sent officials to the main post office on May 31, with orders to stop "suspect agents," naming Bosc specifically, from continuing to work. They also charged them with examining all the correspondence and seizing any letters that were "suspect." The job proved to be a massive one. The following morning, the sections' agent, one Leclerc, sent a note to the revolutionary committee describing having spent the "entire night triaging the letters."[36]

The sections had now learned, as well, the importance of homes and places of business in elite politics. Soldiers were dispatched to intercept suspects across Paris. One detachment went to the home of the Rolands looking for the ex-minister. They found only Madame Roland and their twelve-year-old daughter, Eudora. Madame Roland was arrested and Eudora was sent to stay with friends. Many of the proscribed deputies and their friends scattered. Bosc, though his name was not on the main list of suspects, was also being hunted. He fled to a house he had deep in the forest of Montmorency, north of Paris.[37]

WITH THE EXPULSION OF THE SO-CALLED GIRONDIN DEPUTIES from the National Convention, Robespierre and his Jacobin friends finally seemed secure in their alliance with the sections of Paris. The two groups certainly had broadly shared ideological commitments: a profound investment in republican forms of government, an eagerness to turn away from the "corruption" of the old regime, and a fierce sense that political power should be centralized, firm, and direct. Between June 1793 and July 1794, the Jacobin-dominated republican government tried to reshape aspects of French government and society. Its most important achievement, in the short term, was turning the tide of the war in Europe. A massive conscription drive, matched with an equally heroic organizational and logistic effort, bulked up the republic's armed forces in record time. The government, increasingly dominated by the Convention's Committee of Public Safety, proposed legislation to limit prices and regulate wages in order to aid working people. It revised the calendar, altering the names of the months and eliminating Christian festivals. It promoted the use of the familiar *tu* as a form of address, in place of the more formal *vous*, as a mark of equality. There were few areas of French life its hand did not touch.[38]

The collaboration between the National Convention and the sections had a darker side as well. The Convention, supported by the sections, instituted a campaign of ideological purification and surveillance across France. The Terror, as its opponents called it, entailed the imprisonment of thousands of suspects, summary justice and mass executions, and outright massacres. The Rolands, Brissot, and many of Bosc's other friends were among its prominent victims. Parisians got an early hint of what was to come in September 1792, when crowds murdered over a thousand prisoners being held in the city's jails. Over the next two years, the Jacobin-dominated government waged war on citizens whom it considered disloyal. The city of Lyon, which had the temerity to defy the Convention in 1793, was besieged and its population severely punished. In the west of France, in the region known as the Vendée, republican troops waged a long and bloody campaign against a counterrevolutionary insurgency.[39]

Yet the alliance between the Robespierrists and the sections of Paris, though brutally effective and based on strong agreements on political principles, proved as unstable as earlier alliances across the class divide had been. The two sides, for all their points of agreement, still had fundamentally different approaches to the practice of politics. Robespierre and the Jacobins still saw revolutionary politics through the lens of their prerevolutionary experiences. For them, the pinnacle of political power was exercised in a small room by a group of like-minded elite men. This was indeed the very model of governance that the National Convention established: over the next months, the Convention's Committee of Public Safety, which met in secret, gathered more and more powers to itself.[40] The sections and the popular movement, on the other hand, wanted politics to happen in the streets.

After barely twelve months at the helm, Robespierre found himself at odds with the Paris popular movement. In June and July 1794, he was criticized in the sections for his increasingly autocratic behavior. He continued, as he long had, to socialize within a small group of close allies. The radically different political habits of the popular and elite revolutionaries—even when they were largely in agreement on principles—surged back to the fore. On July 27, 1794, the ninth day of the revolutionary month of Thermidor, a group of deputies in the National Convention staged a coup against Robespierre. This time, the sections sided with the Convention. The following morning, Robespierre went to the guillotine accompanied by several of his closest friends and collaborators.[41]

# 9
# THE ASSAULT ON SLAVERY

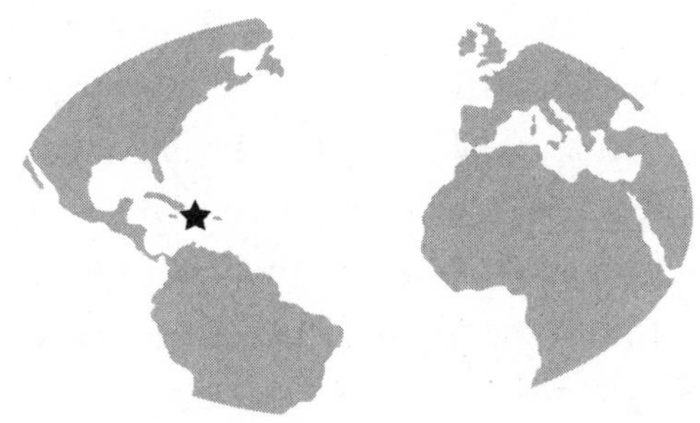

THE ISLAND OF SANTO DOMINGO LIES MORE THAN FOUR THOUsand ocean miles to the west of France. A traveler from Paris in 1789 could expect an arduous two months' journey to arrive on the island's western side, which during the previous century had become France's most important overseas possession. The colony of Saint-Domingue at the start of the French Revolution was a land of sharp contrasts. Fertile coastal plains in the north and west led abruptly to verdant mountain ranges that divided the colony into three provinces. Half a million enslaved people—about ten for every free person on the island—lived there in bondage, cultivating vast quantities of sugar, coffee, cotton, and indigo that brought fabulous wealth to their enslavers. The traveler would likely have landed at one of the colony's two chief ports: Cap Français (Le

Cap), the elegant capital of the north province, or Port-au-Prince, the ramshackle city on the central coast.[1]

The outbreak of the French Revolution ignited embers of conflict that had been smoldering in the island colony for years. The first crisis flared between free people of color and the colony's white ruling elite. Like many of the slave societies in the Caribbean and around its periphery, Saint-Domingue had a tripartite caste system, comprising a small white population, a larger group of free people of color, and an enslaved majority. Free people of color lived under considerable legal disabilities and were the targets of significant racial prejudice. In spite of these handicaps, a nontrivial number of them succeeded in acquiring wealth and power. The free colored community in prerevolutionary Saint-Domingue was especially well-off: its wealthiest members owned large plantations, enslaved hundreds of people, held an important place in local society, and sent their children to be schooled in France. These successes rankled the white population, angering wealthy planters and *petits blancs* (lower status white people) alike.[2]

Both free people of color and the white population of Saint-Domingue sensed an opportunity when the French Revolution began. Some white people hoped to use the occasion to gain greater autonomy and authority for the colonists. This might enable them to expand trade with neighboring colonies and solidify their political and social control over the island's population. When news of the formation of the National Assembly arrived on the island during the late summer of 1789, free people of color saw a chance to address their subordinate status within the colony. The Assembly's hostility to other forms of privilege, such as those enjoyed by nobles and the clergy, made them hopeful that the revolutionaries might also abolish legal distinctions related to color, at least for free people. By the beginning of 1790, the two camps had entered into open conflict. Vincent Ogé, a leading planter of color, attempted an armed rising against the white leadership. It was put down and he was brutally broken on the wheel. The fractious white elite, meanwhile, broke into pro- and anti-revolutionary camps.[3]

With the colony's elite in disarray, many of the enslaved people who made up a majority of the population saw an opportunity to become free. Their revolt, which began in the north province in August 1791, was highly organized on the local level and benefited from a strong yet diffuse leadership. Most of its leaders were relatively privileged enslaved people, many of whom exercised trades. A number of them were African-born, and many were serious practitioners of Catholicism, of African faiths, or of syncretic mixtures of the two. One of the early leaders was a former enslaved man named Toussaint Louverture. Louverture had been born into slavery and secured his freedom in early middle age through self-purchase. He was a devout Catholic, a skilled horseman, and a man known for his probity. In freedom, he became a slave owner himself while remaining intimately connected to the enslaved community by bonds of friendship, clientage, and kinship.[4]

The enslaved people who formed the engine of the revolt were, like their counterparts in France, children of the mid-eighteenth century. But their eighteenth-century experience, and the dispositions and habits that it had formed, were quite different from those of the urban lower classes in places like Paris, Boston, and Cuzco. This was in part because the vast majority of enslaved people in Saint-Domingue lived on plantations, far from the spaces of the city. While in much of the urban Atlantic the classes had grown more separate over the course of the eighteenth century, in slave societies like Saint-Domingue, dominated by rural life, the situation was more equivocal.

Slave societies of the kind that existed in Saint-Domingue simultaneously created great intimacy and tremendous social distance. On the plantations, enslavers in the eighteenth century exercised increasingly close supervision over the people they claimed to own. In the sugar- and coffee-driven economy of Saint-Domingue, especially, the imperative to achieve ever greater productivity, to wring ever more money out of the land, meant that the enslaved were closely watched and supervised.[5] Nor was this surveillance limited to the plantation: enslavers tried to maintain their dominance over public places in cities as well, albeit not without considerable difficulty.

For enslaved people, the hyper-presence in their lives of enslavers—members of the upper castes, both white and non-white—was a formative influence. It produced, in many of them, a driving desire to achieve the kind of liberation from elite supervision that was already the norm across much of the urban Atlantic world. The freedom that an eighteenth-century Paris meat worker or a Philadelphia laborer enjoyed to walk the streets more or less unmolested, all but invisible to the eye of the elite, was the dream of many enslaved and formerly enslaved people.

The first two years of the Saint-Domingue uprising were shaped by the overwhelmingly rural enslaved rebels' efforts to create a degree of autonomy for themselves within the colony. The initial rising, in August 1791, took the form of a coordinated assault on plantation infrastructure and white enslavers. They burned fields and houses, destroyed equipment, and executed a number of those who had held them in bondage. By and large, the rebels did not try to hold onto territory. When they faced counterattacks, they retreated to the hills or mountains. This was good military strategy, but it also represented a way of prioritizing freedom from constraint over anything else: land, revenge, even governance. The rebels largely steered clear of the major cities. This was in part because they were well defended. But even when the rebels did enter the cities, their sojourns—though destructive—were brief. They planned to burn Le Cap in August 1791, but no plans seem to have been made to occupy or hold the town. Port-au-Prince, the main city in the center of the colony, likewise remained outside of the rebels' control.[6]

The French government tried strenuously to gain control over an increasingly chaotic situation in the colony in 1792. A quickly rotating cast of governors, officials, and officers attempted and largely failed to rein in the warring factions and groups. Governance fragmented dramatically. Towns and local governments acted largely independently of any kind of central authority in the colony, let alone the government in Paris. Troops and sailors under the command of several generals took to the field against the self-emancipated rebels. They managed to push them back repeatedly, but any kind of final victory eluded the government's forces. Meanwhile, competing factions within the colony were recruiting ex-slaves and forging alliances with rebel armies.[7]

In September 1792, a trio of "civil commissioners" appointed by the National Assembly arrived in Le Cap to assume governance of the colony. It was Jacques-Pierre Brissot who had pushed their appointment through the National Assembly during his brief period of political ascendancy in the winter and spring of 1792. The commissioners' mission was to reestablish central authority, suppress the rebellion of the enslaved, and, pursuant to a vote in the National Assembly on April 4, 1792, ensure that free people of color enjoyed equal rights. The Assembly granted the commissioners virtually dictatorial powers to carry out these complex and somewhat contradictory tasks. One of the commissioners, Léger-Félicité Sonthonax, a lawyer and low-ranking old-regime official, immediately established himself as the dominant figure of the trio. But their mission was scrambled when shortly after the commissioners arrived, in October 1792, news of the suspension of the monarchy and the creation of the republic arrived.[8]

The advent of the French Republic repolarized the colony's political situation, scrambling the alliances and conflicts. The commissioners' first priority was to secure the republic's position. Within two weeks of the news arriving, in alliance with the *petits blancs* of Le Cap and Port-au-Prince, the commissioners had formed a patriotic club in Le Cap and purged royalists in both cities. At the same time, they continued the long-running war on the formerly enslaved rebels. They put in charge Étienne Laveaux, an officer who had come over with them. He proved an effective commander, pushing back the insurgents on multiple fronts. The commissioners also continued to push their original mission of civil and political equality for free people of color. These missions were somewhat contradictory: many of the *petits blancs* whose support was crucial were vehemently opposed to rights for free people of color. And the insurgent armies, some of which were overtly royalist, posed a continued threat to the republican commissioners.[9]

The commissioners' tricky triangulation of opposing forces exploded in the spring of 1793, leading to the first abolitionist decree in France's colonies. The new National Convention, influenced by Dominguan planters resident in France, appointed as governor of Saint-Domingue François-Thomas Galbaud, himself a planter. The new governor was supposed to follow the lead of the commissioners, but as soon as Galbaud arrived in the colony he allied himself with the planters and the *petits blancs*, who had become disenchanted with the commissioners' politics of racial equality, and led a revolt against the commissioners. Over several bloody days, Galbaud and the commissioners battled for control of Le Cap.

On June 21, Sonthonax and his co-commissioner Étienne Polverel played a trump card: they issued a proclamation promising freedom to any enslaved solider who fought with them for the French Republic. A large force of insurgents responded, helping to drive the royalists and their allies out of Le Cap. Though it was issued in the heat of battle, and with a short-term goal of pushing back Galbaud, the June 21 decree was neither a hasty decision nor a short-lived one. Though it went against his explicit directions and posed a risk that he recognized to the economic life of the colony, Sonthonax was sympathetic to arguments for the abolition of slavery. His decision to issue a kind of interim emancipation proclamation would not have been against his inclinations. It would prove to be the beginning of a much larger emancipation process that encompassed the whole French Caribbean—especially the island colony of Guadeloupe that lay just a short week's sail to the southeast of Saint-Domingue.[10]

After the insurgents joined the fray, Le Cap caught fire. Who caused the inferno and why has never been clear, but much of the town was destroyed. Contemporary images of the capture and burning of Le Cap in 1793, many based on eyewitness accounts, reveal the way in which the formerly enslaved troops were outsiders to the colonial city. In a print of the event, titled *Incendie du Cap Français* (below), the central grouping of former slaves is on

Burning of Cap Français, 1793. Courtesy of Musée Carnavalet, Paris.

a hill overlooking the burning city. They stand at a literal remove from the urban space. Another engraving, entitled *Revolte generale*, shows armed Black men chasing white families through the harbor. But while the soldiers are shown within the boundaries of the city in this print, their action suggests transience.[11]

The sense of outsiderness is present as well in *Pillage du Cap*, an image by the painter J. L. Boquet. He created an intricate scene of pillage set on what appears to be the Champ de Mars, the military exercise field, abutting the hills that hemmed the city in on the west. The picture is divided into three layers vertically—one of sky, one of hills, and a bottom stratum of frenetic activity—and into two parts horizontally by a large tree that dominates the foreground. The picture has a carnivalesque quality: soldiers on horseback mix with women, with carters, with soldiers dressed in outlandish costumes.[12]

*Pillage du Cap* put front and center a representation of an episode that reportedly took place during the seizure of Le Cap: the formerly enslaved soldiers allegedly raided the local opera house, the Comédie, appropriated the costumes, and paraded through the streets with them. These soldiers are depicted in Boquet's image by the base of the tree. One of them holds a military stance, legs akimbo, hands on his belt, gun slung over his shoulder, wearing what appears to be a classical tunic with a towering, seventeenth-century-style wig atop his head. Others are shown trying on women's clothes.[13]

What did the costumes of the Comédie mean to the insurgents? We can safely rule out the possibility that they wore them out of a desire to be ridiculous or because they did not understand what they were. More plausible is that their appropriation of the costumes was a way of seizing the city, of claiming the place. The Comédie du Cap was—as opera houses were in other eighteenth-century cities—the very heart of the elite metropolis. Theaters were public-private spaces par excellence: walled off from

A satirical view of formerly enslaved soldiers wearing costumes taken from the opera of Cap Français. Watercolor, J. L. Boquet. Courtesy of the David M. Rubenstein Rare Book & Manuscript Library, Duke University.

the open streets, zones of relative equality among the well-off who could access them. When enslaved people took the costumes they found there and put them on their bodies—inhabited them, as it were—they claimed that space as their own.

Yet as with so many other efforts in this early revolutionary world to turn the cultural tools of the old regime to the revolutionaries' advantage, the insurgent troops found the going to be treacherous. To white observers, including the creator of the print, the idea of Black soldiers dressed in theater costumes was a farce, not a serious appropriation. They viewed it, as Boquet suggests, as a tragicomic confirmation of Black peoples' alleged lack of civilization and their lack of capacity for self-governance.

What distant printmakers might think about ex-slaves was certainly of less moment to them than the attitudes of the free people of color whom they encountered when they entered Le Cap. The free people of color were connected to the formerly enslaved soldiers by their race, which made them alike as members of a subordinate caste. But their class position had more in common with white people. This gave free people of color an ambiguous place in the troubled colony's social order—and a position as the fulcrum of power, especially in the cities where they predominated.

MARIE BUNEL WAS ONE OF THE FREE PEOPLE OF COLOR WHOM THE soldiers encountered after the burning of Le Cap. She was a woman of many names. She was likely just plain Marie at first; women born into slavery usually did not have a given last name. She later assumed the surname Mouton or Estève. After her marriage, she went by Bunel. Sometimes she was Femme Bunel; other times she used the more "dignified" madame. She also called herself Marie-Françoise, the basis for her nickname, Fanchette. And she had a variety of names by which her kin called her: godmother, aunt, auntie.[14]

As the revolutionary whirlwind descended on her home in 1789, the many identities that Marie Bunel assumed in the old regime became a vital resource for her incipient nation. In Saint-Domingue, divisions within the revolutionary camp, created and accentuated by the politics of caste, yawned wide. Unusual flexibility and creativity would be needed to bring the sides together into a functioning political movement. Would Marie and her intimates, not least among them Toussaint Louverture, be able to make a revolutionary movement cohere with the fickle tools of the old regime?

Marie Bunel had been long established in Le Cap when the insurgents arrived. Though her early years are difficult to trace with any certainty, the likelihood is that she was born on a plantation. By the mid-1780s, at the latest, she was free and living well in Le Cap. Newspaper advertisements show that she kept an inn or tavern. She owned property, including a house up in the Petit Guinée (Little Africa) neighborhood, which was a home and a productive asset when she chose to rent it out. And like many of her group, she owned a number of enslaved people. Contemporary reports gave wild estimates of her property in persons. One newspaper claimed she owned "800 slaves," which would have made her one of the wealthiest planters on Saint-Domingue. Mariette, a woman probably born in West Africa, with the legend "VEUVE SALLE AU CAP" burned into her right breast, was one of them.[15]

Most of Marie's business was as a trader: her correspondents called her a *négociante*. She acted as a kind of eighteenth-century fashion consultant. Surviving receipts and correspondence show her selling cloth, buttons, and finished clothing to a variety of clients, including both other free people of color and white islanders. She was no seamstress herself; she did not produce the clothing. Her role, instead, was as an intermediary. She had a reputation in Le Cap as a lady of style. One of her correspondents said that she "preside[d]" over fashion (the "*toilettes de[s] graces*") in the city. When someone wanted fashionable clothes or household articles, she or he would commission Marie to procure them.[16]

Marie Bunel was set apart from the formerly enslaved soldiers by her education. She wrote with a strong albeit somewhat unsteady hand—not uncommon among those who had learned to write later in life—and had a clear head for figures. Like other members of the free colored elite, especially women, she had mastered the use of complex debt and credit instruments. And she was intent on passing these educational advantages on to her family. She sponsored the education of her niece, Orphise, paying for regular lessons from a schoolmaster.[17]

While her money, education, and modishness set her apart from the insurgent soldiers, Marie Bunel definitely remained connected to them. Most free women of color had connections among the enslaved, either through kinship ties or business relationships. She was unusual in having close connections with two of their leaders, Toussaint Louverture and Henry Christophe. Both men in 1793 were mid-level commanders in the insurgent forces. One white colonist, an eyewitness to events in Le Cap through the 1790s, described Marie as a "good Friend of Toussaint" and even went so far as to suggest that she had a certain "influence" over his "mind." She was close with Christophe's wife, Marie-Louise, another fashionable free woman of color.[18] It seems likely that the two commanders, both of whom were in or around Le Cap in 1793, extended their protection to Marie and her family.

Some years earlier, likely during the 1780s, Marie had married a white man named Joseph Bunel. Born in Normandy into a middling family, Bunel had gone to the Americas, like many other young men of his generation, to make his fortune. He may have first tried his luck in French-speaking Canada, which had been ceded to Britain in 1763. Failing to advance there, he had gone to Saint-Domingue. Like many white merchants in the colony, Bunel was a jack-of-all-trades. He acted as an intermediary between plantation owners and consignees in destination countries such as France and the United States. Trading to Philadelphia, for instance, he sent coffee and other tropical products in exchange for flour, meat, manufactured goods such as cloth, building materials, and sometimes drink. The size of the ventures could be substantial, with values exceeding one thousand pounds per cargo.[19]

With these substantial amounts of money on the line, Bunel, in common with other long-distance traders, engaged in fiscal risk management and lending as a sideline. Bunel regularly lent money to others and received loans in his turn. This included small sums—one Philadelphia merchant sought a loan of fifty dollars—as well as much larger ones. Like many merchants, he helped to insure other merchants' risks. In the mid-1790s, for instance, Bunel agreed to insure a cargo that his business partner Jacques Mussy wanted to send to Saint-Domingue. Bunel insured it for the very substantial sum of three thousand gourdes. The voyage was successful, entitling him to a 10 percent fee for his services. Unluckily for him, Mussy went bankrupt and the fee seems never to have been paid.[20]

The marriage between Marie and Joseph Bunel was, in some sense, a business partnership. By the 1790s, wife and husband had their business affairs thoroughly entwined. Each one acted as an agent for the other's business, and their letters are stuffed with figures, bills of lading, and prices current. Hostile observers of the couple claimed that their motives for marrying had been entirely businesslike: Joseph had married Marie for her connections, so they said, and she married him to gain status in the community. This was not entirely implausible. Transactional sexual relations and relationships between white and non-white individuals were common in the early modern Atlantic world.[21] Neither of the spouses would have been blind to the considerable advantages that their marriage brought to each of them.

But Marie and Joseph's marriage seems to have been based on a genuine bond of affection—and in many respects, Marie seems to have been the dominant partner. Joseph's letters to Marie, which form the bulk of their surviving correspondence, are filled with expressions of love and attention that go well beyond the formulaic style of eighteenth-century letters between spouses. In one letter,

Joseph observed to Marie that the day he was writing, August 15, was the feast day of her patron saint (Assumption), and her birthday. "Not being there in person, I can't give you a bouquet for your special day [*fête*]." But he promised to "pay off [this] just debt" as soon as he returned. Joseph's letters are punctuated with gentle complaints that Marie was not writing back as promptly as he had hoped. In one exchange, he suggested that he had written to her repeatedly over six months without reply.[22]

The Bunels likely joined forces with the insurgents around the time of the seizure of Le Cap, becoming active participants in the revolution and close collaborators with some of its main leaders. The fragmentary state of the archival record makes it difficult to pinpoint the moment at which the Bunels decided to ally themselves with the insurgents, but Marie Bunel had long been connected with Louverture and, by 1798, both Bunels were within his orbit. Starting around 1794, Joseph Bunel assumed important public roles in alliance with the insurgents under Louverture's command. His most crucial job was serving as treasurer to Henry Christophe's Army of the North. He had physical control over the insurgents' funds. At one point, Christophe ordered him to quickly collect "all of the money" that was in the treasury and deliver it up to the local commander. Bunel did it that evening, on three tumbrels with an armed escort. As treasurer he also collected taxes and duties that Louverture imposed once he had gained control of Le Cap, including a new stamp tax. Louverture and Christophe reposed a great deal of trust in Bunel: he was not required to keep books or to give a regular accounting of his collections to the officers. He may have also had a role in counterfeiting money.[23]

The Bunels' public life went well beyond the position of treasurer. Bunel was appointed to one of the newly established departmental superior courts in the mid-1790s. Given his lack of any legal qualifications, this was certainly a patronage appointment that reflected his closeness with the governing group of insurgents. He was a member of an alleged "committee of whites" (*comité blanc*), a group of individuals, mostly *petits blancs*, who worked with the insurgent forces. At one point in 1797 or 1798, the two Bunels had apparently gone "door to door" to secure signatures on an "address . . . begging Toussaint to take the reins of government" from the French government's appointee.[24] In short, building on their long-standing role as commercial intermediaries, they had become political go-betweens and allies of the insurgent forces commanded by Louverture and Christophe.

Yet even as the Bunels immersed themselves in the revolution, there remained a fundamental ambiguity to their position. They kept a close eye on their property—and on the individuals they had enslaved. When Marie Bunel departed Saint-Domingue in the early 1800s, she instructed her agent, a man named Maurin, to "protect and watch over" fourteen formerly enslaved people, seven men and seven women, and to "implement on them all of the laws and regulations concerning them." At the moment she gave these directions, formerly enslaved people were being ordered to return to the plantations they had worked in slavery. Bunel likely hoped to regain control over their labor even if she no longer possessed their persons.

Maurin carried out his charge well, leaving behind a stark and poignant record of Marie Bunel's lingering commitment to slavery. Of the seven men, Maurin marked three "dead," while one (a cook) had gone to Port-Margot, a town a short distance from Le Cap. The other three men—including two watermen—had no annotation at all, suggesting that they could not be found. The women—among them two washerwomen, a cook, and a "merchant"—seem to have been somewhat easier to run to ground. Four of their names carried annotations indicating their location or other information. What use was made of Maurin's list is not clear. But its mere existence shows how the Bunels, for all their sincere commitment to the revolution in Saint-Domingue, remained rooted in the old regime. They did not hesitate to grasp at their former bondspeople when they had the chance.[25]

BETWEEN 1793 AND 1798, THE ARMIES OF FORMER ENSLAVED PEOPLE gained effective control over Saint-Domingue. Toussaint Louverture was the key figure in this triumph, and by 1798 he had become the preeminent leader, in both title and fact, of a colony that was only nominally under French rule. He managed to accomplish this feat by temporarily bridging the divisions between the colony's fiercely competing factions: formerly enslaved people, free people of color, *petits blancs*, and the French civil and military administration. He did it, above all, by creatively repurposing the old-regime models of cultural power, exercised through speech and writing, that he had grown up around during his youth in the 1750s and early 1760s.

Louverture's ascent began in earnest in the year after the pillage of Le Cap in 1793. During the first months of 1794, the republican French government, following the lead of the civil commissioners, formally abolished slavery in the French empire. At about the same time, as part of a drive to seize France's Caribbean possessions, British forces had invaded Saint-Domingue, capturing a band of territory running up the island's coast. Even those who had not been particularly enamored of French rule understood that the British invasion threatened to undo slavery's abolition. Louverture, realizing that French-aligned forces could not hope to resist the British invasion so long as they were divided among themselves, set about uniting the island under his leadership.[26] To do this, he would have to be a bridge between the very different worlds of the formerly enslaved, the free people of color, and the various groupings of white colonists and officials.

By 1794, Louverture had already showed himself to be a highly effective leader of formerly enslaved troops. He was a wily tactician;

his battlefield successes were an advertisement all their own. He won formerly enslaved men over to his side with his unwavering commitment to the abolition of slavery. Because his wife, sons, and other relatives had still been enslaved until the eve of the revolution, and even into its first years, he was personally invested in abolition in a way that some of the other insurgent leaders, who had been born free, were not. Yet at least as important in mustering his men was Louverture's way with words. He was famous for his "lengthy lecture[s]" to his troops, in which he exhorted them to act in "fraternal" fashion with one another and to maintain the highest ethical standards. His eloquence in Kreyol was apparently legendary, although unfortunately no records of these oral speeches have survived.[27]

Beginning in 1794, Louverture began to master the method of communication that he would need to exercise a similar kind of leadership over the more elite segments of Dominguan society: the letter. Unlike the John Adamses and Brissots of the era, Louverture had not grown up writing letters. Like many people born into slavery, he did not learn to read or write until adulthood. After 1793, he suddenly began producing letters at a rapid clip, often several per day. He developed a painstaking and elaborate collaborative process in order to effect this nearly miraculous expansion of his epistolary self. The general dictated each letter in Kreyol to a secretary, who then translated it into French. Louverture then reread and corrected the missive himself, after which a fair copy was made. Signs of the letters' roots in dictation are not hard to find, most notably in Louverture's frequent use of apostrophe and a vocabulary of orality, such as using the verb for "speak" rather than the one for "say."[28]

Many of Louverture's letters, which were written to subordinates or superiors in the French civil-military hierarchy, adopted the genre conventions of formal official or government correspondence. This genre, which was familiar to both Louverture and his secretaries from their prerevolutionary experiences, was characterized by a stylized formality that evoked and reinforced the writer's authority and legitimacy. Louverture's letters made a political claim starting with their physical trappings. By 1796, if not before, Louverture had his own official letterhead, which he often paired with conventional formatting at the top of the first sheet, such as leaving a large space between the addressee's name and the start of the text. Official letters were often produced on larger sheets of paper than were used for regular private letters and frequently numbered or labeled according to their subject matter. The genre also had certain characteristic stylistic features that Louverture and his secretaries adopted. They adhered to the expected formal and direct style of address and rarely mentioned personal matters, except to formulaically offer compliments to acquaintances.[29]

Louverture made deft use of the genre to solidify his dual position as a reliable, loyal subordinate and as a powerful and decisive leader. His letters were exquisitely well tuned to these purposes. In a large number of surviving missives to his superior, French governor-general Étienne Laveaux, Louverture was at pains to present himself as a trustworthy follower. He wrote to Laveaux frequently, usually at length and in great detail. He offered up accounts of his military decisions and point-by-point descriptions of how battles and other events had played out. He enacted his loyalty by reporting on contacts he had with other French officers or with the enemy and by passing along information, often emphasizing that he did so with "haste." When writing to his subordinates, on the other hand, Louverture adopted a very different style. His letters to inferior officers were curt, usually taking up little more than a paragraph. As would have been common for military officers, Louverture couched many of these short missives as straightforward orders or requests. In them, in other words, he presented himself, not as the loyal subordinate that he was in correspondence with Laveaux, but as the busy and powerful commander of an army.[30]

Louverture showed remarkable skill not only in using the existing epistolary forms but in reshaping and remixing them to suit new purposes. In some of his military reports to Laveaux, Louverture threaded in emotive language drawn from the genre of familiar letters, creating a hybrid style seemingly intended to nourish a close personal bond with a superior officer. Louverture also used letters to solve new problems that arose. One that he faced regularly after 1794 was persuading other ex-slave leaders—who had competing interests and allegiances, and did not necessarily recognize his authority as a French officer—to ally with him against both the British and other potential leaders. Louverture used letters as a key part of his strategy for recruiting these important figures. He blended together the conventions of several different genres in these missives, creating an idiosyncratic and persuasive hybrid style tailor-made for his purpose.

Writing in early 1796 to an officer called Dieudonné, the leader of some three thousand soldiers, Louverture began in the conventional style of an official letter. “I send you three of my officers,” he wrote, “to bring you a packet that the general and governor of Saint-Domingue orders me to deliver to you.” But the letter soon veered sharply from that genre’s conventions. Louverture adopted a familiar tone, more appropriate to a friend or colleague, calling Dieudonné his “dear brother,” and declaring that he wanted “nothing in the world other than to see you happy.” He recounted in personal terms his past flirtation with a foreign alliance and urged his correspondent to “follow my example” by remaining allied to France. Louverture added to this intimate, fraternal appeal a heavy dose of revolutionary rhetoric with a distinctly Dominguan twist. Only under the flag of the French Republic, he declaimed, are we "truly free and equal." Together "let us chase the royalists from our country; they are villains who want to put back on us the shameful irons that we broke at such great cost."[31]

The unorthodox mixture of genres in Louverture's letter to Dieudonné reflected at once the general's deep appreciation of old-regime epistolary genres and his clear-eyed understanding of how to deploy it in original ways. The formal framing of Louverture's missive affirmed to its recipient that the general was a trustworthy leader, someone with whom he could safely ally himself. Yet rather than try to command Dieudonné's allegiance, Louverture sought a relationship based on brotherly and patriotic feelings. The mixture of heated rhetoric and fraternal familiarity seemed intended to appeal not only to Dieudonné himself but also potentially to his men. It is not implausible to think that this letter was either read in public or at least shared—as many missives were—with some of the recipient's officers. In the absence of a response from Dieudonné, or an eyewitness account of the letter's reception, it is hard to know just how effective these epistolary strategies were. Yet we do know that, in this case at least, the outcome was almost exactly what Louverture had desired: though Dieudonné proved unwilling to ally with the general, one of his lieutenants led a revolt the next day that brought most of Dieudonné's men over to Louverture's command.[32]

Between late 1796 and the end of 1798, Louverture used his hard-won power to sideline metropolitan French authorities in the colony and consolidate his rule in defense of freedom. In 1796, after having spent more than a year enthusiastically praising Laveaux, Louverture persuaded him to return to France. A year later, he forced Sonthonax, who had returned as civil commissioner, to give up his post and leave Saint-Domingue. The French government, by now aware of Louverture's intention to seize control of the colony, sent Gabriel de Hédouville, a conservative-leaning republican general, as its new agent in mid-1798. Within six months, Louverture had entirely undermined his authority and forced him to depart as well.[33]

Louverture's growing command of letter writing also enabled him to coax British and American officials into establishing independent diplomatic relationships with his administration during the last years of the 1790s. Though Saint-Domingue was still a French colony, France by 1798 was not providing much in the way of either trade or military protection to the island. Louverture hoped to open direct negotiations with representatives of the British and US governments to secure the withdrawal of British troops and the opening of American trade. His position, however, gave him at best a questionable authority to treat with foreign powers—a problem of diplomatic recognition that would continue to bedevil Haiti even after independence.[34]

Louverture created the authority he needed essentially out of nothing by using the conventional language and forms of diplomatic correspondence. His initial November 1798 letter to US president John Adams, proposing that he would protect American ships in exchange for a reopening of trade with the island, presented the general as a regular diplomatic partner worthy of the president's confidence. In a subsequent letter, assuring the president that he would gain control over the southern parts of the island that were then in rebellion, he took pains to rhetorically construct himself as the leader of a peer state at war with the usual forces hostile to state order: "Piracy," "civil war," and "machiavellism." Louverture knew that the right epistolary self-presentation, the construction of the right kind of corresponding self, could help him secure diplomatic recognition.[35]

Joseph Bunel became a key figure in Louverture's diplomacy with the United States in 1798. The loyal treasurer, closely tied to him through his wife Marie, was a perfect emissary to send to the United States. Louverture could trust him completely. But as a white man and an enslaver, and French-born at that, Bunel had a far better chance of gaining a hearing from the US government than any Black or mixed-race official would have. Though hardly trained as a diplomat, Bunel was well acquainted with the worlds of merchants and planters that dominated US foreign policy. Bunel proved to be an inspired choice for the mission. He made an excellent impression in Washington and succeeded in securing an agreement from Adams's government to reopen trade with Saint-Domingue.[36]

LOUVERTURE'S MASTERY OF THE OLD REGIME'S CULTURAL TOOLS, having brought him to the pinnacle of power in 1798, soon began to undo his regime from within.

As soon as Louverture consolidated his power in Saint-Domingue's north, he invited former planters to return and began to press formerly enslaved people to return to their plantations. He hoped to use them to increase production on the island's plantations and so reestablish Saint-Domingue as a crucial part of the Atlantic world economy. Economic strength, he hoped, would support the island's autonomy and secure the freedom of formerly enslaved people. His fluency in the language of property and his ability to incarnate a gentleman were crucial elements in winning the planters back to his side. As he had done so successfully with French officials over the previous decade, he personally made his case to the former enslavers using their own language. And he enjoyed considerable success in the endeavor: many former planters, including some who were quite conservative, rallied to Louverture's regime. By 1800, they were occupying crucial roles in government and administration as judges, treasurers (like Bunel), municipal officials—and, of course, planters.[37]

Louverture's détente with the planter class eroded the bond that he had formed with the mass of Haitian peasants, who formed the backbone of his victorious army. As early as 1799, Louverture and his lieutenants were putting pressure on peasants to return to plantations and to the production of staple crops for export. Matters came to a head in 1801, when Louverture had a new constitution for the island drafted. The Constitution had many provisions that resembled constitutions adopted during the 1780s and 1790s in the United States and France. These included an overhaul of the colony's judiciary, fiscal reforms, and protections for some individual rights. Other, more original provisions—including sections establishing Catholicism as the official state religion, a ban on divorce, and measures intended to protect "collective morals"—seem to have been well calculated to appeal to the population of the island.[38]

Far more controversial for cultivators were provisions in the Constitution that aimed to reimpose something very much like the old plantation regime. The Constitution envisioned most formerly enslaved people returning to plantation labor in the coming years. They would do so under the governance of former enslavers, whom the Constitution tried to reimagine as "father figures." In practice, it was clear that the former enslavers would regain much of the coercive power they had had under the old regime. They would once again have the right to hold workers against their will and to inflict bodily punishment on those who did not perform to their expectations. Even before the promulgation of the Constitution, the moves that Louverture had taken to restart the plantation regime struck many formerly enslaved people as disturbing echoes of the days of slavery. When the Constitution was promulgated, formalizing this return to the practices of enslavement, scattered revolts broke out among the freedmen. The connection between the leader and his followers was under serious strain, and with it the revolutionary movement he had built. Less than a year later, Louverture himself would be gone.

The travails of Louverture's regime in 1801, which would contribute to his eventual fall a year later, were in some sense peculiar to the circumstances of Haiti. In an emergent state negotiating the immense transition from a plantation slave society to freedom, it was probably impossible for anyone to smoothly navigate among the competing constituencies and priorities. And Louverture succeeded beyond any reasonable expectation. He built an effective political and military movement during the 1790s that defeated some of the era's most powerful empires and helped to secure freedom for hundreds of thousands of enslaved people. More than most revolutionaries at the time, Louverture also managed to bridge the social gap, at least for a while, between the elite and working class.

Yet even Louverture, for all of his political genius, could not escape the gravitational forces of the first revolutionary generation's habitus. The revolution in Saint-Domingue had begun as a revolt from below, created and led by a shadowy and widely dispersed leadership drawn from among the enslaved. As Louverture took command in the mid-1790s, he tried to transform it into a revolution from above. Like his counterparts across the revolutionary world of the 1780s and early 1790s, from the plantations of Virginia to the dense cities of the Netherlands, Louverture believed that he as the leader was best suited to shape the revolution's direction. As he tried to exert control, he fell into what his most recent biographer has called an "authoritarian spiral," in which he had to use an increasingly heavy hand to impose his will on the movement below. His efforts to advance the revolution ended up, tragically, alienating the populace without whose support a revolutionary movement could not hope to be sustained for very long.[39]

Louverture's failed effort to direct the Haitian Revolution from above has a particular poignancy given that the leader himself had begun his life in slavery. His struggles, however, were not exceptional in the Atlantic world of the 1770s, 1780s, and 1790s. In region after region, political elites who tried to organize and direct revolutions from above ran headlong into the gap that divided the worldviews of social classes and racial groups from one another. Unable to form robust political mobilizations across these deep divides, political leaders found that their movements could only fly a short distance before they were dragged back to earth.

Even failures, however, can have powerful consequences. Toussaint Louverture did not live to see his vision of a free and prosperous Saint-Domingue come to fruition. His own program of revolutionary reforms was interrupted almost as soon as it began. It set the stage, however, for more conclusive and permanent changes that would sweep Saint-Domingue/Haiti after 1800. In this respect, too, Louverture was more typical than exceptional. For across the revolutionary Atlantic world, the fragile and often evanescent revolutionary movements that burned during the late decades of the eighteenth century acted as a crucible. They molded a new generation of revolutionaries who saw the social world in profoundly new ways that opened up promising avenues for mass political mobilization.

# PART III

# MASS MOVEMENTS AND MASS CULTURES, 1795–1815

# 10
# RUINS AND RECONSTRUCTION

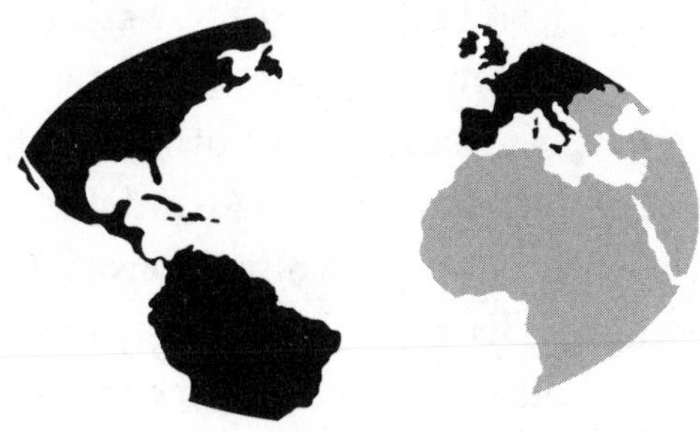

FOR MADRE MARIA DE LA CONCEPCIÓN RIVADENEYRA, THE 1790s were nothing less than a disaster.

Still trapped in Santa Teresa during the early years of the decade, she found her position under attack from all sides. Litigation began over the ownership of a profitable mine in Ocontaya, in the mountainous region to the southeast of Cuzco, that was a source of her family's wealth. In early 1794, she and her sister lost the case and were ordered to pay the "earned income" of the mine to one of the plaintiffs. Her former fellow nuns in Santa Catalina, now under the firm control of her old opponent Madre Trancito, were also doing their level best to get even with their ex-prioress. In her fatter days, Madre Maria had been the administrator of several religious foundations dedicated to particular saints. When Madre Maria had been exiled from Santa Catalina by Don Benito de la Mata Linares in 1786, she had retained control of at least some of the foundations' resources by taking with her all the "books, and papers belonging" to them. She even continued to collect the rents while in exile.[1]

In 1796, the new rulers of Santa Catalina demanded that Madre Maria account for the foundations' funds. She responded with her customary bravado, asserting that a great deal of money was owed to the foundations and asking the bishop to authorize her to use the courts to collect the debts. The new bishop of Cuzco dryly ordered that she turn over accounts of her administration to the convent. By the following year, she had lost control over the foundations.[2]

The burdens of the previous decade's fights, probably compounded by her exile to the unfamiliar convent of Santa Teresa, aged her prematurely. Her health began to fail. In early 1795, she was reported to be quite sick with a swelling in her face. Under the care of physicians, she was allegedly too ill to even leave her room.[3]

Madre Maria's position took another severe blow in 1797 when her sister, Josefa Rivadeneyra, died. Doña Josefa had played an important role in Madre Maria's power network. It was she, as Antonio Ugarte's wife, who linked the Ugarte and Rivadeneyra clans together. She had also been one of Madre Maria's conduits to the outer world of property and power. Doña Josefa had gone into exile with Antonio in the 1780s but had continued to support her sister and a niece, Sor Martina de San Miguel, also in Santa Catalina, from Spain. This support ended with her death. Not long after Doña Josefa passed away, Madre Maria was reduced to writing plaintive letters about her "lamentable situation" and asking others for relief.[4]

It was thus a financially and physically broken Madre Maria who limped into the new century. In 1801, bereft of support, in ill health for years—and, one must imagine, in poor spirits—Madre

Maria died in the convent of Santa Catalina. The passing of her generation had begun.

THE TWENTY YEARS SURROUNDING 1800, COINCIDING WITH THE height of the wars of the French Revolution, brought ruin on a virtually unprecedented scale to the societies that rimmed the Atlantic Ocean.

The strongest impacts were felt in continental Europe, where the armies of France and its allies fought a series of grinding conflicts to the north, south, and east. They began in April 1792, when France declared war on Austria, and continued with only brief interruptions for over twenty years. The master of the wars, for much of their duration, was Napoleon Bonaparte. He was in many respects an archetypical member of the second revolutionary generation. Born in 1769 to a family of minor nobles in Corsica, Napoleon had become an army officer in the 1780s. The French Revolution launched him to prominence: during the dangerous days of 1793 and 1794, he almost always managed to land on the winning side of the political strife while demonstrating genuine courage in battle. In March 1796, having served with military distinction and political acumen in a number of engagements, he was appointed commander of the Army of Italy at the tender age of twenty-six. Six years later, in his early thirties, having gathered most power in his hands, he had himself named "first consul for life"; in 1804, he abolished the vestiges of the republic and proclaimed himself emperor.[5]

European warfare during the 1790s and early 1800s was intensely disruptive in new and unfamiliar ways. Most of the damage was not done by disciplined armies during the campaigns of conquest. Indeed, by comparison to some recent wars—particularly the bloody Thirty Years' War, which ravaged Germany during the first half of the seventeenth century—the French and allied armies by and large showed restraint against their foreign enemies. Nonetheless, the sheer human scale of the armies that France fielded during these decades left a strong imprint. Hundreds of thousands of young men were pulled out of their communities, upending the traditional social order across France. The armies sustained staggering losses, which ran into the hundreds of thousands. The armies also fought a series of much dirtier wars within the bounds of the empire itself. Counterrevolutionary military mobilizations, the first of which emerged in western France as early as 1792, became a perennial thorn in the side of successive French regimes. The French armies treated these internal opponents as illegal combatants and waged war without mercy against them. In western France, Poland, and Spain, armies on both sides committed atrocities that left lasting scars.[6]

The tsunami waves of the French Revolution and the resulting wars quickly reached and broke over almost the entire Atlantic rim and beyond. This process was already well underway in the early 1790s. The most profound impact was of course in Saint-Domingue, where the French Revolution helped create the conditions for a successful revolt of the enslaved, which the government spent a decade trying to control. A destructive and ultimately failed French expedition to Saint-Domingue in 1802 would bring this chapter to a close. But it was only one of several expeditions personally commanded or dispatched by Napoleon, which also included his 1798 foray into Egypt. The United States, though formally neutral throughout the wars, became embroiled in an undeclared maritime war with France between 1797 and 1799 that resulted in the loss of thousands of US flagged ships and American-owned cargoes to French privateers. Reparations for some of these losses were still being adjudicated a century later. The maritime war also hit the commerce of Spanish America hard. As early as 1793, the vital trade links between Spanish America and Europe were under considerable pressure. Over the next decade, war weighed on the economies of all South America, linked to Atlantic trade, beginning to disrupt the social order along with it.[7]

After 1800, war in Europe sparked major military conflicts on land in both North and South America. In 1808, Napoleon's armies invaded Spain and toppled the Spanish king. Spain's American colonies surged into armed conflict with Spain and France—and with one another. The resulting wars were intermittent and initially mostly local in their impact. They varied considerably in their degree of violence. By 1815, however, there were few regions of the Americas that had not yet experienced some measure of military conflict. The United States, which escaped war on its territory for most of the period, eventually began a three-year war with Britain, called the War of 1812 after the year it began. In 1814, the British army invaded the United States and destroyed (among other things) the nation's nascent capital.[8]

For city dwellers and rural residents alike, one of the common experiences of these years was confronting ruin. Ruins of polities, ruins of families—but most of all, ruins of cities and towns. The physical ruins were the most visible sign of the destruction wrought by the wars and political conflicts. But they were also at the root of other kinds of ruin. The loss of homes meant the collapse of family life, the transition to life as a refugee or an itinerant. The loss of neighborhoods and businesses marked the end of familiar politics as well—tied up, as politics always is, with the shape of the community that creates them.

The destruction of the physical fabric of cities and towns was all the more serious because of the tightly meshed fabric of the eighteenth- and early nineteenth-century urban environment. In the premodern city, which still existed into the early nineteenth century, homes were essential sites of productive labor. Women, as well as many professional artisans, manual laborers, and even members of the elite such as merchants, set aside part of their residence as a workplace.[9] The loss of such a building was thus not merely the loss of a home or a workspace but the destruction of everything for a group of individuals and their families.

Perhaps the greatest testimonial to the power of ruins is Francisco Goya's celebrated, terrible series of prints *The Disasters of War.* Etched in the midst of the vicious Peninsular War, which pitted Napoleonic soldiers and their local allies against British forces and Spanish guerillas, the dark-hued images lament the wanton and cruel destruction of war. Goya's subject is not primarily buildings, as it was for so many of his peers in the European north. Goya focuses instead on the human ruins of war. The prints abound with images of bodies destroyed: soldiers and civilians impaled on sharpened sticks, corpses heaped atop one another, and bodies being hewn apart.[10]

Goya puts women at the center of the stories that his pictures tell. An early series shows women being sexually assaulted by soldiers. The captions emphasize their subjectivity: "They do not want it." Subsequent images show scenes of women in combat, firing

An image of war's destruction: a plate from Francisco Goya's *The Disasters of War*. Courtesy of Yale University Art Gallery.

weapons or egging on other combatants. Many show women in the course of everyday life in the midst of war: walking down shadowy streets, collecting bodies, searching for food. Their prominence in Goya's pictures, which echoes the role played by Andean women in the Túpac Amaru rebellion, reflects their central role in the Peninsular War. Women also serve, for Goya, as emblems of home, as metaphors for the Spanish homes and cities being destroyed by Napoleon's troops and allies.[11]

Disaster on this scale is a great leveler. The Atlantic world had never experienced a period of sustained crisis like this one. Earlier catastrophes, however severe, had been local or regional in scope: the great earthquakes of Cuzco and Kingston in the seventeenth century, or Lima and Lisbon in the mid-eighteenth century. Major epidemic outbreaks had periodically ravaged coastal cities, especially those in warmer climates like the Mediterranean or the southern reaches of North America. Man-made destruction from warfare had devastated individual cities and regions. New York City, notably, had been partly destroyed by fire in 1776.[12]

The ruin of the decades around 1800, larger and wider than ever before, also leveled the social and political playing field. Not all the way, to be sure: the rich typically fared better in a crisis than the poor, and many of them succeeded in maintaining their position in spite of the disruptions.[13] But for many, ruin was both a shared experience and a great equalizer. The rubble of a mansion was no more luxurious, after all, than the cinders of a hovel.

Ruin could also be the beginning of reconstruction. The destruction of stable and settled life creates a void that demands creativity to fill it back in. It creates opportunities for flexibility and freedom that were not there before. The ruins of a building require work to bring them back into coherent form, to put the columns back together and reset the roof on the beams—and these processes create opportunities to rethink the structure along the way. In similar fashion, the ruins of societies and polities that were made by war made it possible to imagine reassembling them in new ways. In this sense, crisis created the opportunity to "begin the world over again," as Thomas Paine had suggested in 1776.[14] Indeed, the central question that the ruins posed was precisely this: What should be built in their place, physically as well as socially and politically?

Nobody was more attuned to these experiences, or more likely to be shaped by them, than the children of the revolutionary era. That is, the young men and women born from about 1765 on. They were uniquely situated, biologically and socially, to respond to the stimulus of ruins. We know that the brain, on the whole, is more plastic the younger it is. A child of ten is able to learn more quickly than an adult of fifty: the young person adopts new habits more readily, learns new skills faster, and has a better memory. We also know that there are two great periods of heightened plasticity. Infancy is one. The other is the teenage years and the early twenties. The adolescent and young adult brain is undergoing a massive rewiring, making it uniquely capable of receiving, incorporating, and creatively adapting to the circumstances in which it is being remolded.[15]

This age happened to be a particularly important period for the molding and shaping of the life course in these early modern societies. Eighteenth-century Atlantic societies, by comparison to those of the previous and subsequent centuries, had a fairly extended period of childhood and adolescence. In Europe, most men and women did not marry until they were in their twenties—oftentimes well into their twenties. (Men tended to marry a bit later than women, on the whole.) As Julie Hardwick has observed, this created a distinctive period from roughly ages fifteen to thirty during which young men and women were sexually mature, usually at work, but still not quite full adults, settled and tied to children, careers, and responsibility.[16]

The extended period of young adulthood, in the early modern Atlantic world, was a time of unusual flexibility and freedom within the frame of the existing social order. Those who were younger, prepubescent children, were often working and living under the tight control of their family of origin. Young adulthood, in this society, was the moment when one went out into the world, when men and women figured out their place. The plasticity of the mind thus coincided with the moment of maximum social plasticity. The late teens and early twenties were when an early modern person's sense of the world around them was shaped and set.

What all this adds up to is that those who were teenagers and young adults during the first half of the revolutionary era were particularly primed to be molded by the ruins all around them.

As physical ruins proliferated, representations of ruins became an increasingly important part of Atlantic cultures. For some, the response was to imagine the possibilities of reconstructing the world exactly as it had been before. In an elegant illustrated map of Le Cap created in 1800, intended as an aid to reconstructing the city, C. H. Vincent used color coding to show which buildings had been rebuilt. Much of the map is in light red—the color that indicated the buildings that had been burned and then reconstructed. Buildings that did not burn are shown in dark red.[17] If you look at the map and blur your eyes, the outlines of the fire become apparent: the center of the city was almost completely destroyed, and only the north of the city and a patch hugging the water on the southern end had been spared by the flames.

There is something curious about the image, something a bit jarring in the juxtaposition of the neat grid of the city with the colorful depiction of massive destruction. Seen from the street level, the reconstruction of Le Cap would be messy and visceral: half-ruined buildings, blackened by fire and eroded by the tropical sun and rain, stood alongside new constructions being built by manual laborers. The streetscape was transformed by the work,

Map showing the effects of the 1793 fire that destroyed Cap Français. Courtesy of the Bibliothèque Nationale de France.

with familiar facades replaced by new and updated buildings.[18] The map from above, with its deity's-eye view, imagined the city as unchanging. There had been destruction, to be sure, but the map imagined a kind of infilling of the gaps created by the fire, as though the familiar physical structures of the city—and the urban life that went with it—were being put back together exactly as before.

The map of Le Cap imagines a city in which, in spite of the destruction that swept through it, nothing has changed. In the map, this faithful and exact reconstruction is physical. But it was without a doubt part of a broader project, shared by many in metropolitan France and in the colony itself, that imagined that it was possible to faithfully re-create the racial-caste-based society and economy that had existed before the city's destruction. This vision saw ruins not as a warning or an opportunity to reconfigure society but as a challenge to rebuild the city in exactly the way that it had existed before.

But most of those who meditated on destruction during these years did not imagine that the world would be reconstructed along exactly the same lines. They envisioned a transformation as new growth came out of the ruins of the old.

*The Ruins, or, Meditation on the Revolutions of Empires*, published in 1791 by a former deputy to the French National Assembly, imagined such an umbilical connection between the ruins of the past and the world being made anew. The first edition opens with a frontispiece showing a solitary man in Near Eastern garb, sitting in a contemplative pose beneath a vibrantly arborescent palm tree. The debris of an antique structure surrounds him, and before him is a valley filled with magnificently ruined buildings. These, the reader discovers in chapter two, are the remains of the ancient desert oasis of Palmyra, in present-day Syria.[19] As the narrator looks out over the ruins, he drifts into a reverie and communes with a spirit who instructs him on the history and future of the human race. Like the frontispiece, with its juxtaposition of the robust and living palm with the broken, dead stones of the ancient city, *The Ruins* imagines a new world emerging from the remains of the old.

The painters and draftsmen of the early nineteenth century were fond of such images of new life pushing out of destruction. They dwelled on moments of half-light, solitary figures, and the haunted and ruined landscapes through which they traveled. Most often, these images were set in the countryside, not in the city. In *After the Storm* (1817), Caspar David Friedrich, a northern German

Frontispiece of C. F. Volney, *Les Ruines*. Courtesy of the Bibliothèque Nationale de France.

and strong opponent of the Napoleonic regime, painted a deceptively simple picture of a small boat wrecked just off the shoreline. The painting is all sea and sky. But the knife's point of the mast sticks out at an uneasy angle, piercing the moody atmosphere. This is an image of the power of the sea and of the brokenness of the human endeavor. It is also an image of an irremediable failure: one cannot imagine reconstructing the ship just as it was. This is not the God's-eye view but the much more troubled picture from the ground level, where we can see precisely the damage that has been done.[20]

Another picture by Friedrich, *Graves of Ancient Heroes* (1812), imagines mountain ruins as the scene of a political rebirth. Rocky crags form a cleft that enfolds a shining, gold-white monument to Arminius, a Roman Germanic general who died around the year 21 CE. The tomb is surrounded by many others in various states of decay. At first glance, the image appears to be a pastoral elegy for a lost nation. Then the viewer's eye settles on two small figures: dressed in the helmets and cloaks of contemporary German soldiers, they stand in contemplation near Arminius's grave. The men's presence transforms the picture's story from a scene of mourning to a depiction of new growth—an assertion, one might say, that a new German nation was about to come into being.[21]

THERE WERE NO MOODY PICTURES OF RUINS ON THE LAVISHLY decorated walls of the Santa Catalina chapter house. When the nuns went down to the vaulted hall to choose their new prioresses in the 1790s, they still sat surrounded by the idyllic scenes of aristocratic life that had been frescoed there in earlier decades. But even in this convent high in the mountains, located on the far side of the Americas, that idealized world was slipping away. The waves of destruction and creation spreading across the Atlantic rippled there too.

As Madre Maria declined, others pushed their way upward. Madre Trancito, who had been thwarted by her wealthier rival throughout the previous decade, found her position growing stronger. In 1792, her ally Madre Cecilia de San Sebastian was again chosen as prioress. A few years later, Madre Cecilia finally succeeded in wresting the administration of the convent's finances out of Madre Maria's long-holding grasp. After a few more years had passed, Madre Trancito would return to the priorate herself.[22]

Others used the status ladder that the convent provided to rise from much more humble beginnings. The convents were no stranger to economic mobility. Part of their purpose had long been to provide a refuge for women without sufficient prospects in the secular world. But the convents in Cuzco, at least, had functioned during the previous two centuries as a mirror rather than a ladder, reinforcing the social order instead of providing ways to challenge it.[23]

Doña Manuela Gonsales's story suggests that this was beginning to change as the eighteenth century wound to a close. In the spring of 1791, Doña Josefa Sotomayor, a lay woman, made a complaint to the ecclesiastical authorities requesting that they stop the sale of a cell in Santa Catalina. According to her, the property had been one of two purchased by her uncle, Joseph Sotomayor, as a life estate for his two daughters, Gabriela and Micaela. The doña thought the property was supposed to revert to the family's descendants after the daughters' deaths. When Madre Gabriela died, however, she had willed her cell to "her servant Manuela" out of her "love" for her. Doña Josefa asked that the sale be stopped on the grounds that the cell was not Madre Gabriela's to bequeath.[24]

Manuela replied promptly, and successfully, to the attempt to claim her property. Styling herself "D.na Manuela Gonsales"—presenting herself as a lady—she offered a counternarrative backed by evidence. It was true that she was a "poor woman," she declared, but the cell was rightly hers. It had not been purchased by Don

Joseph; Madre Gabriela had acquired it "with her own money." Doña Manuela even had a document from the early 1770s, a contract between Madre Juana de los Remedios and Madre Gabriela, that backed up her claim that the cell was Madre Gabriela's own property. Doña Manuela went on to explain how she had become the beneficiary of the will. The nun had chosen to give the cell to her because of the "services and personal labor" that she had performed. The cell was, she asserted, her rightful reward for years of loyal and loving care.[25]

The victory that Doña Manuela won in 1791 was literally small: the right to a little corner of a convent she could call her own. But this triumph was emblematic of a much larger process already beginning to transform the empires of the Atlantic world, which moved at an accelerating pace over the coming two decades. The first generation of revolutionaries had struggled mightily to create sustained political movements. The coalitions they built, against the grain of class and racial prejudice, were fractious and fragile. The states some of them managed to create were unstable. But though revolutionaries were not yet triumphant, they had managed to irretrievably fracture the old regime. Out of the disarray, new people and new kinds of politics were beginning to emerge.

# 11
# THE LIMITS OF REPUBLICANISM

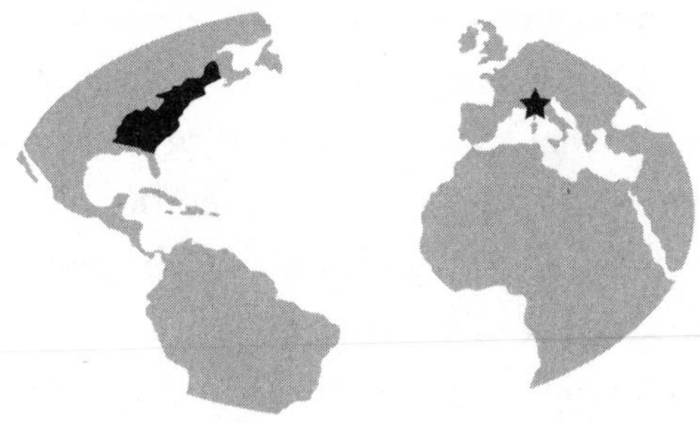

THE SHOCK WAVES OF THE REVOLUTIONARY ERA'S SHATTERING of old regimes buffeted two republics especially hard during the mid-1790s. The United States and Genoa arrived at this common fate by very different routes. The United States was a relatively new, federal state, built in good measure on slavery, with an expansive territory. The Republic of Genoa could trace its history back to the Middle Ages. Occupying a tiny sliver of the Mediterranean coast, it had built its wealth on trade. Yet there were significant similarities between the two republics when the last decade of the eighteenth century rolled around. In both, the political power of the wealthy had become entrenched over the course of the previous century. Republican politics in both countries responded readily to the powerful example of the French Republic. Above all, the instability created by the revolutionary wars generated fears about national unity and independence.

In both the United States and Genoa, revolutionaries responded to the crises they encountered during the mid-1790s by consciously trying to organize political movements that straddled the great eighteenth-century social divide. They were not the first to do so, but patriots in both republics showed a growing awareness of the vital need to shore up their political power by building movements across class lines. Revolutionary leaders tried in a limited way to open up previously exclusive forms of political sociability to non-elite patriots while embarking on self-conscious educational projects to impart what they regarded as proper political practices to the wider populace. The younger generation of revolutionaries, which was just then beginning to come of age, played an important part in this process. Like any generational transition, it was not a sharp handoff. During the 1790s, on both sides of the Atlantic, the two revolutionary cohorts shared the political stage.

As had happened in France during the early 1790s, however, the deep sedimentation of social distinction made most mass-movement building during the 1790s a mirage that seemed to always slip just out of reach. In the United States, the decade brought both a new federal government and intense divisions over the direction that it should give to the new republic. A network of clubs, calling themselves Democratic-Republican Societies, became one of the most important foci for political organizing. The clubs' ambivalent attitude toward social mixing limited their immediate effectiveness, but they became a catalyst for the emergence, at the end of the decade, of the Republican Party, the United States' first mass political party. In Genoa, elite revolutionaries came to power in 1797 prepared for the need to spread their political gospel and instruct the lower orders in the proper revolutionary practices. But the task proved to be even more difficult than they had anticipated.

Over three years in power, the Genoese leaders never succeeded in establishing a stable republican government. Their inability to bridge the social divide was a main cause of this failure.

ONCE THE US CONSTITUTION WAS RATIFIED IN 1788, THE CONfederation Congress provided for elections to the new federal government and disbanded itself. The president was chosen by groups of electors who met independently in their own state capitols on February 4, 1789. To nobody's surprise, George Washington was unanimously chosen as president. Washington was the obvious choice because of his military service during the revolutionary war and his stature as an elder statesman who seemed to stand outside of political conflicts. Elections for members of the first Congress under the Constitution took place about the same time, during the early months of 1789. The vast majority of those elected to both the US House and Senate were strong Federalists—that is, supporters of the Constitution and its aim of strengthening national authority.[1]

The Federalists wasted little time in seeking to establish the authority of the new national government and use it as an instrument of national unity and strength. The driving force behind this program was one of the leading New York Federalists, Alexander Hamilton. Hamilton was one of those rare men who had managed to achieve genuine status mobility in the mid-eighteenth century. Reared in very modest circumstances on the Caribbean island of Saint Croix, he had come to New York City under the sponsorship of a well-placed merchant in 1772. In less than ten years, he had acquired a fine education, served as Washington's aide-de-camp in the revolutionary war, and married into one of New York's wealthiest families. In September 1789, Washington appointed Hamilton as secretary of the Treasury, a position he would hold for more than five critical years.[2]

As secretary of the Treasury, Hamilton advanced a powerful, divisive vision of strengthening the country through commercial and industrial development. It was a program that was unabashedly tilted toward the wealthy and powerful. Hamilton began to articulate his program almost as soon as he took office. In January 1790, he presented a report to Congress that proposed a British-style national debt, which would be created by having the federal government assume the states' revolutionary war debts. To service the debt, the federal government would raise revenue through tariffs and the post office and create a national bank to manage the whole. This set of fiscal proposals flowed together with another set of ideas for strengthening the nation's industrial base, which he detailed in a report on manufacturing two years later. The *Report on Manufactures* proposed protective tariffs and federal subsidies for certain manufactured goods, in the hopes of encouraging the growth of domestic industry. At bottom, these proposals were intended—as many of the Constitution's framers had hoped—to turn the federal government into an engine of national growth and unification. Although Washington tried to remain above the fray, he tacitly (and sometimes explicitly) endorsed the secretary's plans.[3]

The Hamiltonian program elicited strong and growing opposition from a number of quarters. Though there was some overlap between these opponents and the anti-Federalists of 1787–1788, the resistance to Hamilton included many of his onetime Federalist allies. They early on began calling themselves "Republicans." Small-scale white farmers, especially in the western counties of the states, made up one of the largest constituencies in this movement. Farmers believed, probably with reason, that the Treasury secretary's economic program, tilted toward encouraging manufacturing, would harm them. Some, though not all, urban artisans shared this view. The most vocal and certainly most powerful part of the opposition, however, was composed of southern planters and their allies. Thomas Jefferson and James Madison, the latter of whom had been a leading proponent of the Constitution, became two of the main leaders of the Republican opposition. They framed their resistance to Hamilton in terms of high principles of local control and an idealized economy of yeoman producers. But as men whose wealth depended on agricultural production by enslaved people, they stood to lose ground if the republic became more commercial and industrial.[4]

By 1792, the conflict about American domestic policy had begun to map onto Americans' divergent views about the French Revolution and the stance that the United States should take toward it. The French Revolution had a powerful effect on the United States. A web of cultural ties had bound French and North American intellectual and political leaders since France's crucial intervention in the American revolutionary war. Waves of diplomats, merchants, and refugees from France and its colonies flooded into US ports after 1791, making the ties between the two nations concrete.

Federalists, on the whole, were skeptical of the French Revolution, especially after the proclamation of the republic in the fall of 1792. The Terror further polarized their reactions, leading to a more explicitly pro-British stance. The nascent Republican opposition, on the other hand, took on the whole a pro-French position. This Federalist-Republican divide was somewhat peculiar, given that the leadership of the French Republic had a highly centralizing program that was on paper more congenial to the Federalist vision than that of the Republicans. Some Republicans did also nuance their support for France in response to the Terror and its aftermath. But competing views of the French Revolution remained a durable dividing line in American politics until the last years of the century. Views of foreign relations, though not primarily responsible for the emerging division in US politics, gave it some of its hard edge.

RESISTANCE TO THE HAMILTONIAN FEDERALIST PROGRAM SPREAD and grew during the first four years of the 1790s, but it was a struggle to find formal or collective channels through which it could flow. The Republicans lacked control over the levers of power in the national government through about 1795. Some state governments fell under Republican control during the first years of the 1790s. But they were, on the whole, fairly parochial in their outlook and were inhibited by a reflexive resistance to formal party organization. Much of the energy of the opposition to the Federalists was thus channeled into a new institution: the Democratic-Republican Societies that sprouted up in large numbers across the United States starting in 1793.

The Democratic-Republican clubs emerged in 1793, seemingly in imitation of the Jacobin Clubs. But they had local precedents. North America in the 1780s had been lousy with voluntary associations and mutual benefit societies. Some of the most robust associational life had had a strong political slant, with conventions and self-appointed bodies organized by groups seeking to reform state constitutions and the Articles of Confederation. The Annapolis Convention of 1786, the meeting at which representatives of five states had met and called for the 1787 meeting that became the Constitutional Convention, was very much a body in this mold.[5]

The Democratic-Republican Societies' antecedents were decidedly genteel. One public defender of the clubs in early 1795 offered up a list of the associations that were similar to the societies. They were, he wrote, "religious, political, medical, philosophical, mechanical, masonic." The list is hardly exhaustive, but it offers some sense of which clubs the participants in the societies considered part of the same family. Two of the types of clubs mentioned, medical and philosophical, were obviously genteel. One, the "mechanical," referring to artisans (or mechanics), was clearly working-class. The remaining three—religious, political, and Masonic—could be either. Yet the likelihood is that at least two of these were genteel: political clubs in North America until this time had been largely made up of the well-off, and many Masonic lodges were heavily tilted toward elites.[6]

The Democratic-Republicans wholeheartedly adopted the mechanics of these earlier genteel associations for themselves. The prominent Democratic Society of Pennsylvania, based in Philadelphia, adopted a formal constitution in 1793, which it shared far and wide and offered as a model for other societies. By the spring of 1794, after about a year of existence, the society had developed a set of governance procedures, including a system for producing "Certificates of membership" to allow members to participate fully in meetings, and procedures for expelling members who violated its rules. The Democratic Society of New York produced an even more elaborate constitution in 1794, complete with a preamble, divided into seven "Chapters" and numerous "Articles." Even the tiny society in Colchester, Vermont, produced detailed "Regulations for our Government" that included procedures for calling meetings, admitting members, and deliberating on issues. They specified, among other things, that any resolution concerning "the public at large" had to be submitted "in writing" for consideration.[7]

Yet if the clubs took on the appearance of genteel societies, their membership was somewhat more varied. The leadership of the urban societies, it is true, was drawn almost exclusively from the wealthiest and the professional classes. But the societies "united men from diverse economic and occupational backgrounds," including a large share of individuals from the "bottom of the tax pyramid." Indeed, "workmen and mechanics" formed the core of the membership of the new societies. The membership, however, was not indiscriminately admitted. The societies understood themselves as being exclusive rather than inclusive organizations. The New York Democratic Society may have put it best in a public address published in early 1795. The societies, they wrote, "have always claimed the valuable privilege of CHUSING

THEIR COMPANY."[8] In this sense, they took on the coloration of the mid-eighteenth-century models.

Generationally, too, the clubs had a mixed composition. As was the case with many voluntary associations, the membership skewed toward those of middle age, who were relatively established in life and business. These men, averaging around forty, were the children of the revolutionary era; born in the 1750s and 1760s, they came of age during the American Revolution and its aftermath. But the leadership of the clubs was decidedly older. The Democratic Society of Pennsylvania was run by a group of men who were some twenty years older—products of the mid-eighteenth century. They were members of the first revolutionary generation, whose worldviews had been shaped in the unequal and relatively static prerevolutionary world.[9]

The societies took measures to maintain and assert the gentlemanly character of their membership. The Political Society of Mount Prospect, in its constitution, barred from membership any "person of an immoral character" or who had "not punctually obeyed the good laws of this country." The society in Lancaster, Pennsylvania, declared that it "shall be composed of independent citizens." Many of the societies included membership provisions designed to ensure not only political conformity but a certain respectability among their members: the New York Democratic Society required that a candidate for membership provide "positive testimonials of his patriotism and Republican principles" from "five members." One defender of the clubs in Congress, Virginian William Giles, observed that the clubs were similar to those that "the venerable Franklin had been at the head of."[10]

The respectability of the club membership was both manifested by and embodied by its whiteness and maleness. That the clubs had an all-male membership seems to have been a foregone conclusion. Though these criteria were never explicitly stated in their charters, the clubs and their members spoke the language of white, male exclusivity. During one of the interminable newspaper polemics that swirled around the New York society, one of the club's defenders proudly declared that "we eagerly court, the most minute, the most strict investigation into our real characters, either as men or politicians." They intended, he went on, that every member of the society should be "a man of good moral principles, and strict honor." The web of meanings around "honor" in the early republic marked this as an exclusively male space. Similarly, though there was no explicit ban on non-white people joining societies, free Black men seem to have been systematically excluded.[11]

The political views that the societies expressed, in spite of their socially mixed membership, were boldly radical, on the cutting edge of eighteenth-century republican thought. The societies positioned themselves as fierce defenders of freedom of speech. Many of their public statements denounced the "rich," called for "equality," and cast fierce aspersions on any tendency toward "aristocratical or monarchical government." The core of the societies' discourse was hostility to any form of hereditary or undemocratic authority: they were particularly opposed to the alliance that they thought was emerging between conservative politicians and the wealthy to blunt or confine popular democracy. Perhaps even more remarkable was that some of the societies' members publicly took anticlerical or atheistic positions. This fit with the positions of the most advanced French revolutionaries and was in accord with the idea that clerics and religion in general often supported other forms of hereditary authority. But such religiously skeptical positions were regarded as extreme by most others, including even some of the era's dyed-in-the-wool republicans.[12]

Yet for all the radical notions they espoused, the societies' ways of expressing them had a distinctly elite cast. The Democratic Society of Pennsylvania began its first communiqué to the public with language taken from the canon of polite sociability: "We have the pleasure to communicate to you," they wrote, "a copy of the constitution of the Democratic Society." They concluded with the cordial wish that the readers would give an "early attention to the subject." The New York Democratic Society issued a circular in 1794 larded with Latin terms, learned discussions of feudalism, and high-flown metaphors. ("The plot of our political drama is by no means original, but has been copied with some degree of servility from the European stage.") As a rhetorical construction, it was tangibly the product of well-educated gentlemen and clearly aimed at a similar audience.[13]

The patriotic celebrations that the societies organized and hosted were also a mixture of working-class modes with more genteel ones. The societies aimed to create a public, "celebratory" political culture. They particularly favored July 4 as a date for their celebrations, as it allowed them to claim the mantle of American patriotism while they advanced their distinctive political views. They organized probably hundreds of Fourth of July celebrations, which typically took the form of open-air meetings or banquets. Yet even these apparently democratic, public activities were in reality inflected by the groups' genteel character. The banquets were necessarily limited in their social reach. Many of them required a ticket, which cost money that the poor could ill afford. And the publicity given to the toasts and speeches was hardly natural or organic. Toasts at these events were recorded and published in the newspapers. Many of them likely ended up there not because they were so newsworthy but because members of the societies had access to newspaper editors and convinced them to include them in the papers.[14]

So the Democratic-Republican clubs had a kind of double consciousness. They were, on the one hand, formed out of groups of men who shared a common political consciousness and agenda. The groups were largely Francophilic, opposed to the more conservative impulses of the Federalist-dominated national government, and concerned above all with the dissemination and circulation of political information. This ideological orientation brought together fairly diverse groups of white American men, uniting mechanics with the wealthiest members of the urban communities. Yet the societies themselves were still modeled on the consensual and self-contained midcentury club.

The societies tried their level best to stretch themselves to accommodate both the mid-eighteenth-century generation and the revolutionary war generation, the old and the new dispositions. The leaders of the societies recognized that both pieces of the puzzle were important to them. Their connection to the "old Whigs" of the American Revolution gave them credibility and authority. Yet it was their mustering of a rising commercial, artisanal class that gave them numbers and energy. So the societies spoke the language of radical change—they imagined a world in motion, a world that could be entirely renewed—and tried to encompass all of the main politically active groups in a single association.

For all of these bold ideological claims, the societies remained quite limited in their ability to organize beyond the familiar confines of the lettered elite. They failed to challenge the racial order; they remained tied to a highly genteel, even learned mode of communication; and they were tightly bound to a politics of respectability. Neither generational impulse, within the frame of the clubs, could predominate.

THE SOCIETIES HAD A HARD TIME STRADDLING THE SOCIAL DIVIDE in the movement they were trying to create. One of the first and steepest challenges they encountered came with an uprising in western Pennsylvania during the summer of 1794. The rebellion, which had roots in long-standing local grievances, was sparked by efforts to enforce a 1791 federal excise tax law, which included a levy on the manufacture of whiskey. Communities in western Pennsylvania rose up against the tax, forcibly resisting the federal officers who were trying to levy the duties and punishing local distillers who were inclined to cooperate. In July, US marshal David Lenox got into a firefight with protesters, leading to a massive mustering of militiamen near Pittsburgh on August 1.[15]

On its face, the whiskey "rebellion" or "insurrection"—what name one gave it depended on one's view of it—seemed to fit perfectly with the political positions of the Democratic-Republican Societies. Most of the rebels belonged to the lower orders, for whom they claimed to be speaking, and the targets of their anger, including Lenox and President George Washington, were wealthy and respectable. The uprising was also billed by the rebels themselves as resistance to an overbearing and officious government. Even commercial distillers, in their view, represented an arm of the large "interests" who oppressed the ordinary citizen.[16]

In spite of the obvious connections between their political agendas, however, the societies expressed considerable reservations about the Whiskey Rebellion from the moment it became a matter of public debate. Indeed, the most prominent of the local societies in western Pennsylvania opposed the mobilization. The elite-dominated Democratic Society of Washington, the counterpart to the Philadelphia society in the western reaches of the state, pronounced itself opposed to the excise tax. But the Washington society explicitly and repeatedly denounced the use of violent measures to oppose it. Two smaller and more "popular" societies, hastily organized in the same region, took responsibility for recruiting locals to take up arms against the excise tax.[17]

Once the rebellion had become an armed insurrection, Democratic-Republican Societies fell over themselves to express their disapproval. The Democratic Society of Pennsylvania, in Philadelphia, denounced the rebellion repeatedly. In July, a meeting declared that they "highly disapprove" of any extralegal "opposition" to even unjust legislation. Slightly over a month later, after consuming internal debates, the club dispatched a letter to the club in the Washington district (in the western part of the state, where the rebellion was unfolding). The Philadelphia clubmen denounced the federal excise tax that had led to the revolt. But they stood firm in their commitment to finding a "constitutional remedy to the evil." They affirmed, furthermore, that "the genuine principles of Democracy" were "perfectly compatible with the principles of social order." The Republican Society of Newark declared itself in similar terms a bit later in the month: the members denounced the rebels for having substituted "indecent menaces in place of temperate and manly remonstrance." The New York society, likewise, declared in blunt terms that they "disapprove the conduct of their fellow citizens of the western part of Pennsylvania." They should not resist a "constitutional law," however unwise, "with arms and violence."[18]

Shorn of wider political support, the armed rebellion did not last for long. In August, under advice from members of his cabinet, President Washington put in motion a two-pronged plan to end the rebellion. In a peaceable vein, he sent a group of federal commissioners out on a fact-finding mission to western Pennsylvania, with instructions to investigate and report on the situation. They were also authorized to offer amnesty to the rebels. Simultaneously, he took steps to muster the militia in eastern Pennsylvania under federal command, ready to deploy if the rebellion needed to be suppressed by force. Though most of the rebels accepted the proffered amnesty and swore oaths of loyalty, Washington concluded that a show of force was still necessary. In the last days of September, he rode out at the head of a militia. There was no organized resistance, and only a handful of men were arrested. The rebellion had simply melted away.[19]

Even though the armed rebellion had ended peacefully, the Democratic-Republican Societies could not so readily escape from its shadow. Less than two months later, the entire movement found itself under attack from Washington himself, called upon to prove their respectability and, by implication, their political legitimacy. In his 1794 annual address to Congress, in November, President Washington spoke of the recent uprising in western Pennsylvania and lay blame for the rebellion at the feet of what he called "self-created societies." Though he did not name them explicitly, it was clear to everyone that he was referring to the Democratic-Republican Societies. Washington accused the societies of having encouraged unlawful behavior by issuing "threats" against federal officers.[20]

In tarring the societies with the brush of illegality, Washington was echoing a wider Federalist critique of clubs and associations, which invoked the specter of the French Revolution. Congressmen and newspaper articles were not terribly discriminating in their accounts of club life in France. They frequently conflated the Jacobin Clubs, which grew out of a network created by representatives to the National Assembly, and the sectional clubs of Paris, which were more populist in orientation. They also failed to distinguish between the quite distinct roles of both sets of clubs before and after the abolition of the French monarchy in 1792. They merged them together into a single effigy of the dangerous "self-created societies" that had sowed political disorder in France—and threatened to do the same in the United States.[21]

Washington's remark ignited a furious conflagration of charges and countercharges. Federalist-leaning newspapers quickly picked up the baton, critiquing the Democratic-Republicans as a danger to the republic. A number of the societies met, several in a hurry, and issued blistering responses defending their right to assemble and speak. (And, just as importantly, asserting their patriotism.) The most extended, even exhaustive discussion of Washington's address took place in the House of Representatives. From Monday to Friday of the last week in November 1794, the closely divided House devoted itself almost entirely to drafting a response to

Washington's message. How to reply to the "self-created societies" charge became a central issue in this debate.[22]

It soon become clear, as the debate continued, that what really upset Washington and other Federalists was the social hybridity that the members of the Democratic-Republican Societies wore as a badge of honor. Indeed, Washington could hardly have been denouncing club life in general, as he seemed to be doing with his attack on "self-created societies." Associational life, as Alexis de Tocqueville would famously observe a few decades later, was lodged deep in the marrow of the American republic. Washington himself had been involved in the creation of the most celebrated of these associations—the Society of the Cincinnati, a fraternal network of revolutionary war veterans—in 1783. As one congressman had noted early on in the debate over the House's response, "There was not an individual in America, who might not come under the charge of being a member of some one or other self-created society."[23]

Federalist commentators stressed the Democratic-Republican Societies' social breadth as a key element that made them objectionable. Referring to one of the clubs, Massachusetts Federalist Theodore Sedgwick speculated that "perhaps the individuals who composed this society were . . . too despicable to deserve any notice in this place." Another Federalist, who represented the part of western Pennsylvania where the Whiskey Rebellion had broken out, vigorously denounced the members of the local societies as "deluded people," "objects of real pity," who were "grossly ignorant." Another one, who authored a facetious account of a meeting he claimed to have attended, reported that the minutes of the last meeting were "read or rather spelt." Federalist William L. Smith of South Carolina offered a more glancing denunciation. The societies, he fantasized, were secret "nocturnal meetings" that the members held "after they have dined." Smith clearly saw something louche in the idea of a nighttime meeting. But as a New York newspaper polemicist noted in 1795, the societies held their meetings in the evenings because their "private employments . . . prevent them from assembling in the day."[24] "Nocturnal meetings" were not so much a sign of a conspiratorial bent as of the members' occupational profile.

In short, the core of the Federalist critique of the Democratic-Republican Societies boiled down to an elaborate version of "self-created societies" for me but not for thee. Their objection to these clubs was not that they were doing anything different from what other American societies had been doing. It was that the Democratic-Republican Societies, which they imagined as filled with members of the working classes, lacked the requisite social standing to engage in such political activity. The societies, having already tried to distance themselves from their dangerous association with the whiskey rebels, felt the need to further shore up their respectability in response to Washington's charge. The societies' public statements took on a defensive cast, pushing back against the notion that their members' class position made them any less entitled to meet and deliberate on the great matters of the day. As the members of one society wrote in December, "We have as great a right to speak, write, and print our opinions of men and measure as Washington and those great speculators in the funds whom he seems to patronize." They also redoubled their denunciations of extralegal behavior. In a long address published in the newspapers in early 1795, several months after the rebellion had ended, the New York Democratic Society reiterated that its members had already "condemned all unconstitutional opposition to the law of our country."[25]

Most of the Democratic-Republican Societies gradually stopped meeting over the course of 1795. Seen in isolation, their disappearance from the political scene suggests that they had been defeated by the Federalist onslaught. In fact, their energy was beginning to turn into other channels. The most important of these was the Republican political party, which drew on wells of support among southern planters, rural white men, and urban artisans. When the Republican Party emerged as an institution during the last years of the eighteenth century, it became the long-awaited vehicle for a sustained cross-class political movement in the United States.

THE FRENCH GOVERNMENT WAS KEPT WELL INFORMED BY DIPLOMATS in Philadelphia about the rise and fall of the whiskey rebels. Yet looking outward from Paris in 1795 and 1796, the leaders of the French Republic did not find much in the affair to worry or even interest them. Their attention was focused on matters much closer to home: the delicate political situation in France and an ever-expanding European war.[26]

The French government had changed a great deal since the fall of the Jacobin-dominated Committee of Public Safety in the summer of 1794. After Robespierre and his allies were toppled with the support of the Paris sections, the National Convention dismantled the institutional apparatus of the Terror. For the next fourteen months, the Convention governed France through its committees. The political situation in Paris and in France as a whole during this year, summer 1794 to summer 1795, was even more unsettled than usual. The Jacobin Clubs were closed down. Twice, the sections of Paris rallied against the high cost of foodstuffs, with crowds again entering the National Convention to demand immediate satisfaction. Unlike the situation in 1789, however, both occupations were put down promptly by the forces of order. In the provinces, a low-grade civil war broke out as conservatives and victims of the Terror took the opportunity to strike back against those whom they perceived as Jacobins or "terrorists."[27]

During the summer of 1795, a committee of the National Convention drafted a new constitution in an effort to establish a more stable republican government. This document, known as the Constitution of Year III (by the revolutionary reckoning), provided for a bicameral legislature and a five-person executive, the Directory. One of the Constitution's main features was that it limited the franchise, at least by comparison with the Jacobin republic. In general, only taxpayers were eligible to vote; to participate in the electoral assemblies that actually chose officials, one had to own substantial property, equivalent to at least one hundred days' local wages. The Constitution was approved by the National Convention in August and ratified by a national referendum in September. This republican government came to be called by the name of its executive body: the Directory.[28]

As a political regime designed for stability, the Directory left a great deal to be desired. Notwithstanding the referendum that had approved the new Constitution, the Directory lacked broad popular support. This was as evident in lukewarm participation in elections as it was in rumors of discontent that reached the ears of police spies. Lacking a strong political base, the Directory sought stability by balancing and playing off the nation's opposing political forces. It at first conciliated the Left in the latter part of 1795 and early 1796, then tacked rapidly in the opposite direction, having concluded that the former Jacobins were growing too powerful. In 1797, the Directory both put a group of Jacobins accused of sedition on trial for their lives and staged an armed coup that purged newly elected right-wing deputies from the councils. The balancing act continued in 1798: the Directory tightly controlled that year's elections, but when too many deputies with Jacobin sympathies were nonetheless elected, they staged a second coup or purge, nullifying many of the choices.[29]

One of the areas in which the Directory did prove itself effective was in expanding and wielding the republican war machine that had first been created by the Jacobins in 1793 and 1794. In the summer of 1793, the Committee of Public Safety had been facing down destruction by the combined armed forces of most of Europe's military powers. On August 23, it issued an unprecedented order to enlist three hundred thousand men in the army. Guided by Lazare Carnot, one of its members, the committee formed new armies that succeeded in stopping the enemy advance. Over the next two years, the republic's armies gradually pushed the front outward from France's borders. After the Jacobins fell in Thermidor 1794, the army continued to grow and advance. The Directory, unlike the Jacobins and the Committee of Public Safety, saw multiple advantages to be gained from this expansionist foreign policy. Foreign conquests provided sources of funds for the money-starved French state. Military victories helped morale and buoyed the Directory's popularity. And by installing republican governments in the conquered territories, the Directory could cushion its frontiers and better protect itself from the monarchies that threatened it.[30]

Fueled by the Directory's political interests, the French armies waged a war of expansion in Europe. Between 1795 and 1797, French armies conquered modern-day Belgium, the Rhineland, northern Italy, Switzerland, and the Netherlands. Belgium and portions of the Rhineland and northern Italy were incorporated directly into France as *départements*. In the other regions, the Directory, its agents, and its generals—with the active assistance of local revolutionaries—installed republican governments allied to France. (They also tried, unsuccessfully, to aid a revolt in Ireland.) These new republics had names with a classical ring: the Batavian Republic in the Netherlands, the Helvetic Republic in Switzerland, the Cisalpine and Ligurian Republics in northern Italy, and (a bit later) the Roman and Neapolitan Republics in central Italy. Arrayed in an arc around France, they were like so many moons circling the center in Paris. All of the "sister republics" had governments that were modeled on the Directory and all were client states, dependent on France for military protection and strongly influenced by the French government's political line.[31]

The Republic of Genoa, which became the Ligurian Republic in 1797, had for centuries clung to a strip of the rocky Mediterranean shores of northwestern Italy. Speaking a language that lay phonetically and linguistically between French and Italian, the Genoese had long straddled worlds. For much of the early modern period, the republic had been a major maritime power, often allied with the French monarchy. But by the eighteenth century, like its Venetian cousin to the east, it had devolved into a stagnant state ruled by a self-perpetuating oligarchy. Though ostensibly governed by an elected council and a doge (chief magistrate), in practice a handful of powerful families occupied all of the positions of authority. The economy, having lost its medieval and early modern dynamism, was sluggish and weighed down by taxes and feudal dues. A brief popular rebellion in 1746, led by artisans who organized an "Assembly of the People," had come to an end in a matter of months, with the oligarchical government retaining almost all of its power.[32]

The stagnant situation of the republic spurred calls for reform. Genoese reformers, like their counterparts elsewhere in northern Italy, came overwhelmingly from the ranks of the well-to-do. Their proposals were initially very modest: fiscal reforms to make the economy work better, reforms in governance to make the authorities more responsive and effective, and changes to the punitive and archaic legal code. Pressure for change intensified in the 1790s as the French Revolution's ideas, literature, and people flooded the Republic of Genoa. As was the case elsewhere in northern Italy, local reformers organized themselves into clubs like those of the French Jacobins. The Ligurian/Genovese reformers sought both political and social change. They wanted to return the republic to its presumed democratic roots. At the same time, they hoped to reorganize the ossified social and economic structures of the city. A "violent[ly]" worded 1794 letter from Luca Gentile, a reformist member of the governing oligarchy, demanded democratic reforms. Yet during the first half of the 1790s, the oligarchs resisted all proposals for constitutional change from within.[33]

The reformers finally got their chance in 1797 thanks to the French army. Since the start of the revolutionary wars, the Republic of Genoa had maintained a studied neutrality, trying to avoid being drawn into a war between much larger powers. For a time, this served both sides; the French and the Austrians and their allies both violated Genoese territory as they struggled for supremacy in northern Italy, but neither side found it in their interest to threaten Genoa's independence. A series of brilliant military victories against the Austrians and their Piedmontese allies by Napoleon in the spring of 1796 changed the calculus. Having become effective masters of northern Italy, Napoleon and the Directory saw no further advantage in allowing Genoa to continue its balancing act. They put increasingly heavy pressure on the republic to choose sides. On June 2, 1797, the Senate agreed to effectively put the republic under the tutelage of France. A new state was proclaimed shortly thereafter, the Ligurian Republic.[34]

The reformers, thwarted for years, were now suddenly thrust into power. They formed a provisional government, headed by an extraordinary commission with executive powers, and began the process of overhauling the republic. The reformers—or democrats, as they now called themselves—began to lay out their program publicly in a newspaper, the *Gazzetta Nazionale Genovese*, which began publication on June 17, 1797. The plan, as they set it down on paper, drew from the more radical canons of the French Jacobin republic. "WE ARE ALL EQUAL," the paper screamed. Titles and "blood" were now rendered irrelevant. "THE PEOPLE ALONE ARE SOVEREIGN." The democrats concluded with the resounding assertion that "WE ARE ALL FREE."[35] Their vision was of a democratic republic of equal citizens, all of whom would have an equal role to play in the renewed state's politics.

The Genoese democrats of 1797 were well aware that their political utopia, if they were to create it, had to earn the support of the wider public. To this purpose, the democrats articulated a social agenda from the earliest days of the new republic. In July, in its third issue, the *Gazzetta* led with an anonymous address to the legislative commission. The author's central argument was a denunciation of the "inequality of fortunes." An aristocracy of wealth, he argued, "will one day become . . . [a] political aristocracy." To forestall this possibility—this return to the bad old days of the oligarchical republic—he called on the legislators to be "severe" with the "rich." Part of this vision was also an attack on "superstition." Though the democrats paid lip service to the idea of useful and proper religion, they fiercely denounced the "pantomime of false devotion" that was part of the "artifice of the Oligarchs" to maintain their power.[36]

Problems arose for the democrats' political project almost immediately. The provisional government created a commission that was charged with crafting a new constitution. They envisioned a republic modeled on the one currently in use in France, with a powerful executive (the Directory) and a weak two-house legislature. The constitution writers found themselves "subjected to continual criticism" from all sides as they worked: radicals sought major democratic reforms while conservatives strongly resisted the liberalizations—including freedom of religion—that seemed likely to be included. In August, the commission produced a compromise draft, which satisfied nobody, and presented it to the provisional government. The government scheduled a vote to ratify the Constitution in September.[37]

Before the ratification vote could take place, armed revolts broke out in the city of Genoa and outlying towns. These were encouraged and aided by conservative members of the old oligarchy, as well as priests, but they were genuinely mass movements. There was sporadic fighting in the streets of Genoa. In the towns, the situation was even graver: in the fishing village of Camogli, armed crowds tore up every copy of the Constitution they could find and forced local officials to flee to Genoa for safety. In Camogli, Recco, and Rapallo, columns of rebels prepared themselves to march on Genoa to put down the revolutionary government. Frightened and cornered, the provisional government called for help from the French. Within days, Napoleon had dispatched a detachment of French troops. Most of the rebels melted away rather than face battle-hardened soldiers. The government established a special commission that arrested, tried, and executed a number of leading figures in the revolt.[38]

Rattled by the revolt, the leaders of the provisional government pulled back from their initial hopes of radical political transformation. Urged on by Napoleon—who wanted stability above all—the democratic leaders tried to forge a compromise with the leading conservatives, largely men who had been part of the oligarchical government of the old republic. The ex-oligarchs were only too happy to have a hand again so soon in governance. Over the course of the next two months, the constitution writers made a series of fateful compromises. They agreed to smaller-size assemblies (which favored the wealthy), allowed nobles to retain some of their privileges, and gave the Catholic Church special status. When the first elections were held under the new Constitution, conservatives swept the majority of the seats in both assemblies, further limiting any possibility of radical change.[39]

As the democrats realized by now, the trouble was not merely that conservatives were resisting revolutionary change; that was entirely predictable. It was that the dispositions of the Genoese lower orders also made them quite chary of reform and ready to collaborate with the conservatives. The old republic had depended on, and reproduced, a social order marked by a high degree of hierarchy at every level. The most dramatic differences were between those at the top of the republic and those below:

until the revolution, twenty wealthy and powerful families had exercised almost total control over the finances and government of the republic for more than two centuries. The system excluded both poorer nobles and rich non-nobles from the major roles in the government. In order to exert their control over the populace, the governing families extended a laddered system of power downward. Its crucial rungs were the artisanal corporations that dominated the labor market of the city. These closed guilds, which held monopolies on the production of some of Genoa's key exports, formed a hierarchical structure of masters, journeymen, and apprentices that encompassed much of the population.[40]

The exceedingly hierarchical old regime, paired with the relative stagnation of the Genoese economy in the long eighteenth century, made for conservative dispositions on all sides. The magnates, as the oligarchical leaders of the republic were known, had little to lose by maintaining their highly privileged place atop Genoa's society. But the common people, faced with few opportunities for advancement, clung to their limited privileges as well. Even as free trade and free commerce were sweeping European countries in the last decades of the eighteenth century, Genoese artisans clamored for further restrictions on trade and the continuation and even increase in privileges and monopolies. Rather than seeing these restrictions as limitations on their ability to advance, they saw them as protective measures that would shield them from unwanted competition from abroad.[41]

Significant food shortages during the early revolutionary months compounded the difficulties that the revolutionaries faced in forging new kinds of solidarity. The standard of living for the working people of Genoa had been declining gradually throughout the eighteenth century, as static wages fell further and further behind rising prices of necessities. The revolution, instead of making things better, had made some of the problems much worse.

Price supports had kept down the cost of some foodstuffs; as those were removed, prices soared. Other effects of the end of the fiscal old regime on popular subsistence were more puzzling, though equally disruptive. One of the most pressing issues for the new republic, for instance, was maintaining adequate supplies of salt after the abolition of feudal duties.[42]

But the democrats would not be easily discouraged. They embarked on a program of democratic and republican education directed at both the ordinary people and the gentry. "Every Republic," the author of an article in the *Gazzetta* wrote, "flourishes through laws, and habits." The author advocated a program of "patriotic festivals" as a way to educate the public and change their "habits." There was no place better for such festivals than Genoa, the author suggested, since the city was a natural theater: "What City is better adapted to public spectacles than Genoa? Reflected in a beautiful sea, extending in a vast Amphitheatre." The author proposed to use the physical spaces of the city—both terrestrial and maritime—as a giant chalkboard on which to write lessons for the public about the new democratic politics.[43]

The revolutionary decade was no stranger to revolutionary or patriotic festivals. North American revolutionaries had staged a number of festivals during the war itself, and many more in the decade after, especially in the wake of the Constitution of 1787. Festivals with many similar features had taken place in the Netherlands during the Dutch patriot movement and in the Batavian Republic.[44] French revolutionaries had done the most to popularize the revolutionary festival: the Fête de la Fédération of 1790, celebrating the unity of France under the revolution, reproduced in countless images and descriptions, became a model for festivals across France and the entire Atlantic world. All of these festivals had a didactic purpose, aiming at once to manifest the unity and power of the revolutionary nation and to instruct the public in correct, patriotic views.

Festivals in republican France had tried to create a space out of space: they were held by preference in large open spaces or even outside city limits. The patriot author writing in the *Gazzetta* proposed something quite different: four interlocking, recurring festive performances, each to be held twice a month, which would take the city as their stage. There would be public military exercises in four of the city's larger plazas. At the conclusion of these exercises, the author imagined, the soldiers would stack their arms, and dances would be held in the squares with "a mix of Soldiers and Citizens." There would be boat and foot races, the latter of which would take place along major arteries running through the town. Most remarkable of all, the author proposed that twice a month "public lunches should be instituted." Every Genoese household would be instructed to eat lunch "in front of the door of their home." The poor would be provided with food by the "rich" of their parish, and everyone would be limited to "two dishes not including soup." This menu roughly reflected the average meal for the middling artisan in Genoa at the end of the eighteenth century. At the end of the meal, the author imagined, everyone would parade together through the town.[45]

In stark contrast to the French example, with which he was almost surely familiar, the Genoese writer sought to insert the festivals he proposed into the tissue of the city as it existed—even into its individual neighborhoods. The balls, the spectatorship at the military exercises and public games, and above all the collective meals on the stoops would be vivid displays of equality within the face-to-face communities of the city's neighborhoods. The goal of this project was not just to instruct the public or symbolize unity. Its aim was to imbue the everyday spaces of the city with the new politics. One can imagine, if this proposal had come to fruition, the city's gentry seated outside their front doors, forced to take an uncomfortable meal in the streets under the eye of the less fortunate.

By the time the Ligurian Republic was approaching its second year, it was clear that the democrats' efforts to shift popular opinion in their favor through education and culture had failed. They began to see the common people of the republic not as potential allies but as another oppositional bloc to be tamed. The Ligurian Directory, which had remained in the hands of more radical democrats, took an increasingly hard line with them, turning from collaboration to coercion.

The Directory gave ear to negative, even hopeless views of the republic's lower orders. "The ignorance of the People is profound," the police committee wrote to the Directory in 1798, and the "enemies of liberty" are trying to "profit from it." The "multitude," they continued, had not given up their attachment to the "old Government." In their view, this "ignorance" was being stoked by the various elite opponents of the regime. Foremost among these were the priests. In a letter about Monte Liguri, one of the outlying towns that was a stronghold of resistance to the new government, the police committee opined that the priests were trying to keep the people "in the shadows of ignorance" and to spark "aversion to the New Democratic system."[46]

Even within the city of Genoa itself, the Directory was severely limited in its ability to know what was going on and to control possible counterrevolutionary activities among the lower orders. The piazzas near the waterfront, especially San Donato and the Piazza del Molo, were the heart of the working-class city. The reports filed by the police from these areas paint a picture of communities over whom the authorities could hardly exercise any authority. In the first days of 1798, for instance, the police were watching a house on the piazza in front on San Donato where they had heard that a regular "meeting" was being held in the night. They suspected that it was a counterrevolutionary gathering. Only after more than a week of nightly surveillance did they manage to establish that it was nothing more than a meeting of "card players." A couple of months later, the police reported that there was a "large group of young men . . . who roam the City at night and haunt the squares," whether for hijinks or to undermine the government, they could not say. The Directory frequently received queries about opening the gates at night to allow individuals in and out. Even the city's boundaries were porous.[47]

Facing a public whom it regarded as both hostile and hard to watch, the Directory tried to stamp the revolutionary credo on the public spaces of the city. One of their most dramatic efforts was a requirement to wear cockades in public. Dress codes and sumptuary laws had been a familiar feature of the republics of Italy during the old regime, where they served as a crucial marker of social and political status. As late as the 1780s, the government of Genoa prescribed sumptuary laws for the entire population. These laws were remarkably draconian, with restrictions not only on colors but on cuts of fabric, and with severe penalties to enforce them. Given this, it was perhaps natural for patriots to use dress as a way to make the city more manageable. Controversies over the wearing of cockades were not uncommon in the revolutionary Atlantic world: they played a role in crucial episodes in the French Revolution, including one incident on October 1, 1789, that had contributed to fears of a royalist coup.[48]

The use that the Genoese democrats made of cockades and other badges of political belonging in the late 1790s, however, was remarkable. The new government ordered all "outsiders" (*forastieri*) to wear distinctive cockades in order to make it easier for the police to "watch over their equivocal conduct." Genoese citizens were required to wear revolutionary cockades. Repeated conflicts over cockades erupted in subsequent months. In December, a dispute broke out in San Remo over a consul of the Kingdom of Sicily who insisted on wearing a nonrevolutionary cockade. Early the following year, the police reported on a citizen who had worn a red cockade, in violation of the regulations, indicating hostility to the "democratic system." Nor did the authorities limit themselves to cockades. "Republican" hairstyles—short cropped, in imitation of the styles of republican-era Rome—were also in vogue among the patriots. One woman from the countryside was heard, in early 1798, to be denouncing the new government and the "citizens, who had cropped hair."[49]

The non-elite people of Genoa responded in kind by staking their claim to ownership of the streets and public spaces of the city. Religious processions were a particularly visible part of this counterprogramming to the Directory's agenda. As in many Catholic countries, the calendar was rich with public religious celebrations. Among the most important were ones during which the body of Christ, in the form of Communion wafers, was carried through the streets. In the new republic, however, these ceremonies were a provocation, regarded by the more radical members of the democratic party as relics of a bygone age.[50]

In Genoa, 1798 brought repeated conflicts over the religious ceremonies and symbols that remained precious to the ordinary people of the city. In February, the police reported that there were regular disruptions to the public peace as French soldiers mocked the Eucharist as it was being carried to the homes of the sick. In general, the presence of French troops aggravated the conflicts within the city. The Directory received frequent reports of conflicts between Genoese and French troops, often involving the use of firearms. On March 18, 1798, there was a disturbance in the Quartiere dell'Eguaglianza that pitted French soldiers against Genoese workers. A few months later, in June, another conflict occurred in which shots were fired. Yet not all of these conflicts were caused by the French. In March, the minister of police suppressed the performance of a play that depicted the Virgin Mary in a scandalous light. June brought another conflict over processions of the Eucharist, which the new minister of police felt were troublesome to public order.[51]

In sum, the "common people" proved adept at harnessing the freedoms they were afforded to conservative ends. The right to elect representatives produced conservative outcomes as members of the old oligarchy marshaled votes for their candidates, enlisting artisans and the poor in their electoral campaigns. Expanded freedom of speech and printing proved as useful to the conservatives as it did to the patriot cause. The bottom line, as a police report put it, was that there was little to "console" any patriot leader anxious about how the people of Genoa seemed to be resisting the revolutionary project.[52] The gulf between the people and the revolutionary elites was proving too great to be bridged.

The Ligurian Republic limped on for another year and a half. In November 1799, General Napoleon Bonaparte, now back in France, staged a coup d'état and overthrew the French Directory. He replaced it with a system he called the Consulate, in which he and two collaborators took full executive authority. A month later, the Ligurian Republic was overthrown in a similar coup. It moved into close alignment with France. The military and political alliance, which had at first seemed a wise idea, quickly proved disastrous. When French forces fell back in 1800 before a renewed assault by the Austrians, the city found itself in the midst of a grinding, monthslong siege. The city capitulated to the Austrians in June 1800, just three years after the republic's hopeful beginnings.[53]

One might say that the fall of the Ligurian Republic was overdetermined. The ongoing subsistence crisis, which left the city of Genoa lacking everything from grain to meat, pressed hard on the lives of the people and on the legitimacy of the government. The weight of financial exactions from France drained the state's coffers. France's increasingly assertive political interference in the internal affairs of the republic left it with less and less room for maneuver.[54] Even all these insults, however, might not have succeeded in toppling the Ligurian Republic so quickly had the democrats not failed so spectacularly to achieve even a modicum of social unity.

Even if the republic was doomed to be absorbed by France, it might have maintained more power and autonomy, or even regained its independence later in the nineteenth century. Instead, it virtually disappeared as an autonomous actor. This failure was not the result of external disruptions, even if they were many; it was the failure of the republic to knit itself together, through political organizing, that doomed it to irrelevance.

For R. R. Palmer, the Ligurian Republic and the other sister republics of the late 1790s represented the "high tide of revolutionary democracy." To look at their constitutions and the public proclamations of their leaders, as he did, this may be true. The leaders of the sister republics certainly recognized and aspired to create mass mobilizations. They knew better than anyone else just how fierce the resistance was to revolutionary change and so how much they needed to muster a broad-based political movement. But on the ground, the political organizing in the sister republics remained at best in a transitional state, still highly influenced by the hierarchical habitus of the first revolutionary generation.[55]

The limited democracy of the Ligurian Republic was the rule, not the exception, among the sister republics. Studies of political organizing in the Batavian and Cisalpine Republics have found similar patterns of elite control and failures to extend their political movements across class lines. In the Batavian Republic, the revolutionary leadership had to contend with a still vibrant popular Orangism. But even with groups among the lower and middle classes who were sympathetic to their aims, the leaders of the Batavian Republic struggled to build a durable political alliance. The "Jacobins of Piedmont," the Italian region that formed the core of the Cisalpine Republic, faithfully followed the script they had learned from the French Jacobins. As with their French counterparts, they found that sustained popular collaboration with their aims was virtually impossible to secure. They had, even Palmer had to admit, "little contact with the actual masses."[56]

The failure of the Democratic-Republican Societies in the United States during the 1790s for many of the same reasons suggests that these European political failures were not a regional curiosity but part of a much larger pattern. In the United States, as in Europe, the first generation of revolutionaries remained quite politically active during the 1790s. This generation's social and political habits were ill-suited to the messy realities of cross-class political collaboration: the need to socialize with, to eat with, in short to be in fellowship with people of all ranks. At bottom, this inability to straddle the social divide made the political divide unbridgeable as well.

If the United States seemed closer in the mid-1790s to turning the page on the long-standing problem of building cross-class political movements, that is not too surprising either. The society of the United States was less urban, less wealthy, and less aristocratic than that of Genoa or the Netherlands, which meant that the habits of social division that revolution had to overcome might have been a bit less extreme. The transition from the first to the second revolutionary generation was also further along in America. The United States had had an earlier start on the passage through revolutionary convulsion. Now, in the mid-1790s, the revolution's children were beginning—but just beginning—to bring its promises to fruition.

# 12
# THE NEW SOCIAL ORDER EMERGES

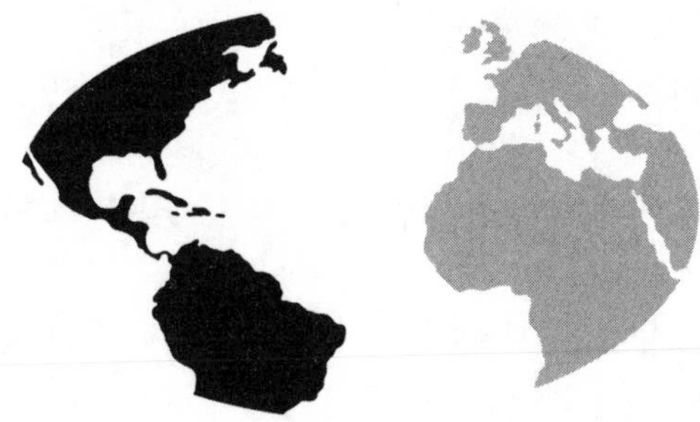

GABRIEL PROSSER WAS A CHILD OF THE AMERICAN REVOLUTION. Born into slavery on a Virginia plantation in 1776, he had known the revolutionary war firsthand. The year before his birth, Lord Dunmore had issued his famous proclamation inviting enslaved Virginians to join the British forces in exchange for their freedom. When Gabriel was about five years old, British troops burned the nearby town of Richmond, Virginia's capital. He grew up in the world of expectant half possibility that the revolution created. The son of a smith, he was apprenticed in his early teens to train in the same profession. By the 1790s he had become a skilled craftsman and knew how to read and write.[1]

At some point in 1799, Gabriel began to plan a revolt. His goal was not just to escape bondage himself. He had a much more capacious understanding of the possibilities for change. The purpose of the revolt, with strong echoes of Haiti, seems to have been nothing less than the destruction of slavery in Virginia. He aimed to seize the state's capital, demand "freedom" for the enslaved, and redistribute the property of the masters by parceling out the state's "treasury" among the rebels. It was a revolt that put its faith in the possibility of a radical transformation of the status quo. Just before it was supposed to be triggered, the conspiracy was betrayed. Gabriel remained at large for two weeks, along with a number of other conspirators, but was eventually captured, tortured, and executed. Had it succeeded, Gabriel's revolt would have been the largest uprising of the enslaved in North America in at least a half century.[2]

Gabriel was bolder than most, but many members of his generation had a good deal in common with him—even if they would not have admitted it. Many of them had early and intense encounters with the era's social, political, and military disruptions. More than a few of them had their own or their family's assumptions about the world, the social order, and their place within it upended at a young age. Each, after their own fashion, had internalized the experience of rapid change that they had lived through. As a group, they viewed social status as impermanent and uncertain. Some, such as Gabriel, showed a striking willingness to seek radical changes to the social order. Others looked with new alacrity for ways to sustain the existing order, recognizing that it would now need to be actively held in place.

As this generation came to maturity around 1800, their dispositions began to reshape political life across the Americas. In the United States, the flexible dispositions of the younger generation fed the rise of political democracy for white men in the nation's growing cities. Easy social fluidity became an especially important part of the way that Washington, the new capital of the United States, functioned as the political center of a fledgling democracy. At the other end of the continent, in South America, the generation that had come of age during the disturbances of the 1780s and 1790s began to break from the patterns of caste that had long defined the social order of Spanish America. People of low birth began to imagine the possibility of rising to prominence. What is more remarkable, they began to find a receptive audience even among the well-off in their change-conscious generation.

In the United States, the more socially flexible world of the second generation was clearly visible in the nation's new capital, which was being constructed throughout the 1790s. George Washington had imagined the Federal City—as Washington, DC, was initially called—in the vein of a grand European capital. The eighteenth century had given rise to new models for how to plan and organize cities of this sort. At the small-scale level of the ordinary streets and dwellings, royal officials in eighteenth-century Europe sought to straighten the roads, improve sanitation and lighting, and clear away debris and private encumbrances on the public ways. On the grander scale, they wanted to create an imposing urban facade that would exalt and reflect the glory of their princes. They sliced stately new streets through the tightly built medieval and early modern city, punctuating them with airy squares formed in surprisingly complex geometric shapes. This was the baroque "grand manner" in city planning.[3]

Through the members of the board of commissioners charged with creating the city, Washington engaged the services of Pierre-Charles L'Enfant to design the new US capital in this grand style. L'Enfant, a painter by training—his father had been employed by Louis XV—was happy to oblige. His plan for the city was a richly imagined ornamental metropolis that drew on European models.

L'Enfant conceived of a city centered on the double poles of the Congress and the executive branch, furnished with wide avenues that opened up perspectives and vistas. These crisscrossed in an irregular pattern, producing many unexpected angular forms. This "dream city" or "elaborate scheme of city planning," as one early historian described it, was intended to provide a grand capital for a future, powerful republic.[4]

For the baroque plan to be a success, Federal City had to be not merely stately but also economically lively. European capitals reflected the glory of their princes because they were economic and population powerhouses. Encouraging economic growth was an integral part of the plan advanced by the commissioners. The city was to be settled by auctioning off vacant lots to developers, who would construct housing and shops and sell or rent to new arrivals. The first sale, which took place in October 1791, was a modest success, selling lots mostly near the future presidential "palace." But overall, the grand design proved an abject failure. The city site had few natural resources or attractions. Speculators in land had better prospects during these years than the cramped and expensive confines of the Federal City (land on the western "frontier" was cheap and plentiful), and it proved difficult to construct any buildings at all, in part due to an acute labor shortage.[5]

Unable in the short term to create the city they had wanted—one of stately public buildings anchored by powerful landlords—the board and the government allowed the emergence of a democratic (with a small *d*) town. The structure of the city, for at least two decades after 1800, was that of three largely autonomous villages surrounding clusters of public buildings: one around the executive mansion, one around the Capitol, and a third near the Navy Yard. Each of the villages individually was a small, face-to-face community: the total population of the central part of the District in 1800 was a mere 3,210 souls, including free people of color and enslaved people, putting the population of each village at roughly one thousand.[6]

In the villages that made up early Washington, there was relatively little space for social groups to live separately. Each of the villages contained a social cross section. Capitol Hill and the executive settlement, for instance, each had their own tavern keepers, washerwomen, shoemakers, grocers, and the like who lived in the village. Unsurprisingly, given the city's location on the northern edge of the slave-society zone of the United States, roughly a third of the population in the first decades of the 1800s was either free or enslaved Black people. They appear to have lived throughout the villages and indeed owned substantial property within each one. White residents lived cheek by jowl with Black neighbors, and the micro-economies of each village confounded social distance. Produce markets were held on the lawn of the executive mansion in the early years of the century.[7]

DURING EXACTLY THE YEARS IN WHICH THIS NEW CAPITAL WAS taking shape, the younger generation was creating the first organized political party in the United States. The Republicans, as they called themselves, grew in part from the rootstock of the Democratic-Republican Societies. But unlike the societies, the Republican Party welcomed all white men, and its organizational techniques explicitly crossed class lines. The party began to define itself as an "interest" as early as 1790 and took a remarkable leap toward collective organization in 1795 and 1796. By 1800, the Republicans had become the most powerful nationwide political force—a position they would retain for nearly a quarter century thereafter.

Discernable factions began to emerge in Congress less than a year into the tenure of the new federal government. The appearance of factions was no surprise to anyone. Competing "interests" had long existed in legislatures. Early modern political thinkers were inured enough to their presence that James Madison argued, in the tenth of the *Federalist Papers*, that a large republic would be more stable precisely because it would spawn so many factions. The "republican interest," however, firmly disclaimed any intention of forming a "party." This attitude, though it appears at odds with some of the congressmen's voting records, was consistent with bedrock principles of early modern republican thought. Their ideal of a republican government depicted the rule of virtuous, disinterested men who worked toward the common good. Most genteel political leaders imagined themselves in these terms, rejecting overt electioneering or formal party organization as antithetical to true republicanism.[8]

From 1790 to 1794, the "republican interest" nationally did very little to constitute or operate a political party in anything like the modern sense. One of the marks of this genuine lack of party organization was that candidates continued to stand for election individually, with minimal filtering or nomination mechanisms in place. In the South, elections were often virtually uncontested; in New England, the lack of any filtering mechanism meant that elections featured huge slates of candidates for the same office. Only in New York and Pennsylvania did a system of nominating conventions and committees begin to come into existence during these years. Even that system remained embryonic and was oriented more locally than nationally. In Philadelphia in 1792, for instance, two slates of candidates were nominated, but they shared a number of names, and both were assembled by ad hoc committees and mass meetings.[9]

In 1796, the Republicans took major strides toward creating a formal party organization. An important spur to this process was the deep partisan divisions that had been on public display during the debate in Congress over a new treaty with Great Britain negotiated by John Jay. Jay's treaty, which was seen as favorable to British interests and likely to strengthen US bonds with Britain, was hotly contested. After an acrimonious debate, the Senate approved the unpopular accord in June 1795 by the barest possible margin. When Washington announced his intention to retire from politics in the summer of 1796, after two terms as president, it set up the first truly contested presidential election. The sharpness of the partisan divisions that had emerged over the previous several years made the stakes seem exceptionally high to both Republicans and Federalists.

In the mid-Atlantic states of Pennsylvania and New York, a cohort of younger Republicans took the lead in organizing the party. One of the organizers, John Beckley, an immigrant to the United States who had grown up in Virginia during the imperial crisis, took Pennsylvania by storm. Beckley was a typical member of the middling sorts, neither wealthy nor poor. He had experienced upward mobility, especially during the revolution, when he had risen to hold a number of clerical offices, including clerk of the House of Representatives during the early 1790s. In 1796, he became the trailblazer of party organization. He and his allies handwrote more than thirty thousand tickets listing the Republican Party's preferred candidates, which were distributed throughout the state by a network of travelers and correspondents. Major John Smith, one of his collaborators, described having ridden deep into the countryside to distribute the tickets and rally voters for Jefferson. Nothing on this scale had ever been attempted before in the United States. Pennsylvania's Republican Party, with Beckley at the helm, may have been precocious, but it was not alone: similar Republican Party tickets were created and publicized in 1796 in New York City, Delaware, and other key districts.[10]

What is most remarkable about the organizing of the Republican Party 1796 is how wide its social reach was. In Pennsylvania, the party led by Beckley engaged in outreach to tens of thousands of voters, implicitly bringing many individuals who were members of the lower orders into their political fold. Over 50 percent of free white male Pennsylvanians were voting by the end of the decade—and the figures went up from there. In New York City, the Republican Party gained a powerful following among artisans, which would last for years. Even in Virginia, the Republicans were engaging in elector "mass mobilization" by the end of the decade. Not coincidentally, the key players in this emerging mass politics were members of the second revolutionary generation, who had grown up during and after the war years. This included Beckley, of course, but also Stephen Allen in New York City, an artisan who became mayor in the early 1800s. Beckley and others like him created a series of standing party committees, which kept in touch with one another and with national leaders. The Republican Party that took shape in the second half of the 1790s was not just a mass organization that united elite and working-class voters. It also had a durable structure, with emerging institutions that were capable of sustaining the mobilization over time.[11]

The Republican organization of 1796, for all of its precociousness, was not enough to win Thomas Jefferson the presidency. He fell short of John Adams, his longtime friend and sometime rival, by three electoral votes. But the party continued to organize over the next four years. In 1797 and 1798, the Republicans found themselves on the back foot. The French Directory targeted US shipping in a conflict that came to be called the Quasi-War. War fever gripped the United States, and the Anglophile Federalists gained ground at the Republicans' expense. But by 1799, the worm had begun to turn. With the Quasi-War calming, and the Federalists overreaching in their militant response to the crisis, the Republicans began to regain the ground they had lost. Eighteen hundred brought the second contested election for president, once again pitting John Adams against Thomas Jefferson. This time, the Republican Party machinery did not fail: Jefferson defeated Adams, and the Republicans won large victories in Congress. The Federalists were pushed into the minority in both houses—a status from which they would never reemerge.[12]

THE SECOND REVOLUTIONARY GENERATION, WITH ITS DISTINCTIVE acceptance of social mobility, set the cultural tone in the US capital. The majority of the members in the first Congress that convened in Washington in 1800, and for at least a decade thereafter, were men born in the 1760s and 1770s who had grown up during and after the revolutionary war (John Quincy Adams, a senator from 1803 to 1808, among them). Many of the prominent individuals in other parts of the government or its orbit were also of that age, including William Cranch (Abigail Adams's nephew, born 1769), who became an important federal judge, and Samuel Harrison Smith (publisher of the capital's first newspaper starting in 1800, born 1772).[13] Of course, both John Adams and Thomas Jefferson were members of the generation born before 1750, and that remained the case for the presidents and vice presidents over the next sixteen years. But these old men at the helm were the exception in Washington, not the rule.

The new generation looked at the world in a different way than their elders. US senator from Pennsylvania Jonathan Roberts, whom the future president John Quincy Adams viewed as an exemplar of the self-made new man in the early US republic, described in his memoirs the moment at which he had realized that the world had changed completely. As a teenager, he claimed, what he read about the French Revolution had shattered in him any tolerance for the "policy of casts [*sic*], and classes." From then on, he was opposed to all forms of fixed social status—including the institution of slavery. Adams himself, who was no friend to "inconstant Democracy," acknowledged that "too great a degree of inequality among the Citizens" was inconsistent with representative government. It followed that even though he was never an enthusiastic proponent of social mobility, neither was he reflexively opposed to it.[14]

The new arrivals to Washington more than accepted the socially mixed character of the existing city; they embraced it. In these early years, Congress was only in session during the winter months. As a result, members of Congress and their entourages, as well as judges and others who were not in constant service, lived in boardinghouses. They did the government's business there too: the justices of the Supreme Court, for instance, held their private conferences for decades in the Capitol Hill boardinghouse at which they all stayed. The houses were open to anyone who could pay and typically included a wide range of individuals. Because boardinghouse life was communal—boarders shared rooms and usually meals—it gave at best modest scope for social distance and hierarchy. A well-known anecdote about Thomas Jefferson, recounted by Margaret Bayard Smith (wife of Samuel Harrison Smith), has it that during the end of his time as vice president, Jefferson lodged in Conrad's boardinghouse on terms of "perfect equality" with thirty other men. He supposedly cheerfully took the least-favored spot at the common table. On another occasion, Smith described a teatime visit from two senators from the backcountry. She was shocked to find that they did not know what written music was. But, she concluded in a conciliatory tone, "do not think now these good men are fools, far from it, they are very sensible men and useful citizens, but they have lived in the back woods, that's all."[15]

Social mixing was characteristic of most forms of sociability in early Washington. The city's first dedicated theater, opened in 1804, was a small and not particularly salubrious space. It offered a mélange of popular entertainments, including "songs, magic, dancing and acting automatons," in addition to plays. Its clientele seems to have included Black people as well as a cross section of the white population. The "annual horse races" were a major event that drew the entire (male) community together, with "persons of all descriptions" present on and around the track. So important was the event perceived to be in the city's social life that in 1803 the Senate adjourned for several days to allow its members to attend. Early religious services in Washington offered little more in the way of social distinction or discrimination. Until the first church building was completed in 1806, services took place in the chamber of the House of Representatives, with the public in attendance.[16]

The leaders of the government after 1800 made affirmative efforts to open some of the spaces of power to the ordinary people of the city. They did so in part so that the working people of Washington could stand in for "the people"—a Jeffersonian desideratum—but the public's presence was more than metaphorical. In the galleries of the Senate, notices had to be put up to warn spectators against putting their feet on the railings, since dirt from their shoes then rained down on the senators. At James Madison's inauguration, the Capitol was thrown open to the public and "high and low were promiscuously blended on the floor and in the galleries." These choices represented more than just an accommodation of the relatively rough-and-ready conditions of early Washington. They were a deliberate rejection of the formality, exclusiveness, and gentility of the "republican court" that had been characteristic of the Philadelphia-based federal government of the 1790s.[17]

The processes unfolding in Washington during the early years of the 1800s had echoes in other US cities during the same period. In New York and Philadelphia, the existing cultural and social infrastructures helped elites maintain the separate lives that they had created for themselves across the mid-eighteenth-century Atlantic urban landscape. But in those cities, too, there was motion both on the surface and beneath it. Popular entertainments and media with a mass audience, including the theater and the newspapers, expanded around 1800. The ordered world of artisanal labor, with its theoretically close-knit hierarchical relationships, was fraying; in its place emerged more fluid (and often more unequal) labor and employment relationships. The shape of the cities themselves was in the process of being reordered as the densely settled colonial-era "walking city" gave way to a sprawling urban landscape in which social relations were increasingly anonymous. Throughout the United States, the second revolutionary generation was rising—and reshaping the nation's culture and politics as it grew in strength.[18]

A SIMILAR SET OF CULTURAL SHIFTS WERE UNDERWAY, ALBEIT A few years behind the United States, in Spain's continental viceroyalties. People in several large and important regions of Spanish America who were in their twenties and thirties during the 1790s had grown up in a social world of political and military disruption. The political crises had begun with a series of large-scale revolts during the 1780s. The fact that their protagonists often articulated traditional aims, including expressing loyalty to the Spanish king, did not make their effects any less disruptive. The Túpac Amaru rebellion was the most violent and traumatic, with thousands dying during the fighting and in the repression that followed. Just as consequential were the Spanish government's post-rebellion attacks on the power of criollos and Native elites. As Luis Durand Flórez has argued, the government's desire to limit both groups' power meant pushing them both into a subordinate position. The groups found themselves, for perhaps the first time in the region's colonial history, squeezed into closer alignment.[19]

The Viceroyalty of New Granada (present-day Colombia and neighboring countries) was the scene of another major rebellion in 1781, the Comunero revolt. This rebellion first took shape in the prosperous hill town of Socorro, in immediate response to efforts by royal officials to impose a new tax regime on the region. In a matter of weeks, local rioting turned into an armed rebellion that set out for Bogotá, the capital of the viceroyalty. Unlike in Peru, royal officials compromised with the insurgents, effectively withdrawing the tax reforms. Most of the insurgents lay down their arms without significant loss of life. In the aftermath of the rebellion, as in the Peruvian highlands, the imperial government engaged in a campaign of repression that left significant scars on the region and was not quickly forgotten by those who experienced it.[20]

These revolts, though quite localized and relatively short in duration, struck some of the most economically important and dynamic regions of the Spanish Americas. Cuzco and its region formed the core of the Viceroyalty of Peru, the main source of labor and food for the silver-mining operations of the Andes. Socorro was the de facto capital of a rapidly growing agricultural region in New Granada. These revolts, in other words, did not occur in marginal or peripheral areas. The people who were revolting were relatively prosperous and were well integrated into the empire and its economic and political system. Though the circulation of news is hard to track, it is probable as well that knowledge of these uprisings was well disseminated in much of South America.[21]

The revolts had noticeable effects on the life courses of those who grew up in their shadow. The early lives of two very different men, both born in Peru around the Túpac Amaru revolt, suggest how these changes had affected this generation. Agustín Gamarra was born into a lower-middle social rank in Cuzco in 1785. An ambitious young man fluent in both Spanish and Quechua, the language of the region's Native majority, he made it his mission to rise in this stratified society. He started out for a career in the church, the traditional route upward. But he changed course abruptly around the age of twenty-four. The quick-witted young man likely recognized that the church's power was on the wane and that a closer connection to the empire, recently reinforced by its victory over the criollos after the rebellion, offered a surer path to success. He entered the royal army instead, rising quickly through the ranks aided by his command of the "language . . . and terrain of the Sierra [highlands]." Gabriel Aguilar, born in 1773 in the central Peruvian town of Huánaco, came from another lower-middle-class family. He felt the impact of the Túpac Amaru rebellion directly: a "close relative" was involved in the revolt. The damaged post–Túpac Amaru economy left him struggling throughout his young adulthood. He had an itinerant early life, wandering through South America. He also began to have religious visions that centered on a radical change in his social position. The first, he reported later, occurred shortly after the Great Rebellion had been crushed: he was transported to a church where numinous beings informed him that he was one of God's chosen and that he would become "one of the greatest [men] on the earth."[22]

The French revolutionary wars seeded further economic and political instability in continental Spanish America starting in the early 1790s. As soon as the French wars began, long-distance trade in the Atlantic and the Caribbean came under attack, with effects that rippled through ports and coastal regions across the Americas. For the first two years of the war, before French commerce raiding had fully engaged, the damage to Spanish trade remained minimal. Indeed, in both the viceroyalties of New Granada and the Río de la Plata (including present-day Colombia and Argentina, respectively), 1795 to 1796 was a banner year for trade between Spain and its colonies, with exchanges reaching previously unseen heights. In 1796, however, a sharp drop-off in transatlantic trade began, which struck a hammerblow at all regions of South America. Major trading firms went from having their best year ever to a complete cessation of trade. Goods became scarce or far more expensive; bankruptcy loomed for merchants who found themselves suddenly unable to move their wares. These commercial disruptions stretched into the hinterlands along the web of trade routes that connected the coast to the inland areas.[23]

War, and especially the war on trade, troubled the economies and social orders of the Spanish American viceroyalties. In the Río de la Plata, which remained socially rigid in this period in spite of its economic dynamism, members of the younger generation began thinking about reimagining their society and their position within it. Manuel Belgrano, who would become the leader of Argentine independence, had been born in 1770 into one of the city's merchant families. In the 1790s, he was in Spain studying, at the beginning of a brilliant career. He described his work during these years, influenced by the "ideas" of the French Revolution, as a long series of proposals to reform the society and economy of his native viceroyalty. In the Caribbean-facing littoral of northern South America, others saw opportunities for more direct action against the existing order, inspired by the Haitian Revolution. In 1795, 1797, and again in 1805, rebellions broke out in the Viceroyalty of New Granada. These rebellions were socially diverse, involving enslaved people, free people of color, and Natives, in addition to white Spaniards. Though all of these uprisings were suppressed, they contributed to the strengthening feedback loop between military and economic crisis and social and cultural transformation on the South American continent.[24]

By the early nineteenth century, practices of social mobility and ideas of social flexibility had penetrated even the most conservative regions of Spanish America. An alleged criminal conspiracy in Cuzco in 1805 gives us a window into how the younger generation was reimagining the social order. The two main coconspirators were the visionary from Huánaco—Gabriel Aguilar, now settled in Cuzco—and his friend and sometimes patron, a man named Manuel Ubalde. This incident has been analyzed as an early precursor to the independence movements and as one of a long string of manifestations of an "Andean utopia" centered on the revival of a mythologized Inca past. What is most striking about the conspiracy is how it reveals the ways in which the fixed statuses that had for so long dominated the Peruvian highlands had begun to shake loose by the first years of the nineteenth century.[25]

The exact contours of the alleged conspiracy remain vague. It was not clear, even at the time, whether the conspirators intended to overthrow the monarchy or had some more limited goal in mind. In any event, they had made virtually no practical preparations. But they had for months been feverishly discussing the corruption of the government, the visions that Aguilar received, and a potentially redemptive revolt. Aguilar and Ubalde were arrested in June, after being denounced by a man who had initially been drawn to the conspiracy, and interrogated along with others whom they named in their statements to the authorities.[26]

Aguilar and Ubalde were men of quite different social statuses. Aguilar had begun life on the lower rungs of the social ladder. After his wanderings, he had eventually become a miner. It was a potentially lucrative profession for those who owned mines but a dangerous and risky one for those who operated them. Ubalde, on the other hand, was a member of the colonial elite. He was a lawyer and a royal functionary (*teniente asesor*), in the employ in 1805 of the Real Audiencia in Cuzco. He had a substantial personal library and was versed in theology, politics, and history.[27]

In spite of the clear status difference, Aguilar had long been the dominant figure in their partnership. The two had first met in Lima in 1800 or 1801 when Aguilar came to Ubalde for legal assistance. After they had done their business, Aguilar disappeared from view for a few years. He resurfaced, this time held in prison in Chachapoyas (northern Peru), asking for Ubalde's assistance, which he provided. Already, Ubalde reported, he was drawn to this "extraordinary man." After Ubalde had moved to Cuzco, Aguilar walked unannounced into the lawyer's new office. Ubalde greeted him as a hero, believing that Aguilar had been sent "by Divine providence" to help him. He moved the visitor to his own home and provided him with a field for his animals. He "tried by every means to gain the goodwill of this man and keep him in [Cuzco]."[28]

Over the next several months, Aguilar shared his visions with Ubalde, and the lawyer worked hard to support the visionary. Aguilar reported having seen angels and other divine messengers, who told him that he would be crowned a king. In other dream visions, he spoke with the devil, a crucified Christ, and other numinous beings, who made specific predictions about his glorious future and gave him directions on how to achieve it. Ubalde listened and sought confirmation of the validity of the visions from churchmen, including his own chaplain, Padre Barranco.[29]

The religious visionary from a lower-status group who entrances or cons a well-off person is an old story. But there is a strong suggestion in the trial transcript that it was precisely the fact that the two men were working together across lines of class that was so threatening in the eyes of the Spanish royal authorities. Aguilar had long been telling everyone he could about his visions, not excluding the ones that included seditious and sacrilegious notions of his anointment or coronation. He had recounted his first visions, when he was nine years old, to his "masters and his parents." Neither royal nor ecclesiastical authorities had ever reacted before.[30] Once Ubalde, a member of the elite, began to take Aguilar seriously and to recruit others to join him, the government's view of him and his visions changed.

Aguilar's visions, centered on the idea that the low (led and exemplified by himself) would be made high, formed the political heart of the alleged revolt. Some of what he saw was undoubtedly fantastical: himself being crowned king or elevated to a position of "greatness." His visions also included other elements, consistent with these fantasies, that suggested a more concrete vision of growing social flexibility in the Andes. More than half of Aguilar's visions revolved around marriage. He first reported that he was destined to marry a woman who was an Indian and "poor." But as the visions progressed, the social character of his intended seemed to shift. On April 26, 1805, in one of his last visions before the conspiracy was exposed, Aguilar described his future bride in explicitly upper-class terms: she would be a woman who "knows how to play piano, to read and write," and her father "is a notary." In his own mind, at least, his low origins were no barrier to an advantageous match—or perhaps he had come to believe that there was no real difference between the "poor" Indian and the educated girl. Either way, Aguilar's visions of his intended reflected a keenly felt sense of the fluidity of social position.[31]

Aguilar's visions, populated by Natives and Spaniards, said little about Black people, whose numbers were lower in the Peruvian highlands than elsewhere in Spanish America. But the mobile social imaginary that he advanced could be extended to Black people as well, even in Peru. A comic Christmas play (*entremés*), probably written by a Carmelite nun in Arequipa around 1797, suggests these possibilities. The play featured a "Negra" (woman of African descent) as one of its four main characters. Like the other characters, she is initially depicted in caricatural terms: a bit slow on the uptake, illiterate, and speaking with a thick accent. But in the course of the play, the audience discovers that she has learned how to read—in fact, she has apparently paid the trickster-like Indian character, named Huamanguino, to teach her. The play ends with the four characters each delivering a brief excursus about Christmas. The "Negra" gets the last word, reflecting on the possibility that the newborn savior and his mother might resemble her. *Could Mary be dark-skinned like her?* she wonders. And perhaps the Christ child, whom she calls "my little Angolan boy," has a "face as flat as mine."[32] The ending note of the play, for all the stereotypes and racism in which it traffics, is thus the striking image of a Black redeemer.

We do not know how many saw the 1797 *entremés*, but we can be sure that Aguilar's visions found a receptive and fairly broad audience in Cuzco. The trial transcript implicates some two dozen individuals in the conspiracy. A number of them were reported to have specifically affirmed the validity of Aguilar's visions. The priest Bernardino Gutiérrez, for instance, who served as *capellan* of San Andrés, had an ecstatic vision of his own one night, in which he saw Aguilar with a halo about his head. This vision served as confirmation for him and others, a "very clear indication of the truth of this vision" that Aguilar had, and a sign that his visions represented "the will of God." The *capellan* went so far as to try to enter into marriage negotiations on Aguilar's behalf.[33] Whether all of these alleged conspirators thought Aguilar would be crowned a king is far from clear. But the idea that a social inferior like Aguilar might be a divine guide, and that he might himself be elevated to the top of the social order, was clearly well within the scope of what they and others in early nineteenth-century Cuzco could imagine.

Like Túpac Amaru's twenty-five years earlier, Aguilar's life came to an end in Cuzco's Plaza de Armas. On December 5, 1805, just a few months after their arrest, Aguilar and Ubalde were both hanged in Cuzco's central square. Their bodies were left up overnight and then taken for a quiet burial at the cathedral that stands on the eastern side of the plaza—the same one in which Aguilar had imagined his coronation would take place. The ending of Aguilar's life did not signal that the social changes he envisioned were dead. The other two-dozen individuals who were implicated in the alleged conspiracy survived, some with no punishment at all. They and many others, in subsequent years, would carry on the transformation of Andean society that Aguilar boldly envisioned.[34]

In continental North and South America, the years around 1800 saw the second revolutionary generation begin to come to maturity. They had been shaped by the first-wave upheavals of the 1770s and 1780s. The uprisings in the Americas during this period had not been evenly spread across the landscape. Even in North America, which had experienced a war that lasted more than five years during the 1770s and early 1780s, there were regions that had been more and less affected. Rural New England, for instance, experienced far less disruption than the major cities that changed hands multiple times or contested areas like Long Island or the southern backcountry, which became scenes of partisan wars. This was true in Spanish America as well. Upper Peru and the Viceroyalty of New Granada had been the most directly affected by the revolts of the early 1780s. Yet the Spanish Americas, unlike North America, had remained under imperial control. As a result, all the colonies had been subjected to an ongoing campaign of political repression from Spain, which lasted through the 1790s.

The common experience of upheaval had left formative imprints on this entire generation. For them, the world of fixed status in which their parents and grandparents had grown up—that is, the world of the mid-eighteenth century—was a distant memory. In its place was a strong conviction, indeed a certainty, that changes of status were possible and even inevitable. White men and women who belonged to the elite, whether in Washington, DC, or in Cuzco, were far more willing than their parents or grandparents had been to mix socially with members of the lower orders. In some cases, indeed, they might even see these low-status individuals as bearing spiritual or political power. Members of the lower orders, in some cases including Black North and South Americans, began to move somewhat more freely through spaces marked by political and social power.

As the second generation began to take control of the political and cultural spheres, the implications of these distinctive attitudes began to become clearer. They were far from monolithic. In North America, the late 1790s saw the creation of the first mass political party, the Republicans. Built on a strong cross-class political collaboration, it was at the same time racially exclusionary. It was challenged by, and eventually vanquished, the more socially exclusive but racially liberal Federalists. In Spanish America, cross-class politics in the 1790s and first years of the 1800s remained largely in the realm of dreams and visions. The imperial state retained a close grip on the power that it had consolidated during the 1780s. But beneath this imperial surface, new ideas of social equality, with political implications, were percolating.

# 13
# THE HAITIAN STATE

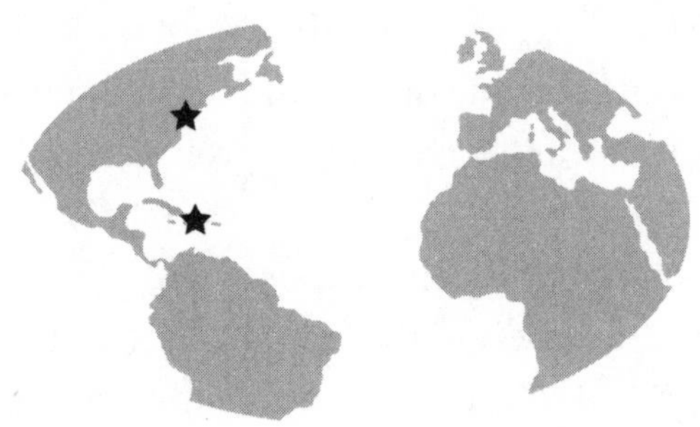

NOWHERE IN THE ATLANTIC WORLD HAD THE REORDERING OF society sped forward as fast and as far as it did in Haiti during the decade after the revolution began in 1791. Marie and Joseph Bunel had witnessed this transformation firsthand. The men and women whom they held in bondage were freed by decree. The Bunels experienced the violence of war: the burning of plantations and then Le Cap, the British invasion, the many smaller moments of destruction that ran through the civil war that consumed the colony. The couple became close along the way with the revolution's leaders. Toussaint Louverture brought Marie Bunel into the circle of his close confidants. Joseph Bunel was appointed to key posts of responsibility, including as a judge and as treasurer to Henry Christophe, at the time commander of Le Cap.

Between 1802 and 1804, Haitians lived through one last crescendo of violent struggle. In the space of twenty months, Saint-Domingue was invaded by a French expeditionary force, Louverture was deposed and exiled from the island, and a new Black-led revolt burst onto the island. The Bunels faced prison and exile. By 1803, both Marie and Joseph had left Saint-Domingue and eventually established a temporary home in Philadelphia. The French invasion, however, proved a failure. Under the leadership of Jean-Jacques Dessalines, one of the revolt's longtime military leaders, the armies of formerly enslaved people united and drove the French from the island. On January 1, 1804, Dessalines proclaimed the independent State of Haiti.

With the coming of independence, the Bunels were positioned to take a place as members of the Haitian state's emerging elite. The creation of a new governing class, loyal to the new regime and capable of sustaining the post-slavery order, was an essential aspect of Haitian revolutionary politics after 1802. The main features of this elite and how it functioned have been well fleshed out by several generations of Haitian Revolution scholars. Its members comprised Black freedpeople and people of color who had been free before the revolution, most of them island born. It operated in a highly stylized and formalized fashion, through courtly rituals and carefully structured political bodies.[1]

The Bunels left behind a rare record of how this new governing class came into being and began to assert its authority during the first years of the nineteenth century. One of the most pressing tasks facing Haiti's emerging rulers, many of whom had risen from slavery during the previous decades, was to consolidate their position as a social elite. Everyday practices, from gift giving to managing property, were crucial to this collective and individual refashioning. The formation of this social elite took place both beyond and across the new nation's borders: the movement of people and information in the Atlantic world, including between Haiti and the

United States, was essential to how they formed themselves into a ruling group. And even though Haiti was officially a "Black" state, its rulers still made a significant place in the ranks of the elite for white collaborators like Joseph Bunel.

The events that led to the end of French rule in Saint-Domingue began quietly enough, with a string of unanswered letters. By the fall of 1799, when Napoleon and his allies overthrew the Directory and took power in France, Toussaint Louverture thoroughly dominated Saint-Domingue. He had expelled the British from the island colony, marginalized officials sent from France, and consolidated his rule over all its regions. By now a practiced hand at navigating shifting French political regimes, Louverture did not delay in trying to win the confidence of France's new ruler. He wrote a series of letters to Napoleon and dispatched envoys to Paris in the hopes of persuading the consul of his importance and his willingness to collaborate with France. Napoleon, however, proved impervious to his overtures. All the letters went unanswered, and the envoys were largely ignored.[2]

The truth was that Napoleon had become more and more determined to reassert control over France's onetime colony. In the fall of 1801, in consultation with his ministers and the unofficial lobby of ex-planters who had become influential in the government, Napoleon decided to dispatch an expeditionary force to bring Saint-Domingue back under direct French rule. The expedition was put under the command of an experienced soldier, Napoleon's brother-in-law Victor-Emmanuel Leclerc. In his secret directions to Leclerc, Napoleon indicated that the general was not only to dislodge Louverture from his hard-won position but to re-create the plantation regime. He may have intended for Leclerc to prepare to reimpose slavery on the people of Saint-Domingue, as he would do in the rest of the French empire in 1802.

In due course, in February 1802, a fleet of fifty French warships appeared before Cap Français bearing over forty thousand soldiers and sailors. Henry Christophe, following the orders he claimed that Louverture had given him, withdrew his forces from Le Cap. He took with him the contents of the treasury and set the town alight. For the second time in just over ten years, Le Cap was devastated by fire. Flames consumed the lion's share of the town before the French landed and extinguished them. Marie Bunel's house, number 893 (as the census takers called it), was somehow not seriously damaged, though the acrid smell of ash surely clung to the drapes and breathed from the upholstery. Most of the other houses on her block were destroyed.[3]

Leclerc landed his forces and took control of the coastal areas of the colony. As the French force extended its reach, Marie Bunel's position grew increasingly fragile. Louverture had some initial success in holding back the expeditionary force. By the spring, his resistance was crumbling, undermined by the French army's superior weaponry and desertions among his commanders—Christophe among them. In early May, Louverture accepted Leclerc's offer of an honorable surrender; he gave up his command and withdrew to his country estate. But Leclerc, following Napoleon's directive to eliminate the island's Black leadership, had him arrested in June and deported to France.[4]

Severe repression followed the exile of Louverture. The Bunels, whose allegiance to the rebels was a matter of public notoriety, felt the hand of chastisement almost immediately: Joseph, perhaps with Marie, was arrested in the weeks after the French took possession of what remained of Le Cap. Joseph was sent by ship to France, to the eastern city of Besançon. (Louverture was imprisoned in France at the Fort de Joux, not far from Besançon, under much more severe conditions.) Marie was held in the notoriously insalubrious jail of Le Cap. The government sequestered all of the couple's property. By the spring, Marie Bunel was reduced to asking for loans of small sums of money to keep body and soul together. The months after were punctuated by arrests and assassinations of Black officers, inciting fear and hatred toward the French army. In October, after Leclerc died of yellow fever, command of the French forces passed to Donatien-Marie-Joseph de Rochambeau, the son of a celebrated French general of the American revolutionary war. The younger Rochambeau prosecuted the war with great cruelty, ordering mass slaughters of Black prisoners, including women and children.[5]

Marie Bunel managed to secure her release from jail in the midst of this especially brutal phase of repression. How exactly she accomplished this feat is not entirely clear. It may be that her strong connections with prominent members of white society in Le Cap swayed French officers in her favor. When she petitioned Rochambeau for her release, she included the signatures of nearly thirty well-known residents of Le Cap, including lawyers and notaries. But her actions during the invasion itself may have played a role. In her petition, she was at pains to note that she had "devoted her being and her means to helping and serving *all* of those who had . . . suffered" in the war. The suggestion was that she had been helping white residents as much or more than Black folk. This evidence of her friendship to white Dominguans, if that is indeed what it was, might have convinced Rochambeau that she could be set free.[6]

Although Marie Bunel was released from jail in late 1802, she was not set at liberty. Shortly after she got out of prison, a mysterious visitor came to her house and advised her to "leave this country as soon as possible." Hearing of the situation, a friend wrote back: "I shudder" to hear of "your woes." We do not know who this mystery visitor was. But the best guess is that he was a representative of either the expeditionary force or of locals allied with the French occupiers. He seems to have come carrying a threat: white

Dominguans and their allies were prepared to deal with the loyalists of the Louverturian regime even if, like Marie Bunel, they had been formally cleared of any charges.[7]

Even with vigilantes roaming her home city, Marie Bunel's decision to leave Saint-Domingue could not have been an easy one. She had probably never left the island before setting foot on the ship in 1802. There would have been fear of the voyage: travel by ship in the long eighteenth century, especially in wartime, was risky. British Navy ships and hungry privateers intercepted many of the vessels that left the island. Bunel probably had politics on her mind as well. How must it have appeared to others when someone like her left Saint-Domingue at a moment of crisis? One can imagine that leaving, even under duress, might seem to represent an abandonment of the cause. For someone who was personally close to the revolutionary leadership, whose husband had held positions of responsibility under the new regime, it might tar her as a turncoat.[8]

But leave she did. As was the case with many of those who fled Saint-Domingue in the 1790s and after, her route upon leaving the island is hard to retrace with precision. She took passage from Le Cap with one Captain Tremel, a Philadelphian. Tremel sailed the North America–West Indies routes frequently: we catch glimpses of him at Le Cap in 1800, Havana in 1802, and Saint Thomas in 1803. There are hints that the voyage that carried Marie to the United States was out of the ordinary. Tremel later ended up in litigation with the Bunels. In one of the documents related to the case, a witness attested that the Bunels had enticed Tremel to come to Le Cap with an empty hold on the promise of being sent back with a full cargo. They then failed to give him a return cargo, causing significant losses. A plausible explanation for this otherwise peculiar behavior is that the Bunels needed a safe means of escape for Marie. They used their commercial connections and reputation to get Tremel to come to Le Cap, knowing that they could rely on him to take Marie safely away from the island.[9]

Her route to the United States was probably not direct. A fragmentary document, dated "Kingston Jamaica 1802," suggests that she may have stopped there on her way. It is possible that she, like many other refugees, also stopped at Havana. She arrived in the United States around March 1803—plenty of time for a month or more stopover in Cuba. As was the case with many of the Dominguan refugees, she settled in Philadelphia, which offered close commercial links to the French Caribbean and a generally cosmopolitan air—at least insofar as such cosmopolitanism existed in the United States.[10]

During the twelve months after Marie Bunel departed from Saint-Domingue, the situation in the colony experienced another abrupt shift of course. Already by the end of 1802, when she departed, Black troops and citizens across the colony had risen in revolt against the French. These included both Christophe and Dessalines, another formerly enslaved commander who had risen to prominence during the 1790s. By early 1803, Dessalines had consolidated almost all of the rebel forces under his command. Over the course of the spring and summer of 1803, the armies under his command grew and won repeated victories against the French expeditionary force. The early Haitian historian Thomas Madiou asserted that French troops were so weakened by disease and casualties that even their occasional successes on the battlefield only made the situation of the army worse. The end of a brief peace treaty between France and Great Britain in May put further pressure on the French forces, with British cruisers starting again to harass and attack the expeditionary force and French shipping.[11]

By the fall of 1803, the expeditionary force had been reduced to a rump that controlled only a handful of ports around the island. Dessalines and other commanders took them back one by one. In October, Dessalines reclaimed Port-au-Prince, in the colony's narrow geographic middle; a few days later, a separate army recaptured Les Cayes in the south. Dessalines at last turned to Le Cap, Marie Bunel's home, the final redoubt of French forces in Saint-Domingue. The campaign proved brief. The insurgent troops overran the fortresses surrounding the town on November 17 and 18 and took control of the heights overlooking the city. On the nineteenth, Rochambeau sent his envoy to negotiate terms of surrender; most of the French troops departed the next day. Ten days later, the insurgent troops led by Dessalines occupied Le Cap.[12]

The same day that the insurgents entered Le Cap, November 29, Dessalines and two other generals, Christophe and Augustin Clerveaux, issued a "proclamation of independence." The proclamation, which may have been written by Dessalines himself, circulated to the United States and would certainly have been seen by Marie Bunel. A little more than a month later, Dessalines issued a more elaborate *Acte d'indépendance* (declaration of independence). The declaration of January 1, clearly intended as a document in international law, proclaimed the "State of Haiti." It established the new state's oppositional posture toward France and its commitment to the "Native Citizens" of the island. A separate, simultaneous declaration named Dessalines governor-general of the new country. Nine months later, on October 8, 1804, Dessalines crowned himself emperor.[13]

As the new state was coming into being on Saint-Domingue, Marie Bunel was moving quickly to reestablish herself in Philadelphia. The money funding this new life was itself wrapped up with Haiti and the revolution. She very likely drew on a sizeable sum of money in her name—nearly four thousand dollars—that she had directed to the United States from her commercial activities in Saint-Domingue. In 1801 or 1802, Marie had dispatched to the

United States an agent, the Le Cap lawyer Gellibert, to collect the money owed to her. He succeeded in securing the payment of several thousand dollars. But when the French invasion occurred in 1802, the consulate claimed the money, arguing that it belonged to the colonial government and should remain at the disposal of the expeditionary army. Shortly after she arrived in Philadelphia, Bunel sought to have the money released to her. Whether it happened immediately or later, it seems likely that she managed to get control of it.[14]

By 1804, Bunel was well established in Philadelphia, with a house in the city on Lombard Street and a country "farm" in Bucks County. The house was amply if not very luxuriously furnished, with a full array of furniture and cookware. Already an expert at conveying power through dress, Bunel rebuilt her wardrobe in the United States: her surviving receipts show that she purchased fine clothing and materials, including yards of tulle, shoes, cloak pins, and much else. Bunel does not seem to have made much of an impression among the fashionable ladies of Philadelphia.[15] But she certainly understood the power of respectability to help her blend in and shield herself from the dangers that stalked people of African descent.

Just as important for someone aiming to establish herself as a respectable citizen, Bunel became an employer. She may have favored Black employees. By 1807–1808, a few years after she had arrived in the United States, she had several African Americans working for her. In 1807, her property manager hired a young "Black man from Mr Jacob Ashton my neighbor" to "take care of the place." He contracted for a wage of eight dollars per month. Around a year later, Bunel paid a bit over a dollar to Jonathan Scholfield for the "use of John Richardson"—probably an apprentice or bondsman in his household.[16] This seeming preference for Black workers could have been a matter of convenience. Or it might have represented a form of solidarity. Then again, it could also have been driven by the calculation that she, as a woman of color, might find herself more easily wrong-footed or disrespected by white employees.

As she got her affairs in order in Philadelphia, Marie Bunel kept an eye on her standing back in Saint-Domingue. The news that reached her during her first year or two in the United States cannot have been encouraging. In September 1804, Joseph Bunel's nephew, the well-educated Louis-Ambrose Grandjean, wrote to her from Le Cap. Grandjean had kept his residence in Saint-Domingue and had been acting in part as his aunt's go-between. He told her about an audience that he had heard someone had had with Dessalines, in which the subject of Marie Bunel had come up. The emperor had expressed the "friendship, attachment, [and] esteem that he has" for her, as well as his "ardent desire" to see her back in Saint-Domingue. But he added that it would be the "height of his desires" if he were to "see [her] make common cause with the Haitians." Dessalines's words hint that the governor-general found Marie Bunel's loyalty to Haiti wanting in some fashion. Perhaps Dessalines doubted how committed a well-off former enslaver like Marie Bunel could be to the "common cause" of ordinary Haitians. Or maybe, stressing *Haitians*, Dessalines wanted more evidence of her support for the independent nation. Not without some justification, he and his close allies harbored suspicions about the loyalties of anyone who had relations with the French.[17]

Whatever precisely it was that made Dessalines skeptical about Marie, so long as he ruled in Haiti the Bunels were relegated to the margins of the political universe. Marie Bunel's correspondence with Haiti during the years 1804 and 1805 was primarily of a purely personal nature: letters, for instance, from the widow of a merchant, Tardieu, and another friend in Le Cap, both rejoicing in her safe arrival in the United States and sending greetings to their relatives and friends. Nothing of a political or public nature. Joseph Bunel did return to Haiti at least once, in late 1804. He was relieved to find that he was received with some degree of friendliness by Madame Dessalines. Evidently a warm welcome from Dessalines and his court was not a given at this point.[18] But neither Bunel, as far as we know, was asked to carry out commissions for Dessalines directly.

So Marie Bunel, resident of Philadelphia and Bucks County, set to work in 1804 to erase the label of refugee or émigré that had attached itself to her and her husband. From a distance, she sought to refashion herself into a member of the Haitian elite. She used her command over property in Haiti and the United States to display and affirm her attachment to Haiti and its government. She turned to the practices of charity and gift giving, long an integral part of life among the free colored elite of Saint-Domingue, to stake her place. She used her transnational networks of friends and business partners to make this image of herself visible, even tangible, to those whom she had left behind in Haiti.

Property ownership was a powerful mechanism for staking a claim to place and position in the eighteenth-century world. Marie Bunel made it a priority to hold on to her home in Le Cap and her plantations in the Haitian countryside even after she herself had left Saint-Domingue. There were obvious economic reasons to retain them: both were valuable pieces of property that could produce income. But they were also important markers of rootedness and belonging. Around the Atlantic, including in the United States and France, owning property was a common criterion for exercising political rights. In a post-slavery society, property ownership could be even more crucial as a marker of one's freedom and respectability.[19]

The house that Marie Bunel owned in Petit Guinée must have seemed very empty after she left Le Cap in 1802. Built for a family with servants and enslaved people in attendance, the house had just three people living in it now: Hélène Mouton, Orphise Bunel, and Edouard Coursault. Two women from one family and an unrelated man living together; this was not a common arrangement. They seem to have been there taking care of the house, perhaps keeping looters and squatters at bay. Once it was clear that the house was secure, Marie moved again to make it productive property. In 1804, Grandjean wrote to Joseph indicating that he was expending considerable effort to "rent" the house "in its entirety." In the meantime, however, the Bunels had evidently agreed that it could be used gratis by members of the family. Keeping the house occupied was important. Since Hélène Mouton no longer wanted to "occupy" the house, Grandjean allowed "cousin Marotte" to stay there.[20]

The Bunels also worked to retain control over their plantations and to turn them back into sources of income. Marie Bunel seems to have owned two plantations in her own right—a large one and a small one. Though we have only scant details, the Bunels had most likely held considerable numbers of enslaved people in bondage during the old regime.[21] By the early nineteenth century, the cultivators had been freed but the land remained in the Bunels' possession. Both plantations had been sequestered by the French expeditionary force. Though the land was not immediately returned to them when Dessalines took power, the Bunels seem to have regained control of it by 1804.

Putting the plantations back into a productive state was a more difficult task for the Bunels and their agents. Across Haiti, agricultural laborers were in short supply. Revolt and warfare had drawn many freedmen away from plantations and into the armed forces. Others had been killed. Yet others simply wanted to cultivate their own land. The shortages are reflected in the figures for exports from the plantation economy, which dropped precipitously during the 1790s and were slow to recover even in the face of strenuous efforts by early Haitian leaders to restart the plantation economy. Marie Bunel's plantations were no exception. The larger one had been leased to another planter, J. B. Papazel. This presumably ensured a stream of income for Bunel but limited the gains she was likely to realize. The smaller one, however, had nobody remaining to farm it, except for "old Scipio," presumably a freedman.[22]

Giving away her property, like holding fast to it, provided another way for Marie Bunel to rebuild hierarchical connections with the Haitian world she had left. Charity was one important avenue. Her papers include a large collection of small slips, roughly two by three inches in size, marked "Bon pour quatre pains d'un escalin. Femme Bunel." These were vouchers for bread, which the bearer could redeem for four loaves worth an escalin (a small coin) each. The system likely worked through the circulation of the vouchers like commercial debt slips: Bunel handed out the vouchers, the poor gave them to the bakers in exchange for bread, and the bakers then exchanged them with Bunel for payment. The purpose of this charitable giving was not merely to provide relief to those in distress. It bound the recipients to her by obligation and necessity. And giving charity that was visible in public, as these bread vouchers were, helped fashion one as a member of the elite.[23]

Bunel had a consistent practice of charity that spanned multiple decades. She was already widely known as a "protector of the poor" in Le Cap in the 1790s, and she continued to distribute bread in Philadelphia after 1802. She does not seem to have changed her practice much when she moved from Saint-Domingue to the United States. It is likely that the recipients of her charity, in both cities, were primarily if not exclusively the enslaved and poor free people of color. She continued to write her vouchers in French, using a common French unit (the escalin). It is even possible that she brought over with her from Saint-Domingue some of the physical vouchers she used in Philadelphia. Several of them are written on paper fabricated by a family of French papermakers, the

Pignion, whose products would not have been readily available in the United States after 1800.[24]

Bunel's giving took on a new meaning in Philadelphia. The fact that all the surviving vouchers are written in French, including those that were probably created in the United States, strongly suggests that they were intended for the use of the French-speaking community. Philadelphia had one of the largest free Black populations in the United States, so Bunel would have been deliberately channeling her charity into the Dominguan diaspora. It may be that this was simply the community to which she felt most attached. But it is equally if not more plausible that she knew she could count on the circuits of information and commerce to bring news of her beneficence toward Dominguan exiles back to Haiti. She could fashion herself, in this way, into a protectress not just of the poor but of the Haitian poor.[25]

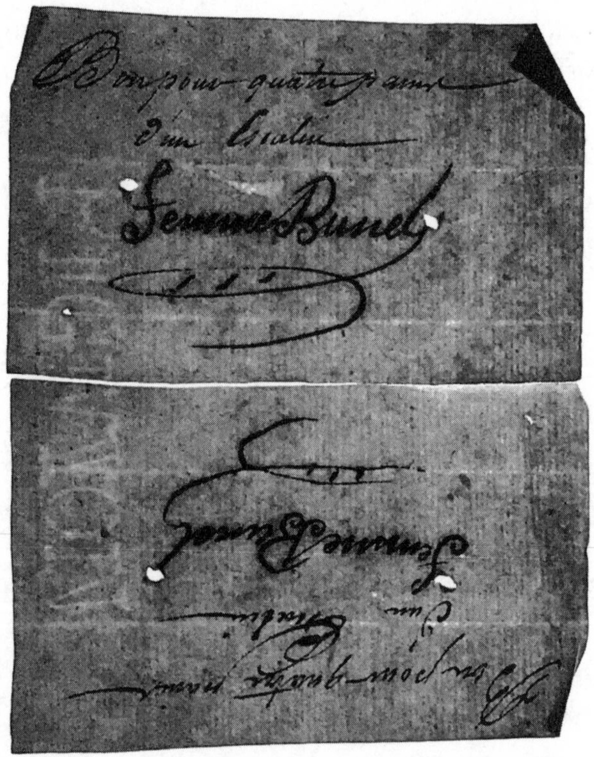
Femme Bunel

Charity vouchers on French-made paper used by Marie Bunel in Philadelphia, early nineteenth century. Courtesy of Historical Society of Pennsylvania.

Gift exchanges with other members of the Haitian elite helped Bunel clarify her place within the revolutionary state's new hierarchy. Gift giving was common in eighteenth-century merchant circles as a way to grease the wheels of commerce. Marie Bunel's gifts were a bit different. She liked to send and receive luxury or fashion items that could help her present herself as a gentlewoman. In 1810, her niece Orphise, whom she had helped to educate, sent her aunt a "*redicule*" (a reticule or small purse), among other items, asking her to accept it as a "costly gift." A few years earlier, in 1807, Bunel had accidentally sent a box of sweetmeats to the wrong recipient, a Philadelphia merchant by the name of Bond. When she discovered the "error," Bunel apologized profusely—and sent another gift to Bond in its stead.[26]

Marie Bunel's gift giving reached all the way to the revolutionary leadership in Haiti. An 1810 letter to Bunel from Marie-Louise Christophe (née Coidavid), the wife of the now president of Haiti, paints the picture of a lively economy of exchange between the two women. Madame Christophe began her letter by complaining gently that she had not received the goods that Bunel had promised to send her from Philadelphia. (She entrusted Bunel with her orders for intimate apparel—stockings—asking for ones that were "very large.") Madame Christophe described the gifts that she was sending back with the captain of a ship: pots of mango jam and jellies, guava and lemon jams, and other delicacies. "Please accept these," she wrote, using the polite language of gift making rather than the imperious language that one might have expected of the wife of a paramount military and political leader.[27]

Many if not most of Marie Bunel's gift exchanges, like that with Madame Christophe, took place within the circles of free women of color. In old-regime Saint-Domingue, such exchanges could have been a way to create bonds of community and trust to help them survive in the hostile environment of a slave society. With the abolition of slavery and the exodus of white people from Haiti, women of color who had been free before the revolution, like Marie Bunel, could move near the top of the local status hierarchy. Their gift exchanges took on a new meaning. What had served before as a way to forge necessary bonds among members of a subaltern community became a means to solidify a new elite. An elite of color, to be sure, but one no less sure of its privileges and bent on dominating those lower down the social ladder.

Marie Bunel's tireless efforts to make a place for herself in Haiti began to bear fruit once Henry Christophe took power, first as commander of the northern provinces under Dessalines and then, after Dessalines's 1806 assassination, as head of state himself. Since Louverture's arrest and deportation, Christophe had been the Bunels' closest ally. This may be because Christophe, who had commanded Le Cap under Louverture, was already quite familiar with the Bunels and trusted them. As early as 1804, shortly after Joseph Bunel was released from French prison, Christophe had begun to turn to him again as a supplier. In November of that year, the Haitian general asked Bunel to buy a variety of goods for the army, including a detailed list of items for officers' uniforms. He concluded his letter by calling Bunel "Mon Cher Diplomatique"—roughly, "my dear diplomat"—suggesting an ongoing sense of his role as an intermediary between Haiti and the wider world.[28]

Once Christophe took power, matters took a distinct turn for the better for the Bunels. Their fate was indeed closely entwined with Christophe's during the first decade of the nineteenth century. Following the assassination of Dessalines, Christophe and Alexandre Pétion, leader of the armies in the south of Haiti, became the main rivals for the mantle of overall leader of the new state. Pétion tried to sideline Christophe, offering him a titular position as head of state while retaining most of the power in his own hands. He then presented a new constitution that he had rigged up. Christophe rejected the empty offer and the constitution and broke decisively with Pétion. Not long after, on February 17, 1807, he promulgated his own constitution. Barely two weeks earlier, clearly following the news from the Caribbean closely, Joseph Bunel had been preparing himself to return to Haiti: he wrote his will, which directed that all of his property should go to his wife. It seems safe to assume that he either expected to be called back soon or had in fact been recalled by Christophe. By that summer, he was back in Haiti, where he would remain in Christophe's good graces until 1812.[29]

Though Joseph Bunel had served along with Christophe in Le Cap during the later 1790s, it was Marie Bunel who seems to have established the real bond with him. When Joseph Bunel finally returned in 1807, Christophe's intendant of finances, Jacques Simon, wrote to Marie Bunel. Simon called Joseph an "old friend and acquaintance" and expressed admiration for his "principles and his constant love of liberty." He went out of his way to assure her that he would do "everything possible to be useful and agreeable to Monsieur your husband." The strong impression that the letter leaves is that it was important to Christophe and his government to assure Marie Bunel that her husband was being well treated; she, not he, was the principal figure.[30]

Christophe had good reason, on his side, for wanting to rebuild relations with the Bunels. The regime that Christophe created starting in late 1806 was one based, even more than the earlier Louverturian system, on centralized and autocratic power. As early as 1805, when he was again in charge of Le Cap, Christophe kept those within his jurisdiction under the closest surveillance. He directed the movements and labor of individual artisans for the army, ordered the arrest and release of prisoners by name, and commanded his officers to come before him personally to explain themselves when they failed to fulfill his orders. He extended and expanded the system of semi-forced agricultural labor. By 1811, he had caused an elaborate militarized bureaucracy to be created, which supervised farmers and ensured that they produced what the state commanded. He even went as far as to return freedmen to the plantations on which they had been enslaved before emancipation.[31]

Christophe's dictatorial powers depended on support from the outside—just the sort of assistance the Bunels were able to provide. One element that was essential to securing Christophe's new domain was foreign trade. Given that Haiti did not reliably produce its own food and that its wealth came from the export of commodities, anyone who hoped to dominate the island had to gain access to foreign markets. For Christophe, the Bunels were one such conduit. Joseph Bunel spent much of 1808 in Le Cap managing the couple's trade. In letters to Marie, he outlined the goods that would sell best in Le Cap. Yet this mission of personal gain always dovetailed with a public mission. In a letter in early November, he reported on the capture of a ship that had carried a large cargo of his, which had also included some of Christophe's goods. In another letter, he explained that he could not make it to the court of Christophe and his "Dame" because he had to be "in his store morning and night," receiving "very large quantities of foodstuffs for the inhabitants."[32]

The other necessity for Christophe's government was arms and armaments. On this count, too, the Bunels proved to be vital players. In 1809 and 1810, the Bunels were working to purchase and outfit a warship in the United States intended for Christophe's use. Christophe at this moment was under considerable military pressure from Pétion, whose superior naval forces threatened to blockade the north. To counter this eventuality, Christophe ordered the Bunels to equip a twenty-eight-gun corvette for him in Baltimore. The American newspapers, which got wind of it via rumor networks stretching from the Caribbean to North America, viewed this as male work and attributed it to Joseph Bunel. But there is strong evidence that both Bunels were involved. Robert Cooke, a ship's captain based in Baltimore, sent several updates on the progress of a ship under construction to Marie Bunel during the summer of 1810. In one of them, he indicated that she had sent him a letter from Joseph Bunel under cover of her letter. This letter, which included some instructions from Christophe, at least passed through Marie's hands—if she did not in fact execute the instructions herself.[33]

It must have been strange for Marie Bunel, the elegantly dressed leader among Le Cap's women of taste, to be in the middle of an international arms deal in 1810. Yet it was no accident that she found herself there. The mutually beneficial military and commercial alliance that blossomed between the Bunels and Christophe after 1806 grew precisely out of Marie Bunel's mastery of eighteenth-century cultures and her skill in adapting them to the revolution's purposes. Her deftness in refashioning herself into a member of the Haitian elite in good standing after 1802—even as she lived thousands of miles away from the island—was part of what made it possible for trade and arms to flow to Christophe after he took control of Haiti. And Christophe, for his part, had begun with their help to fashion the stable albeit illiberal nation to which both Joseph and Marie would eventually return.[34]

# 14
# A CULTURAL TRANSFORMATION

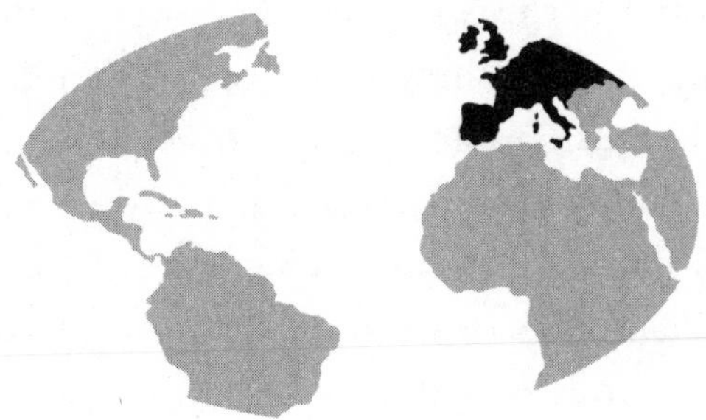

In 1803, the year that Marie Bunel settled into life in Philadelphia, Ludwig van Beethoven completed his Third Symphony in Vienna. The *Eroica*, as he came to call it, may have originally been intended to honor Napoleon Bonaparte. It aimed to be every bit as transformative as its erstwhile namesake. From the pair of slashing chords that open the first movement's portrait of a hero to the propulsive, suspenseful, dance-like themes of the symphony's ending, Beethoven wrote the *Eroica* as the opening salvo of a "revolution in music."[1]

In the second movement, Beethoven seems to both reflect the era's crises and transmute them into a new order. The movement begins solemn and steady—it is a *marcia funebre*, a funeral march—dominated by gentle violins. A few minutes into the movement, a series of crescendos, drawing on the full forces of the orchestra surmounted by trumpets and drums, come in like waves. This drama appears to resolve, and the movement resumes the initial theme. Instead of continuing with the opening melody, however, the violins mount gradually—and then a sudden change takes us into a new realm. Over a percussive beat of staccato notes on the cellos, the violins spiral upward. The violins then take the beat and the cellos rise up. The string groups swap back and forth, going higher and higher, until in a moment of unbearable tension they seem to have reached the extent of their powers. But then the winds come in, rising up in a similar fashion. For another astonishing half minute, the tension somehow continues to build.[2]

Then, as suddenly as it began, it is over. Six notes on the strings—long, short, short, short, long, long—bring us back down from the mountain. The original theme, transformed, briefly reasserts itself, the melodic violins playing sotto voce.

What makes this passage so remarkable is how Beethoven manages to turn this abruptly found mountain of sound, emerging from the flat plains of the second movement, into what seems like a fact of nature. The listener feels, against all evidence, that there has been an almost inevitable logic to both the mountain's appearance and its disappearance. The conductor and music scholar Wilhelm Furtwängler saw this as the heart of Beethoven's genius: his ability to bring together "subjects of entirely different individual characteristics" into a "new and all-embracing unity." The successful synthesis of two or more incommensurate things was Beethoven's special gift. He could, as another critic put it, unite fragments into a coherent-seeming whole.[3]

The fusion of disparate parts was indeed a fact of Beethoven's daily reality. Ever since he had settled in Vienna in 1792, he had worked as a freelancer for customers. Already very well known by 1803, he still supported himself with a hodgepodge of musical jobs.

Just during the months in which he was composing the *Eroica*, he had accepted a contract to write an opera with a local theater, performed his earlier symphonies for a paying audience, composed a sonata (the *Kreutzer*) for publication, and was engaged in fighting off an unauthorized edition of his keyboard works.[4]

Beethoven's achievement in the *Eroica* was not merely a mark of his individual genius. It was a reflection of a wider cultural moment. The longer, slower, and deeper generational reverberations of the revolutionary era were beginning to be felt in Europe just as they were on the other side of the Atlantic. The mid-eighteenth-century certainties, the confidence that the social and cultural orders were stable, had been deeply shaken by the events of the previous quarter century. For some, this fragmentation was a catastrophe from which they would never recover. But for others, among them Beethoven, it was the beginning of a rebirth, which required a reorganization of expectations and ways of being in the world. In the second movement of the *Eroica*, as he fused incommensurate parts, Beethoven showed that a start had been made on this process of giving the new dispositions a coherence and rationality all their own.

DURING THE EARLY NINETEENTH CENTURY, THE GREAT URBAN centers of Europe—Paris and London especially—entered a phase of rapid growth and equally speedy transformation. Paris went from having about five hundred thousand people in 1800 to nearly a million by the middle of the 1840s. London, which had already almost doubled in size between 1750 and 1800, grew again by almost half between 1800 and 1821. This was the leading edge of a mounting demographic wave that would see the population of Europe and some of its colonies grow threefold during the nineteenth century.[5]

As cities expanded, a double movement took form, combining sharper physical separation with greater cultural integration. In most cities before the early nineteenth century, only the rich had lived truly apart. Full physical separation did not exist between the indigent, the working poor, and the middling classes. In eighteenth-century Paris, for instance, class separation was vertical rather than horizontal. The century saw the construction of a vast number of multifamily dwellings in the French capital. These new buildings had a vertically oriented class structure: The lower floors, which had high ceilings and were relatively cooler in the summer heat, were occupied by the well-to-do. The upper stories, divided into smaller apartments, were rented to the working classes. The very top floor—too hot in summer and icy in winter—went for low rates to the poorest residents.[6]

The early nineteenth century saw the full flourishing of separate working-class and impoverished neighborhoods. In Paris, the poor congregated in the center of the city in the early nineteenth century, in the arrondissements that surrounded the Île de la Cité, the original center of the city, on both banks of the Seine. In London, already jam-packed after a century of explosive growth, the first decade of the nineteenth century brought a slight thinning out of the population in the center of the city, driven initially by the construction of docks and warehouses and eventually (after the 1830s) the expansion of railroads. The thinning corresponded to a growing division between the neighborhoods of the rich and the poor.[7]

The iconic working-class neighborhood in London was Wapping, which took shape during a major expansion of the dockyards. Between 1802, when construction began, and 1805, when the process was completed, the London Dock Company building the docks in Wapping demolished some thirteen hundred houses. As Gareth Stedman Jones has shown, the individuals and families who were displaced from these destroyed homes did not go far. Unable to move away from their places of employment or (for pieceworkers and laborers) the worksites where they could look for casual work, they were forced to settle into ever more crowded apartments and houses in adjacent areas.[8]

For members of the gentry, the concentrations of poverty that resulted from the dock project and similar efforts elsewhere in the Atlantic world were a blight. In *Afloat and Ashore*, American author James Fenimore Cooper's thinly veiled autobiographical account of his youthful career as a sailor, Cooper described Wapping in dark terms. Its "scenes of atrocity," he declared, were worse than anything he had seen elsewhere—with the possible exception of the wealthiest London districts. For it was still true that the "long train of low vice," he wryly observed, was "neither so long nor so broad as that which is chained to the chariot-wheels of the great." Charles Dickens, visiting the Five Points of New York in 1841, which played a roughly equivalent role in that city, declared it the home of "all that is loathsome, drooping, and decayed."[9]

Yet in Wapping, as in many other areas of the Atlantic world in this period, concentrations of the poor contributed to the formation of a new kind of lower-class sociability. In the crowded working-class neighborhoods, distinctively lower-class forms of leisure proliferated. Bars and clubs, workingmen's associations, and the rougher amusements of cockfights and gambling all catered to working-class men who could no longer use workplaces, homes, or the streets for their socializing.[10]

City dwellers were increasingly interested in the spectacle provided by these new, lower-class, and distinctively seedy bits of the city. A series of infamous murders that took place in and around Wapping in 1811—dubbed the "Ratcliff Highway murders," after the street off of which they occurred—were among the first of the grisly *fait divers* of the nineteenth century to mesmerize the public. The murders were gruesome and brutal, but there was no obvious ideology or motive behind them. In part because they seemed to be so senseless, so utterly without reason, they received wall-to-wall coverage in the English press. The area in which the murders took place became a kind of pilgrimage site for locals and tourists alike.[11]

Sixteen years after the murders were committed, the English critic Thomas De Quincey made them the center of a celebrated essay, "On Murder Considered as One of the Fine Arts." Writing in the form of a club oration, De Quincey claimed to be working out criteria by which murders ought to be judged by connoisseurs as a form of performance art. The pseudo-lecture mocked the hyper-aestheticized attitudes of late Georgian gentlemen and made a sidelong critique of the sensationalism of the press. But De Quincey's essay hit on something deeper about the early nineteenth-century city. When gentlemen shared a cultural sphere with lower-class folk, they no longer stood apart from the messier bits of urban life. "In these murders of the amphitheatre," wrote De Quincey, the person who "sits and looks on" shared in the guilt of the crime. Gentlemen were no longer passive observers of poverty and mayhem in the growing city; they were implicated in it.[12]

Growing residential segregation paradoxically drove greater mobility within the city, which in turn produced more contact of a certain kind among classes in urban public spaces. Eighteenth-century people had seen the city as a stage, with dramas that played out in many different spaces, from the private home to the public square. Nineteenth-century observers in Paris saw the city differently: as an organism animated by its many parts. This change of focus can be attributed in good part to the growth of residential segregation around 1800. Individuals now needed to move substantial distances through the city in order to get to and from work, creating more and more of a sense that the core of urban life was not place but circulation.[13]

A rethinking of the nature of what a city was as a political and cultural organism accompanied this change in social practice. Émile Zola's famous metaphor, which called the wholesale market at Les Halles the "belly of Paris," is a late indication of this shift.

In this new vision, the central functional process of the city, the thing that made it a city, was the movement of the population. Not coincidentally, it was during this early nineteenth-century period that urban engineers and city planners refocused their attention on how to move people and things smoothly through the city. Circulation became not just a metaphor but a real and practical obsession of those whose job it was to manage the movement of the cities.[14]

The figure of the flaneur, who first appeared in literary works beginning in 1806, was a manifestation and epitome of this new vision of the city. The flaneur was an urban spectator, a person who was imagined as wandering the city and observing its interconnections and organic life. His particular domain was the streets—the public arteries that now, in the wake of the disruptions of the previous decades, had become a space that was again shared by elites and non-elites. As he circulated through the streets, he took cognizance not of spaces but of the flows of people, objects, and ideas. The flaneur was particularly fascinated by the mixed society that he would observe: the original flaneur, an invented "M. Bonhomme," spent much of the day watching the "lower ranks of society."[15]

There were antecedents of the flaneur. The early eighteenth-century writings of Joseph Addison and Richard Steele in the *Spectator* foreshadowed some of its elements. Others were hinted at by the writings of Louis-Sébastien Mercier or the popular prints of urban workers known as the *cris de Paris*.[16] But the flaneur was the product of the particularly nineteenth-century vision of the city that emerged from the first phase of the revolutionary era. The idea of watching the parts of the city work together would have been nonsensical to the eighteenth-century observer; to him or her, those pieces were already in motion together, and that motion was always visible to the city dweller.

Étienne de Jouy, the man most responsible for creating the nineteenth-century figure of the flaneur, gave him an explicitly generational cast. Jouy's series of newspaper essays under the pseudonym "the Hermit of the Chaussée d'Antin," first published between 1812 and 1814, set out the traits of the nineteenth-century flaneur: his peripatetic interest in the city, his bourgeois sensibility, his attraction to the exoticism of the everyday. Jouy, born in 1764, was squarely a member of the second revolutionary generation; he had even fought in the French revolutionary army. He made his creation, the Hermit, part of the previous generation: in the first essay, published in 1811, the Hermit describes himself as having been born in 1741. Imagining his protagonist as a man of the eighteenth century helped Jouy capture more dramatically the transformation of the revolutionary decades. "I could believe I have lived more than two centuries," the Hermit exaggerates, "when I think about the changes that have occurred around me over the past forty years."[17]

Seventy years old or not, however, Jouy's Hermit was peripatetic almost beyond belief, a whirlwind of motion circulating through the city. He began his day, most days, at Les Halles—the wholesale food markets—where he claimed to know more about the business than the workers themselves. From there he made his way along the river to the Palais Royal, where he ate lunch. He carried on to cafés, reading clubs, visits to friends and lovers, and promenades in the park. The day would end, "every evening," with a frenetic tour of the theaters. "It is not unusual to find me during the same evening," he wrote, "at the Opera, the Feydeau Theatre, and the Comedie Française."[18] As he moved through the city, he reconciled and integrated its disparate fragments, from the rough work of the market to the glissandos of the imperial opera, into a single story.

Mobile crowds became increasingly central to the cultural and political life of the city. Crowds had hardly been absent from the eighteenth-century city. Royal entries and executions had long collected large crowds. Crowd actions had also played a crucial role at junctures during the French Revolution and other major political upheavals of the age of revolution's first phase. The most famous of these, undoubtedly, were the taking of the Bastille in July 1789 and the march on Versailles in early October 1789. Similar actions had taken place in London in the 1780s (the Gordon Riots) and in New York and Boston during the 1770s, but they had been exceptional and in most cases were rapidly contained. The mobile crowds of 1789 gave way in short order to the stage-focused, static crowds of the Fête de la Fédération and its successors. In the United States, the actions of the crowds were even more quickly tamed. What came instead were orderly parades—spectatorial in their orientation—and the quasi-royal entries of George Washington in the 1790s.[19]

The years after 1800 were when a mass of moving people became the hallmark of urban life—and a key element of political activism. In London, the architect John Nash designed Regent's Park in the early 1810s with the aim of channeling and guiding the "stream" of crowds through the city. The second decade of the nineteenth century saw growing numbers of mass demonstrations and marches in the United States—a departure from the old model of orderly, spectatorial parades. The iconic *Liberty Leading the People*, painted in 1830 by Eugène Delacroix, son of a member of the National Convention, is an emblematic summation of this transition. Its image of bodies blending into an indistinct mass suggests the power of the mobile populace, poised to overrun its enemies.[20]

WITHIN THESE TRANSFORMED CITIES—RESHAPED BY A GENERATION of war, social disruption, and profound political upheaval—a distinct second-generation revolutionary culture took place. It was visible in every area of life: in the composition of the crowds that jammed the streets, in the clothes that men and women wore as they circulated around the city, even in the graves to which they eventually made their way after the end of their lives.

The crowds that the early nineteenth-century flaneur watched and that played a growing role in the European city's life had a greater social diversity than the crowds of previous decades. Indeed, the mobile crowds were a kind of symphony of their own, uniting the diverse classes and communities of the growing European metropolis.

Eighteenth-century crowds tended to have a very specific class or social identity. Most of them were imagined as composed of the lower classes, even when they were somewhat more mixed. The Orangist crowds that resurrected the stadtholderate in the Netherlands in 1747 were figured as "popular" or lower class, though they actually included a fair number of more elite individuals. The 1789 march on Versailles was imagined as composed almost entirely of "fishwives"—though a considerable body of research has shown that it was far more heterogeneous.[21]

During the first years of the nineteenth century, the crowd changed its complexion, becoming less homogenous in image—and perhaps in fact as well. An important part of this change was the development of forms of early mass entertainment. Theaters and other spectacles, such as museums and galleries open to the public, as well as musical entertainments, had long been part of the urban landscape in Europe's cities. In the early nineteenth century, they grew dramatically in size and scope. The showman or "exhibitor" William Bullock opened his first "Museum" in London in 1809, which was visited by over eighty thousand spectators during its first months. In 1811, he constructed the Egyptian Hall, which instantly became one of the most visited sites in London. In Paris, the boulevards to the north of the old city center developed into formidable rivals to the Palais Royal as hubs for theatrical performances and shopping.[22]

All these entertainments depended on attracting large crowds, and they were, in the estimation of many contemporary observers, more diverse than those of the late eighteenth century. Étienne de Jouy, writing about the Palais Royal in the early nineteenth century, described its transformation. The "physiognomy of the inhabitants of the Palais Royal has changed," he wrote. The crowd was now a kind of "camera obscura where one sees everything that happens in the capital . . . all of the vices . . . all of the pleasures and all of the miseries of humanity." The Paris boulevards, too, attracted a mixed multitude. There was some difference among the main theaters, with those to the west more mixed and those toward the east hosting a more exclusively working-class clientele. But like Jouy's Hermit, many patrons were clearly ecumenical in their attendance.[23]

One may doubt whether these impressions of the early nineteenth-century crowd were truly accurate. Since nobody at the time conducted scientific studies of crowds, it is difficult to tell just how much class diversity there really was among the men, women, and children who constituted them. It is difficult to rule out the possibility that there was relatively little actual change in their composition, at least from the mid-eighteenth century onward. What is certain, however, is that even if their actual composition did not change radically, public perceptions of the mixed nature of some crowds underwent a major alteration. Social heterogeneity, regarded by eighteenth-century observers as a countercultural oddity and vaguely disreputable, had by the 1840s become the normal condition of urban crowds.[24]

Even as the early nineteenth-century crowd grew more mixed, a sartorial revolution meant that it presented a more homogenous face to the viewer than crowds of earlier eras. The early nineteenth century brought a rapid homogenization of clothing for both sexes. Jouy described it as nothing short of a "revolution." The first phase in the process was the disappearance of the famously elaborate fashions of the late eighteenth century. The passing of breeches and the adoption of trousers brought elite men's costumes into closer alignment with those of the middle and even working classes. Women's clothes, as well, became simpler and less clearly demarcated by class. The second phase, which began around 1800 but accelerated after 1810, was the development of what the French called the *habit noir*: the iconic dark-colored suit that became the uniform of the nineteenth-century man. The clothes of the wealthy were still better made, with higher-quality materials, but the distinctions became far more subtle than they had been in the eighteenth century.[25]

The increased homogenization of clothing, for both men and women, created—in the eyes of many observers—a simulacrum of equality among the members of the crowd. Jouy's imagined flaneur complained that the fashions of the era promoted an "equality in the manner of dressing oneself," which resulted in people "conflating all of the ranks and all of the professions." (He admitted that his dislike for this manner of dressing might be a generational quality: "A prejudice of my age.")[26] Where dress had once served as a clear and readily visible marker of differentiation among members of different professions and classes, clothing now became a marker of sameness.

Even the modest degree of homogeneity fostered by early nineteenth-century dress could be perceived by some as quite threatening. During the same years that Jouy's Hermit was fretting about changing fashions in Paris, the rabbi and Hasidic leader Menachem Mendel of Rimanov was worrying about the potentially homogenizing effects of these same fashions in the Polish lands. Unlike most Hasidic rebbes, Menachem Mendel had grown up in a relatively assimilated context—the Germany of the 1760s and 1770s. The Jewish enlightenment was already well underway, and growing numbers of Jews were moving away from traditional religious practice. An apocryphal story has it that the young Menachem Mendel himself attended a reforming school with the great Jewish enlightenment thinker Moses Mendelssohn.[27]

Menachem Mendel kept up with the latest fashions but only to ensure that his followers avoided them. In an early nineteenth-century sermon, he likened the situation in eastern Europe ("this exile," he called it) to the Israelites' exile in Egypt. In Egypt, too, there had been Jews who "put on foreign [i.e., non-Jewish] clothing." These Israelites had become so spiritually polluted by this practice that they were excluded from the Jewish people and "not redeemed" from Egypt when the Exodus occurred. A similar fate, he suggested, awaited Jews who did the same in the present day.[28]

The Rimanov rebbe could be quite specific about the styles of dress and comportment that his followers were supposed to avoid. In an 1812 letter that doubled as a decree in Jewish law, Menachem Mendel ordered his followers to avoid some of the very latest fashions. He was vehement in his denunciation of the new men's jackets among "the gentiles." He described the style—which had come into vogue after 1800 and is familiar to anyone who has seen a film based on a Jane Austen novel—as one in which "the left side is doubled over the right side and buttoned there." In the same letter, he called for Jews to stop promenading with parasols on the Sabbath, in imitation of a common early nineteenth-century pastime. The Rimanov rebbe's rejection of the latest styles was a form of Jewish particularism, born of a desire to remain distinct from the gentile world. That a Hasidic rebbe in east-central Europe was aware of the latest styles and needed to warn his followers of them, however, attests to the reach of the early nineteenth-century cultural revolution.[29]

The growing crowds and changing fashions that were leading toward superficial forms of equality, which so worried both Jouy's Hermit and Menachem Mendel of Rimanov, paradoxically had their most visible manifestation not on the streets but in cemeteries.

The traditional manner of burial in the Christian West had been interment in the parish graveyard. (This option was not available to nonconforming Christians and non-Christians, who had long made separate but similar arrangements for their dead.) These graveyards were attached to the churchyards, most were relatively small, and they were dispersed throughout the city. This age-old model began to break down during the late eighteenth century as urban growth accelerated. Newly built areas did not necessarily have churches immediately available for the burial of the dead. And the sheer scale of growth—with its inevitable outcome, the production of more and more dead bodies—threatened to overwhelm the churchyard system that had been adapted to populations that were largely stable over time.[30]

To deal with the growing problem of finding places to bury the dead, governments in western Europe created the rural or garden cemetery during the early nineteenth century. The first of these large-scale cemeteries to be created was Père Lachaise in Paris, whose construction Napoleon set into motion in 1804. The government commissioned Alexandre-Théodore Brongniart, one of the most eminent architects of his generation, to design the cemetery. He happened to be the father of one of Louis-Augustin Bosc's contemporaries and collaborators, also named Alexandre Brongniart. Once the Brongniart-designed Père Lachaise opened, it was followed in quick succession by a series of other large cemeteries constructed on the then outskirts of Paris: the cemeteries at Montmartre, Montparnasse, and Passy. The government handed down new rules for funerals, too, strictly regulating burial costs and processions.[31]

The new cemeteries were intended to house the remains of people from different social classes—all corners of society. The result was a kind of social mixing of the dead. Napoleon signaled this new disposition by having the remains of a French queen, Louise de Lorraine, reinterred in Père Lachaise. Other celebrated individuals followed in relatively short succession, including the medieval monastic couple Abelard and Héloïse, who were reburied in the cemetery in 1817. Under the old regime, such celebrated and sacrosanct figures would have been buried far from commoners, usually in their own dedicated tombs. Over the next decade, Père Lachaise became a magnet for famous corpses, with dozens of others buried there during the first decades of the nineteenth century. Yet the vast majority of those interred in the cemetery were quite ordinary: by 1816, just a decade after it had been opened, thousands of Parisians had already been buried there.[32]

Just as social mixture in urban crowds and the homogenizing effects of clothing elicited hostility, the social mixing of the dead in the new cemeteries called forth disapproval in some quarters. Of course, churchmen were none too happy about losing their monopoly on the care of the dead. French priests objected to the explicitly non-Catholic nature of the public cemeteries. Others objected more to the way in which the social mixing of the cemetery echoed and reinforced similar fluidity among the living. In one of his early pieces, which described a promenade through the various new cemeteries of the city, Jouy's Hermit made this a focus of his disapproval. Seeing "so many graves jumbled together without order" made him "wish for the old practice of private mausoleums," in which families would be buried together. He longed to bring back the old churchyard in which the "rich man would still have his palace, where the poor man would still have his shack."[33]

For all of Jouy's complaints, distinctions of rank were still quite visible among the individuals buried in the new cemeteries—as they were among the crowds and their clothes. The wealthy and the famous acquired the best plots and built elaborate monuments to themselves and their families. The middle classes opted for more modest headstones. Indeed distinctions of wealth were built into the early regulations for the cemeteries, which created a two-tiered price list for plots. Temporary concessions, suitable for a simple burial, were priced in the 1820s at a relatively affordable fifty francs for six years. Perpetual concessions, which might include a monument, cost 125 francs per meter, with a minimum size of two square meters for the monument.[34]

The crowds of visitors who came to the cemeteries mirrored the modest degree of mixing that was present among the permanent inhabitants. Naturally, if people of all classes were buried there together, more or less cheek by jowl, the mourners who would be drawn to the cemetery would also come from many classes. Contemporary observers noted the mixed multitudes who came to visit their dead. Yet the ambition of the designers of Père Lachaise, at least, went well beyond this. The growing numbers of famous men and women interred in the cemeteries drew the curious as well as the bereaved. As early as 1816, Paris editors were publishing guidebooks. One published by Roger in 1816, *Le Champ du Repos*, promised a detailed map of the cemetery and a list of all the names and epitaphs of those buried there and included depictions of many of the monuments.[35]

The new cemetery was thus a social space as well as a house of the dead. Yet its sociability was different from that of eighteenth-century public spaces like the Allées de Tourny in Bordeaux or the Palais Royal. Those quintessentially eighteenth-century places had a rectilinear organization with long sight lines, designed to allow individuals to see and be seen. The politics of elite display were written into their ground plans. Père Lachaise was different. Much of the cemetery is composed of winding paths and nooks and crannies. People of different classes could be together there without the need to be in constant view of or contact with one another. It actually became known as a place for solitude. In *Les Amants du Père-Lachaise*, an 1896 novel by the renowned popular writer Clémence Robert, a character writes that she loves walking in Père Lachaise for the pleasure of "being with strangers, alone, always alone!" In this way, the cemetery served as one of the models for the kind of anonymity that would come to be seen as a characteristic feature of the nineteenth-century city.[36]

Once the cemetery had become a sociable space, it was only a matter of time before it became a political space as well. Under the Napoleonic empire and after, funerals and gatherings in cemeteries became one of the preferred means for opponents of the governing regimes to express their discontent. During the 1820s, funeral corteges for leading members of the political opposition drew crowds that were estimated to be as large as one hundred thousand people. Aware of the possibilities that funerals and other gatherings created for the opposition to rally, the government exercised close control over politically sensitive funerals. In 1820, for instance, the prefect of Paris ordered the concierge of Père Lachaise to close the gates and not allow anyone to enter the cemetery to prevent it from being used as a site to protest the recent death of a politically engaged student, Nicolas Lallemand.[37]

Cultural revolution spread rapidly in Europe and throughout the Atlantic world during the early nineteenth century. Mobile crowds dressed in relatively homogenous clothing became the norm in western Europe and began to extend their empire beyond the fashionable capitals. The diffusion of the Père Lachaise model of burial serves as a kind of tracer dye for the spread of new ways of living as well. The garden cemetery found acceptance almost immediately in France's nearest neighbors, among them Britain and Denmark. Its influence took somewhat longer to reach across the Atlantic. The first burying ground of this type in North America, Mount Auburn Cemetery in Cambridge, Massachusetts, began in 1830. But by the middle of the nineteenth century, there could be no question that the Père Lachaise model had conquered the world: it was the undoubted "international standard . . . for a new space of the dead."[38]

The cultural revolutions of the early nineteenth century looked both backward and forward, to the revolutions past and the revolutions yet to come. The political upheavals of the previous three decades had set the stage, in myriad ways, for a transformation of Atlantic cultures. They had at least temporarily broken the authority of traditional rulers, kings, and nobles and called into question the power of established churches. Revolutionaries had elevated the standing of ordinary citizens and given some of them a political voice for the first time. It is not so surprising that these tectonic political changes prompted new ways of living in society and brought previously marginal cultural practices into the mainstream. These new ways of living were second nature to the rising generation, children of the first revolutionary era, who were now coming of age and taking command in Europe and across the Atlantic Ocean. Their political imagination would be fueled not just by the ideas of the previous decades but by the new cultures that they had helped to create.

# PART IV

# REVOLUTION, FULFILLED AND FAILED, 1805–1825

# 15

# THE WORLDS NAPOLEON MADE

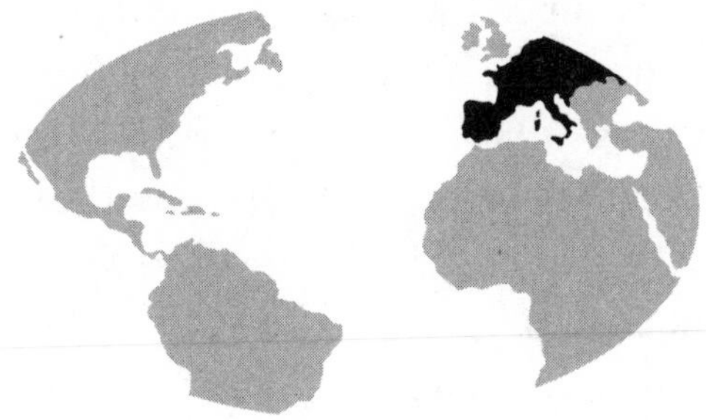

THE TURNING OF THE NINETEENTH CENTURY IN EUROPE brought with it a distinct shift in the continent's revolutionary politics. At first blush, it might appear that Europe experienced an abrupt about-face, a return to the prerevolutionary past. The powerful representative assemblies that had spread across the continent during the 1790s either disappeared or were significantly weakened after 1800, giving way to forms of one-man rule. By 1815, almost all of Europe was back under the rule of kings. Many were scions of the same dynasties that had been overthrown a decade or so earlier.

What did not change after 1800 was the slow but steady progress that political actors made in organizing large-scale, sustained movements to power their political projects. This consolidation continued even as the continent's politics took a conservative turn because the rise of mass movements was being propelled not by revolutionary ideals but by a cultural and generational shift. Around 1800, in Europe as in the Americas, the first revolutionary cohort began to give way to a younger generation. This second revolutionary generation's worldviews and cultural habits, shaped in the uncertain and turbulent society of the previous two decades, gave them a knack for large-scale mobilization that their elders had lacked.[1]

The mass turn in Europe's early nineteenth-century politics took different forms across the region's diverse human and political landscape. Looking at how people experienced this shift in three very different parts of the continent—France, the Polish lands, and the Netherlands—makes visible both these variations and some striking commonalities.

In France, Napoleon's regimes after 1800 pursued the centralization and homogenization of the national terrain that had begun during the 1790s. The successive governments he headed built up the state through administrative and military reforms. The regime's policies were successful in no small part because they were both implemented by and particularly targeted at members of the younger generation. The reforms that the Napoleonic state carried out contributed in turn to leveling certain social and political distinctions, even as they fortified other forms of hierarchy.

In east-central Europe during the decades around 1800, a small Jewish pietistic movement led by spiritual leaders who called themselves tzaddikim exploded into a different kind of mass movement, Hasidism, which reshaped Jewish religious practice and communal life. This "Hasidic revolution," though not state based, followed a similar trajectory to many of the era's other revolutions. What had begun as a struggle for spiritual liberation by a small, elite group became a movement that promised, in some respects, a democratization of spiritual elevation. As the movement grew after 1800, its leaders flexibly imagined new techniques for governing their flocks and fulfilling both their spiritual and their temporal promises.

When Napoleon's empire collapsed in 1814, the coalition of states that had brought it down aimed to reconstitute a version of Europe's old-regime order. It proved impossible, however, to turn back the clock. In the aftermath of Napoleon's fall, the Netherlands had a hereditary monarchy imposed on it for the first time. The new king, William I, proved to be a highly active, modernizing monarch. He made enlisting the populace in support of his regime a central goal of his early reign. Though the king—who had been a child during the patriot revolution of the 1780s—was adamantly opposed to the ideologies of republicanism and democracy, he self-consciously sought to strengthen and protect his new regime through a heavy dose of popular mobilization.

France under the rule of Napoleon Bonaparte acted as the political motor of Europe during the first fifteen years of the nineteenth century. In 1799, the youthful general overthrew the French Directory in a virtually bloodless coup d'état. He replaced it with a so-called Consulate, in which he and two co-consuls held most political power. In 1802, he had himself named consul for life, centralizing most of the power in his hands. Then, in 1804, he abolished this regime as well and declared himself emperor of France.

Napoleonic France dominated the European continent militarily and politically during these years. Although it worked through local collaborators, and with considerable regional variation, France under Napoleon reshaped the continent in its image, in ways both large and small. To understand the course of mass politics in Europe after 1800, there is no better place to start than the successive Napoleonic regimes.

NAPOLEONIC EUROPE, 1804–1812

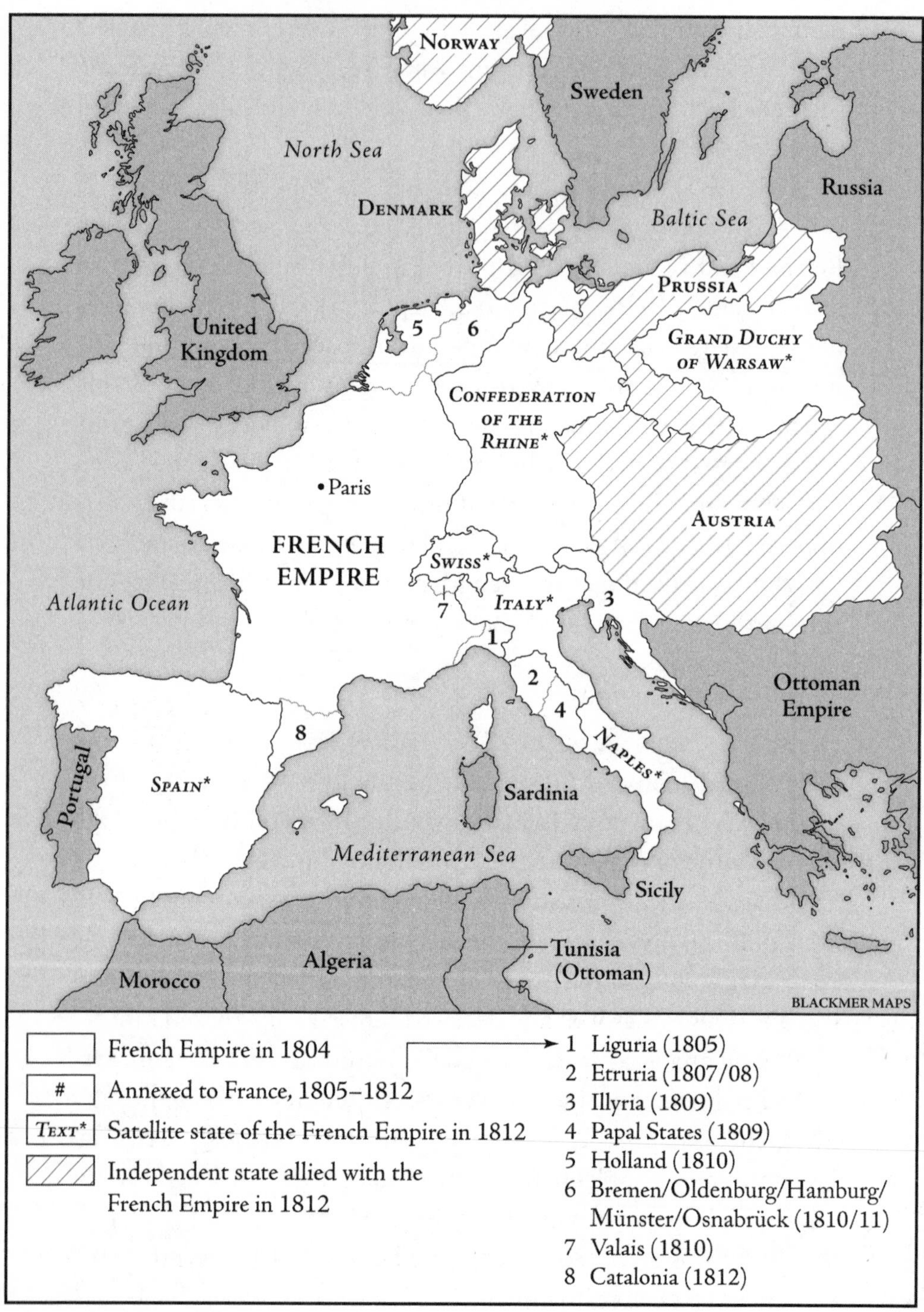

There is no avoiding the fact that the regime Napoleon created was in many respects quite conservative. From 1802 onward, the overall structure of the government was an increasingly explicit callback to the old regime, eventually including the full panoply of dynastic trappings. Napoleon and his government rolled back some of the important reforms of the previous decade. His regimes aggressively targeted the rights of workers and women. The Civil Code, the new laws promulgated in 1804 at Napoleon's direction, sharply curtailed women's rights in and out of marriage. It deprived married women of control over their property and children while severely limiting their ability to divorce. The Civil Code incorporated a 1791 law against labor organizing, and Napoleon's officials enforced the prohibition with vigor. Most strikingly, he reversed the abolition of slavery, reimposing a regime of human bondage in the French empire. Other decisions taken by the Napoleonic state that confirmed or extended reforms of the previous decade, particularly in the areas of property rights, worked to the advantage of the wealthy and powerful.[2]

Though Napoleon's regime was conservative in many respects, its political organizing was anything but. It was, in fact, very much of a piece with the patriots' efforts under the republic to mobilize the populace. This was most evident in Napoleon's repeated use of elections as a way to demonstrate his legitimacy. During the course of his years in power, he instituted regular elections for a number of offices, from local justices of the peace to members of the national legislature. Some of these elections had high participation rates, drawing over 50 percent of the eligible electorate. Most striking in this regard were the four plebiscites or referenda that he staged in 1800, 1802, 1804, and 1815, which involved impressive numbers of citizens. The 1802 referendum was scheduled when Napoleon, then serving as "first consul," wished to be appointed consul for life. Over 1.5 million French men voted in that referendum. This was approximately ten times the number who voted in

US presidential elections during the early years of the nineteenth century—and France had only about six times the population of the United States. The government then falsified the number, claiming that over three million citizens had voted. In the next referendum, in 1804, to legitimate the empire, actual participation did rise to over three million voters. These referenda, in other words, involved an order of magnitude more voters than participated in early US elections.[3]

It would be easy to dismiss the Napoleonic elections and in particular the referenda as window dressing for an authoritarian regime. But they were more than a cynical ploy; they reflected a shrewd understanding of how the second-generation revolutionaries imagined the world and their place within it. In choosing to hold elections, and particularly referenda on major constitutional changes, Napoleon signaled that he, unlike his royal predecessors, did not believe that he was born to rule. The ratification of the public—and indeed, of a large proportion of the public—was needed in order for him to claim the legitimacy he craved. In this sense, the government's falsification of the vote from the 1802 referendum was an effort, however misguided it may seem in retrospect, to prove that the regime had genuine mass support.

THE FRENCH GOVERNMENT HAD LONG BEEN ENGAGED IN A PROcess of centralization of power. Since the mid-seventeenth century, the monarchy had been seeking to diminish the power of local nobles and constituted bodies while bolstering the authority of the Crown's agents. Intendants, royal officials dispatched to the provinces, became a linchpin of this effort in the eighteenth century. Responsible directly to a government ministry in Paris and endowed with broad administrative powers, they became powerful conduits through which the state worked its will at the local level. The early revolutionary government had done away with the intendants but otherwise accelerated the centralization of authority in Paris. The National Convention even dispatched its members on "missions" to the provinces, giving the government in Paris direct access to and authority over local affairs. The Directory established a network of agents at every level, from tiny town governments to vast armies, who were responsible for ensuring that the government's directives were followed by all subordinate officials.[4]

The revolutionary and republican regimes of the 1790s had begun an intersecting process of homogenization, diminishing distinctions and making all French territory and population more standardized and nominally equal. This effort was multipronged. The first revolutionary National Assembly had formally abolished distinctions of rank and condition within France after August 4, 1789. This had entailed an equalization in principle of taxation, which in the old regime had long fallen more heavily on commoners, and the abolition of all the privileged corporate bodies that had been a foundational structure of the old regime. Large numbers of male citizens were granted the franchise—though except for a brief period in 1792–1793, various forms of wealth and income requirements remained in place. The revolutionary assemblies also reorganized the territory of the state, creating out of the old-regime provinces a grid of departments of roughly uniform size.[5] By 1799, when Napoleon took control, the republican governments had made significant albeit uneven strides in remaking France's territory and population.

The Napoleonic regime pursued the goals of both further centralizing power and homogenizing the state internally. The most important agents of this transformation were the prefects, the chief upper-level administrators created by Napoleon, who served as the "true intermediar[ies] between Paris and the departments." "Everything," as one scholar has put it, "rested on the prefect." The prefect corps was overwhelmingly composed of individuals who were part of the second revolutionary generation. Their average age, between

1800 and 1814, never exceeded forty-eight. Two-thirds of the prefects appointed during the Napoleonic regime were in their thirties and forties—meaning that most had been in their teens or twenties during the 1780s and 1790s. Over time, the corps of prefects got "younger," as Napoleon's government increasingly promoted young men who had begun their careers under the empire.[6]

The prefects came from a variety of social and ideological backgrounds. There has been some dispute about how many formerly committed republicans actually became prefects. (Some 30 percent of the prefects had previously served in a revolutionary assembly.) Aside from a few well-known cases, it appears that most of the men who were named prefects were either republican moderates or "weathervanes" who swung with the prevailing political winds. When the Bourbons returned in 1814, the vast majority of the prefects transferred their allegiance to their new masters. The social origins of the prefects were equally mixed and malleable. A majority were initially of commoner origin; after 1804, the corps came to include growing numbers of members of the former nobility. Yet in either case, all the prefects and their families had experienced significant mobility during the previous decade, with their families moving up or down the social ladder. The prefects, like their generation at large, were forged in an unstable and changeable social and political matrix.[7]

Flexibility and adaptability were the key elements of the job that these agents of the Napoleonic state performed. The prefect was a jack-of-all-trades, the interlocutor among the various individuals, interest groups, and bodies that made up the state. He had to be as able to assert his authority against powerful military commanders or local notables as he was to hear and adjudicate complaints from farmers and the mayors of small towns. This intermediary role was most pronounced in the departments that had been added to France out of conquered territories along the Belgian, German, and Italian frontiers (the *départements réunis*).

The prefects in the Italian *départements réunis* were responsible for imposing French administration on the annexed provinces. They engaged in a complex dance of co-optation with local grandees and ordinary people, mixing hard-edged authoritarianism with incentives to sweeten the deal for subject populations. Though they fell short of complete success—especially in extracting money and men from the new departments for the French war effort—the prefects' flexibility certainly made the best of the situation.[8]

The Napoleonic regime took concrete action intended to unify and homogenize the empire's far-flung lands. One particular fixation was the empire's road network. Since the old regime, the main highways had been maintained directly by a royal administration, a commitment that Napoleon maintained. The Directory and the Napoleonic regime also created state schools for engineers and administrators; their graduates would be a reliable and loyal corps of civil servants to expand and maintain the state's infrastructure. Small local roads, which had been the responsibility of local notables under the old regime, were now drawn into the orbit of the central state. The prefects began paying close attention to road maintenance. Battles between prefects and towns that would not pay for the upkeep of the local roads became a regular feature of departmental life. The state's obsession with improving the road network was canny: an integrated system of highways, by making movement easier and more predictable, facilitated mobility that could further knit the national territory and populace together. And the fact that good roads facilitated military mobilizations was a happy side effect.[9]

Using the flexible and powerful institutions at its disposal, the Napoleonic regime encouraged limited new forms of equality under the close watch of the state. A massive reform of the legal system swept away the patchwork of old-regime jurisdictions and legal orders that had survived the initial revolutionary changes of the 1790s. The Civil Code, promulgated in 1804, created a new legal scaffolding that claimed to be comprehensive, universally applicable, and systematic. The implementation of the code was accompanied by a wholesale reorganization of the court system, which created a hierarchical order of tribunals of first instance and appeals courts, culminating in a court of final appeal in Paris. Elections were another area in which the Napoleonic regime extended equality while also subordinating everyone to the state. The Napoleonic state narrowed the already fairly narrow franchise that had been permitted under the Directory, reconverting citizens into equal if subordinate subjects. As René de Chateaubriand acidly put it, "Equality and despotism have hidden links." When Napoleon "ascended the throne," he jibed, "he seated the people there with him."[10]

The Napoleonic state brought a similarly firm hand to the matter of religion, subordinating and equalizing religious life under its aegis. Catholicism was tamed by means of an 1801 concordat between France and the Vatican, which gave the state considerable control over the clergy. Protestant churches were reorganized under a consistorial system: a central administration in Paris, under the close supervision of the ministry, governed and funded each of the authorized churches. Even Jewish religious life, which was radically decentralized, was brought into this system. In 1806 and 1807, an Assembly of Jewish Notables, convened in Paris by Napoleon's ministers, advanced a far-reaching consistorial plan for the Jewish communities of the empire. The proposal aimed to create a hub-and-spoke model for the empire's Jewish communities, with a Central Consistory in Paris, which would be the community's interlocutor with the government, and regional consistories throughout the empire. These regional consistories would be supervised by the Central Consistory and would in turn supervise Jewish communal life in their respective regions.[11]

The regime's crowning accomplishment was finishing the process of turning the army into a mass political entity. The republic, faced with enemies on all fronts in 1792 and 1793, had instituted one of the first efforts at mass enlistment in modern history. Though the initial *levée en masse* had achieved some success, the system of recruitment and retention had been haphazard and only moderately effective. This was especially the case in regions of the country that had no strong tradition of military service. The Directory had reorganized and expanded the army, molding it into a powerful hammer against republican France's many enemies. Napoleon, who owed his political rise to his military genius, made the army his power base. By 1803, the army had become by far the most important single institution in Napoleonic France, and certainly the institution that brought together the most members of the population for a single purpose. It was the means of conquest abroad but also a tool for internal policing and an instrument for integrating and ordering French society.[12]

Napoleon's conscription system, as it evolved from 1799 to 1814, became an ever more efficient machine for the mobilization of men in this state-centered mass movement. The Directory, in 1798, authored a conscription law, the so-called *loi Jourdan*, that established a system of "classes" of potential conscripts, with no exceptions for wealth or rank. Over the course of the next decade, the army conscription system touched virtually every family in France, from the wealthiest to the indigent. Loopholes were built into the system to allow the wealthy to buy their sons out of service, but the administration made it increasingly expensive to do so as time went on. The experience of conscription into the army was a genuinely democratic one in Napoleonic France. Remarkably, there seems to have been increasing acquiescence to the system rather than greater resistance. Even as the pressure of recruitment grew fiercest, in 1811–1813, young men continued to appear for their enlistments.[13]

All in all, the Napoleonic regime in France and Europe more broadly sought to strike a novel bargain with the new mass society that was coming into being. The regime nominally drew its legitimacy from the consent of the public. It recognized and even encouraged a significant equalization of rights and duties—at least formally. Yet all this took place under the tutelary eye of the state, which retained close control over any kind of collective activity. And all roads flowed toward recruitment for the army, the biggest mass institution of the era, in which all citizens were equal and equally subordinate to the needs of the state.

Over the course of the French empire's ten years in existence, Napoleon's armies extended his rule over much of the European continent. In 1804, when Napoleon created the empire, France's power already reached well beyond the farthest extent of the country's old-regime borders. Under the Directory and the Consulate, French forces, some under Napoleon's personal command, had seized effective control of much of Italy, the Low Countries, and the Rhineland (present-day western Germany). Now, in 1805, under the leadership of Britain (at war with France again since 1803), most of Europe's remaining powers, including the Austrian and Russian empires, banded together against Napoleon. Prussia, though reluctant at first, joined the following year. This shifting group of allies, the third coalition against France since 1792, sought to bring an end to France's overweening power.

Instead, in a series of brilliant campaigns Napoleon and his generals crushed the members of the Third Coalition one by one and made France the undisputed dominant power in Europe. Austria, Prussia, and the other belligerents accepted humiliating treaties of peace that included significant territorial concessions.

The Treaty of Tilsit, signed in 1807 between Napoleon and Tsar Alexander I of Russia, confirmed the radical reordering of western Europe under French domination. Only Britain remained standing among France's foes. In 1806, the two powers moved into economic warfare: Britain imposed a blockade on the continent and Napoleon retaliated with an embargo on British trade. The French expansion continued in 1808 and 1809, with invasions of Portugal and then Spain.[14]

As they took control of Europe, Napoleon's armies spread the empire's political innovations across the continent. The armies themselves carried out some of the first reforms. When they captured a new territory, they removed the old government from office. In some instances, they immediately abolished feudal duties or key old-regime institutions. (Though in many other cases, they left the fiscal apparatus intact, the better to extract tribute from the conquered region.) The men who were doing this were, on the whole, members of the second revolutionary generation themselves. The recruits who filled the army were, of course, almost all young men. Even the generals were fairly young on average. Out of the initial group of marshals of the empire created in 1804, more than half were born in the 1760s or after. These men, part of Napoleon's age cohort, included many of the officers who would be most important in Napoleon's military successes, including Michel Ney, Joachim Murat, Jean-Baptiste Bernadotte, and Jean-Baptiste Jourdan.[15]

Once French control had been established, whether directly or through local allies, new administrative, legal, and political structures were put in place. The Napoleonic regime dispatched proconsuls to newly conquered territories, who were responsible for implementing the French legal code and then managed a wholesale reconstruction of the political system to mirror that of France. In regions that were annexed to France, the full French administrative apparatus was brought into existence in the newly added departments. This included the extension of the French way of policing and schooling, aiming to remold the residents of these regions entirely into simulacra of Frenchmen.

Napoleon's conquests in 1806–1807 and subsequent years brought his empire into close proximity with a rapidly expanding empire of an entirely different kind in central Europe: the Hasidim. A spiritual empire rather than a temporal one, the Hasidic movement in the early nineteenth century was also the product of a generational revolutionary shift. Like its Napoleonic doppelgänger, the religious empire of the Hasidim was undergoing a significant transformation in the early nineteenth century under the influence of a younger group of leaders.

The Hasidic movement had its roots in the eighteenth-century Polish-Lithuanian Commonwealth, a vast state that had covered much of central Europe during the early modern period. This region encompassed the "most urbanized, industrialized areas" of central Europe and had one of the largest populations of Jews on the continent. The eighteenth century had brought rising economic inequality to the Jewish community, just as it had in other European societies. A wealthy merchant class emerged and fused with the community's longtime political leadership, known as the kehillah, already composed of wealthier men from prominent local families. They worked closely with the religious leadership, headed on the local level by a town rabbi. Most rabbis came from established rabbinical families, usually with a strong dynastic character.[16]

The Hasidic movement began as an internal uprising in the heart of this relatively prosperous and peaceful Jewish community. It percolated first among hermetic pietistic groups (*havurot*) that had long been a part of the community's religious and social landscape. Usually composed of well-educated and wealthy men, these groups engaged in complex ascetic and mystical practices that they believed would assure a special connection to the divine. On the whole, they considered these practices and the higher spiritual life they offered to be beyond the capacities and needs of the vast majority of the community. Beginning around midcentury, a growing number of pietists recast this special connection to the divine as something to which all Jews should have access. The key figure in articulating this more democratic notion of spiritual elevation was a rabbi named Israel ben Eliezer, who became known as the Baal Shem Tov (or, using an acrostic, as the Besht). The doctrine was genuinely revolutionary: it threatened not merely to upend the authority of rabbis but to call into question the structures of Jewish communal life that were deeply imbricated with ideas about spiritual authority and capacity.[17]

In order to make spiritual elevation available to the ordinary Jew, the Besht and his followers created an innovative economy of spiritual leadership and followership. Its two poles were the spiritual adepts, the tzaddikim, and their followers, the hasidim. The tzaddik served as a channel or conduit for spiritual power from the divine, which he would convey to the hasidim through prayer, individual guidance, and even physical touch. The relationship between the two groups, tzaddikim and hasidim, was hierarchical. But it was considerably more inclusive and accessible than the older pietistic practice. To be a hasid, unlike an old-fashioned pietist, required no specialized knowledge. There was also a strong sense that the tzaddik and the hasid, though on different spiritual levels, were interdependent: as Yaakov Yosef of Polnoye, one of the leading thinkers of early Hasidism put it, if a tzaddik did not transmit the divine energy he received to others, it would stop flowing through him altogether.[18]

During the last third of the eighteenth century, small Hasidic groups spread throughout the Jewish communities of eastern and central Europe. In this early period of Hasidism's formation, the groups were usually similar in scale and tone to the old pietist *havurot*: that is, relatively small, self-selected groups of men who met together. Although the Hasidim were not very numerous, they drew attention by challenging key elements of communal life as the earlier pietists never had. Particularly vexing to communal leaders were the Hasidic practices of meeting separately for prayer, in unofficial prayerhouses called *kloyzn*, and insisting on distinct standards for slaughtering kosher meat. The former challenged the synagogue's role as the locus of communal life. The latter threatened the community's finances: much of the funding for the kehillah came from the monopoly that it held on kosher slaughtering. As early as the 1770s, leading rabbis and communities were denouncing the Hasidim as sectaries or even heretics.[19]

The scale of the Hasidic world underwent extraordinarily rapid growth during the early nineteenth century. The "mystical circles of the eighteenth century," as one history has it, "coalesced into a genuine mass movement." When exactly this happened is hard to pin down; figures are notoriously hard to come by. The causes of the sudden growth spurt are equally hard to decode. But the change was real and strongly felt. Right around 1800, the problem of scale began to appear regularly in the sermons and other writings of Hasidic rebbes. Shneur Zalman of Liadi, a major figure in turn-of-the-century Hasidism, framed his 1796 magnum opus, *Likutei Amarim Tanya*, as a way to give guidance to his followers in writing, since there were simply too many of them for him to receive and counsel individually. He suggested the newness of this approach by noting in the text his worry about whether his hasidim would understand his message correctly if they did not hear it from his mouth. In a commentary on the story of Abraham written in the early nineteenth century, Kalonymus Kalman Epstein, another leading rebbe, obliquely hinted at the growing scale of the Hasidic community when he described Abraham as receiving "sometimes thousands of souls who come . . . to hear Torah and ethical teachings from him." The biblical text on which he was commenting presents Abraham as the leader of a small band of followers at most. Epstein was projecting onto the biblical character the scale of followership with which he was familiar in the early nineteenth century.[20]

The rapidly growing scale of Hasidic life in the early nineteenth century created new issues of financial and administrative as well as spiritual governance. One of the hallmarks of the Hasidic movement was that the tzaddikim received significant sums of money from their followers, which supported their households, networks of religious schools and study halls, charity work, and (in many cases) Jewish communities in Palestine. Managing these income streams was always an important part of what the rebbe and his closest aides had done. As the Hasidic movement gained vast numbers of new adherents in the early years of the century, the scale of the financial and administrative challenges grew apace. Epstein, for instance, expatiated on how much money he imagined Abraham had had to spend on receiving his followers.[21]

The rising Hasidic leaders who had to manage this growing population of followers had a different background from the generation that had predominated before 1800. Many of them had been born around 1770, including Dovber Schneuri (born 1773), Nachman of Breslov (born 1772), Naftali Zvi of Ropshitz (born 1760), and Simcha Bunim of Peshischa (born circa 1765). Like their revolutionary counterparts to the west, they had grown up in a period of political and social turbulence. Most salient for many of them had been the dismemberment of the Polish Commonwealth, which began with a first partition among Russia, Austria, and Prussia in 1772 and continued with two further partitions during the 1790s. These divisions of the Polish lands placed the vast majority of eastern Europe's Jews under new temporal authorities. A wave of political and administrative reforms, such as the curbs on serfdom in Alexander's Russia, set a cultural tone of ferment and rapid change.[22]

The rise of mass Hasidic society forced these rebbes to institute changes to the face-to-face organization that had been a core element of the movement during its eighteenth-century development. One route, which several influential rebbes followed, was to institutionalize the hierarchical relationship between the tzaddik and his followers. Israel Friedman of Ruzhin (1796–1850) developed what one scholar has called the "regal way": leaning hard on the core Hasidic idea of "worship through corporality," he created a Hasidic court that imitated the princely courts of eastern Europe. Friedman lived in a palatial home, wore fine clothing, and otherwise lived as a nobleman. Rather than meet with their tzaddik individually, most hasidim of Ruzhin were spectators. They received religious guidance from a distant, king-like rebbe. Russia's leading tzaddik, Shneur Zalman of Liadi, took another route to the same end. He published elaborate regulations for visitors, which were designed to parcel out the tzaddik's precious time, enabling both new hasidim and "veterans" to have intimate time with him. He also created a well-structured, hierarchical network of underlings who administered his growing community of followers, channeling directions outward and queries and money back to the center.[23]

The most widespread response to the development of mass Hasidic society was for rebbes to place a growing emphasis on more "horizontal" forms of spiritual development among the Hasidim themselves. Late eighteenth-century leaders such as Elimelech of Lizhensk had stressed the centrality of the "vertical" relationship between the tzaddik and his followers. The rebbes of the early nineteenth century showed considerably more interest in how members of the community could and should shape one another. This did not mean, by any stretch, that they had abandoned the idea that the tzaddik was the privileged conduit between ordinary hasidim and the divine. This was still a given.[24] Yet there was a distinctly more democratic tone to the writings of the early nineteenth-century rebbes: the tzaddik remained the essential conduit to the divine, but the ordinary hasid, and especially the community of hasidim, had an important role to play.

One of the most original strategies for organizing a mass Hasidic movement was developed by Menachem Mendel of Rimanov, Elimelech of Lizhensk's former student and the author of the 1812 decree against wearing gentile fashions. Menachem Mendel's communication with his followers, as with many Hasidic rebbes, centered on *divrei Torah* (discourses) that he delivered during meals on the Sabbath and holidays. The practice of discourse making threw into stark relief the problem of how to communicate esoteric, mystical concepts to ordinary followers. The discourses were by nature fairly short (conducted over and around meals) and delivered to an audience that varied from day to day and week to week. The listeners could have widely disparate levels of knowledge and preparation for spiritual elevation. The discourses had to provide insights that were deep enough for the spiritual elite among them while still being accessible to the ordinary Jew.[25]

The Rimanov rebbe's solution to the problem of communicating mystical ideas to a mixed audience was to focus his teachings, to a remarkable degree, on a seemingly mundane subject: food. The major theme of his discourses, as recorded by his students and published several decades after his death, was manna, the quasi-mystical foodstuff that fell from the sky and nourished the Israelites during their forty years wandering in the desert. The subject was particularly well suited to the task at hand. Food and the nourishment it provides are innately accessible subjects; every person understands the importance of food and knows intuitively the sensations and desires attached to it. It surely did not hurt that many of these discourses were delivered over a meal, lending an immediacy and even tangibility to the subject. Menachem Mendel lauded the table as a place for spiritual self-examination: "It is good advice to weigh and consider [*l'fales*] one's deeds when it is time to eat."[26]

Manna, as Menachem Mendel interpreted it in his discourses, was at once a means for the masses to achieve direct spiritual elevation and a gateway to higher learning. One of the rebbe's constant themes, as he discussed manna year in and year out, was that it was a "nourishment of the spirit" that entered the body not through the "esophagus" but via the "windpipe." The simple act of ingesting this numinous foodstuff improved one's spiritual condition, as he explained in an 1805 discourse about the redemption of the Israelites from the deep impurity into which they had fallen in Egypt. Yet even as he touted manna's almost magical efficacy as a spiritual cure, the rebbe used his intricate discussions of its qualities to open up sophisticated discussions of mystical doctrines aimed at enhancing the spiritual condition of his best-educated followers.[27]

Menachem Mendel gave close attention to the horizontal dimensions of spiritual uplift—the ways in which hasidim might elevate one another, as opposed to the action of the rebbe on them. He gave several discourses on a passage in Exodus describing when the manna first descended: when the children of Israel saw it, they said "one to the other, what is it [*man hu*]? For they did not know what it was [*mah hu*]." On its face, the question in the passage is clearly about manna: the pronoun "it" (*hu*) refers to the manna on the ground. But in one of his discourses, the Rimanov rebbe chose to read the pronoun *hu* as "him," which rewrites the question as "What is he?" The Israelites asked this question, he explained, because ingesting the manna had transformed them from "vessels of clay" to "vessels of glass." This made visible the divine "sparks" of their Jewish souls within them, which had thus far been hidden. This sudden transformation allowed them to see one another anew, to perceive the divine "sparks" in one another. Then they asked of one another in wonder, as he paraphrased,

"Who is this person whose heart is so full of the knowledge and the fear of God?"[28]

Other Hasidic leaders in the early nineteenth century found their own ways to encourage their hasidim to enhance one another's spiritual condition. Early leaders of Habad, the group founded by Shneur Zalman of Liadi, developed communication strategies to inform and channel the enthusiasm of the ordinary hasid. Menachem Mendel's chief disciple, Simcha Bunim of Peshischa, whose followers became one of the largest groups within Polish Hasidism in the nineteenth century, shared his teacher's interest in spiritual influences among the mass of followers. He and his heirs encouraged their hasidim to be unusually independent of the tzaddik. They were expected to be well educated in Jewish sources and to engage in critical thinking. In the dynasties that stemmed from Simcha Bunim's disciples, while attachment to and obedience to the rebbe was expected, there was a strong notion that the hasidim should be as self-sufficient and self-directed as possible in their spiritual lives. This was hardly democratic in an absolute sense. Within the framework of the Hasidic movement, however, it represented a relatively democratic solution to the problem of the tzaddik's authority.[29]

Hasidism may have been the most conservative of all the revolutionary movements of the late eighteenth and early nineteenth centuries. Hasidic theology marked a significant break from the dominant religious practice among the era's Jews. Its goals were democratic, in the sense that Hasidism aimed to enable every Jew to have access to the divine to the greatest extent possible. As it exploded in scale around 1800, the problem of how to organize and govern such a mass spiritual movement became a key puzzle for Hasidic leaders. Their flexible solutions, many of which drew on powerful notions of equality and horizontal social relations, are an exemplary illustration of the way that the practice of mass movement building could be put to the most conservative of ends.

If the Hasidim had quite a bit in common with Napoleon and his minions in their methods of organizing their followers, they would not have liked to admit it. With few exceptions, Hasidic rebbes were intensely hostile to Napoleon's regime. Dovber Schneuri, the second rebbe of the Habad Hasidic movement, likened the French emperor to the devil (the "arch-enemy") in an 1813 letter to his followers. Some seem even to have imagined using their spiritual power to destroy him. A small genre of Hasidic tales features various rebbes spurring on Napoleon's defeat on the battlefield and eventual fall from power by means of magic and prayers.[30]

The real reasons for the fall of Napoleon's empire were a bit more prosaic. On the last day of 1810, Tsar Alexander withdrew Russia from Napoleon's continental blockade. This followed more than two years of worsening relations between the two emperors. In response, Napoleon began to prepare for an invasion of Russia. It took two years to prepare the campaign, including the Grand Army six hundred thousand men strong—the largest military force ever assembled in Europe to that date. The campaign initially proceeded well, but Napoleon proved unable to decisively defeat the Russian forces. The Grand Army captured Moscow in September, but Russian saboteurs burned the city, leaving it to all intents and purposes uninhabitable. Napoleon concluded he had no choice but to withdraw. The Grand Army, which casualties had already reduced by a third, was forced to beat a long, wintertime retreat through hostile territory. Losses of men and matériel along the way were catastrophic, leaving France and its allies seriously depleted.[31]

The 1812 campaign had marked the apogee of Napoleon's empire. Like a balloon that has risen too high, the empire, just as it reached these commanding heights, began to tear open. The following year, Napoleon and his government made strenuous efforts to reconstitute the Grand Army and to meet the reinvigorated allied forces—now including Russia, Prussia, and Britain—in the field. The bled-dry French army could not hold. France faced defeat on a growing number of fronts, from Spain to Germany, and Napoleon's armies were forced to retreat from territories that they had controlled for a decade or more. In November 1813, the remnants of his northern army crossed the Rhine River back into French territory. His German satellite kingdoms promptly collapsed behind them.[32]

As it became clearer that the empire no longer had the wherewithal to resist its external enemies, the political outlook for Napoleon darkened. By the end of March 1814, the troops of the anti-Napoleonic alliance had come within a few miles of Paris. After protracted negotiations, realizing that he had few remaining options, Napoleon agreed to abdicate the throne. The allies decided that it would be best for them if the Bourbon dynasty, in the person of Louis XVI's long-exiled brother, was to return to the French throne. In April, the allies dispatched Napoleon to the Mediterranean island of Elba, which was to be his new "empire" in exile, and the French Senate formally invited Louis XVIII to reestablish his kingdom. The new king entered Paris in the first days of May on a wave of goodwill and the same month signed a favorable treaty with the allies to end the war. The good mood of the early Restoration did not last much beyond that point. The newly minted king, nearing sixty years of age, had an imperious manner and poor political instincts. In short order, he had alienated a good segment of the French populace, France's political leadership, and the allies as well.[33]

General discontent with the new king helped to create an opening for Napoleon to make one last bid for power. On March 1, 1815, he returned to France, called on the army to rally to him, and marched on Paris. The Hundred Days, as his final, brief return to rule is known, is probably best remembered for how it ended, with the cataclysmic battlefield defeat at Waterloo and the second restoration of the Bourbon monarchy. Even as he was frantically organizing his army for this climactic battle, though, Napoleon did not neglect his political movement. In April, less than two months after his return from exile, Napoleon staged one last mass referendum, a vote on a new constitution that would make him emperor again. This referendum, like the one more than a decade earlier in 1802, elicited the participation of some 1.3 million Frenchmen.[34]

THE PASSING OF THE NAPOLEONIC REGIME DID NOT MEAN AN END to mass political organizing in the authoritarian key. Indeed, even as Napoleon's empire was crumbling, its opponents had been adopting for themselves many of the same policies and approaches to creating mass politics of their own. This phenomenon was Europe-wide, but one of its most striking manifestations was in the Netherlands, which in 1814 became Europe's newest monarchy.

Since the fall of the patriot movement in 1787, the Netherlands had passed through a dizzying series of political regimes. Conquered by French arms in 1795, it became a client state of republican France, its foreign policy effectively dictated from Paris. In 1806, Napoleon transformed it into a kingdom and installed his brother Louis as its king. In 1810, he abrogated this arrangement as well and incorporated the Netherlands directly into France. The prefect whom Napoleon appointed to complete this integration, Charles-François Lebrun, was a translator of Homer and former co-consul with Napoleon who had just completed a tour as the French proconsul in Genoa. The new regime that Lebrun put in place would only last a handful of years. The disaster of 1812 left the French unable to maintain their military control over the Netherlands. The French armies withdrew and, with allied armies massing on the other side of the Rhine, "spontaneous localized" revolts began against French rule.[35]

William of Orange landed on the beach of Scheveningen, a sea-swept town in Holland, close to The Hague, on the last day of November 1813. William, like so many of his generation, had experienced the turbulence of the first revolutionary wave first-hand. Indeed, he had been in the eye of the storm for longer than most. His father, the stadtholder of the Netherlands, had been the main target of the Patriot movement in the 1780s. (The stadtholder, a uniquely Dutch position, served as elective head of the military and civil governments.)[36]

In 1785, when he was just thirteen, William, his mother, and his siblings had been forced to leave The Hague and their palace, Het Loo, and flee to Nijmegen in the far east of the country. His father, with his army, was on the front lines of a civil war. In June 1787, his mother, Wilhelmina, made the bold choice to travel personally to The Hague to lobby for the stadtholder's reinstatement. She was intercepted and held briefly by the Gouda Free Corps. Her arrest ultimately spurred Prussia to enter the conflict on the stadtholder's side, which resulted in the rapid end of the revolt. Eight years later, William and his family were again forced to flee into exile, this time by the onrushing army of revolutionary France. He and his family had fled first to Brunswick, a small Rhineland kingdom under the sovereignty of the British kings. Over the next decade, William spent time in Berlin, London, and elsewhere across northern Europe.[37]

The young William responded to these multiple dislocations with brio. His biographer describes him during the 1780s as more or less a typical teenager: a bit rebellious but also eager to take an active hand in adult business (in his case, politics and the military). Even in this early phase of his life, he had more of the sprezzatura and creativity of his mother than the stolidity of his father, who was himself surely representative of the mid-eighteenth-century scene of economic and social stagnation that Dutch historians have dismissively labeled the *pruikentijd* (era of the wigs). By the time of his return to the Netherlands in 1813, William had imbibed the lessons of another nearly twenty years of exile in revolutionary Europe. He had learned, beyond the shadow of a doubt, the lesson that political power was never secure; to keep it, one had to be adaptable and flexible.[38]

William soon had occasion to apply his hard-won knowledge: at the end of 1814, he was declared the first in a new line of kings of the Netherlands, the first the country had known since the sixteenth century. (Sovereignty before 1795 had resided primarily in the Dutch Republic's seven provinces.) This alteration in his status was part of a much wider reconfiguration of the European order after Napoleon, the most important developments of which took place during the so-called Congress of Vienna—in fact a congeries of meetings, negotiations, and treaties that stretched over nearly a decade. The aim of the congress was to assure the continued peace of Europe; the mission was one of creating "security and repose" rather than any revival of the old regime.[39] The principal players in the congress and in the ongoing negotiations, alongside France, were the major allied powers that had defeated Napoleon in Europe: Russia, Austria, Prussia, and Great Britain.

The allies had granted the new sovereign a greatly enlarged kingdom. Under the impulsion of the British government, which wanted to create a strong Netherlands and to keep the port of Antwerp out of French hands, the allies decided that all the Low Countries should be united under a single sovereign. This meant folding the former Habsburg Netherlands (present-day Belgium) into the new Kingdom of the Netherlands. The fusion of the two territories was an audacious if not downright wild move. The two lands, though they partially shared a language and had some common cultural heritage, had not shared a sovereign since the Dutch Revolt a quarter of a millennium earlier. More recently, the Belgian lands had been incorporated into France directly for nearly twenty years; their recent past was quite different than that of the Netherlands.[40]

The new country that William had handed to him was in a state of considerable disorder and fragmentation. After a decade of punishing extraction of its resources in both money and manpower by the French empire, the Dutch economy was barely limping along. Deep political divisions within the north over the House of Orange and the power of the most populous provinces, hardened by the dramas of the previous two decades, remained intractable. Repeated invasions, changes of regime, and administrative reorganizations had left the administration in far from pristine condition.

The Belgian fusion had created a fresh, profound fissure at the heart of the new kingdom. The divide had many dimensions. There were the different political histories of north and south: one with an almost unbroken past as an imperial province, the other formerly Europe's preeminent kingless republic. These differences were doubled and reinforced by disaccords over language and culture. Many of the leading figures in the Belgian lands spoke French, not Dutch. They were mostly Catholics, unlike the mostly Protestant northern Netherlanders. The Catholic hierarchy in the south objected strongly to the need to swear allegiance to a non-Catholic sovereign, and there were concerns that the court would favor Protestant interests and churches.[41]

The first problem that William faced was how to assert his legitimacy and authority over the new country. Unlike many of the other royal houses of Europe restored by the Congress of Vienna, the House of Orange as stadtholders had never been thought to be kings by divine right. There had even been two so-called stadtholder-less periods in the seventeenth and eighteenth centuries, during which the provinces and the States General had simply refused to elect a new stadtholder. There was no preexisting model for legitimating or crowning a king in the northern Netherlands. Though the southern Netherlands had a tradition of royal rule, it had not seen an actual king set foot on its territory in centuries.[42]

William and his advisors invented a novel pastiche of different authorizing bodies and symbols of authority to establish him on the throne in 1815. Separate Estates General held in the northern and southern Netherlands ratified his selection as king. He wielded regalia of kingship borrowed from the practice of other kingdoms, including an ermine robe and an orb and scepter, and modeled his triumphal coronation processions on a mix of local precedents and French and other foreign models. While these adaptations might seem ridiculous or artificial, they represented a canny effort to co-opt the materials of European kingly authority for the Dutch context. Like other successful inventors of tradition, William and his ministers were engaged in a flexible and creative endeavor, albeit in the service of a conservative ideology.[43] This flexibility, which contained within it an implicit acceptance that the world was changing, was one of the long-reverberating echoes of the revolutionary era in early Romantic Europe.

With his coronation, William made himself into a visible sovereign in a way that few stadtholders had been before. The lands of the former Dutch Republic had a long Orangist tradition, especially among the ordinary people. Its emblems included orange flags, clothing, and objects, as well as prints of the stadtholder and his family. William, however, became a public figurehead in a way that more closely resembled the visibility of French kings of the old regime than that of prerevolutionary stadtholders. He put his face on the realm's coin—a first since the sixteenth century—and had public ceremonies and celebrations organized around himself.[44] The effect, as with his coronation, was to emulate the centripetal model of the French state.

The new king saw centralized power as the antidote to the fragmentation that he perceived in the kingdom. He moved rapidly to lodge authority in his own person, and within a couple of years of his accession to the throne he had effectively taken over hands-on management of the polity. He was a remarkably involved ruler. The king was often at his desk conducting state business from morning until evening. No detail seems to have been too small to merit his notice. Ministers and visitors recalled that the king's study was full of papers and dossiers; one said that it resembled nothing so much as a "paper factory."[45]

The king exercised his power so actively, indeed, that almost any other center of power within the central government found itself stripped of authority. Ministers came under close questioning when they reported to the king. Those who dared discuss issues outside their purview found themselves quickly silenced or dismissed. The king's authoritarian turn did not pass unremarked. The moderate liberal minister and nobleman Gijsbert van Hogendorp, who had been one of the central players in William's return to the Netherlands and a key figure in the first year of the kingdom's existence, moved into opposition by 1816. As he acidly explained, the king had "ministers, and no ministry"—that is, the ministers had no independent authority. They functioned, as another observer put it, as mere "commissioners" to enact the king's will.[46]

Though the new king took power away from his advisors, he aspired to build a collaborative political relationship with his ordinary subjects. Petitioning the authorities had been a common practice in both the old Dutch Republic and prerevolutionary Belgium. An important part of the political culture of both regions, it was understood to be a way for the voice of the public to enter into the government's deliberations. The practice continued unabated after William's accession to the throne and even expanded in some regions. Many petitions after 1813 went to the king directly: in 1832, he personally received some twenty-five thousand. William saw petitions not as an annoyance to be dismissed but as a valuable way to connect directly with the mass of his subjects. Though he and other political leaders did not respond to every one, some petitions were treated at the highest levels of the government and played a significant role in shaping policy. In this way, William sought to build autocratic rule on the foundation of mass politics.[47]

During the first decade or so of William's reign, the government's policies focused especially on unifying the territory and people of the kingdom. He wanted to "amalgamate the very different parts of the state into a cohesive whole." The government pushed administrative and judicial reforms, mimicking the strategies that Napoleon had used to form his state. One of the most important areas in which the government took action was the language question. Northerner that he was, William envisioned that this unification would involve reshaping the south to make it more like the north. The government pushed hard to impose Dutch as the language of government in the French-speaking Belgian lands. "I am convinced," wrote an official in 1822, "of the utility, the necessity even, of propagating the use of the national language [Dutch] as much as possible." The purpose of language unification was of course more than just to make administration smoother. A "national" language would help knit together a growing and diverse populace. But even this enthusiast had to admit that it would take a "new generation" to secure the adoption of Dutch in the most Francophone parts of Belgium.[48]

The royal government made a strong push to increase and expand domestic industry, again as a way both to strengthen the country's international position and to knit it together. The government imposed tariffs on manufactures in a bid to increase the country's industrial base. Through loosened trading regulations and the creation of new overseas trading companies, the government gave a spur to overseas trade with both the former Dutch colonies that had been returned (notably Indonesia) and the rest of Europe. Dutch industry and trade did indeed grow rapidly in the fifteen years after William's accession to the throne. Yet this growth did not always help to bring the country together in the way that he had hoped. The two regions that were joined in the kingdom had already diverged economically in the eighteenth century: the once moribund southern provinces had revived while the Dutch

Republic stagnated. Many of the post-1814 government's economic measures managed, at least in the short term, to further widen the gap as the Belgian lands were best able to take advantage of the openings provided to them.[49]

William I's strategy of mobilizing and unifying the populace under his rule was, in the end, half successful. Within the Dutch-speaking lands of the former republic, William successfully built on the foundation of Orangist sentiment to make the new monarchy popular and, by the end of his reign, secure for the long term. He did not succeed in fully stamping out the old republican tradition, but he marginalized it. In the Belgian lands, however, his efforts had the opposite effect, driving a wedge between king and people. The king's language policies proved to be one of the biggest sticking points. As a Belgian subject put it in a missive to the monarch in early 1816, it was the "greatest injustice" for the government to "demand that we speak Dutch before we can manage to learn it." He added veiled hints that pushing too hard in this area could bring about the fall of William's new kingdom. That was precisely what occurred fifteen years on: in 1830, political factions in Belgium set aside their differences, mounted a revolt against William, and declared their independence.[50]

A NINETEENTH-CENTURY HASIDIC TALE RECOUNTS THAT WHEN Napoleon's empire was just beginning to teeter, the emperor disguised himself as a Polish peasant with chickens to sell and went to visit the home of a famous rebbe, the Maggid of Koznitz, seeking his help in the war. The Maggid saw through the emperor's disguise, refused any assistance, and foretold the emperor's fall from power. Although the story is pure fantasy, the Hasidim who told it may have hit upon a nugget of truth: for all the differences between them, the leaders of the Hasidic movement and the monarchs of Europe were not entirely dissimilar. They each espoused a conservative ideology that rejected republicanism and secularization but was nonetheless forward-looking. All of them, in their own ways, intended not a return to former glory but the creation of a new social, political, or spiritual order that conformed to their conservative vision. They also had in common the desire to spread these conservative ideologies to a growing population of followers.[51]

Hasidic rebbes and crowned heads alike after 1800 embraced the easy egalitarianism of the second revolutionary generation in the service of their conservative projects. It was a powerful combination. Hasidic masters, recognizing that they could not hope to sustain the face-to-face leadership styles of the prior generation, developed new methods of communicating with and guiding their followers that drew on the practices of contemporary mass culture. Over the first half of the nineteenth century, the Hasidic revolution conquered the heartland of European Jewry. Napoleon discovered that by reducing all his subjects to equal subordination, he was able to extract extraordinary amounts of money and labor and put them in the service of his state. They fueled an unparalleled imperial expansion in Europe during the early nineteenth century. Though Napoleon's system eventually failed him, the methods he had used outlasted the fall of his empire. William I employed many of the same tactics as he worked feverishly in the years after 1814 to settle himself and his dynasty securely on the throne of his new kingdom.

# 16

# THE JOURNEYS OF LOUIS-AUGUSTIN BOSC

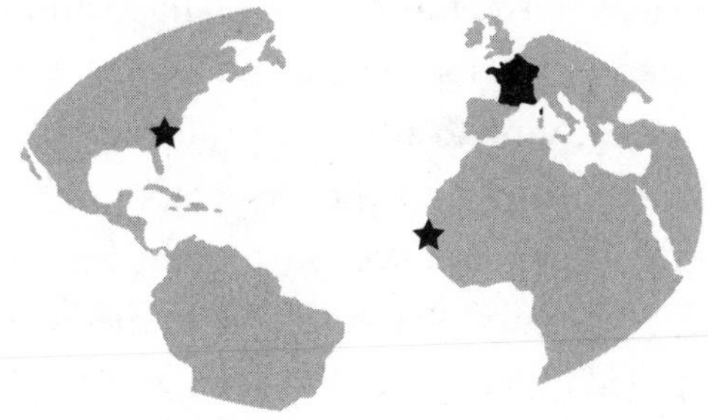

NOT EVERYONE MANAGED TO ADAPT AS WELL AS NAPOLEON OR the Hasidic masters to the second wave of revolutionary transformations, cultural and political, that swept the Atlantic world in the early nineteenth century. The transition was especially jarring in France, which whipsawed from republic to empire in just over five years straddling the year 1800. Many leading political figures of the French Republic, having survived the Terror, faded quickly from the political scene during these years. Some did so voluntarily, disappointed by the collapse of their republican dreams. Others were spurned by the new regimes that Napoleon created on account of their overtly republican sympathies. But for many, no great break or decision took place. They simply could not play the game that the second revolutionary generation was playing. Formed in the vanished world of old-regime France, the new political world was incomprehensible to them.[1]

Louis-Augustin Bosc was one of this group of revolutionaries from the first generation who ended up virtually shipwrecked once the nineteenth century began. Bosc was just a bit over forty in 1800, hardly an old man. But he was very much a child of the French old regime, with mental reflexes tuned to the hierarchical scale of mid-eighteenth-century society. After 1800, those habits of mind, which had served him relatively well during the 1780s and 1790s, proved far less useful. The music had changed and he struggled to learn the new steps. Still a striver, as he had been since his youth, Bosc never stopped trying to advance professionally. But his efforts after 1800 were awkward, and the successes few and far between. The only place he seemed to have any success was inside the walled compound of the Muséum d'Histoire Naturelle, where he lived and worked, surrounded by a coterie of other aging revolutionaries who formed the tight circles of friendship that had defined his political and scientific life since before the revolution.

By the time Robespierre's government was overturned in the last days of July 1794, most of Bosc's close friends from before the revolution were gone. The Rolands and Jacques-Pierre Brissot were dead, François Lanthenas had switched to Robespierre's side, and Henri Bancal had fled the country to save his hide. Bosc himself had become politically suspect and was fired from his longtime job in the postal service. He seems to have been in a kind of haze for months after the Terror ended. He refused to rejoin the postal service in 1795, unwilling to serve along unrepentant Jacobins. "I am in a distressing [state] of indecision about what I ought to do," he wrote to an acquaintance.[2]

When his friends the Rolands died, they made him the caretaker for their young daughter, Eudora, as well as the custodian of their papers. Eudora, born in 1781, had just turned twelve at the time of her parents' death in November 1793. Though Bosc was over twenty years her senior, he became enamored of the girl. It did not happen all at once. He spent a great deal of time with her, particularly to ensure that she would inherit her parents' property. By 1796, when she was fifteen, her "beauty, by then very striking," caused him to "fall madly in love" with her. His "passion" for her was overwhelming. Eudora, he claimed, returned his affections and had wanted to get married. According to him, it was he who had resisted Eudora's proposals: since she was "richer," he worried that the marriage would be seen as inappropriate. Bosc repeatedly delayed fulfilling her wishes, and these hesitations, in his telling, wore away at Eudora's affections. Her heart "cooled" toward him, and eventually she seems to have grown positively hostile.[3]

Bosc had good friends in the Directory, not least among them the director Louis-Marie Larévellière-Lépeaux, whom he had personally helped to save from the guillotine. They were ready to take care of him. In early 1796, he asked Larévellière-Lépeaux to find him a position as a French consul in the United States. He was looking for new government patronage, to be sure. By his own account, Bosc's decision to depart for America was also a way of treating his feelings about Eudora's rejection. Describing himself as "sick for her," he decided that only an "act of firmness" could help him get over her. A few months later, in July, he departed Bordeaux for Charleston.

Bosc spent two years in the United States. Though the French government named him first vice-consul in Wilmington and then consul at New York, because of the state of low-grade hostilities then prevailing between France and the United States, he was never able to take up any official appointment.[4] Instead, he cultivated a botanical garden, corresponded with his French and European colleagues, and collected specimens.

Bosc in the United States focused on work as a collector and classifier of species. He had become interested in taxonomy, the science of classifying living things, during the prerevolutionary years, when taxonomy had been the great drama of the natural history world. Bosc came of age amid a major controversy over the Linnaean system of classification. Carl von Linné, a Swedish botanist, developed the system for classifying plants and animals primarily according to their sexual organs (flowers and the like). In France, powerful opposition to this system came from the comte de Buffon, France's premier naturalist. He rejected Linné's hierarchical scheme of species, genera, and families and flogged his own system, which focused almost exclusively on the species, which he considered to be the only "real" basic unit of life.[5]

Bosc and his friends were immersed in this controversy during the prerevolutionary era: he was a charter member of the Linnaean Society of Paris, organized in 1788 to advance the Linnaean system against the acolytes of Buffon. The struggle was indeed a difficult one. The Linnaeans in Paris were "small in numbers and mainly outsiders," heavily outgunned by the state-sponsored, royally sanctioned Buffon and his followers. The revolution had radically shifted the balance among scientists, helping the Linnaean Society and its allies make considerable inroads in both the scholarly and political realms. By the time Bosc left for the United States, Linnaean taxonomy was in the ascendant.[6]

Yet Bosc's interest in taxonomy was not compelled merely by the fact that it had been a major controversy when he was starting out in natural history. Taxonomy, regardless of which system one used, was an art of stasis. Taxonomists aimed to fix the vast, complex, and heterogeneous natural world into a single, stable whole. What was in dispute between the Buffonians and the Linnaeans was how best to capture a complete and orderly picture of the natural world; they agreed that there was such a fixed order to uncover. One can imagine this orderliness making sense to the young Bosc, stuck in his dead-end, old-regime jobs. Linné's system, with its classification of greater and lesser creatures, seemed even to faithfully map the social hierarchy of the old regime onto nature itself.[7]

Bosc threw himself into the job of collecting and classifying the flora and fauna of the United States. He conducted a close study of the "Carolina grasses," penning detailed physical descriptions of each type of grass that he identified, along with its geographic range and the animals that lived in and on it. He took over the garden that had been created by André Michaux, another French naturalist and a friend of his who had recently departed from Charleston. Bosc also went on a veritable collecting spree among the local fauna. In the span of less than a year, he identified four new frogs, three turtles, three fish species, and a lizard. In August 1797, he reported to Alexandre Brongniart—whose father would be commissioned a few years later to build Père Lachaise—that he had dispatched a large collection of birds and amphibians preserved in bottles back to France.[8]

Being in the United States gave Bosc his first extended exposure to people of African descent. During the 1780s and 1790s, Bosc and others in the Roland circle, especially Brissot, had been involved with France's leading antislavery organization, the Société des Amis des Noirs. The *société* took a leading role in urging the revolutionaries to abolish or at least curb the slave trade and slavery in the French empire. There is every reason to think that Bosc shared their views. Like many antislavery activists in this period, Bosc's opposition to slavery went along with hostility toward people of color. On the voyage across the Atlantic, he wrote disparagingly about a "Black man" among the crew. Shortly after arriving in the United States, he wrote a note in his journal about the enslaved women whom he had met. His language was patronizing and shot through with racist tropes. "My eyes are not yet accustomed to appreciating the beauty of their black faces," he wrote, though he believed them to be "good girls or women, because many have children."[9]

There are nonetheless glimmers of the suggestion that Bosc may have been more willing than many white North Americans to recognize the enslaved as equals. Bosc employed Black men as assistants on collecting expeditions that he undertook during his time in Charleston. A story was told about a time when one of Bosc's Black collaborators captured a viper and was bitten by it. When he brought the snake to a shocked Bosc, the collaborator waved off the danger that he had run. "It is nothing," he is quoted as saying. "I am content if this animal suits you," using the familiar *tu* to address Bosc. Though white people regularly used *tu* with enslaved people, for a Black person to use it when addressing a white person would have been unusual, a mark of familiarity and intimacy.[10]

Running short on funds and finally realizing that he was not going to be able to take up a consular post, Bosc returned to France in the fall of 1798. He arrived at a delicate moment. The Directory was teetering. Torn between resurgent conservatives and Jacobins, it struggled to hold the center. By the time Bosc came back to France, two purges of the government had already taken place, the first in September 1797, intended to suppress right-wing tendencies, and another in May 1798, targeting the Left. Though these moves were intended in part to strengthen the Directory against the legislature, over the next twelve months the Directory grew weaker and more divided. In June 1799, the legislature purged the Directory, forcing Bosc's protector Larévellière-Lépeaux to resign. In November 1799, Napoleon Bonaparte returned from a failed military expedition to Egypt and delivered the final blow, overthrowing the Directory and instituting a new government, the Consulate, in which he was the central figure.[11]

Bosc finally married shortly after the Directory's end. In 1799, he was on a "secret mission" to the south of France. While there, he went and visited his father's family. He "found a pretty cousin, whom they were trying to marry against her will, whom I thought would be suitable to get me to forget the Roland girl." Although she was not rich, he "obtained her consent, and that of her mother, and took her back with me." In his memoir, Bosc did not so much as give her name—Suzanne—and not a single document in her hand appears to have survived in his papers.[12]

The disgrace of his closest allies and the advent of the Consulate sharply shifted Bosc's trajectory again. Unable to get the kind of administrative post on which he had lived since he was a teenager, Bosc turned to "literary work" as his "means of existence." Over the next several years, he collaborated on encyclopedias, works of natural history, and other scientific publications. The collapse of republicanism in 1799 threw Bosc into something of a psychological crisis as well. During the republican decade, Bosc had devoted himself to trying to "help his fellow man directly." He had invested deeply in the republican project and saw himself as working through politics to improve social conditions. With the failure of republicanism in 1799, he had to look elsewhere for "consolations," as an early biographer put it.[13]

The Consulate marked the beginning of a sharp turn toward applied research in Bosc's professional interests. Bosc had always had a great interest in what was known as "useful knowledge." Starting around 1799 and 1800, he shifted his focus to more practical projects, including improving crops and yields, studies of soil, and identifying "useful" flora and fauna. This shift was politically expedient. Napoleon and his new government were eager for national glory and power, and they had learned from the preceding decade that enlisting the energy and expertise of outsiders could contribute a good deal to their mission. The price they demanded in return was that those whom they enlisted devoted themselves to the state's mission and uncoupled their work from any notion of political liberty.[14]

If Bosc was trying to regain the state's favor by turning toward applied research, he succeeded. In 1803, he was hired by Jean-Antoine Chaptal, then occupying the powerful post of minister of the interior, as "inspector of Gardens and nurseries at Versailles." Bosc's new role, which led him to move his family to Versailles, entailed intensive care for the trees and gardens originally established around the Château de Versailles by Louis XIV and his successors. As Napoleon seized the center of the political world after 1800, Versailles again became a seat of authority. The role of gardener, similarly, took on some of the same shading that it had had during the old regime: as an agent of the court's glory, responsible for assuring the resplendence of its setting. Bosc certainly saw and felt the ceremonial of Napoleon's new court. Decades later, he still recalled that his son had been born in 1804, "nine days before the coronation of the Emperor."[15]

For Bosc, taking on the role of gardener at Versailles proved to be a major change. His nomination to this post, he wrote later, "influenced my future, perhaps as much as" any other event in his life. The Versailles posting required that he very quickly learn a great deal about plants. He built on the foundations he had formed as an amateur in earlier years: his "promenades in the Jardin des Plantes" and among "students of foreign plants." But he also "avidly read the works on agriculture that I could get my hands on" and sought out guidance from scientists of "repute," including his old teacher, the botanist André Thouin. Bosc was a quick study. By 1807, he was up to speed enough on silviculture that he was admitted as a member of the Société d'Agriculture de Paris. Within a few years after that, in 1811, he was sufficiently well-known that he was asked to take over a journal in the field, the *Annales d'Agriculture*.[16]

Alongside promoting the grandeur of the French state, agricultural improvement was at the heart of Bosc's new role. One of the major projects that he undertook was a study of the collection of grapevines Chaptal had assembled at the Jardin du Luxembourg, in central Paris, drawn "from all of the wine-growing regions of France." There were, Bosc wrote, more than fourteen hundred varieties that Chaptal had collected there. Chaptal himself was a leading figure in the development of French viticulture and enology. The goal of Bosc's work in these years, as he put it later, was "for the amelioration of the wines of France and consequently for the augmentation of the wealth of our territory." It would be hard to find a more forthright statement of the mission of science in Napoleonic France.[17]

Burrowing ever more deeply into the practical, Bosc lost touch with the cutting edge of scientific work. After 1800, the controversy over taxonomy that had burned so hot during the previous decades went on the back burner. A new generation of scientists became interested in how the order of nature—as expressed in individual species—had changed over time. The idea that animals and species changed was not an entirely new one; even the old comte de Buffon had thought that species "degenerated" with time. But it was not until the 1790s, and even more so the first decade of the nineteenth century, that primary natural historical debate turned to considerations of "transformism." The early nineteenth-century debate took as its premise the idea that nature was flexible and changeable, not fixed—a sharp departure in focus from the Linnaean ideal. This shift was certainly produced in some measure by the internal logic of scientific inquiry. However, it can also be connected to the society-wide experience of social decomposition and recomposition that the first revolutionary era provided.[18]

Though Bosc was closely associated with the protagonists of the discussion about transformism, he remained almost entirely absent from the conversation. The leading figures in the debate were Jean-Baptiste Lamarck and Georges Cuvier. Cuvier, though younger than Bosc, was considerably more successful. A canny political actor, he had managed to gain significant government patronage in the 1790s, when newly arrived in Paris, and had been appointed a professor at the Muséum d'Histoire Naturelle. Bosc knew him well and was one of his close collaborators, including working on several of his books.[19]

THE COLLAPSE OF THE FRENCH EMPIRE IN 1814 AND 1815 WAS NOT kind to Bosc. The disgrace of his onetime patrons, including Chaptal, left Bosc bereft and nearly destitute. During the first years of the Restoration, he found himself so constrained that he was obliged to hold onto lodgings in Versailles that he had rented for an appointment he had received just before the final collapse of Napoleon's regime, because he knew selling his furniture in that moment would produce "nothing." In an 1816 letter to a longtime colleague, Picot de Lapeyrouse, he stolidly remarked, "I would have many things to say to you, but the time for effusions is past."[20]

Bosc eventually returned to his work at the Jardin des Plantes, continuing his steady stream of undistinguished publications. But in the first year of the Restoration he made an attempt to salvage his fortunes by engaging in a risky colonial venture.

Starting in 1814, a group of adventurers and financiers called on his expertise as a botanist in order to work up a plan for a new French colony in West Africa. The site would be in present-day Senegal, a longtime French colony that the British had seized during the Napoleonic wars. Bosc accepted the position of "Administrator of agriculture" in the organization, which named itself the Colonial-Philanthropic Society of Senegambia. The society's plan was deeply shaped by the well-documented failures of French colonization in the New World and by the situation in the early nineteenth century. They intended for the project to grow on the model of the English North American colonies: a group of individuals, associated in a self-governing chartered company, would purchase land and create their own government. Doing so, they argued, would mobilize the "personal interest" of the company members, "the most powerful motive" to achieve the society's goals. The government would not have a direct role.[21]

Africans had crucial roles to play in the society's projects. They were, first of all, one of the imagined beneficiaries of the plan. One of the stated goals of the colony, as Bosc put it in his 1817 memoir to a powerful government body, the Conseil d'État, was to "assist in the civilization of the Negroes" by "spreading . . . the light of Religion and . . . the Sciences and useful Arts." (Though this seems to have been distinctly secondary to the goals of making money for the investors and providing a dumping ground for "thousands of unfortunate Frenchmen.") West Africans were also, in a rather opposite sense, imagined as the current owners of the future colony's land. The society admitted that the lands of the peninsula were held by the "black Chiefs of the villages, from whom the private property . . . must be acquired." They intended to do so "legitimately"—though Bosc, at least, wildly underestimated the prices they would have to pay for it.[22] In the sense that they held a key resource that the colonists needed, Africans might also hope to benefit from the scheme.

Mostly, however, the society's leaders—including Bosc—imagined the Black inhabitants of Senegambia as potential laborers. Bosc and the others presumed that the region's hot climate made it impossible for Europeans to cultivate the land themselves. They therefore proposed to recruit an African labor force. But they imagined a novel approach. Rather than enslave free people, they proposed to purchase already enslaved Africans and free them in exchange for a term of service that corresponded to their purchase price. They would be, in effect, engaging in something quite similar to the gradual emancipation schemes then popular in the New

World. Bosc even deployed the same language of education that was common among the advocates of gradual emancipation in the Americas: the colonists would "instruct" them in "Christian morals" and useful arts.[23]

Bosc's involvement in the Colonial-Philanthropic Society of Senegambia suggests that his views of people of African descent had changed little since the 1780s. They were, in his view, primarily laborers and proprietors whose efforts and lands would help enrich France. Bosc had retained some grain of his long-ago enthusiasm for equality: in his 1817 memoir to the Conseil d'État, Bosc was at pains to note that the "current inhabitants of Senegambia, or free Blacks," would "keep all of their rights." Indeed, he asserted, the society's legislation would "consolidate their property rights and their social existence equally with the Whites [*à l'égal des Blancs*]" and would "closely unite the interests of the free inhabitants."[24] The old paternalism of the Société des Amis des Noirs was never far off.

Like so many of Bosc's projects, the Senegal scheme was beset by troubles and ended in disaster. In mid-1816, the French government dispatched a small expedition to take possession of the retroceded colony. The ships carried soldiers and officers as well as several representatives of the society and twenty artisans and workers who were supposed to supply the skills needed to establish the colony. At least one of the society representatives had studied botany with Bosc. The voyage went horribly wrong when the incompetent captain of one of the vessels, the frigate *Medusa*, ran his ship aground off the coast. Most of the survivors were set adrift on a large raft in the Atlantic ocean; of 150 passengers, only 15 survived. The wreck became a cause célèbre in Paris, with liberal politicians using it as a cudgel against the Restoration government. The event was immortalized by the painter Théodore Géricault in a celebrated picture, *The Raft of the Medusa*.[25]

Though Bosc had stalwartly refused to take on any financial stake in the project, he still found himself mired in the disaster of the Senegal scheme. Because of a torturous series of developments connected to the formal organization of the society, he became responsible for a part of its considerable debts. After the project failed, he found himself dragged into a messy and protracted litigation, which cost him (by his estimate) several thousand francs that he could ill afford to lose.[26]

If Bosc had any great virtue, it was his winsome attachment to collegial friendships, a resolutely eighteenth-century quality. Indeed, eighteenth-century man of science that he was at heart, he built his career on these deep and sustained ties with a circumscribed group of peers. This tendency had already been well in evidence during the 1780s and 1790s. He remained attached to this form of friendship into the nineteenth century. His colleague André Duméril, eulogizing him in 1828, encapsulated the man well: Bosc was "devoted to his friends, to the point of sacrificing everything for them, of braving everything for their sake."[27]

Bosc sought out places where he could form these kinds of friendships. In 1806 or so, when he was appointed to a position at the Muséum d'Histoire Naturelle, Bosc and his family moved onto the museum grounds. The large walled compound on the Left Bank of the Seine, not far from the Île Saint-Louis, housed some fifty extended families of scientist-members during the early nineteenth century. The museum and the Jardin du Roi from which it grew both had a distinctively democratic spirit: the professors formed a partially self-governing corporation, and in spite of significant differences of income and status, the sense of community seems to have extended to underlings and employees as well.[28]

Within the grounds of the museum, the scientists, their families, and their employees after 1800 forged a close-knit sociability strikingly redolent of the eighteenth century. Because the appointments of professors were for life, the community within the walls was unusually stable. Many of the families had deep and dense connections with one another. One of Bosc's neighbors, for instance, was his former teacher and now superior, André Thouin, the professor of botany. Thouin lived with his sister and her husband, J. B. Leclerc, who had been a deputy in the National Assembly. Leclerc was close friends with Larévellière-Lépeaux, Bosc's ally in the Directory. That many of the residents of the museum grounds were republicans and liberals further cemented their tight-knit community.[29]

The vast number of plants and animals named after Bosc was one of the most lasting legacies of his friendship-based scholarship. Bosc had at least five plant species named after him, including three in which his name figures in the scientific (Linnaean) name, and two that use "Bosc" as the common name. These include *Paspalum stoloniferum Bosc* (a New World perennial grass), *Pinus adunca Bosc* (Monterey pine), and *Boscia senegalensis* (and others in genus *Boscia*, members of the caper family native to Africa).[30]

Bosc also eventually had two pears named after him: the Beurré Bosc and the Calebasse Bosc. The former remains one of the most common variety of pears grown today in the United States. Bosc had his first pear variety named after him during his lifetime. It was probably discovered by an unknown nurseryman in Belgium, in the garden of one "M. Swates" near Brussels. It was then shared with Jean-Baptiste Van Mons, one of the country's leading pomologists. Van Mons had a past not unlike Bosc's: like him, he had been a revolutionary (a member of the Belgian National Convention) in the 1790s. By the 1810s, though, he had accommodated himself to the new political reality. Van Mons named the variety after Bosc, "a celebrated name." "We could not have chosen . . . a more respectable scientist than M. Bosc."[31]

It is no accident that the best-known Bosc namesakes are pears. They were fruit-bearing trees and thus "useful," which was Bosc's great preoccupation after 1800. Pears were second only to apples as the king of useful fruits. Some varieties provided good eating fruit, which was valuable in itself. Others, as with apples, provided the main ingredient for cider (or perry, for pears) and distilled alcohol. Pear trees were also capable of growing in a wide variety of climactic conditions. They were an unusually important fruit. It was a mark of Bosc's friends' enthusiasm for him that they attached his name to these valuable plants.

Bosc died in 1828 following a painful illness. When his body was opened for an autopsy, twenty-eight hours after his death, the coroner found his stomach had been perforated by a cancerous growth and his liver was distended and filled with foreign masses. It was the final, cruel irony of his life that it was only during these last, difficult years that Bosc attained the recognition he had long coveted. In 1825, after more than a decade of impatient waiting, he had finally been appointed to a chair at the Muséum d'Histoire Naturelle, replacing Thouin. Bosc had managed to discharge the duties of this long-awaited office for barely a year before his body began to fail him.[32]

For all of Bosc's abilities, the last three decades of his life had been a study in frustration. Over and over again, Bosc had in his grasp what seemed to be promising avenues of advancement, only to find them closed off or transformed into dead ends. His inability to keep hold of success owed something to his unwillingness—or inability—to dance the new dance of the later revolutionary era. And as the years went by, he more and more affirmatively turned away from the nineteenth-century world and its shifting intellectual and political currents. He retreated into a familiar, shielded bubble of scholar-friends, pursuing worthy but hardly cutting-edge research. The world had changed around him. He, like so many others of his generation who had lived through the transition from one world to another, would not or could not adapt to the demands of the new.

# 17
# THE REVOLUTIONS CURTAILED

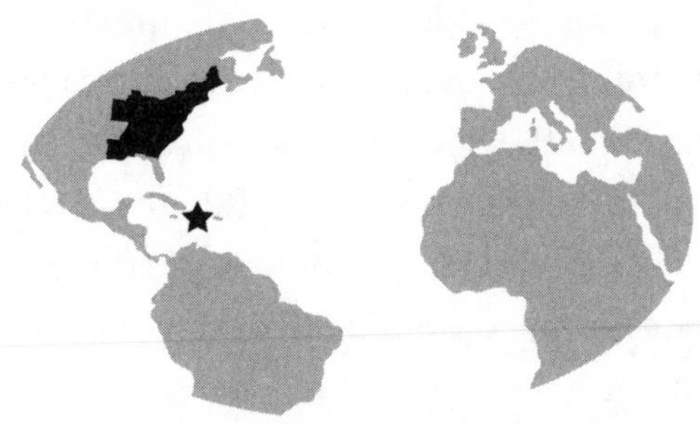

In the Americas, the second revolutionary generation fully took command during the second and third decades of the nineteenth century. They made their new power felt first in the two already established revolutionary states, the nations in the Americas that had already gained their independence from European empires: the United States and Haiti.

On the surface, Haiti and the United States in the 1810s appeared to be opposites. The United States was a large republic in which slavery was protected and expanding, and in which enslavers held a virtual hammerlock on the highest national political offices. Haiti was an island nation divided politically between an oligarchical republic in the south and a monarchy in the north. It was ruled by Black people, many of whom had formerly been enslaved themselves; antislavery was its foundational principle. The two countries certainly imagined themselves as opposites, and political leaders eyed one another warily.

What the two nations had in common during the 1810s was as consequential as the things that set them apart. Second-generation political leaders in both countries managed during these years to build national political movements that effectively did away with any meaningful opposition. The Republicans in the United States became the sole national party, and King Henry I held unchallenged sway over his kingdom in Haiti's north. Integral to the success of both political movements were illiberal policies that curtailed or impinged on the liberty of those at the bottom of the social hierarchy. The dominant faction in the Republican Party embraced universal suffrage for white men, but it blocked Black men from the ballot box and encouraged the spread of slavery. Henry Christophe created a highly militarized society in which the personal liberties of the vast majority of the population were curtailed in order to maintain plantation production. In both countries, leaders viewed these trade-offs as essential to the survival of their republic as a single nation. The illiberal revolutionary turn was neither a particularity of Haiti, as has sometimes been claimed, nor was it an exceptional feature of the antebellum United States.

The development of illiberal revolution in both countries came to a head in 1820. In the opening months of that year, the US Congress voted in the so-called Missouri Compromise, a cluster of legislation intended to address the issue of slavery in US territories. The compromise blatantly prioritized national unity and the preservation of the national political party over the rights of the enslaved and free people of color. That fall, in Haiti, Christophe died unexpectedly. His passing, which ushered in a rapid transformation of Haitian politics, paradoxically ended up solidifying the regime he had created over nearly fifteen years in power—a regime that subordinated Haitians' individual liberty to the imperative of protecting their collective freedom.

THE REPUBLICAN PARTY, HAVING WON A SMASHING VICTORY AT every level of US politics in the elections of 1800 thanks to its superior political operation, continued to build up its organization over the next two decades. The already "sophisticated" party apparatus that had come into being in the mid-Atlantic states (especially Pennsylvania and New York) during the 1790s expanded apace after 1800. By the 1810s in New York City, the Republican Party had become a highly effective political machine capable of mobilizing a large majority of the city's voters at every election. During the same years, an elaborate party structure with filaments that reached deep into the grassroots spread to New England and the South. These regions, though they had voted increasingly Republican by 1800, had not had party machinery. In Connecticut and Massachusetts, a multilayered party bureaucracy came into being: town and county party committees reported to a statewide Republican committee, all of which coordinated their efforts at election time and during the rest of the year. The trend in the early 1800s across all the states was toward "more democratic party procedure." Increasingly, candidates were selected not by committee members but in mass meetings or "conventions" to which all Republican voters were welcomed.[1]

The expansion of the Republican Party's political machinery was accompanied by a halting expansion of suffrage to white men. What this meant, across the country, was the removal of legal barriers to voting, which included requirements that individuals own a certain amount of property, that they have resided in a place for a certain amount of time, or that they had paid a certain amount in taxes. The expansion of suffrage was most rapid in the states on the edges of the republic with largely rural populations: Kentucky and Vermont were the two states that by 1815 had completely eliminated property requirements. More populous and urban states were not far behind. States as different as Maryland, New Jersey, and Connecticut all adopted measures that significantly expanded the franchise for white men. In New Jersey, notably, these gains for white men came at the expense of Black men and propertied solo women, who lost the right to vote that had been conferred on them by the state's independence-era constitution.[2]

What made these political measures so effective, and the Republican Party so dominant after 1800, was the way that the Republicans' political practice dovetailed with the second revolutionary generation's native egalitarianism. Electioneering for Republicans after 1800 meant sharing drinks, long days spent in political discussion, and mass meetings at which gentlemen rubbed shoulders with laborers, artisans, and farmers. Their political strategy, as it had from the beginning, rested on the assumption that among white men, at least, all were equal. The Federalists fought against these tendencies. The hallmark of Federalism was a belief in a hierarchical social order and forms of natural superiority. In 1798, a number of Federalist orators explicitly lay claim to political virtue through their "fathers," suggesting a kind of bodily transmission of political values from members of the first to the second revolutionary generation. Federalist authors in Connecticut in the 1810s alluded to the importance of having a "superior caste" in command of national politics. Small wonder that they had a more and more difficult time mustering a majority in any region.[3]

Yet even as the Republican Party expanded its social reach, it remained firmly connected to the gentry. A succession of Virginia aristocrats remained at the head of the party throughout this period. Thomas Jefferson served two terms as president, from 1801 to 1809. He was succeeded by James Madison, coauthor of the *Federalist Papers* and the titular head, with Jefferson, of the "republican interest" during the 1790s. Madison served two terms as president as well, from 1809 to 1817. Following Madison in office was James Monroe. Like his two predecessors, he was a propertied member of the Virginia gentry with legal training. Yet he was more nearly a child of the American Revolution than either of his predecessors. Though only seven years separated him from Madison, these were crucial years: Madison, born in 1751, had been in his twenties during the war years. Monroe was still in his teens when the American revolutionary war began. Monroe's worldview took shape in Virginia during the very turbulent war and postwar years.

The Republican political synthesis or coalition, stretching across the class divide of white America, proved remarkably resilient. During the first decades of the nineteenth century, the party withstood a number of political shocks. Though the party was dominant on the national level, it remained quite fractious internally. The Federalists, though much weakened as a national political force, remained a live opposition at the state level. This was especially the case in New England, where the Republicans had to beat back repeated attempted revivals. They were able to do so even when the Federalists had the political wind at their backs. In 1807, in a dramatic attempt to maintain US neutrality in the Napoleonic wars, Jefferson declared an embargo of all foreign trade to the United States. The measure attracted ridicule and disobedience in equal measures: the sharp drop in US trade brought on an economic crisis that hit every part of the Republican coalition, from small farmers to commercial planters to urban artisans. In spite of this economic near disaster for which the leading Republicans were solely responsible, Madison handily won election to the presidency the following year, and the Republicans did not suffer any serious electoral consequences.[4]

Dramatic economic and territorial expansions accompanied the political evolution of the first two decades of the nineteenth century. Jefferson had been elected to the presidency in 1800 on a promise to create a paradise for the small producer: the yeoman farmer, the independent artisan. By the end of Monroe's second term in office, that utopia seemed further away than ever. Early industrialization was well underway in much of the northern part of the country. Spurred on by innovations in shipbuilding and land transportation—notably the construction of canals—US merchant houses were growing rapidly. Just as important was the vast expansion of the nation's territory that took place on the Republicans' watch. During his first term in office, Jefferson had been offered the chance to purchase the Louisiana Territory, a swath of the middle of the continent, from France. Though he lacked specific constitutional authorization to do so, Jefferson seized the opportunity to nearly double the nation's land area. Over the next several decades, US settlers and governments seized the land from the Native peoples who lived on it and carved more than a dozen states out of it.[5]

The institution of slavery grew significantly under the Republican ascendancy as well. It had not been a foregone conclusion during the 1790s that this would happen. Though the Constitution and the early federal Congresses had protected property in persons, a number of informed observers had believed that the plantation system would gradually give way to an economy based on free labor. The invention of the cotton gin in the late 1790s, which made it possible to efficiently clean the short-staple variety of cotton that was suited to cultivation across the South, had made enslaved labor a viable mode of production in more of the country. But what most boosted North American slavery, paradoxically, may have been the decision by Congress in 1807 to legally close the transatlantic slave trade. By the time that took place, the enslaved population in a number of states in the upper South, primarily Virginia and Maryland, had stabilized and started to grow through natural increase. For enslavers in those states, the closing of the external slave trade became a boon: it meant that they held a monopoly on the supply of enslaved laborers to the rest of the country. Over the next half century, the enslaved population in the United States would quadruple.

The twinned expansions of US territory and the population of the enslaved made the spread of slavery an increasingly volatile problem in US national politics. In 1819, the issue burst into the center of the national discussion, propelled by a debate about the admission of Missouri to the union.

By the time the Missouri issue came before Congress, second-generation revolutionaries had come to be in nearly full control of the US government. President James Monroe had been born in 1758, on the cusp between the two revolutionary generations. Aside from him, the leading players were all children of the revolution. John Quincy Adams (born 1767) was secretary of state. Secretary of War John C. Calhoun (born 1782) and Attorney General William Wirt (born 1772) were both members of the cabinet. And Henry Clay (born 1777) was the powerful Speaker of the House of Representatives. Almost all the backbench members of Congress by this point belonged to the second revolutionary generation.[6]

Members of this generation from across the ideological spectrum took for granted the reality of social mobility and a rising tide of social equality. We have already seen how Pennsylvania senator Jonathan Roberts rejected, almost reflexively, the idea of distinctions by "class." This view was not limited to the antislavery party. The Maryland proslavery tribune William Pinkney, born in 1764, had in his earlier life given free voice to notions of equality between Black and white Americans. In an impassioned 1789 speech, he had declared Black Americans "men as well as we are, sprung from the same common parent," and "in all respects our equals by nature." His opinions had since changed, but the recognition of this social fact cannot have dimmed with the passage of the intervening years. Even John C. Calhoun, who would become known as the nation's proslavery ideologue par excellence, had in his youth developed an appreciation for social mobility as he clawed his way into the ranks of the South Carolina gentry.[7]

The political crisis that this divided-but-united group of politicians confronted in 1819 and 1820 emerged out of some of the same transformations that had shaped their own worldview over the previous four decades. The central driving force of the controversy was the growth of the US population in the Missouri territory: it more than tripled from just over twenty thousand, recorded in the 1810 Census, to over sixty-six thousand ten years later. This migration made the territory eligible for admission as a state. The population included a substantial share of enslaved Black people, brought there as part of the ongoing expansion of the economy of slavery in the South after 1800. Southerners hoped to set the precedent, with Missouri, that slavery could continue to expand westward.[8]

When Missouri applied for statehood in early 1819, a ferocious congressional debate erupted. Its first phase took place during the last days of the 1818–1819 congressional session. When the issue was left unresolved, it was picked up by the newly elected Sixteenth Congress in December 1819. In the meantime, Massachusetts had given permission for the District of Maine to split off into its own state. It also now demanded admission to the union. Southerners moved to link the admission of the two states, arguing (as Speaker Henry Clay put it) that it was a long-standing practice in Congress to admit free and slave states together.[9] The debate that took place in Congress in December 1819 and January 1820 was notable for its no-holds-barred quality and the intransigence of each side.

The debate's ferocity did not come from any great novelty in the issues that Missouri's admission to the union had raised. Indeed, most of the points of contention were ones that the political classes had already been wrestling with for decades. The United States had been a coalition of slave societies and societies with slaves from the beginning. Nine other states had been admitted to the union previously without arousing similar strident conflict. While abolitionist sentiment had certainly grown in the North during the years after 1800, it remained relatively moderate and marginal. Indeed, it was the Missouri controversy that did a great deal to heighten antislavery feelings in the North; rising abolitionist sentiment was effect, not cause.[10]

Part of what generated such acrimony was that restrictionists (those who favored closing Missouri to slavery) and opponents of restriction shared much of the same worldview. Both sides framed their arguments about the Missouri question in terms of how it affected social status and political systems that they thought of as being in a state of flux.

Restrictionists regularly cited worries about how the institution of slavery, were it to be extended to Missouri and beyond, would lower the status of white freemen and Black people. The most eloquent restrictionist spokesman, Rufus King, used language to describe slavery that suggests he viewed it as a status-changing practice: "Man could not enslave man." Many of the restrictionists, as was typical among antislavery actors in the period, expressed more concern about the effect that slavery would have on white people. Slavery threatened to degrade the status of work and thus erode the position of white laborers. Conversely, free labor was elevating: a New York newspaper asserted that if Missouri were a free state its settlers would feel themselves not "degraded, but elevated, by the idea, that the soil [is] cultivated by *freemen*."[11]

Defenders of slavery, though they disagreed vehemently about the issues, approached the controversy with similar kinds of worries, which they expressed through anxieties about how social and political statuses might be in motion. Southern defenders of slavery, such as John C. Calhoun of South Carolina, used the controversy as an occasion to articulate their belief that the subjugation of Black people formed the basis for equality among white people. By "descend[ing]" in status, Calhoun claimed, the enslaved "produced an unvarying level" of equality among white people. Clay, for his part, imagined a future in which, as a result of population growth, "the price of labour shall have reached a minimum." This, he argued, would make "free labour" cheaper than the labor of the enslaved, leading to disappearance of slavery.[12]

The debate over the Missouri question simultaneously brought out threats and anxieties about the instability of the union. All sides expressed a fear of—or was it a desire for?—the collapse of the republic. John Taylor of New York, who had just been elected the new Speaker of the House, hinted broadly at the conclusion of his speech in favor of restriction that "extreme measures"—by which he clearly meant a breakup of the union—might be called for if Missouri joined as a slave state. Former senator Abner Lacock, writing to President Monroe, expressed "fear," "concern & uneasyness" that the controversy might end with "a dismemberment of the Union." Henry Clay, the former Speaker, noted that the "words, civil war, and disunion" seemed to be on everyone's lips.[13]

The fiercest calls for disunion came from southerners. Senator Pinkney of Maryland apparently voiced the idea of disunion repeatedly in his speeches on the matter—although they were not recorded. Senator James Barbour of Virginia was worried enough about the tenor of the debate that he wrote to James Madison to ask for "advice." "The Missouri question . . . threatens the tranquility if not the dissolution of the Union," he opened his letter. He blamed it largely though not entirely on "many . . . of our Southern Brethren who seem to think it is better to risk at once a dissolution of the Union than agree to a Compromise." According to some reports, Barbour himself was part of the problem that he claimed to be worried about: he had apparently broached the idea of an extra-congressional convention to begin dissolving the union.[14]

The vividness and sharpness with which the men of 1820 dreamed their nightmare of disunion may be chalked up to their generation's formative political experiences. This was far from the first moment in US politics when actors considered the possibility that the republic would dissolve: there had been hints of it during the heated party controversies of the 1790s and among New England Federalists during the Jefferson and Madison administrations.[15] Yet earlier discussions of disunion had been more abstract, colder in tone. For the men of 1820, it was a palpable danger, a foreboding reality. And why should it not be so? These politicians—whose political consciousness had been formed during the rough-and-tumble 1790s, buffeted by the French revolutionary and Napoleonic wars—had grown up seeing centuries-old states fall and empires shatter into fragments.

What Congress encountered in 1820, in other words, was a head-on conflict between two dimensions of a shared worldview. The members of the second generation heard calls, on the one hand, to limit the practice of enslavement, which lowered the status of Black people and consequently either (depending on one's view of slavery) lowered or elevated the position of white workers. On the other hand, all of them realized that any effort to stop enslavement, even in a limited fashion, could shatter the Democratic-Republican Party and the union itself.

This conflict within the politicians' worldview ultimately set the stage for the so-called compromise that Congress struck in 1820 to end the standoff. The compromise itself was simple. Missouri was admitted as a slave state, as its representatives and other southerners had demanded, without restrictions. Maine came in as a free state, which did not change the extent of slavery's reach in the union at all. The only concession made to antislavery was that a separate bill prohibited the institution of slavery in territory to the north of the Mason-Dixon Line. This was not as substantial a concession as some believed: the region covered by the prohibition was Indian country, and US settlement and statehood were far off in the future.[16]

A small number of northern representatives—eighteen in all—provided the critical votes that allowed the Missouri bills to pass: four absented themselves from the House, and fourteen voted down the restriction on Missouri. They provided the bare margin of victory (three votes) by which the House decided to admit Missouri as a slave state. Their opponents pilloried these representatives as "doughfaces"—soft and pliable in the face of hard southern sentiment—and most of them would lose their seats in Congress at the next election. Posterity has not been much kinder to these politicians, who have been roundly criticized for their apparent inconsistency and failure to hold to the moral principles of antislavery.[17]

Yet the "doughfaces" were quite clear about why they had decided to vote as they did: most of them placed maintaining the integrity of the union above their antislavery principles. Charles Kinsey of New Jersey was one of the prominent voices among them. In a speech explaining his vote, Kinsey called slavery "the greatest of evils." But he explained that his central concern was avoiding having the republic "break asunder" over the issue of slavery's extension. The "advancement, the consolidation of the Union," he argued, was of paramount importance. In the confrontation between the two principles, his "conscience" dictated that he choose the collective. John Holmes of Massachusetts, another "doughface," justified himself in a slightly different fashion. In his own long speech on the controversy in late January, he expressed his deep "fears" and "forebodings" about the prospect of disunion. Like Kinsey, he also denounced slavery as an evil. Where he differed was in attempting to justify his choice by linking the two together. He posited that the union was necessary to freedom: "Kindle the flames of civil discord," he declaimed, "destroy the Union, and your liberties are gone. And then, where will your slaves find the freedom which you proffered them?"[18]

Perhaps the most precise and honest account of the compromise, however, came from a man who was only peripherally involved in the discussions: John Quincy Adams. In his diary, Adams observed that the decision that Congress had made was an extension of a "bargain between freedom and slavery contained in the Constitution of the United States." As a longtime opponent of slavery as an institution, whose antislavery beliefs were by now beginning to grow stronger, he believed this bargain to be fundamentally "vicious." Yet he still "favored this Missouri compromise . . . from extreme unwillingness to put the Union at hazard."[19] To preserve the American republic, even Adams was willing to accept a radical curtailment of personal liberty in the form of an extension of slavery westward.

The Missouri Compromise did not so much resolve the conflicts over slavery in the United States as shove them under the rug. It was a "deceptive nationalist truce," which maintained the cohesion of the Democratic-Republicans and the union by placing a thin antislavery veneer over the extension of slavery.[20] Within the context of the United States, that compromise has seemed oddly exceptional: the debate over slavery, which was ready to explode, was silenced in the name of keeping the nation whole. But it was not so unusual.

AS SECOND-GENERATION REVOLUTIONARIES IN THE UNITED States were hammering the Missouri Compromise into place in Washington, DC, the last days of Henry Christophe's kingdom were approaching in Haiti.

Since shortly after Jean-Jacques Dessalines's assassination in 1806 by a coalition of his generals, the former French colony of Saint-Domingue had been divided between Christophe, who ruled in the north, and Alexandre Pétion, the wellborn son of a French planter and a free woman of color, who controlled its south and west.[21] Both men were children of the revolutionary era. Christophe, born in 1767, most likely served in the American revolutionary war. He had experienced firsthand the earliest wave of destabilizing political and military change that rolled across the Atlantic world. Pétion, born in 1770, had been a well-informed nineteen-year-old when the French Revolution began. When Saint-Domingue erupted in a revolt from below in 1791, he quickly established himself as one of France's most useful military leaders.

The leaders of both Haitian states had imbibed the reflexive sense that social and political status were in flux. Given their different social positions, they had not absorbed precisely the same lessons from this set of facts. Christophe seems to have been acutely conscious of the possibility of re-enslavement: just as he had risen, so could he find himself thrown back down into legal non-personhood. He constantly invoked the threat "of irons, of slavery" that he thought Europeans and their henchmen were still trying to fix on Haitians. The discourse coming from Pétion and his republic was a bit different. As befit a man who had always enjoyed a privileged life, Pétion shaped his language around the pursuit of respect and sustaining the republic's status rather than the dangers of enslavement.[22]

The rival states had different political organizations and a history of conflict. Christophe named himself president of the State of Haiti in 1807 and then, in 1811, declared himself the first king of Haiti. Pétion adopted the forms of a democratic republic and served as the Republic of Haiti's president until his death in 1818, at which point he was succeeded by Jean-Pierre Boyer. The states were locked in conflict. Christophe and Pétion were both "ambitious" leaders, eager to increase their power. Each controlled an army, drawn from their respective regions and with a different social base: Christophe led mostly freedmen, while Pétion's army included many of the free people of color who like him had been free before the revolution. With both men claiming to be the rightful ruler of all of Haiti, conflict was inevitable. An initial war between the states in 1807–1808 left a stalemate. A second war that broke out in 1812, spurred by the seizure of some of the kingdom's vessels and an alleged conspiracy against Christophe ginned up by Pétion, ended after less than three months with the status quo ante intact.[23]

In spite of their enmity, however, the two states were both shaped around the existential fact of Haiti's vulnerability. Both leaders thought that Haiti and Haitians remained under grave threat from European powers in the early nineteenth century. Christophe's messages on the anniversary of Haitian independence, January 1, returned regularly to the idea that both Haitians' "freedom" and Haiti's national "independence"—the two were linked—were under threat. "So long as our independence has not been solemnly acknowledged," he declared in early 1819, "we are and must ever remain on the alert." Such worries were far from imaginary: the Restoration French government, urged along by ex-planters, had been trying since 1814 to reassert its sovereignty over Saint-Domingue. In secret, the French ministry made clear that it intended for most Haitians to be effectively re-enslaved.[24]

How best, then, to protect both Haitians' "freedom" and Haiti's national "independence"? Christophe, first and foremost a military leader, looked to a strong army to secure Haitian independence and freedom. Within a few years of taking power in the north, Christophe had built one of the first standing armies in the New World, known around the Atlantic for its impressive size, discipline, and effectiveness. The army occupied the center of the kingdom's political world. The Code Henry, the new legal regime that Christophe promulgated in 1812, established a starring role for the army in the northern state's social and political functioning. It divided the law into just three main domains: civil law, criminal law, and military law. The very first provision of the "Military Law" made "commanders of provinces, of divisions, and of districts" responsible for ensuring that "the inhabitants maintain the obedience they owe to the king, and that they are living together in harmony." Article 5 of the military law gave general officers "the same authority . . . over the inhabitants as over the soldiers."[25]

For Christophe, "union"—a word he invoked ceaselessly—meant that the state or kingdom would be like a single organism governed by a strict hierarchical order. The kingdom's propaganda harped on the idea of the army as the guarantor of "harmony" among the nation's inhabitants. Responding in an address in 1814 to the ham-fisted diplomacy of the Restoration government, Christophe apostrophized the people and invoked the principle of union as the necessary condition of their continued freedom: "On the unanimous concord of our union, of our efforts, depends the quick success of our cause." The sense that the army stood in for the people was internalized by the generals. When a group of them addressed the Republic of Haiti after Christophe died in 1820, they described themselves as "the generals, organs of the people and of the army"—speaking, as it were, for both. As late as the early twentieth century, historian Vergniaud Leconte could assert that the army under Christophe was the "incarnation of the cohesive force" of the nation, "the representation of the people."[26]

The military model that predominated in the Kingdom of Haiti effectively protected the nation's independence at the expense of internal liberty—that is, the personal liberty of freedpeople. This was visible, first and foremost, in the organization of the army itself. The Christophean army was hierarchical even by the standards of other contemporary military organizations. By far the longest section of the military law in the Code Henry was devoted to "Discipline." It took up 43 pages out of a total of 112 (nearly 40 percent). It began with the king's exhortation that there "shall be established . . . a graded subordination . . . which keeps the subordinates faithful to their duty." This was followed by an almost ritualistic reiteration of the hierarchy: "The king orders . . . that the soldier obey the corporal, the corporal the sergeant, the sergeant the sergeant major . . . the lieutenant colonel the colonel, the colonel the major general"—and so on. The rules that followed were minute in their detail, including instructions on matters as granular as how to keep a notebook for receipts (Article 296).[27]

Military discipline extended outward from the army to pervade the wider society, which Christophe and his ministers imagined as part of a single mass mobilization. Christophe's state/kingdom developed a "militarized" plantation system in which workers were formally tied to plantations and a significant share of plantation income was paid directly to the state. There was some precedent already for this: Toussaint Louverture, during the years from 1798 to early 1802, when he had been the undisputed ruler of Saint-Domingue, had sought to reestablish plantation agriculture. Louverture's measures, which were quite unpopular with freedpeople, were at least framed as temporary, more or less emergency actions. Christophe's new plantation system, on the other hand, was clearly intended to last. Peasants found themselves being forcibly returned to the same plantations on which they and their families had been enslaved before the revolution and forced to resume production of staple crops. The whips and irons might be gone, but their freedom was still severely curtailed.[28]

The internal unfreedom of Christophe's state extended to the literary and cultural spheres as well. The kingdom had by far the most successful printing and publication operation on the island of Saint-Domingue; by comparison with the south, it had the better presses and more effective publicists. This was just one part of its elaborate official cultural scene, which included (by the end of Christophe's reign) an Academy of Fine Arts and a Royal Theatre. Yet all the productions of the northern state/kingdom were carefully coordinated with the government's political line, functioning as little more than cultural arms of the army-state. The kingdom's literary productions, like its agriculture, were "militarized," with the aim of ensuring that Haiti remained independent and secure. (It was only in the southern republic that literary journals and a growing culture of letters began to develop.)[29] In this domain as well, Christophe sought to build up the "union" of the nation at the expense of individual autonomy.

In August 1820, the king fell gravely ill while attending church services. It may have been a stroke. Throughout August and September, with his condition weakening, small revolts began to break out across the kingdom. On October 1, a larger revolt began among the troops stationed in the western port city of Saint-Marc. Christophe was forced to mobilize his forces to put the revolt down. His generals, who had apparently been waiting for this moment, took the opportunity his orders presented to muster the troops against their king. On October 8, as rebel troops approached his palace, Sans-Souci, Christophe took his own life. Within a matter of days, the president of the republic, Jean-Pierre Boyer, had begun to reach out to the rebel generals, trying to sway them to his side. He succeeded: on October 26, the republic's army entered Le Cap, unifying Haiti for the first time since Dessalines's death.[30]

The unification of the country under the republic's aegis seemed to offer an opportunity to reconceive the illiberal revolutionary bargain that Christophe had struck. On the face of things, the republic was far more liberal. It had some democratic forms—though honored more in the breach than in observance—and its publicists espoused notions of private and public liberty. Unlike the Christophean regime, the republic spoke the language not of "union" but of "brotherhood." It was also far less coercive in its notion of labor and economic organization. Pétion's regime had distributed a great deal of land to wealthy planters and soldiers, but it left them to cultivate it as they wished. The state earned its income primarily from export duties that it laid on cash crops leaving Haiti.[31]

Yet although the republic had formally triumphed, the illiberal revolution that Christophe's kingdom had consolidated could not be easily undone. Over the next decade, Christophe's generals—many of whom had retained significant power after the consolidation of the two states—kept Haitian society functioning along militarized lines. Boyer, who was also a general, increasingly based his power on the support of a military elite that held substantial landholdings. They strengthened, rather than eliminated, the "feudal system" of land tenure and labor that had taken shape during Christophe's reign. Nearly two decades after Haiti had won its independence, most Haitians remained less than fully free in the name of protecting their freedom.[32]

THE EVENTS OF 1820 HELPED TO SEAL BOTH HAITI AND THE United States into long-term commitments to their respective illiberal revolutionary settlements. The Missouri Compromise set the United States on a path toward an ever growing series of political confrontations over the future of slavery and the place of Black people in the American polity. The 1820 agreement contributed materially to the sectionalization of American politics over the next three decades: slavery expanded rapaciously below the Mason-Dixon Line, while the North became increasingly hostile to slavery. By the 1850s, the long shadow of the Missouri Compromise was looming ominously over the union that John Quincy Adams and others had been so desperate to preserve at all costs. In 1857, Roger Taney, chief justice of the US Supreme Court, declared in his opinion in *Dred Scott v. Sandford* that the Missouri Compromise was unconstitutional: Congress, he ruled, had never had the power to restrict the institution of slavery from US territory. Less than three years later, after Abraham Lincoln was elected to the presidency on an antislavery platform, the defenders of slavery shattered the United States into civil war.

Christophe's coercive revolutionary state became all but impossible to undo in 1825, when President Boyer was forced into signing an agreement with France to pay an enormous sum of "reparations" to the former colonial power. Boyer had little room to maneuver: The French were threatening a new war on Haiti, which the nation could ill afford. And the threat of re-enslavement, if France succeeded this time in reconquering Haiti, was very real. The agreement that Boyer signed committed the Haitian state to paying 150 million francs in five installments—the equivalent of billions of dollars in today's money—in exchange for which France would recognize Haiti's independence. Since Haiti lacked the funds to pay even the first installment of the bill, it was forced to take out a massive loan from French bankers at extortionate rates of interest.[33]

Paying back the loans and making the remaining payments placed enormous fiscal pressure on the Haitian treasury over the next century. (The loan was not fully paid off until 1947.) In order to keep funds flowing, Boyer and his immediate successors maintained and even expanded the coercive labor system that Christophe had installed. In 1826, Boyer issued his own rural code, which brought back many of the most hated aspects of Louverture's rural code from nearly three decades earlier. These measures included tying cultivators to a particular plantation and depriving them of the right to organize or to keep most of their earnings. As it had in the United States, the illiberal revolutionary settlement remained a dose of arsenic in Haitian politics for decades to come. Nearly two decades later, farmers with a long memory supported a coup that ousted Boyer, helping to inaugurate a period of increased political instability.

# 18
# THE CONSTITUTIONS PROMULGATED

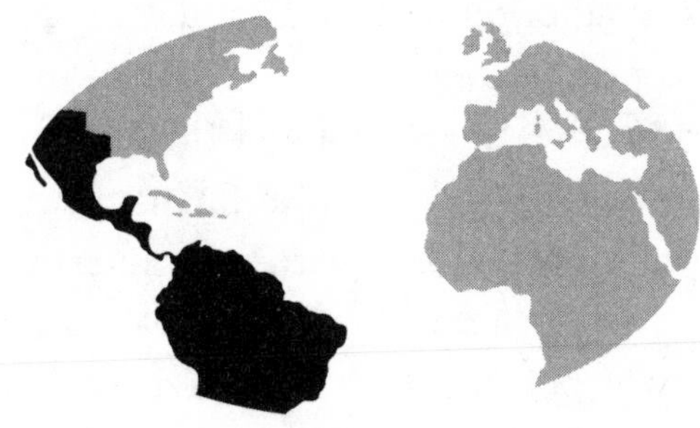

IN SPANISH AMERICA, AS HAD HAPPENED ELSEWHERE IN THE revolutionary world, the second revolutionary generation began to take command after 1800. It was about 1799 when Gabriel Alexandrino Ugarte, nephew of Madre Maria Rivadeneyra, returned to Cuzco. Born in 1783 near the height of the Spanish government's campaign against his family, he had gone into exile with his father as a child. He returned to his homeland to enroll in the seminary of San Antonio Abad, Cuzco's premier institution of higher education. It was familiar ground: the seminar's aged rector, Josef Pérez, had been the priest in charge of Santa Catalina during the 1770s and 1780s.[1]

The seminary young Ugarte joined was known as the "headquarters of insurrection," a place whose aspiring lawyers were aflame with eagerness to radically reform the empire. In 1804, having completed his studies, the young Ugarte petitioned to be admitted to the bar of the Cuzco audiencia (superior court). When his request was accepted on June 11, he became part of an institution that was at the center of a growing political debate in Spanish America. Just a few years later, in 1810, an up-and-coming young jurist, Manuel Lorenzo de Vidaurre, penned a blistering attack on the audiencias. He denounced them for (among other things) their "arbitrariness and notorious injustice," and demanded that they be reformed from top to bottom.[2]

In the decade after Ugarte entered the audiencia bar, a new wave of political uprisings swept over Spanish America. Though parts of Spanish America were already simmering with discontent, the catalyst for open revolt was the decapitation of the Spanish monarchy by Napoleon, when he forced the abdication of the Spanish king in 1808. Deprived of its head, the empire entered a period of intense political turbulence. Leading the charge were members of the younger generations, like Alexandrino Ugarte. Born in the 1770s and 1780s, and having come of age during the 1790s, this generation was habituated to social mobility and readier to collaborate, politically and otherwise, across the lines of social division.

Spanish America, covering much of two continents, was nothing if not diverse; its political responses to the crisis in the Spanish empire varied accordingly. Yet there was much in common in how the rising generation of political leaders in these different regions reacted. One commonality was a remarkably quick turn to large-scale electoral politics that crossed, even if they did not obliterate, caste and class distinctions. The electorate who chose new cabildos or city councils in 1812–1813 was especially broad, among the most democratically inclusive of any electorates that convened during the revolutionary decades. Another commonality was a gradual turn toward strong, centralized forms of government. As declarations of independence or autonomy spread over the continent in the two decades after 1805, new constitutions followed. By the early 1820s, most South American constitutional thinkers had come to favor strong, centralized governments. They justified this choice on grounds that would have sounded familiar to any second-generation revolutionary: the need to adapt rapidly and decisively to changing conditions.

Continental Spanish America in the year 1805 was a vast territory divided into four viceroyalties: New Spain (present-day Mexico), New Granada (present-day Central and northern South America), Peru (including modern Peru and Chile), and Río de la Plata (including present-day Argentina, Uruguay, and Bolivia). These large units overlapped with the jurisdictional areas of the various audiencias and with other administrative units such as captaincies general. With a total population of over thirteen million, Spanish America had more than twice as many people as the United States, and as many as a number of contemporary European countries. The population was far more varied in its ethnic and racial origins than in any other Atlantic region: Roughly 40 percent of the total population was Natives. Mestizos, people who were understood to be of mixed race, accounted for about a third. Some 20 percent of the population were "Spaniards," either migrants from Spain or their allegedly purebred descendants. Less than 5 percent of the total population, on the order of 650,000 souls, were classified as Black. This included both enslaved people and some of the free people of color.[3]

The geography of the viceroyalties, like their populations, was a study in contrasts. Spanish America contained extreme variations of climate and geology, from the tropical forests of the

Amazon and the Yucatán to the arid highlands of Peru and central Mexico to the plains of Colombia and the Río de la Plata. The human geography was equally varied. Spanish America contained the largest cities in the hemisphere, including Mexico City, Lima, and Cuzco, in addition to a host of smaller but important and wealthy cities. It had huge amounts of farmland and grazing land. The population of Spanish America as a whole was overwhelmingly rural. But even the most remote rural regions were hooked into the networks of trade and political governance that passed through the cities. Specific demographic groups dominated certain regions. "Spaniards" were concentrated in the cities. People of Native ancestry dominated the countryside in most regions, especially in New Spain and Peru. New Granada had the highest proportion of Black and mixed-race people. Some areas of New Granada, indeed, had a Black majority.[4]

By 1805, the political and fiscal situation in the Spanish empire on both sides of the Atlantic was already difficult. At first glance, the Spanish empire seemed to be in far better shape than most other European powers. Spain had managed to avoid the worst of the revolutionary and Napoleonic wars. The empire had participated in the war of the first coalition but had made peace with France in 1795 before any serious effort to conquer Spanish territory. The Bourbon monarchy had then become a reluctant ally of revolutionary France, starting in 1796. Though Spanish territory was mostly untouched by direct warfare, Spain and Spanish America suffered from its effects. The empire was obliged to increase military spending, as a French ally, and to bear the expenses of defending its colonial possessions. The fiscal strain was considerable. The government increased its exactions from the Spanish colonies. When these proved insufficient, the government began to ask for voluntary contributions to the war effort from corporations and individuals.[5]

The spread of books, newspapers, pamphlets, and rumors from the Atlantic regions that had already embarked on the revolutionary voyage further fed the region's discontent. There is no shortage of evidence that information from France, Haiti, the United States, and other revolutionary hot spots percolated into the Spanish realms. Enslaved people circulating through ports, especially mariners, passed word of the emancipations in Haiti and Guadeloupe, and other sites of rebellion. Reading and discussion societies called *tertulias* continued to spring up in the continent's urban centers, where (mostly) men could converse about the latest news and perhaps read a smuggled pamphlet or book. Yet it is important not to overstate the influence of this rumor mill on the political life of Spanish America. After all, by 1800, it was hardly necessary to receive secret information to know that revolutions were burning all over the Atlantic world or to understand that they could arrive on one's own doorstep.[6]

Signs also began to appear that, at least in some areas of Spanish America, the imperial government might be getting overripe and ready for the plucking. Since most of mainland Spanish America remained untouched by direct warfare until after 1808, there were few occasions for this weakness to be revealed. In 1806, however, a British invasion of Buenos Aires laid bare the government's vulnerability. The commander of a large contingent of British troops, who had recently captured Cape Town in South Africa, was ordered to occupy the city, one of the most commercially important ports in South America. The viceroy fled ahead of the arrival of the British forces, leaving the local criollo elite in charge. Though they initially welcomed the British, many of these criollos rapidly became disillusioned and sought a return of Spanish governance. A force of mostly criollo militiamen, under the command of a French-born officer, attacked and recaptured the city about a month later. Though in theory this feat of arms restored the imperial government's authority, it was the criollos whose authority was maintained. The viceroy himself, now much despised in the city, never returned.[7]

Events in Europe in 1807 and 1808 transformed the rumblings of revolt in Spanish America into a full-blown revolutionary situation. In October 1807, the Spanish government, nominally allied with Napoleon (though a cool ally at best), signed a treaty that would allow forty thousand imperial troops passage through Spain to invade Portugal, a British ally. After invading and quickly subduing Portugal—though the royal family escaped to Brazil aboard British warships—Napoleon invaded Spain as well. In the midst of the invasion, on March 19, the crown prince staged a coup against his father, Charles IV, the current monarch, overthrowing him and his government at the monarchy's springtime palace in Aranjuez. Four days later, French imperial forces under Joachim Murat entered Madrid without resistance.[8]

The new king, Ferdinand VII, reigned for barely more than a month. On May 5, 1808, in the French port of Bayonne near the border with Spain, Ferdinand abdicated the throne. Under orders from Napoleon, he directed his subjects to acknowledge a new sovereign: Joseph Bonaparte, Napoleon's brother. With this move, the authority that had bound Iberian Spain and the sprawling kingdoms of Spanish America together, tendon-like, for nearly three centuries, snapped.[9]

Napoleon's decision to remove the Bourbons from the Spanish throne sparked a powerful backlash among both ordinary people and the Spanish elite. Rebellions began almost immediately across Spain, with local juntas (governing councils) taking power. The organizers of the juntas understood themselves to be caretakers or "depositors" of sovereignty while the king was unable to exercise it. This meant having a rather modest notion of their authority and, in practice, leaving a vacuum of power. The juntas were soon organized, albeit loosely, under the authority of a Junta Central, led initially by a high-ranking elder statesman, the Count of Floridablanca. The Junta Central first met in Madrid, then retreated to Seville in Andalucía (in the south), and finally to the port city of Cádiz, under the protection of the British fleet.[10]

The decapitation of the Spanish monarchy tolled powerfully in the Americas. In legal form, the Spanish American lands were independent kingdoms, each ruled by a viceroy appointed by the king. (This made them different from the colonies of other European powers, which were constructed as bodies subordinate to the European nation.) The kings' forced abdications left viceregal authority in the Americas on shaky ground. Yet many of the other obvious pretenders to power in Spanish America faced a similar deficit of authority: the audiencias and the church each drew their power from the king. In 1808 and 1809, a number of local juntas formed across the Spanish American lands, claiming the power to govern. These early American juntas arose across the territory, largely in response to existing conflicts; most faced quick suppression by vice-regents and other authorities.[11]

In January 1810, the Junta Central in Spain dissolved itself in favor of a new Council of Regency. Before it did so, however, the junta declared that the Council of Regency would convene a parliament, or Cortes, in Cádiz, which would serve as the ruling body of the empire. It would be composed of elected representatives from Spain and Spanish America. The Cortes had an ambivalent stance toward the empire. On the one hand, it was the first governing body that included representatives of the Spaniards on both sides of the Atlantic. (The representation, however, was not equal: peninsular Spaniards were deliberately overrepresented.) Yet by speaking in the name of a fictive, unitary Spanish "nation," the Cortes claimed the same kind of sovereignty that the king had formerly exercised and denied any possibility of imagining the Americas as separate.[12]

News of the formation of the Council of Regency and the Cortes sparked synchronized and sustained revolts across Spanish America in 1810. By dissolving itself, the Junta Central had strengthened the argument that the royal sovereignty that had bound the empire together was in abeyance. Without the king's authority, powerful groups in the Spanish American kingdoms believed they were free to establish their own governments. The dam burst first in Caracas, on the Caribbean coast; its proximity to the independent states of North America and Haiti may have helped to make it the first. A group of prominent locals, using the cabildo (city council) as a vehicle, formed a junta that overthrew the governor. A similar revolt occurred a month later in Buenos Aires. This revolt soon went even further, asserting its authority over the entire Viceroyalty of the Río de la Plata.[13]

As political turmoil began to consume the Americas, the Cortes in Cádiz was working its way toward a dramatic decision to craft the first constitution for the Spanish empire. Though both conservatives and liberals initially embraced the idea of writing a constitution, as a way to shore up the authority of the monarchy and hold the empire together, it was the liberals in the Cortes who gained control of the process and shaped the result. Instead of re-creating the old regime, the law sought to create something quite new in the Spanish imperial world: a constitutional monarchy. It changed the king into a figurehead, with most power residing in the Cortes; the viceroys were demoted to something akin to chief executives; and it instituted powerful elected assemblies and representative bodies at every level of the polity in both hemispheres, from the town to the province.[14]

The Constitution made the cabildo an elected body and gave it considerable political weight in the new system. By the late old regime, the cabildo had shrunk from its origins as a powerful urban corporation into a shell of its former self. During the early modern era, the Crown had made its membership hereditary and stripped it of most of its powers. The reforms of the 1770s, which had strengthened the hand of royal intendants (like Cuzco's Don Benito de la Mata Linares) in local affairs, had further demoted the cabildo in the political pecking order. The Constitution abolished its hereditary character and made it into one of the most important elected bodies of the multilayered constitutional order.[15]

The Constitution specified that the cabildos were to be elected by the "citizens" of each circumscription. This term, as used in the Constitution, was on its face something of a novelty in the Spanish imperial world. In early modern Spain and its empire, the concept of *vecindad*, defined as full membership in the community based on long residence and deep attachments, had been the key form of political belonging. The category of "citizenship" in the 1812 Constitution built on and expanded this notion. (Exactly how much it changed the older definitions is a subject of dispute among scholars.) What is clear is that the Cortes made the category of "citizen" more explicitly ample than it had been before: it "recognized Creoles, Indians, and *mestizos* as both Spaniards and citizens." Only those of African descent, among the major population groups of the Spanish Americas, were explicitly excluded by the Constitution from the status of citizens. The Constitution did nonetheless define them as part of the community of "Spaniards," insofar as they were free and native-born.[16]

The Cortes dispatched the Constitution throughout Spain and the Spanish overseas empire. The official diffusion was slow and quite uneven. The Constitution, dated March 19, 1812, arrived in different regions and cities at a staggered pace. The colony of Panama officially received it on August 10. It did not arrive in most of New Granada, which had busy ports on the Caribbean coast and close connections to Atlantic trading networks, until September or early October. For it to reach the Peruvian highlands, far from any ocean routes, would take longer still. But the people of Peru were no means in the dark about the dramatic events taking place in Europe. By the early summer of 1812, they already knew that a constitution had been drafted and were awaiting its arrival.[17]

The official ceremony of promulgation was an essential part of the entry into force of the Constitution. The Cortes ordered that when the Constitution arrived in a town, the mayor (or other top official) and the town council were to arrange a formal public reading of the document. This was to take place in the "most public place" in town. They were to read the entire text—all fifty-odd pages and 384 articles of it—and accompany it with the signs of collective rejoicing: peals of the bells, "illuminations," and artillery salutes. The following day, the officials were to visit the local prisons and release some of the prisoners. At the next public holiday—most likely a Sunday—the townspeople were to assemble, hear a celebratory mass with a "brief exhortation" by the priest, and then swear fealty to the Constitution. The various public corporations and the army were also required to explicitly swear their fealty. Scrupulous records of all these events, and proof that the oaths had been taken, were to be kept.[18]

The 1812 constitutional ceremony was a new ritual with much older resonances. Public ceremonies had long been an important part of Spain's imperial world. Conquistadores declaimed a long Latin text to claim territory for their monarchs, and the entries of new viceroys had for centuries been marked with multiday extravaganzas that bedecked cities with processions, public dances, and long speeches. Promulgating the Constitution was not intended to be much of a departure from these rituals. As when a new viceroy arrived, the people were supposed to play their assigned role. They were there to witness, to celebrate—and to be silent.[19]

The document, so much anticipated in Peru and especially in Lima and Cuzco, was slow in arriving. The first delay was the typical slowdown caused by distance in the pre-telecommunications age; Peru was among the most distant of the Crown's domains from Spain. By the time the document reached Lima, it was already September 1812. Only on the last day of that month did Viceroy José Fernando de Abascal finally promulgate the Constitution in that city. Now the wait began in Cuzco to get a copy. The text itself had long since arrived thanks to the trade routes that linked Cuzco both to the Pacific and Atlantic coasts (the latter via the Plate River estuary and Buenos Aires). But the official copy was needed in order to promulgate it formally. That finally arrived on December 10, 1812, more than two months after its publication in Lima.[20]

Here the ceremonial script began to deviate from what had been planned. According to the wishes of the Cortes, and seemingly of Abascal as well, the Constitution should have been promulgated as soon as possible. But there were "rumors" that the conservative audiencia and its allies in the cabildo were resisting its publication. The rumors were given weight by the lack of any public preparations for the elaborate festival that was expected to follow the promulgation. (Given the massive size of the ceremony, the preparations would have been visible to everyone.) Four days after the document's arrival in Cuzco had become known, a group of lawyers led by Rafael Ramírez Arellano wrote and published a petition demanding that the Constitution be promulgated and enter into force. "Everything has been ready since the tenth to inaugurate the happy year [i.e., the first year of the Constitution], and to obey the Cortes," the lawyers wrote. But nothing had been done.[21]

In petitioning the cabildo, Arellano and his fellow lawyers were refusing to play by the rules of the old-regime ceremony. In the tradition of the viceregal entry, they would have been at most silent players, marching in their designated spot in the processions and offering their obeisance to the new ruler: they literally kissed his hand. Their role was to form part of the pageantry and to bear witness to the legitimation of new power. Now, they were positioning themselves as actors in the drama. When the Constitution arrived and was not promulgated, they interposed themselves as its advocates. The ritual of petitioning was itself an age-old practice in Spanish America. But this petition was a departure from the old-regime model. In the old regime, a petition was a personal appeal to the sovereign or his representatives for personal or collective help. The petitioner sought grace for him- or herself. The lawyers were not doing this. They presented themselves, both implicitly and explicitly, as speaking "in the name of the people."[22] Their petition sought a general, public goal, not a personal favor.

According to Mateo Pumacahua, the prominent Indian who was the titular president of the Real Audiencia, Arellano's petition and his activism had a substantial deleterious effect on the constitutional ceremony. Pumacahua wrote to his superiors that "nobody was present or concurred in its celebration as the Constitution ordained for its full formalization." The president painted a dreary picture of a failed ceremony, with only himself and the leaders of the cabildo "carrying the weight" of the proceedings. One can easily imagine the solemn clip-clop of the horse's hooves echoing through the largely empty streets beneath the searing summer sun. Convinced that Arellano was an "agitator," the government ordered his arrest on February 1, 1813. He, along with one of the other signatories to the lawyers' petition, Manuel Borja, was held in the prison near the Plaza de Armas in the heart of the city.[23]

As the Constitution of Cádiz arrived and was eventually promulgated, Spanish Americans went to the polls. As in much of the rest of the Euro-American world, elections in and of themselves were hardly unknown. However, the elections that took place in 1812 and 1813 were of an entirely different kind from what had been seen before in Spanish America. These elections drew voters in strikingly large numbers and from a wide cross section of the population: they included poor white men, Native people, and those of African descent. Some credit for this enormous shift goes to the framers of the Constitution, who defined membership in the polity in an unusually capacious way. But the fact that this principle was immediately accepted by a wide range of political actors on the ground is a sign that the terrain had already been well prepared for an extension of suffrage. The cultural shift that had been percolating over the previous two decades helped to make the elections for the constitutional cabildos into an unprecedented, continent-wide exercise in democracy.

The electoral system for the new cabildos and other offices that the Constitution envisioned was not obviously radical or innovative. First the local officials would conduct a census of the population to determine how many eligible voters and representatives were needed, and then they were to establish electoral districts. The election itself was to be a highly choreographed ceremony that would help link together the forms of authority in the city and the empire. A staid, formalized election day, modeled on solemn royal and religious festivals, would be staged by the political leadership. The elections themselves would be indirect: the voters chose electors who would in turn choose the members of the cabildo and other offices. Though the Constitution's language was not precise, the assumption seems to have been that "*vecinos*" (residents) would mean well-off heads of household.[24]

The reality on the ground in Spanish America turned out quite differently. In Mexico City, one of the places where the elections for the constitutional cabildo have been most thoroughly studied, the distinctive character of the new vote was on clear display. The scale of the election in Mexico City was impressive in itself: there were over nineteen thousand qualified voters in the city, and between 40 and 70 percent of them participated. These figures compare favorably with those in North America and France during the first decade of the nineteenth century. The electorate, as suggested by the somewhat vague wording of the Constitution, included all the *vecinos*, Spaniards and Indians. There is evidence that people of mixed race, and even men considered Black, voted as well. Just as remarkable, a robust "campaign organization" was in place to shape this mixed-race, mixed-class electorate. Soon after the vote took place, it emerged that hundreds of *papeletas* or electoral tickets had been distributed to voters before they had gone to the polls. To some at the time—particularly, defeated candidates—this practice smacked of corruption. But it shows just how much the early nineteenth-century generation was conscious of the political role to be played by ordinary people. The turnout for the first cabildo elections seems to have been similarly robust and socially broad in the towns of rural Mexico, though in the rural areas members of the traditional elite largely retained their dominance by getting themselves elected.[25]

Similar stories with local variations can be told about the cabildo elections in other Spanish viceroyalties. The port city of Guayaquil, in present-day Ecuador, was the capital of a growing, economically dynamic region. The city and its region had been moved back and forth administratively between the Viceroyalty of Peru and the Viceroyalty of New Granada over the course of the eighteenth century. The cabildo elections there in 1813 were similar in their key aspects to those in Mexico City. The officials charged with organizing the election in Guayaquil took an ample view of who should get the right to vote, allowing Native people and many people of African descent to participate. Social class and education were not considered a barrier either; the organizers took care to accommodate illiterate men. In Cuenca, an Andean city also located in present-day Ecuador, at least one constitutional official argued that women, because of their economic and social importance, should also have access to the "rights of full citizenship," including the right to vote. This proposal does not seem to have been approved, but it is indicative of the degree to which actors on the ground in Spanish America were ready to rethink political and social hierarchies in this moment.[26]

Back in Cuzco, the elections for the new constitutional cabildo and other offices had been scheduled for February 7, just a few days after Arellano's arrest. In Cuzco, the decision-makers had adopted a more restrictive view of the electorate than that which prevailed in other jurisdictions. Suffrage for the new cabildo was limited to those who were descendants of Spaniards on both the mother's and the father's side. Indians were encompassed under the title of *vecinos*, but in Cuzco only those who were members of the hereditary elite (*caciques*) were considered eligible to participate in elections. People of African descent seem to have been firmly excluded.[27]

Even with this limited suffrage, however, the people of Cuzco took a leading role in the election—and not at all the traditional one or the one that the formal rules prescribed. When election day came, officials arrived to find a large crowd gathered in front of the Convento de la Merced, a stone's throw from the Plaza de Armas. The protestors blocked the entrance to the church, preventing voters from entering to begin the electoral proceedings. To cries of "Viva la Constitución," they demanded the immediate liberation of Arellano and Borja from prison. After some tense negotiations, Audiencia president Pumacahua, who was present at the election, granted the prisoners' release and the crowd went to the prison, extracted the two men, and carried them back in triumph to the election site. The vote then proceeded, resulting in the election of Borja to the new cabildo. Yet even after the crowd allowed the election to go ahead, the people in it remained active participants in the action. Electors, as they went into La Merced to cast their votes, had to pass through the crowd.[28] One can imagine the intimidation they might have felt, the pressure to vote in the way that the crowd clearly wanted.

As with the celebrations of the promulgation of the Constitution, the February election revealed that politics in Cuzco had changed. The Cortes, like the Constitution itself, expected that members of the populace would act as witnesses to the ceremonies of power. The "people," though present, would be a passive screen on which the drama of authority would be acted. Instead, the crowd became an active force: the abstraction of the people gave way before the actual populace making its choices known. The insistence on Arellano and Borja being freed, making them eligible for election, and the crowd's vocal embrace of the liberal group the men led clearly gave shape to the election results. While the election remained a highly restricted affair—perhaps 10 percent of the total population was eligible to vote—the crowd's presence and demands shaped the outcome. Conservatives in the city government made the argument that the "riots, and tumults" by the general public had tainted the election. The five elected deputies were forced to produce a dossier of evidence to show that they were rightfully elected.[29]

Once Arellano and his allies had gained control of the cabildo, they did not hesitate to exercise their new authority. They seem to have claimed sweeping powers to protect the city and the region from military threats, to raise and disburse funds, and to dispense justice. (Some of these were part of the traditional portfolio of a cabildo, but not to the extent that Arellano and his allies claimed.) Other constituted bodies and authorities took umbrage at the cabildo's attempts to exercise far-reaching authority. Pumacahua, in a letter to the viceroy, complained bitterly of the presumptuous manner of the constitutional cabildo. Manuel Pardo, another audiencia official, complained that the cabildo was trying to "sweep away all of the legitimate authorities," including the Audiencia. The Audiencia, for its part, sent an official report that described the cabildo as seeking to "make war" on the other "authorities" in the region.[30]

It was no idle or foolish enthusiasm that led to the constitutional cabildo's aggressive exercise of its authority. The Audiencia and its allies tried to portray the cabildo's actions as the product of "ill intention[s]" or a thirst for power. But the situation was more complicated than they realized or were willing to admit. The cabildo did in fact, in its own eyes and in the eyes of many in the city, have a unique claim to authority: it was the only representatively elected governing body in Cuzco. The members of the cabildo believed—not without some reason—that as the first officials elected under the Constitution, their authority trumped that of even higher-ranking officials who owed their offices only to royal appointments.[31]

The triumph of the constitutional cabildo in Cuzco marked a coming of age for mass politics in the city. Cuzco and the highlands had not been without impulses toward political reform in the previous decades. The profound divisions of caste within the region had stymied every effort to build a durable mass constituency. Even Túpac Amaru, who had managed to unite criollos and Indians for a brief period, had been betrayed by the criollo leadership. The election of the constitutional cabildo, however, was the product of a collaborative alliance between liberal elites and the multiethnic, multi-caste lower orders of Cuzco. The younger generation had finally set Spanish America's long-delayed revolution into motion.

Nearly a decade of political strife and open warfare in Spanish America followed the entry into force of the Constitution of Cádiz in Cuzco and its region. In December 1813, Napoleon released Ferdinand VII and sent him back to Spain. He sought to reestablish the absolutist monarchy both in European Spain and Spanish America. In Spain, a "white terror" purged the administration of both French sympathizers and even liberals who had remained loyal to the Crown. Spanish America proved more resistant. Across the continent, the individuals and bodies who had gained power since 1808—including criollos, army officers, and city officials—showed little willingness to hand over their hard-won gains. Governing juntas in Buenos Aires, Colombia, and Venezuela refused to simply accept the reimposition of the old order. In 1814, efforts by the Crown to regain control sparked a major rebellion in Cuzco, led in part by Mateo Pumacahua, who abandoned his longtime loyalty to the *peninsulares*. The deft viceroy of Peru, José Fernando de Abascal, sent an army to put it down and brutally executed its leaders. Like the Túpac Amaru rebellion, revolt in the old Inca capital was a warning sign of more turbulence to come. In 1816, at Tucumán in present-day Argentina, a congress of representatives from more than a dozen provinces in present-day Argentina, Uruguay, and Bolivia met and declared an independent United Provinces of South America.[32]

As independence became an increasingly live possibility in Spanish America, the question of the form of government that would follow became an important topic of debate. That the independent countries would adopt a republican government was not obvious. Part of Haiti had followed the monarchist path after independence. France, another onetime republic, had become an empire after 1804. These and other possibilities were all open to the new states, in theory. Most of the leading Spanish American actors fell into one of two camps. Some, like Vicente Rocafuerte, a Colombian independence-era politician, argued for republican government. Others favored a constitutional monarchy not unlike that which the Cortes had tried to implement in 1812. The first Peruvian declaration of independence in 1821 sparked similar debates there.[33] Within the republican camp, there was a further deep division between advocates of centralism and federalism: Should the new republics adopt a strong central government or be essentially federations of regions and states?

The influence of North America was strongly felt in South America during the constitutional debates in the late 1810s and early 1820s. The texts of the US and state constitutions were one source of this influence. The United States had been a pioneer in written constitutionalism, and the US Constitution and state constitutions were widely admired among liberals and revolutionaries around the Atlantic during the 1790s and after. These documents circulated widely in Spanish America during the early nineteenth century. A complete translation of the US Constitution into Spanish appeared in 1810, and numerous partial translations, excerpts, and discussions were visible in publications and public debate during that decade. The US Constitution—and the prosperity of the United States, which was often attributed to it by political authors—was held up as a demonstration of the virtues of choosing a republican form of government. In the "Preliminary Discourse" to his 1811 translation of the US Constitution, the New Granada politician Miguel de Pombo adduced the US Constitution as evidence for the "path which we ought to follow" after independence.[34]

The other source of North American influence—and a strange one at that—was Thomas Paine's *Common Sense*. Paine died shortly before the Cortes had first met in 1810, and the last years of his career had been difficult. He had gained a public following in 1776 with *Common Sense*, a slashing attack on the British constitutional monarchy, and hereditary monarchy more generally, that led to an impassioned call for North American independence. Between 1790 and 1797, he had published some of his most enduring works: *The Rights of Man*, which so enraged Edmund Burke; *The Age of Reason*; and *Agrarian Justice*. Meanwhile, *Common Sense* had largely disappeared from public view. Though it was translated into French in 1790 and 1791, it had little impact in France: the spread of strong anti-monarchical sentiment would not come for another two years.[35]

After 1810, *Common Sense* enjoyed a sudden revival in Spanish America. The reasons were obvious: Paine's denunciation of a far-off monarchy and the vices of hereditary kingship were directly applicable to the situation in which Spanish America found itself in the wake of Napoleon's invasion of Spain. The first translation of the pamphlet into Spanish appeared in 1811, in a book published in Philadelphia, *La independencia de la Costa Firme justificada por Thomas Paine*. The translator, Manuel García de Sena, was a Venezuelan-born lawyer living in Philadelphia. After 1820, several other Spanish versions appeared in quick succession.[36]

*Common Sense* spoke to Spanish American authors because it combined an attack on monarchy and an advocacy of republicanism with an endorsement of powerful and centralized government. Though often mistaken for a kind of proto-libertarian, Paine was a lifelong advocate for strong government, provided that it was democratic and responsive to its constituents. The Pennsylvania Constitution of 1776, which Paine endorsed enthusiastically, had a single house of legislature and frequent elections. It was regarded as a dynamic and empowered government that was highly responsive to popular demands. In the 1780s, Paine advocated for a stronger central government. He was disappointed by the US Constitution of 1787 in part because he feared its complex structure would make it weak.[37]

Paine's rejection of balanced and limited government, which had largely fallen on deaf ears in the United States, found a receptive audience in South America. The Peruvian intellectual and jurist Manuel Lorenzo de Vidaurre was one of those who took up the baton of the "Divine Paine" after 1820. Vidaurre, born in Lima in 1773, had lived through the repression of the criollos in Peru during the 1780s. (Vidaurre was already conversant with Paine's works, including *Common Sense*, as early as 1810, when he was living in Cuzco.) Throughout the 1810s, as conflict raged in Europe and in the Americas, Vidaurre had been a firm advocate for American rights while opposing independence. Once Vidaurre embraced independence, however, Paine became one of his major influences. In an important 1824 speech, Vidaurre gave a biting denunciation of the British monarchy: "There was never a monarchy more avaricious, more venal, more unjust, more ferocious, more baleful." In a discourse on the opening of the Gran Asamblea Americana (Congress of Panama) held in 1826, he echoed *Common Sense* in denouncing the "ancient, complicated, defective architecture" of constitutional monarchies. He favored simplicity—and centralized authority.[38]

South America's constitutions, especially those written during the 1820s, followed Paine's model of favoring strength over balance. The first Peruvian Constitution, promulgated in 1822 by the First Constituent Congress, divided government among the three branches, legislative, executive, judicial, as was typical of balanced constitutions. Within each of the power structures, however, the Constitution prioritized strength. The legislative power was "one" and indivisible, and conferred on a single chamber. Executive power, similarly, was imbued in a single head of state, the president. With the exception of the first Venezuelan Constitution of 1811, which modeled itself on the United States, most of the dozens of South American constitutions created a "strong centralist state."[39]

The inclination toward centralism in South American constitutions had many sources. The circumstances of late Bourbon Spanish America, many commentators noted, made it important to have a strong central government. The diversity of the population, the fragmented economy, and the relative weakness of royal authority under the old regime all placed a heavy burden on the new governments to forge states that could maintain their internal cohesion and fend off external enemies. The prevalence of the centralist model also owed something to the French revolutionary and Napoleonic constitutions, which had demonstrated just how much change a centralized state could force through even a recalcitrant society. Geographical proximity mattered too: Mexico, which had much closer ties to the United States, adopted a federal model that more closely resembled that of its neighbor.

Like the political leaders in Europe during this period, South American constitutional thinkers sought to create strong governments to shape and direct mass movements. When they looked to the United States, they did not initially find much that would help them in this direction: US constitutionalism was decentralized and generally favored relatively weak governance. The turn to Paine, and to *Common Sense* in particular—a book that had been largely neglected for decades until they revived it—is a measure of how intent the younger generation of South American constitutional thinkers were on creating powerful governments to match and master the mass movements they saw emerging from the revolutionary waves of the early nineteenth century.

# 19
# THE NATION UNDER ARMS

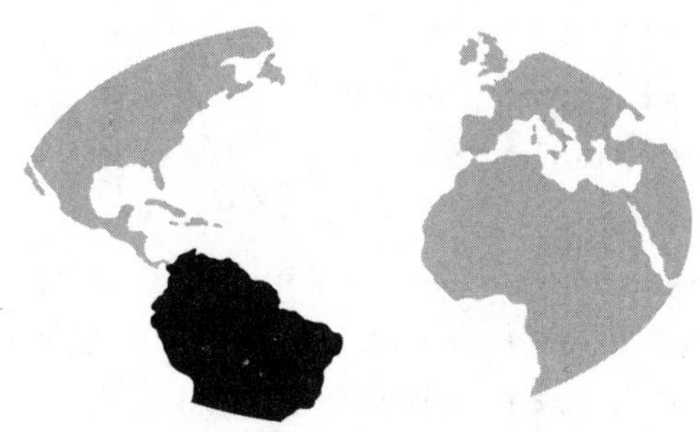

On August 21, 1820, an army operating from Chile under the command of General José de San Martín made landfall on the coast of Peru. Over the next ten months, the self-appointed "Peruvian Liberation Army," comprising soldiers belonging to several racial caste groups, made slow but steady progress capturing the loyalist strongholds along the coast. In June 1821, the army entered the capital, Lima, and on July 15, 1821, San Martín declared Peru independent of Spain. Just under a month later, on August 12, he issued a decree of gradual emancipation for Peru's enslaved population.

The conjuncture in 1821 in Peru of an army, a powerful military leader, and a decree of emancipation, all in close proximity to a declaration of independence, was no accident. Scholars of Spanish American independence have long recognized the very significant place that military conflict occupied in the overall process. Traditional narratives have focused in particular on how charismatic caudillos (roughly translated as "strongmen"), among them San Martín, dominated the independence movements. This political pattern has been used to explain why independent South American states were supposedly less stable and less democratic than the postrevolutionary states of North America and Europe. The slow abolition of slavery in the Spanish-speaking Americas has also been closely connected by scholars to the supposedly exceptional circumstances of early national Latin America, especially the liberal views of some of the caudillos and the exigencies of fighting a series of long wars.

These features of the Spanish American independence movements were not so exceptional after all. In Europe after 1800, revolutions took a hard turn toward institution building and a reconstituted form of one-man rule. In Haiti after independence, the leadership deemed it necessary to curb the exercise of political rights and to maintain a repressive labor regime in the interests of preserving the island nation's collective freedom. This was not so much a counterrevolutionary turn—it was, after all, dictated by leaders with impeccable revolutionary credentials—as a prioritization of one kind of freedom over others. North America, under the single-party rule of the Democratic-Republicans, cannot be said to have been much more enlightened. There, the slow opening of the franchise for white men was paired with a radical closure of access to formal politics for virtually every other social group, notably African Americans, and the growth and reinforcement of the regime of American slavery. Spanish America was not the anomaly but the epitome of the second revolutionary wave.

The three elements that came together in Peru during the summer of 1821—a charismatic general, a socially diverse army, and emancipation of the enslaved—were each in their way expressions of the distinctive habitus and practices of the second-wave revolutionaries. A condition of the Peruvian Liberation Army's existence was the characteristic early nineteenth-century acceptance of social mobility and cross-class socializing, especially among men. The army functioned because the men who joined it were willing to work together, in a single group, with men of other races, castes, and classes. This acceptance of social mobility cannot be traced back to the political ideologies of autonomy or independence: the armies of loyalists were, if anything, even more marked by racial and caste diversity.

The generals who played an important role in shaping the armies and mobilizing them to bring about independence—including San Martín and Simón Bolívar, but also the likes of Argentine independence leader Manuel Belgrano—were children of the revolution. They understood, like Napoleon, that their authority rested on personal qualities and individual accomplishments ratified by the endorsement of a mass following, not on inherited social position. Gradual emancipation was a product of the troubled outer limit of this generation's reflection on the permanence of social hierarchy. The legislators and leaders of the independence era were deeply uncomfortable with the idea of heritable status. But many of them were also fearful of the consequences of rapid social mobility. Their solution was a generational one, freeing only the children of enslaved people born after a certain date. This strategy and the legislation that gave it full effect mirrored, implicitly and at times explicitly, the revolutionaries' own experience of the apprenticeship of revolutionary politics over the prior quarter century.

The role of the armed forces in Spanish American independence was thoroughly entangled with the vexed, halting political processes of revolt and rebellion. For roughly a year and a half after the forced abdication of the Spanish kings in the spring of 1808, political authority in Spanish America remained in a state of suspended animation. Almost all the viceroys and subordinate

SOUTH AMERICAN INDEPENDENCE, 1808–1825

royal officials remained in place, continuing to act in the name of the Crown. On the surface, the situation was peaceful. But it was a watchful peace, filled with doubts and uncertainty about what would happen next. This tense peace collapsed in early 1810, around the time that elections were being held for the Cortes of Cádiz. Within a few weeks of each other, in April and May, the cabildos of Buenos Aires and Caracas (a port city in the captaincy general of Venezuela, vulnerable to invasion) ousted the local royal officials and established new governments. Both cities were careful to say, however, that they were not declaring their independence.[1]

Over the course of the next year, dozens of towns and cities in various parts of South America followed the lead of Caracas and Buenos Aires. From Cali and Santa Fe de Bogotá in New Granada (present-day Colombia) to Santiago, far to the south in Chile, localized revolts toppled royal officials in the name of the sovereign. As more towns overthrew their royally appointed officials, loyalists entrenched themselves in other cities and towns. The entirety of the Viceroyalty of Peru, governed by the skilled Viceroy Abascal, remained for the time being in the hands of the loyalists, but many other loyalist towns and regions sat in close proximity to centers of the rebellion. Montevideo, just across the Plate River from Buenos Aires, formed itself into an armed loyalist camp in direct opposition to the rebellious city across the estuary. In New Granada, the coastal town of Santa Marta stayed loyal to the existing royal authorities. There were also considerable differences among the loyalist regions; some adopted a fervent revanchism while others retained officials more out of habit or convenience.

The multilevel patchwork of loyalist and rebel towns, cities, and regions drove both sides to speedily develop military forces suitable for both attack and defense. In short order, much of the continent was at war with itself. Many of the wars were micro-conflicts, fought between neighboring towns on opposite sides of the political divide. Others were major, long-range expeditions: among the most spectacular was the campaign by Buenos Aires to conquer Upper Peru. Warfare, in turn, further radicalized both sides politically. By 1811, Venezuela and New Granada had given up the pretense of autonomy and had formally declared themselves independent republics. On a far smaller scale, numerous towns and regions used the occasion of imperial upheaval to try to throw off the yoke of regional and viceregal capitals.

Over the next four years, from 1812 to 1816, the initial burst of rebellions, independence, and military confrontation gave way to a grinding reassertion of imperial authority across the continent. The republics in Venezuela and New Granada each collapsed, revived, and collapsed again. In 1814, as Napoleon was retreating from his European conquests, Ferdinand VII was restored to the Spanish throne. He and his advisors immediately sought to reverse the political changes of the past six years. In early 1815, a large expeditionary force set out from Spain to reconquer South America. In a "brisk and uncompromising campaign," the royal forces under General Pablo Morillo regained control of New Granada and Venezuela. A separate campaign in Chile crushed the movement for autonomy there. Of the major rebel regions, only the Río de la Plata held out, and their war in the Andes with loyalist forces from Peru was not going well.

Starting in 1816, and at an accelerating pace over the next five years, the rebels regained the initiative. In the north, armies under the command of Simón Bolívar, fighting in the name of a re-resurrected republican regime, gradually took back Venezuela and New Granada. To the southeast, Buenos Aires finally declared itself independent of Spain in 1816. Its armies also began to make progress against the loyalists nearby and farther off. In Chile, a reborn republican army first cleared loyalist forces from the province and then mounted an attack on Peru to the north. In 1821, San Martín conquered Peru, the last major redoubt of Spanish imperial authority in South America, and declared it to be an independent state.

As was the case almost everywhere in the revolutionary Atlantic world, armed forces played an essential role in protecting, extending, and consolidating revolutionary politics. Everywhere, the creation of armies had resulted in some degree of popular mobilization and social mobility and mixing within the ranks. This had certainly been the case in the North American Continental Army of the 1770s and 1780s, and even more so in the French revolutionary army of the 1790s. The Napoleonic era had supercharged both of these movement-building aspects of revolutionary armies. The military mobilization in the Spanish American revolutionary wars was transformative in similar ways: the armies were formed through mass mobilizations, which militarized their societies over sustained periods, and the forces themselves became crucibles for further social mixing. Since the armies' ranks were almost exclusively composed of men, they helped to strengthen the link between male sociability and citizenship that had emerged earlier in the revolutionary period.

Militias and standing armies were a familiar part of life in colonial-era Spanish America. During the seventeenth and early eighteenth centuries, most of the military muscle in Spanish America had been provided by locally recruited militias. Though the laws changed over time, in general it was expected that able-bodied householders in every town or city would be prepared to bear arms in its defense. The eligible men were organized into an elaborate system of militia companies, which were structured as civic corporations. These corporations played a very important role in the rituals and everyday ordering of urban life in Spanish America, alongside guilds and religious societies (confraternities). The militia companies' great utility in organizing urban life was not matched by a similar degree of military value. The militia were "proverbially ineffective" as a military force; it was well-known that they could not stand up to disciplined troops. It may have been partly for this reason that the Spanish government gradually expanded the number of regular soldiers garrisoned in Spanish America over the course of the eighteenth century. Yet these troops, though a more effective fighting force, remained relatively small in number: only about thirty thousand regular troops were posted in all of Spanish America in the 1780s and 1790s.[2]

Starting in 1808, sustained military mobilizations took place across many of the regions of Spanish America. Given the continent's politically fragmented character after 1808, there was no equivalent to the centralized enlistment systems that Napoleon's regime brought into being. Each autonomous city and region organized its own military recruitment. This decentralized quality, seen from the point of view of the region as a whole, did not make military recruitment any less effective. Indeed, it has been argued to the contrary that the highly local scale of recruitment may have made it that much more difficult for men to avoid enlisting: it was, after all, often literally their neighbors who were calling up the prospective recruits. The depth of the mobilizations is visible in both their absolute and relative numbers. In the Río de la Plata during the later 1810s, one scholar has calculated that nearly half the adult male population was enlisted in the armed forces (militia or regular army). By comparison, France during the *levée en masse* of 1793–1794 attained a maximum of just one out of every nine men under arms. In New Granada, the size of the autonomist armed forces grew fivefold during the five years from 1817 to 1822, from around five thousand to over twenty-five thousand men. This massive recruitment yielded armies that were of unprecedented size for the region. This fact can be somewhat obscured by comparisons with the Napoleonic armies, which were much larger in absolute terms. But the Napoleonic armies were drawn from a far larger population. The scale of the Spanish American armies, on the order of tens of thousands at their largest, were proportionally as large as the European ones.[3]

The Spanish American military call-up of the 1810s, like those of the Napoleonic era in Europe, penetrated deeply into the society at large. One scholar has described it as effecting a gradual "militarization of civil society." The experience of mobilization was in many ways a new one for South Americans. With the exception of a few of the mainland's key Caribbean-facing ports, South America had not been under regular threat from enemy armies during the colonial period. As these societies experienced large-scale enlistment, it had knock-on effects throughout the social order. In Buenos Aires, where members of the city's working class were pressed into military service in large numbers, the group's collective military experience gave them new leverage in internal political struggles within the city. It was not so much that they functioned internally as an armed force—though that did occur—but that the experience of military service gave them a heightened moral authority and rhetorical platform to pursue their goals. On the flip side of the coin, large-scale mobilization brought with it the same kinds of social and economic challenges that were familiar in European contexts: challenges of provisioning, desertion from the army and violence by off-duty soldiers, and the need to maintain household economies while men were away at war.[4]

The mass mobilization that began after 1808 also took place in loyalist cities and regions during these years, and in a manner that was virtually indistinguishable from that of their opponents. This similarity was most apparent in New Granada, where many of the loyalist towns had to form armies from scratch to meet the challenge posed by freshly armed autonomists in and around 1809 and 1810. In 1809, as the first military confrontations were beginning in New Granada, royal officials in Pasto (present-day Colombia, near the border with Ecuador) successfully negotiated to have the local Indian communities mobilize in order to thwart a planned autonomist attack from the south. Two years later, in 1811, the cabildo in the town of Popayán, facing an attack from the forces of the nearby Confederated Cities of the Cauca Valley, crafted a plan to recruit enslaved people into the town's armed forces. The cabildo promised the enslaved people freedom in exchange for their service, underscoring the degree to which loyalists were also willing to disrupt the social order to mobilization manpower.[5]

As the examples of Indian and enslaved soldiers from New Granada suggest, one of the distinctive and remarkable features of the South American military mobilization was its considerable racial and ethnic diversity. Such diversity in a military context was not novel in Spanish America. There was already a long tradition in the region of people of color and Indians serving in the Spanish empire's armed forces. Indeed, from the standpoint of other European empires, the reliance of the Spanish Crown on non-white soldiers during the colonial period was quite remarkable. In the Caribbean and colonial Mexico, for instance, free people of color formed a major part of the militia establishment through most of the colonial period. Soldiers of color did not get equal treatment with their white counterparts, whether in pay, opportunities for command, or working conditions. In some regions, soldiers of color were charged with menial or dangerous jobs. Even where the treatment was unequal, however, there were significant advantages to military service, including the right to bear arms and (in some cases) legal privileges that were conferred on members of the military.[6]

Both loyalists and autonomists (and later, republicans) built on the tradition of military service by free people of color. Free people of color formed an important part of almost all the independence-era armies, serving in every theater of the conflict. Indeed, their presence was so universal as to occasion relatively little comment or objection. More controversial was the incorporation of growing numbers of enslaved people into the various armies. The actions of the Popayán cabildo had only been a beginning in this regard.

Though hard figures are difficult to come by, it is clear that "thousands" of enslaved people served under arms during the 1810s and early 1820s. Generals and other officials promised enslaved people their freedom in exchange for voluntary enlistments. Since these promises were often broken, and military service was not the only route to freedom in Spanish America, such promises do not seem to have enticed very many enslaved people to enlist of their own accord. Many of the armies resorted instead to conscripting enslaved people, often by dint of effectively purchasing them from their enslavers. This created the paradoxical phenomenon, in the republican armies, of enslaved people being forced into the service of a self-proclaimed liberation movement.[7]

The class and caste diversity of the South American armies gave them a potential role as a crucible for new kinds of social equality among men. In this sense, the independence-era armies in South America could be an engine of social equality even more potent than the armies of revolutionary Haiti had been. The extent to which military service in the Spanish American armies unsettled or softened racial, ethnic, and class lines is difficult to determine with any precision. There were certainly moments of camaraderie and precocious social mixing. Yet racial and class distinctions did not dissolve among those who served in the armies, either during the wars themselves or in their aftermath; veterans of the South American armed forces were not necessarily tribunes of equality. What's more, whatever leveling or equalizing effect service in the armed forces did have, it was limited to male citizens or subjects.[8]

More certain is that the social diversity of the South American armies gave them a unique symbolic role, especially in the republican regimes that emerged after 1810. The armies could stand in, symbolically, for the sovereign "people." One of the problems that bedeviled the fledgling independent republics of Spanish America was the difficulty, in the midst of constant civil strife, of locating the fictive "people" whom the republics claimed were the true font of sovereignty and authority. The revolutionary armies, as Clément Thibaud has argued, were uniquely well suited to fictively "incarnate the People," imagined as a unitary and homogenous source of sovereign power. In this way, they resembled the army of Henry Christophe's Haitian kingdom, which also stood in for the people in general.[9]

Military mobilization, in short, became a crucial engine of the large-scale political organizing that took place during the Spanish American imperial crisis. The mobilization reached deep into the continent's societies, bringing a cross section of the population, from all classes and castes, into the heart of the political struggle.

THE REPUBLICAN ARMIES OF THE SOUTH AMERICAN INDEPENDENCE movement fueled the rise of a new generation of leaders during the 1810s. The three most prominent members of this group were Simón Bolívar, José de San Martín, and Manuel Belgrano. Bolívar was based in the north, in New Granada and Venezuela; San Martín and Belgrano had their base in Buenos Aires and the southern Andes. All three men fused political and military leadership roles and exercised their authority in a highly personal manner. With Spanish America in the midst of rapid political and military transformations, these republican patriot-generals became essential figures, the bedrock around whom durable political regimes could be constructed.

The role that the patriot-generals played in South America beginning in the 1810s had clear antecedents in the age of revolutions. As David A. Bell has argued, the Atlantic revolutionary era catalyzed the emergence of a new model of charismatic political authority around the Atlantic. Forms of personal leadership had a long history, but the eighteenth-century spread of a language of sentimental emotion, coupled with the rapid expansion of print, created the conditions for a new form of personal leadership to develop. It rested on a mythologizing of the supposedly superhuman virtues—martial and otherwise—of the leader. This pattern first became visible around the person of Pasquale Paoli, hero of Corsican independence, during the 1760s. Over the next four decades, Bell argues, George Washington, Napoleon Bonaparte, and Toussaint Louverture all drew on this model of charismatic authority to build, shape, and govern revolutionary political movements. Bolívar and, to a lesser extent, San Martín and Belgrano were part of this same tradition.[10]

Central to this new form of power was the idea that the leader's authority flowed not from his high birth or God-given right but from exceptional personal qualities that were recognized and acknowledged by his followers. It was no accident that none of these leaders came from a house of rulers. Napoleon, Washington, and Bolívar were all literally to a manor born, but none came from political dynasties, and Louverture, of course, had been born into slavery. Recognizing the importance of personal qualities and public acclamation in this new form of authority helps to explain the turn toward one-man rule that so many of them took. It was not a very long step, after all, from being adored for one's personal virtue and genius to concluding that it would be far better to gather the reins of power in one's own hands alone.

Yet while the South American patriot-generals took part in this tradition of hero-style leadership, their version of it differed meaningfully from that espoused by Washington and Louverture. The contrast with George Washington is particularly instructive. It is certainly true that Washington, Bolívar, and San Martín read many of the same enlightenment texts and were imbued with similar ideals of military valor and honor. But the social worlds in which they had been formed, and thus their understanding of the relationship between leaders and followers, differed in fundamental ways. Washington was a pure product of the first half of the eighteenth century. The serene self-confidence in his own superior social position that he had imbibed as a youth never really left him. The patriot-generals of South America, on the other hand, never knew such social fixity. Bolívar, born in 1783, had grown up in Venezuela at a moment when the Caribbean was a major theater of warfare and revolution. San Martín (born 1778) had spent the 1790s and early years of the 1800s fighting in Spain's European wars. He, even more than Bolívar, had been a firsthand witness to the tremendous creative destruction—social as well as physical—of the Atlantic revolutionary wars.[11]

Like Napoleon—their closest analog among the other charismatic political leaders of the era—the South American patriot-generals were nothing if not members of the second revolutionary generation. They always had a weather eye out not just for political changes but for social ones as well. And their political vision was profoundly entwined with ideas about transforming and reshaping the social world, either by advancing equality or, in a darker vein, actively reinforcing or reconstructing social hierarchies that were threatened by the shifting cultural sands.

As the slow-motion collapse of Spanish authority in America unfolded from 1808 to 1820, a wave of gradual abolition laws swept across South America. The spread of abolition was deeply entwined with the military conflicts, and the process came to be closely identified with a number of leading generals.

The initial phase of emancipations was propelled by liberal legislators and presented largely in terms of humanitarian principles and enlightened ideals: As a Colombian advocate of gradual emancipation put it in 1813, how could slavery persist "when everywhere else the eternal rights of man [are] proclaimed?" The first enactments of emancipation decrees came in the Southern Cone—present-day Chile and Argentina—which had small populations of enslaved people. Chile acted in 1811, emancipating enslaved people at birth. Buenos Aires declared gradual emancipation in 1813, with a period of "apprenticeship" before freedom was granted (though the abolition of slavery there in fact took decades, slowed by resistance and civil war). In the Viceroyalty of New Granada, the fragmented political authorities of the early 1810s produced a number of gradual emancipation projects, laws, and constitutional provisions, all of which revolved around making children born to enslaved women eventually free.[12]

More broadly, the thirty years from 1790 to 1820 were the heyday for the gradual abolition of slavery in the Atlantic world. Most of the scholarly attention has long focused on the few instances in which slavery was abolished with immediate effect. Yet these were very much the exception. More typical were the successive gradual emancipation acts in North America, which preceded and may have offered a model or inspiration to Spanish American political actors. In 1780, the newly created state of Pennsylvania decreed that children born to enslaved women after March 1 would be freed at the age of twenty-eight. Connecticut and Rhode Island followed suit in 1784, with slightly different provisions. And New York and New Jersey enacted similar legislation in 1799 and 1804, respectively. All of these jurisdictions had small enslaved populations, making it relatively easy for them to follow the logic of a humanitarian, principled argument against slavery.[13]

Advocates of gradual emancipation consistently emphasized the important role of education and self-improvement as one of the keys to the success of the emancipation movement. "First movement" abolitionists in the early United States "sought to prove the capacity of people of color for freedom by . . . making them virtuous and independent citizens." In similar fashion, publicists in Colombia justified the 1821 gradual emancipation law that eventually subsumed the others as an instrument for the "gradual and prepared transition of slaves into *libres*."[14]

There was thus already a rich set of precedents and rationales for emancipation in place when San Martín attacked Peru in September 1820. The expedition, though it ostentatiously presented itself as an army of liberation, was very much an invasion. The expedition was mounted from Chile and went under the Chilean flag. During the years from 1813 to 1818, forces under San Martín had laboriously defeated the royalists in Chile. But their control remained threatened by royalist forces in the Viceroyalty of Peru. It was in this context that Bernardo O'Higgins, Chile's liberal revolutionary leader, who was passionately committed to "beloved equality," dispatched San Martín to seize Peru from the royalists.[15]

For San Martín, arriving in Peru as an armed "liberator," gaining the support of a critical mass of the population was a crucial and also a difficult problem. Socially, Peru was far more akin to the northern Andes and the Caribbean region than it was to Chile or Buenos Aires. It had an Indian majority and an enslaved population that, though small as a percentage, was highly concentrated in Lima and the surrounding regions. These populations had been key to resilient royalist armies in a number of areas.[16] As in the northern Andes and Caribbean region, however, the balance of power was held by criollos and mestizos (in theory, people of mixed Indian and Spanish ancestry). Many of these creoles and mestizos were economically dependent on the labor of enslaved people or Indians. Building a successful mass movement thus required a deft process of steering between these large and important population groups, which had quite different political, social, and economic interests.

The emancipation decree of August 12, 1821, was part of a cluster of orders that San Martín issued during the weeks after independence that were clearly intended both to fulfill liberal promises and to rally parts of the Peruvian populace to the cause of independence. These included a decree abolishing forms of "personal servitude" for Indians, including the hated corvée or labor service to which they had been subjected, and a decree protecting Spanish-born individuals who were willing to be loyal to the independent nation. The emancipation decree, like these other liberalizing reforms, was simple and declarative in its wording: it proclaimed that "all the children of slaves who were or shall be born . . . after July 28 . . . shall be free and shall enjoy the same rights as other citizens of Peru."[17]

San Martín's efforts to build political support through emancipation of the enslaved immediately ran into trouble. Even before the decree had been issued, creole elites had been hinting that they would be strongly opposed to what they regarded as an attack on their labor force. In a series of petitions to the general, prominent Lima-area creoles objected to any possible emancipation project. "Without extra hands and beasts of burden, there is no agriculture," began one of these petitions, which called on San Martín to maintain the status quo. Other petitions asked that fugitive enslaved people be returned to their plantations, since they were the "only hands" for cultivation. Implicit in these petitions, and explicit in others that came before San Martín in substantial numbers, was the threat that the powerful creoles would withhold their support from the Peruvian Liberation Army.[18]

By November, less than two months after he issued his proclamation, San Martín had pulled back significantly from his initial emancipation program. He issued a new decree that revised the emancipation act by putting limits on what had initially seemed to be an expansive project. The November regulations emphasized the importance to the "social order" of *libertos* (freedmen) being properly educated about the "principles of the religion of the states" and their "duties to the fatherland." *Libertos* were directed to work for their enslavers until early adulthood as a "just payment" for the costs incurred in rearing them. The biggest blow, however, was that only after they had been freed and were "exercising some useful profession or industry" would they "enjoy the rights" of citizenship.

The August decree's promise of "the same rights as other citizens of Peru" was effectively a dead letter.[19]

At the same time, San Martín's November regulations tried to turn the abolition of slavery, in a peculiar fashion, into a kind of educational process for the slaveholders. The decree devoted one of its six substantive sections to creating a system by which a "*regidor* [councilman]" from each municipality would be charged with keeping a "list of the masters who fulfill [these regulations] with the most zeal and humanity." That list was to be "published by the press every year" as a "special title of recommendation" that would entitle them to a commendation from the government as "worthy and virtuous citizens."[20] Enslavers' cooperation with the decrees on gradual abolition would be used as an index of their civic virtue. The enslaved, in this twisted vision, became a means by which San Martín could gain the support not of the enslaved themselves but of their masters.

San Martín paired this curtailment of the original emancipation decree with a new program for emancipation of enslaved men via military service, which was carefully calibrated to maximize his mass following. In a series of orders starting in November 1821, San Martín created routes for enslaved men of military age to join the Peruvian Liberation Army, with emancipation as a reward. Yet he was careful, as he had not been in his earlier decrees, to limit the application to enslaved people who would be of no direct concern to the creoles whose support he badly needed. A decree of November 17 freed those who belonged to Spaniards who had departed from Peru. Another decree, dated November 23, emancipated enslaved people who had deserted from the Spanish royal army. These measures, by linking emancipation to the political choices of their enslavers, emphasized the increasingly instrumental nature of San Martín's emancipation program.[21]

San Martín's political strategy was successful in rallying creoles to his banner. Over the next four years, he and his successor,

Bolívar, succeeded in gaining the support of most of the creole population in coastal Peru. By 1825, when the war for independence ended in Peru, the creole population, which had begun the war largely on the fence, was solidly in the patriot camp. At the same time, San Martín's actions had slowed the abolition of slavery to a snail's pace. The immediate changes in 1821 had already impeded the progress of gradual emancipation. The years after brought further regulations limiting the freedom enjoyed by former slaves, including requirements to register and carry with them freedom papers. These and other rules impeded the abolition of slavery in Peru, just as had happened in the Río de la Plata. Not until the end of the 1850s—and even then only with compensation paid to the enslavers—was human bondage finally eliminated in Peru.[22]

Of all of the revolutions that rumbled through the Atlantic empires during the eighteenth and nineteenth centuries, none was more fully the handiwork of the second generation than the independence movements in South America. By the time the calls for autonomy began sounding in Spanish America after 1808, members of the older generation—like Maria Rivadeneyra and her brothers-in-law, the Ugartes—were either already dead or well past the peak of their political leadership. From the start of the conflict within the empire, a large share of the protagonists in South America, on both sides, were members of the second revolutionary generation. Whether they had grown up in Peru in the wake of the Túpac Amaru revolution, in New Granada as the Haitian Revolution burst open across the Caribbean Sea, or in the Río de la Plata under the eye of foreign fleets, the disturbances of the earlier revolutions were part of their formative years.

The Spanish American independence movements became, in a number of ways, the canvas on which the second generation's revolutionary habitus could be most fully expressed. Political leaders in South America, aided by their generation's acceptance of status mobility and ease with social mixing, had a far easier time organizing men across lines of class and caste than their revolutionary precursors. By 1812, less than four years after the Spanish monarchy was overthrown, sizeable, diverse armies were marching across the continent and tens of thousands of Spanish American men had voted in elections with a wide franchise. This organizing far exceeded, in both its speed and its breadth, the first efforts at revolutionary movement building that had taken place in North America and Europe during the 1770s, 1780s, and 1790s. Yet this impressive political mobilization came at a steep cost. The movements were rapidly co-opted by charismatic, autocratic political leaders, adept at using social mobility to foster personal loyalty. As they consolidated their rule, these leaders strengthened their coalitions for the long term by closing off avenues for political engagement and freedom to women and people of color.

# CONCLUSION

BY 1826, THE YEAR AFTER PERU BECAME INDEPENDENT, THE last members of the first revolutionary generation, most of whom had long ago retired from active involvement in politics, were dying out. Jacques-Louis David, the prodigy painter who had been an enthusiastic member of the Jacobin republic's government back in 1793–1794, passed away in the last days of December 1825. Death found him in Brussels, where he was living in exile after the restoration of the French monarchy. In the United States, John Adams and Thomas Jefferson both died—by an astonishing coincidence—on the fiftieth anniversary of US independence, July 4, 1826. Túpac Amaru's long-exiled brother, Juan Bautista Túpac Amaru, finally returned to South America in 1822. He died in Buenos Aires in 1827, without ever having seen the Andes again.

The wave of revolutions that Adams, David, and Túpac Amaru had lived through over the previous six decades had made the Atlantic world into something that their younger selves would hardly have recognized. It was a world of emerging republics, growing mass cultures, and emancipation—but also of repressive dictatorships, deepening racism, and exclusion. The double face of the revolutionary transformation was visible in every region that the upheaval had touched.[1]

More than sixty years ago, both R. R. Palmer and Eric Hobsbawm offered explanations for the revolutionary era's Janus-faced political transformation. Palmer—who saw the revolutions as emerging from a three-way confrontation among monarchs, "constituted bodies," and "democrats"—interpreted the illiberal outcomes of the revolutionary era as evidence of the resilience of "conservatives" and "established interests" in the face of democrats' push for "equality." Because he saw the pursuit of "equality" as the essence of revolutionary politics, Palmer viewed forms of inequality that persisted as external to the "revolution" properly speaking, products of the revolutionary movement's failures or the compromises that it made with conservatism. Hobsbawm's explanation was nearly the reverse: the revolutionary era's conservatism came down to the ideology of the French Revolution itself. As a "bourgeois revolution," he argued, it had been fought "against the hierarchical society of noble privilege, but not . . . in favour of democratic or egalitarian society." French revolutionaries had always aimed to create a government "by tax-payers and property owners." Anti-egalitarianism and illiberalism were, in his account, fundamental elements of the era's revolutionary ideologies.[2]

The argument I have made in this book is that the revolutionary era's illiberalism was neither intrinsic to revolutionary ideology nor external to the revolutionary movement: it emerged in good measure out of the dynamic of revolutionary political organizing. Durable, large-scale political movements were a new phenomenon in the late eighteenth century. Revolutionaries required a long apprenticeship to learn how to create and sustain them. As they embarked on a long struggle to learn how to build mass movements, they had to wrestle not merely with the hierarchical structures of their societies, imposing as those were, but with their own ingrained assumptions about the nature of the social order and their place within it.

The revolutionary era's double-edged outcomes were forged by the distinct struggles that the two revolutionary generations faced in trying to organize mass political movements. For the first generation, who dominated the revolutions from the 1760s through the mid-1790s, the central challenge was overcoming the hierarchical reflexes of the mid-eighteenth-century Atlantic old regime in which they had grown up. These deeply ingrained habits, though inextricably connected to actors' social position in the old regime, did not equate to membership in distinct or well-defined social classes. The society in which they grew up was hierarchical but not, as yet, consciously organized around social class. Elite revolutionaries during these years repeatedly sought to direct political change by fiat from above, while revolutionaries from below struggled to adapt their tactics, informed by old-regime experiences, to a more transformative political moment. As a result, many of the early revolutionary coalitions failed quickly. Important and enduring institutions that emerged from this period, of which the US Constitution of 1787 is a striking example, had a strong elitist bias.[3]

This approach to the first wave of revolutions has something in common with an older "social" interpretation of revolutionary history. Scholars working in this vein, who dominated the historiography of the French and American Revolutions for the first half of the twentieth century, viewed struggles among social groups and classes as the motor of revolutionary politics. This approach was in eclipse by the end of the last century, as cultural and intellectual historians showed that the earlier scholars had too often collapsed all aspects of political ideology into social class and reduced complex political contestation to simple binary oppositions. Yet in spite of its failings, the "social" interpretation got one crucial thing right, which has sometimes been lost in subsequent scholarship: all the revolutionary movements were coalitions between members of the elite and groups of ordinary people. To understand how the movements came together and what made them succeed or fail, we must pay close attention to their social composition and how their coalitions were formed and came undone.[4]

As mass culture and large-scale political organization spread after 1800, they deepened some of the revolutionary changes that were already underway while creating new divisions between haves and have-nots. Mass political organizing consolidated republican governance in North America and the abolition of slavery in Haiti. It enabled Napoleon to extend many of the legal transformations that had begun in France during the republican decade. But the successful beginning of mass politics had a darker side as well. It quickly became the foundation for modernized forms of one-man rule. It also became an instrument of exclusion: across the revolutionary world, the capacity to build large-scale movements went hand in hand with putting racial minorities and women on the outside of the political sphere. Even in Spanish America, which was more politically inclusive of non-white men than any of the North Atlantic nations, the ambiguous treatment of slave emancipation pointed to a trade-off between large-scale organizing and the extension of personal and political liberty as widely as possible.

Though it can be dispiriting to reckon in this way with the pervasive illiberalism of the revolutionary era, the work is both necessary and useful. One of its uses is to point to an exit from today's heated debates about the illiberalism of the American Revolution. Scholars and public figures have argued fiercely over the past several years about whether exclusion and violence against Native people and Black Americans were foundational to the American Revolution and US nationhood. The generational history of the revolutionary era suggests that this debate has been taking place on too narrow a terrain. The American revolutionary experience was far from unique in this regard. Rather than scour the North American experience for the unique virtues or vices that made the revolution illiberal, we should be tracing the contours of the North American variation on the larger theme: how eighteenth- and early nineteenth-century revolutionaries struggled to enact radical ideas through old-regime practices. To understand why the first and second generations of American revolutionaries embedded class and racial hierarchies into US politics, that is, requires looking beyond the United States.

Few people knew better than Eudora Roland Champagneux how to live with the Atlantic revolutions' bittersweet and contradictory legacies. She had lost nearly everything, including her parents, Jean-Marie and Marie-Jeanne Roland, during the Terror. Over the next decades, she expertly rewove her family and created an original political synthesis for herself that harmonized disparate elements of the two generations' political credos.

After the Terror—after her parents were gone—the teenage Eudora had spent an itinerant three years as Louis-Augustin Bosc's ward. Between 1794 and 1796, she was a member of perhaps half a dozen households. When Bosc departed for the United States, he placed Eudora under the guardianship of Luc-Antoine Champagneux, the onetime Lyon editor, government official, and friend of the Rolands. Champagneux, a political moderate, became quite attached to Eudora. In his preface to an 1800 edition of Madame Roland's writings, Champagneux apostrophized his lost friend's "spirited" young daughter, promising to protect her against a "wicked and ungrateful world."[5]

Eudora integrated into Champagneux's family—and, in 1796, married into it, in the person of Champagneux's younger son,

Pierre-Léon. The Champagneux brothers were good republicans in the 1790s, and the match was initially a happy one. The young Champagneux considered himself lucky to be joining such a distinguished family. "Everything that came from the pen of Mr. or Mme. Roland is valuable for educated and feeling people," he averred to a correspondent. In one letter he wrote early in their marriage, he signed himself "L. Champ. Roland," assuming the family name of his wife in a sign of his respect for her heritage.[6]

As she settled into married life, Eudora remade her family. She adopted Louise and Henri-Albert Gosse, close friends of the elder Rolands who lived in Geneva, as fictive parents. She called other friends of her parents her "second father" and "second mother." Her beloved nanny, who had managed to survive the Terror, remained with Eudora for the rest of her life. Some decades after their abrupt break in 1796, she even welcomed a renewed acquaintance with Bosc.[7]

Eudora's inventiveness in family affairs was matched by a creative political consciousness. Around 1805, her husband was called to Paris for an extended period by his government job, leaving Eudora undisputed mistress of the ancestral country estate, the Clos de la Platière, which she had inherited from her parents. Over the next decades, she turned her home into the canvas for an imaginative personal political synthesis.[8]

The heart of Eudora's synthesis was a commemoration of her parents and others with firm republican associations. To this day, virtually every room in the house contains images of Jean-Marie and Marie-Jeanne Roland. There are fine paintings of members of Champagneux's family and Eudora's uncles. But it is her parents' visages that dominate the rooms. She carefully preserved the library that her parents had assembled, which contained a number of enlightened and republican classics, and members of the family used it through the early nineteenth century. There were intangible memorials as well. A bedroom on the second floor is still known as "Lanthenas's room," in memory of the Rolands' friend who was said to have stayed there. As a member of the National Convention, Lanthenas had voted for the king's execution. Recalling his name after the restoration of the monarchy in 1814, even in this private fashion, could be read as a quietly defiant act of remembrance.[9]

Eudora seamlessly fused the memory of these republicans with appreciations of the constitutional monarchy and Napoleon on the walls of her home. Eudora seems to have owned a number of engravings of prominent figures from the early revolution. An image of the marquis de Lafayette in the house may have belonged to her. An important figure during the early revolution, he had become a symbol, under the restored Bourbons, of a moderate path that the revolution had not followed.

A large portrait of Napoleon executed in embroidered silk around 1802 represented another thread in Eudora's complex political tapestry. The general is represented in profile, his hair in a Roman republican style, with the legend "Bonaparte the Repairer" below his visage. One imagines what the legend might have meant to Eudora. Perhaps she looked to Napoleon as the "repairer" of the many kinds of damage that had been wrought on her by the previous decade's political hurricanes. If so, she was taking part again in a family affair: both Pierre-Léon and his brother had secured government employment during the Consulate, and Zélia, her daughter, later married a "fervent" Bonapartist named Joseph Chaley.[10]

In the hands of Eudora Roland Champagneux, the Clos was transformed into a brilliant and idiosyncratic private commentary on the political world through which she and her family had lived. Deeply rooted through her parents in the enlightened republicanism of the late old regime, Eudora had adapted herself to the political exigencies of the new century. She married loyalty to her republican parents with an embrace of the constitutional monarchy and the Napoleonic regime. Like her fictive family, which she never stopped reshaping and reorganizing, Eudora's political vision was a work of radical inclusivity. Her vision is an exhortation, born of experience, that to understand the age of revolutions one must see it as a whole: its proud accomplishments and vexing contradictions inextricably linked across generations.

# ACKNOWLEDGMENTS

Books are the most solitary and the most collective of endeavors. I have accrued more than the usual number of debts working on this one, and I am grateful to be able to acknowledge them.

Many colleagues were generous with their time: answering questions, guiding me through unfamiliar terrain, and helping me think through problems. The very partial list includes Jay Berkovitz, Jerome Chanes, Manuel Covo, Brian DeLay, Madeleine Dobie, Lois Dubin, Marcela Echeverri, Elizabeth Fenn, Julia Gaffield, Jonathan Gienapp, Carrie Glenn, Jim Heft, Jane Kamensky, Sarah Knott, Noah Millstone, Stella Nair, Scarlett O'Phelan Godoy, Francisco Ortega, Thomas Piketty, Siân Reynolds, Meghan Roberts, Jesse Rodin, Claudia Rosas, Nancy Sinkoff, Sujit Sivasundaram, Marcela Ternavasio, Wyger Velema, Cécile Vidal, David Waldstreicher, and Arthur Weststeijn. Kate Blackmer taught me quite a bit in the process of making the maps. I have to offer special thanks to two Latin Americanists who took the time to educate me about their field: Charles F. Walker and Clément Thibaud. They both have my deep gratitude for the gift of their time and expertise.

I am especially grateful to the colleagues who read and commented on large sections of the manuscript: David Armitage, David A. Bell, Guillaume Calafat, Quentin Deluermoz, Glenn Dynner, Mathieu Ferradou, François Furstenberg, Maya Jasanoff, Antoine Lilti, Daniel Mason, Guillaume Mazeau, Joris Oddens, Arnaud Orain, Romy Sanchez, Miranda Spieler, Geneviève Verdo, and the Revisionists, Scott Heerman and Molly Warsh. Their perceptive comments improved the book immeasurably.

I cannot list all the seminars, classes, conferences, and talks at which I was able to share my work. I am grateful to everyone who participated and whose commentary enriched my thinking. Four workshops stand out in my mind as having been especially fruitful: the 2014 USC Huntington EMSI-*William and Mary Quarterly* annual workshop convened by Sarah Knott; the 2016 workshop at the American Historical Association meeting on "Rewriting Revolutions, 1750–1850"; and the 2018 and 2022 *écoles d'été* I co-organized with Clément Thibaud at the Ecole des Hautes Etudes en Sciences Sociales and at USC.

Colleagues at the University of Southern California have provided a great deal of encouragement and constructive criticism along the way. Thank you to all of my colleagues but especially Alice Baumgartner, Daniela Bleichmar, Alice Echols, Kate Flint, Joan Flores-Villalobos, Richard Fox, Anne Goldgar, Rebecca Lemon, Peter Mancall, Steve Ross, Hilary Schor, and Vanessa Schwartz. My thanks to the chairs of my department over the past eight years: Bill Deverell, Phil Ethington, Karen Halttunen, Jay Rubenstein, and Paul Lerner.

Thanks to François Fierens for his warm welcome to the remarkable Clos de la Platière, and for generously sharing his family's oral history.

Friends near and far have made the process of writing enjoyable. Gratitude to Max Bean, Gavi Bogin-Farber, Michal Scharlin, Michai Mazar, Jeremy Deutchman, Michelle Deutchman, Aryeh Cohen, Andrea Hodos, Sara Houghteling, Eve Goodman, Jon Hatch, David Myers, Nomi Stolzenberg, and the whole Shtibl Minyan crew.

It has been a delight to work with Brian Distelberg and the wonderful people at Basic Books. Brian has a well-deserved reputation as a hands-on editor; I was lucky to be the beneficiary of his expert eye. Michael Kaler's chapter-by-chapter reactions were gold. Alex Cullina made short work of many complicated queries. The production process ran smoothly in the skilled hands of Shena Redmond and Liz Dana. The design and publicity teams made the whole package shine. I'm very grateful to Jennifer Lyons, agent extraordinaire, for landing the book in such a great home.

Thanks are due as well to the institutions who funded the research for this book: the Institut d'Études Avancées (Paris), the Shelby Cullom Davis Center (Princeton), the USC Dornsife Dean's Office, and the USC-Huntington Early Modern Studies Institute. A shout-out to the university staff who provided so much assistance, especially Amy Braden, Will Cowan, Lori Rogers, Simone Bessant, Sandra Hopwood, Lisa Itagaki, and Ida Morodome-Castilla at USC; Simon Luck, Geneviève Marmin, and Cécile Durand at the IEA; and Jennifer Goldman at Princeton. Thanks as well to Taka and Paradocs for providing a place to write.

My family helped nourish this project over many years. I enjoyed discussing it with my aunts, uncles, and cousins, especially Liza Kramer, Jonah Rosenthal, and Tracey Rattray, and with my grandmother, Teri Perl. Steve Marglin answered my questions about eighteenth-century wealth distribution and finally coaxed me onto a horse—a taste of the early modern era. Reading a *farsa* with Frédérique Apffel-Marglin was a high point in my research, and the book will always be connected in my mind with the beautiful Centro Sachamama.

Jessica Marglin has been with me every step of the way. There are three bits of evidence in this book that I uncovered during the first months of our relationship. In the twenty years since then, she has given me more love and hope and encouragement than I could have imagined possible. As a co-parent, she made this book possible, enabling me to travel and work late on many occasions. Her scholarly savoir faire has made it so much better.

The joy, curiosity, and sheer energy that radiate from our daughters, Suzanne and Emmanuelle, amaze me every day. They each contributed to my writing: Suzanne offered good advice when I got stuck and Emmanuelle listened with rapt attention to stories from its pages.

I dedicate this book to my parents, Deborah Rosenthal and Jed Perl. A small gesture to honor them, for everything.

# ABBREVIATIONS

For reasons of space, I have abbreviated the names of archival repositories, publishers, and printed collections and journals that I have used frequently. I have not included the place of publication for books unless necessary for clarity.

## ARCHIVES

| | |
|---|---|
| AAC | Archivo Arzobispal del Cuzco, Cuzco, Peru |
| ADG | Archives Départementales de la Gironde, Bordeaux |
| ADR | Archives Départementales du Rhône, Lyon |
| AGI | Archivo General de Indias, Seville |
| ANP | Archives Nationales, Paris |
| APS | American Philosophical Society, Philadelphia, Pennsylvania |
| ARC | Archivo Regional del Cuzco, Cuzco, Peru |
| ASG | Repubblica Ligure, Archivio di Stato di Genova, Genoa |
| BDG | Bibliothèque de Genève, Geneva |
| BHSP | Box 4, Bining Collection, Historical Society of Pennsylvania, Philadelphia, Pennsylvania |
| BHVP | Bibliothèque Historique de la Ville de Paris, Paris |
| BLL | British Library, London |
| BNF | Bibliothèque Nationale, Paris |
| HLH | Houghton Library, Harvard University, Cambridge, Massachusetts |
| JCB | John Carter Brown Library, Providence, Rhode Island |

| | |
|---|---|
| MHS | Massachusetts Historical Society, Boston |
| MNHN | Muséum National d'Histoire Naturelle, Paris |
| NAF, BNF | Nouvelles Acquisitions Françaises, Bibliothèque Nationale, Paris |
| NYHS | New-York Historical Society, New York |
| NYPL | New York Public Library, New York |
| SHD | Service Historique de la Défense, Vincennes |

## PRESSES

| | |
|---|---|
| Alabama | University of Alabama Press |
| Basic | Basic Books |
| Belknap | Belknap Press of Harvard University Press |
| Brandeis | Brandeis University Press |
| California | University of California Press |
| Cambridge | Cambridge University Press |
| Chicago | University of Chicago Press |
| Clarendon | Clarendon Press |
| Colorado | University Press of Colorado |
| Columbia | Columbia University Press |
| Cornell | Cornell University Press |
| Delaware | University of Delaware Press |
| Duke | Duke University Press |
| EHESS | Éditions de l'École des Hautes Études en Sciences Sociales |
| FSG | Farrar, Straus and Giroux |
| Georgia | University of Georgia Press |
| Harvard | Harvard University Press |
| JHU | Johns Hopkins University Press |
| Kentucky | University Press of Kentucky |

| | |
|---|---|
| Liverpool | Liverpool University Press |
| LSU | Louisiana State University Press |
| Metropolitan | Metropolitan Books |
| Missouri | University of Missouri Press |
| Nebraska | University of Nebraska Press |
| New Mexico | University of New Mexico Press |
| Northeastern | Northeastern University Press |
| Norton | W. W. Norton |
| NYU | New York University Press |
| Ohio | Ohio University Press |
| OIEAHC | University of North Carolina Press for the Omohundro Institute of Early American History and Culture |
| Oxford | Oxford University Press |
| Penn | University of Pennsylvania Press |
| Princeton | Princeton University Press |
| PSU | Pennsylvania State University Press |
| PUF | Presses Universitaires de France |
| PUR | Presses Universitaires de Rennes |
| South Carolina | University of South Carolina Press |
| Stanford | Stanford University Press |
| Tennessee | University of Tennessee Press |
| Texas | University of Texas Press |
| Toronto | University of Toronto Press |
| UNC | University of North Carolina Press |
| Universidad Católica | Pontificia Universidad Católica del Perú, Fondo Editorial |
| Virginia | University of Virginia Press |
| Wisconsin | University of Wisconsin Press |
| Yale | Yale University Press |

## COLLECTIONS

| | |
|---|---|
| *CDBTA* | *Colección Documental del Bicentenario de la Revolución Emancipadora de Túpac Amaru*, 6 vols. (Lima: Comisión Nacional del Bicentenario de la Rebelión Emanciapadora de Túpac Amaru, 1980) |
| *CDIP* | *Colección Documental de la Independencia del Perú*, 86 vols. (Lima: Comisión Nacional del Sesquicentenario de la Independencia del Perú, 1971–1976). NB: This collection is subdivided into twenty-seven named subseries; citations indicate the subseries name and volume number within that subseries. |
| *DAJA* | *Diary and Autobiography of John Adams*, 4 vols., eds. L. H. Butterfield et al. (Belknap, 1961) |
| *JCC* | *Journals of the Continental Congress*, 34 vols., eds. Worthington Chauncey Ford et al. (US Government Printing Office, 1904–1937) |
| *LPJA* | *Legal Papers of John Adams*, 3 vols., eds. L. Kinvin Wroth and Hiller B. Zobel (Belknap, 1965) |
| *PJA* | *Papers of John Adams*, 20 vols., eds. Robert J. Taylor et al. (Belknap, 1977–) |

## JOURNALS

| | |
|---|---|
| *AHR* | *American Historical Review* |
| *AHRF* | *Annales Historiques de la Révolution Française* |
| *FHS* | *French Historical Studies* |
| *JER* | *Journal of the Early Republic* |
| *JMH* | *Journal of Modern History* |
| *WMQ* | *William and Mary Quarterly* |

# NOTES

## INTRODUCTION

1. Thomas Paine, "The Rights of Man, Part First" (1791), in *The Complete Writings of Thomas Paine*, ed. Philip S. Foner (Citadel, 1945), 1:344. I favor an inclusive definition of the term "revolution," as discussed in Nathan Perl-Rosenthal, "Ideas of Revolution in the Age of Atlantic Revolutions," *Modern Intellectual History* (2023). For influential definitions of the term that are more restrictive, see Theda Skocpol, *States and Social Revolutions: A Comparative Analysis of France, Russia, and China* (Cambridge, 1979), 4; Jack A. Goldstone, *The Encyclopedia of Political Revolutions* (Fitzroy Dearborn, 1998), xxxi; and Eric Hobsbawm, "Revolution," in *Revolution in History,* eds. Roy Porter and Mikuláš Teich (Cambridge, 1986), 7.

2. R. R. Palmer, *The Age of the Democratic Revolution: A Political History of Europe and America, 1760–1800*, 2 vols. (Princeton, 1959–1964), and E. J. Hobsbawm, *The Age of Revolution: 1789–1848* (Weidenfeld & Nicolson, 1962). For an excellent discussion of the two, see David Armitage and Sanjay Subrahmanyam, eds., *The Age of Revolutions in Global Context, c. 1760–1840* (Palgrave Macmillan, 2009), xvi–xix. A number of other scholars have pushed in similar directions in recent years, including comparatist studies by Wim Klooster, *Revolutions in the Atlantic World: A Comparative History* (NYU, 2009), and John H. Elliott, *Empires of the Atlantic World: Britain and Spain in America, 1492–1830* (Yale, 2006); studies focused on inter-revolutionary connections, including Janet L. Polasky, *Revolutions Without Borders: The Call to Liberty in the Atlantic World* (Yale, 2015), and Patrick Griffin, *The Age of Atlantic Revolution: The Fall and Rise of a Connected World* (Yale, 2023), 6; and David A. Bell, *Men on Horseback: The Power of Charisma in the Age of Revolution* (FSG, 2020), which sees the era through the lens of five key political-military leaders. There has also been important new work on the age of revolutions outside the Atlantic basin, esp. Sujit Sivasundaram, *Waves Across the South: A New History of Revolution and Empire* (William Collins, 2020), and Maurizio Isabella, *Southern Europe in the Age of Revolutions* (Princeton, 2023), the latter of which appeared just as I was completing this book.

3. My quarry in this book is not how groups "imagine" a common identity, for which see Benedict Anderson, *Imagined Communities: Reflections on the*

*Origin and Spread of Nationalism* (Verso, 1983), but how they build movements in practice, for which see Jeffrey L. Pasley, Andrew W. Robertson, and David Waldstreicher, eds., *Beyond the Founders: New Approaches to the Political History of the Early American Republic* (UNC, 2004), 9–15, and Lynn Hunt, *Politics, Culture, and Class in the French Revolution* (California, 1984), 13–16. I use "organization" in a way similar to Charles Tilly, *From Mobilization to Revolution* (Addison Wesley, 1978), 7, 62–64, 69, but my use of "mobilization" is narrower, referring primarily to degree of public involvement. I argue that the social and political disruptions wrought by the revolutions before 1800 were the "trigger action of the social and cultural process" required to produce generational differentiation: see Karl Mannheim, "The Problem of Generations" (1927/1928), in *Karl Mannheim: Essays*, ed. Paul Kecskemeti (Routledge, 1952), 310. Bobby Duffy, *The Generation Myth: Why When You're Born Matters Less Than You Think* (Basic, 2021), 8–9, calls these "cohort effects." See also below, n5.

4. Pierre Bourdieu, *Outline of a Theory of Practice*, trans. Richard Nice (Cambridge, 1977), 72, 83; Nathan Perl-Rosenthal, "Atlantic Cultures and the Age of Revolution," *WMQ* 74, no. 4 (2017): 680–681; David Swartz, *Culture and Power: The Sociology of Pierre Bourdieu* (Chicago, 1997), 100–112; and the deft explications of the implications of Bourdieu's argument in Michel de Certeau, *L'invention du quotidien: Arts de faire*, new ed. (Gallimard, 1990 [1980]), 91–96. On the "social fact," see Emile Durkheim, *Les règles de la méthode sociologique* (1937; PUF, 2013), 3–6.

5. See Duffy, *Generation Myth*, 13–15; Mannheim, "The Problem of Generations," 293–294; Alan B. Spitzer, "The Historical Problem of Generations," *AHR* 78, no. 5 (1973): 1358–1359; and the discussions in Abosede George et al., "*AHR* Conversation: Each Generation Writes Its Own History of Generations," *AHR* 123, no. 5 (2018): 1505–1546, esp. 1516–1517, though the focus in this discussion is on conflict between generations.

6. Alexis de Tocqueville, *Democracy in America*, ed. Eduardo Nolla, trans. James T. Schleifer (Liberty Fund, 2010), 1:89.

7. For a call for this type of history, see Clément Thibaud, "Pour une histoire polycentrique des républicanismes atlantiques (années 1770–années 1880)," *Revue d'histoire du XIXe siècle* 56 (2018): 151–170.

8. On West Africa in this period, see esp. Paul E. Lovejoy, *Jihad in West Africa During the Age of Revolutions* (Ohio, 2016); and the somewhat countervailing view in Bronwen Everill, "Africa and the Early American Republic: Comments," *JER* 40, no. 2 (2020): 213–215; on Native histories in this period, see esp. Kathleen DuVal, *Independence Lost: Lives on the Edge of the American Revolution* (Random House, 2015); Alan Taylor, *American Republics: A Continental History of the United States, 1783–1850* (Norton,

2021). See also Joanna Innes and Mark Philp, eds., *Re-Imagining Democracy in the Mediterranean, 1780–1860* (Oxford, 2018); see also above, n2.

9. Exemplary models of biographical approaches to the history of the revolutionary era are François Furstenberg, *When the United States Spoke French: Five Refugees Who Shaped a Nation* (Penguin, 2014); and Maya Jasanoff, *Liberty's Exiles: American Loyalists in the Revolutionary World* (Knopf, 2011).

10. See also Ashli White, *Revolutionary Things: Material Culture and Politics in the Late Eighteenth-Century Atlantic World* (Yale, 2023), 3–7, which emphasizes the "dynamism" of objects and their meaning.

11. For accounts of the long tail of political turning points in France, see Michael P. Fitzsimmons, *The Night the Old Regime Ended: August 4, 1789, and the French Revolution* (PSU, 2002), esp. 168–172, and Isser Woloch, *The New Regime: Transformations of the French Civic Order, 1789–1820s* (Norton, 1994), esp. 15–16. On the United States' slow efforts to achieve cultural independence, see esp. Kariann Yokota, *Unbecoming British: How Revolutionary America Became a Postcolonial Nation* (Oxford, 2011).

12. See, e.g., Bernard Bailyn, *Atlantic History: Concept and Contours* (Harvard, 2005), 103–111, esp. 110–111.

13. Albert Mathiez, *La révolution française* (Armand Colin, 1951), 1; Gordon S. Wood, *The Radicalism of the American Revolution* (Knopf, 1992), ix, 7; Nikole Hannah-Jones, *The 1619 Project: A New Origin Story* (One World, 2021), 11; David A. Bell, "American Exceptionalism," in *Myth America: Historians Take On the Biggest Legends and Lies About Our Past*, eds. Kevin M. Kruse and Julian E. Zelizer (Basic, 2022), 14–16, 23–24.

## CHAPTER 1: A HIERARCHICAL WORLD

1. *Procès-verbal de ce qui s'est passé au lit de justice . . . le mardi douze mars 1776* (Imprimerie Royale, 1776); Abraham Girardet, *Le Lit de Justice tenu a Versailles, le 6 aout 1776*, engraving, 62.8 x 48.9 cm, Louvre, Paris, https://collections.louvre.fr/en/ark:/53355/cl020578660#.

2. *Procès-verbal de ce qui s'est passé*, 6–7.

3. Ibid., 7.

4. Ibid., 12–16, 31–32.

5. Ibid., 95.

6. James C. Scott, *Against the Grain: A Deep History of the Earliest States* (Yale, 2017), x–xi; Walter Scheidel, *The Great Leveler: Violence and the History of Inequality from the Stone Age to the Twenty-First Century* (Princeton, 2017); of the vast literature on the formation of race, see esp. Joyce E. Chaplin, *Subject Matter: Technology, the Body, and Science on the Anglo-American Frontier*

(Harvard, 2001), 14–15, 158–161, and Jean-Frédéric Schaub, *Race Is About Politics: Lessons from History*, trans. Lara Vergnaud (Princeton, 2019), 130–143.

7. Thomas Piketty, *Capital and Ideology* (Harvard, 2021), ch. 2, esp. 86–87; S. Epstein and Maarten Prak, eds., *Guilds, Innovation and the European Economy, 1400–1800* (Cambridge, 2008), 1–4 (with a positive view); Elliott, *Empires of the Atlantic*, 169–177; David Eltis, *The Rise of African Slavery in the Americas* (Cambridge, 1999), 3–12, 17–18.

8. Jan de Vries, *The Economy of Europe in an Age of Crisis, 1600–1750* (Cambridge, 1976), 16–21; John Miller, "The Long-Term Consequences of the English Revolution: Economic and Social Development," in *The Oxford Handbook of the English Revolution*, ed. M. J. Braddick (Oxford, 2015), 503, 508–509; Ben Coates, *The Impact of the English Civil War on the Economy of London, 1642–50* (Ashgate, 2004), 231–232; Guido Alfani et al., "Economic Inequality in Preindustrial Germany, ca. 1300–1850," *Journal of Economic History* 82, no. 1 (2022): 104, 116–117; Christopher Hill, *The World Turned Upside Down: Radical Ideas During the English Revolution* (Viking, 1972), 114–116.

9. Shelby Thomas McCloy, *The Negro in the French West Indies* (Kentucky, 1966), 15–34; Alejandro de la Fuente and Ariela J. Gross, *Becoming Free, Becoming Black: Race, Freedom, and Law in Cuba, Virginia, and Louisiana* (Cambridge, 2020), 77–78; Ira Berlin, *Generations of Captivity: A History of African-American Slaves* (Belknap, 2003), 99–108; Edmund S. Morgan, *American Slavery, American Freedom: The Ordeal of Colonial Virginia* (Norton, 1975), 334–337.

10. Sheilagh Ogilvie, "The European Economy in the Eighteenth Century," in *Short Oxford History of Europe*, ed. T. C. W. Blanning, *The Eighteenth Century* (Oxford, 2000), esp. 97, 107–108; Robin Blackburn, *The Making of New World Slavery: From the Baroque to the Modern, 1492–1800* (Verso, 1997), ch. 9; John J. McCusker, "Estimating Early American Gross Domestic Product," *Historical Methods* 33, no. 3 (2000): 156; Regina Grafe, "Latin America: 1700–1870," in *The Cambridge Economic History of the Modern World*, eds. Stephen Broadberry and Kyoji Fukao (Cambridge, 2021), 1:231–232. See also Jan de Vries, *The Industrious Revolution: Consumer Behavior and the Household Economy, 1650 to the Present* (Cambridge, 2008); Sidney W. Mintz, *Sweetness and Power: The Place of Sugar in Modern History* (Viking, 1985).

11. J. L. Van Zanden, "Tracing the Beginning of the Kuznets Curve: Western Europe During the Early Modern Period," *Economic History Review* 48, no. 4 (1995): 661; Scheidel, *Great Leveler*, ch. 3; Daniel Roche, *The People of Paris: An Essay in Popular Culture in the 18th Century*, trans. Marie Evans (California, 1987), 145–152; Guy Chaussinand-Nogaret, *The French Nobility*

*in the Eighteenth Century: From Feudalism to Enlightenment*, trans. William Doyle (Cambridge, 1985), 87–91, 126–129.

12. Guido Alfani, "Economic Inequality in Preindustrial Times: Europe and Beyond," *Journal of Economic Literature* 59, no. 1 (2021): 10–13; James A. Henretta, "Economic Development and Social Structure in Colonial Boston," *WMQ* 22, no. 1 (1965): 92; Jackson Turner Main, *The Social Structure of Revolutionary America* (Princeton, 1965), 195–196; Piketty, *Capital and Ideology*, 85–86, 214–217, 258 (quotation).

13. See the discussion in Nathan Perl-Rosenthal, "Cultural Practices and Revolutions, c. 1760–1825," in *The Cambridge History of the Atlantic Age of Revolutions*, ed. Wim Klooster, 1:134–159, esp. 136–139.

14. Paul Bosc d'Antic, "Mémoire sur la cause des bulles dans le verre," in *OEuvres de M. Bosc d'Antic*, 2 vols. (Serpente, 1780), 20.

15. For this and subsequent pages, see Louis-Augustin Bosc, "Notes sur ma vie pour aider ceux qui s'occupent de biographie," MS 1007: Bibliographie et voyages, Papiers Louis-Augustin-Guillaume Bosc d'Antic, BHVP.

16. Steven L. Kaplan, "Social Classification and Representation in the Corporate World of Eighteenth-Century France: Turgot's 'Carnival,'" in *Work in France*, eds. Steven L. Kaplan and Cynthia J. Koepp (Cornell, 1986), 178–180, 183–185.

17. Bosc, "Notes sur ma vie," describes the commission, which I have not been able to track down, as "une Commission pour faire rentrer les domains du Roi qui avoient été aliené sans motif suffisant." Laura Auricchio, *The Marquis: Lafayette Reconsidered* (Knopf, 2014), 23–26.

18. See Will Slauter, "News and Diplomacy in the Age of the American Revolution" (PhD diss., Princeton University, 2007), 23–25; Eugène Vaillé, *Histoire générale des postes françaises* (PUF, 1953–1955), 6:10–13; Antoine Da Sylva, *De Rousseau à Hugo: Bosc, l'enfant des Lumières* (Le Chemin du philosophe, 2008), 34–37. See also the case of Benjamin Franklin and the purloined letters in 1774: Carl Van Doren, *Benjamin Franklin* (Viking, 1938, repr. 1952), 456–467; and Sheila L. Skemp, *The Making of a Patriot: Benjamin Franklin at the Cockpit* (Oxford, 2013).

19. David Garrioch, *The Making of Revolutionary Paris* (California, 2002), 237–238; 2 Oct 1789, Registre des délibérations . . . de l'Administration des Postes, 31 Jul 1772–24 Dec 1790, F/90/20304, f. 47–48, ANP.

20. Bosc, "Notes sur ma vie"; Vaillé, *Histoire générale des postes*, 6:149–151.

21. There is a long tradition of scholars overstating North American equality: see esp. the foundational Louis Hartz, *The Liberal Tradition in America: An Interpretation of American Political Thought Since the Revolution* (Harcourt Brace, 1955), 3–8; the notion of a "truncated society" in Gordon S.

Wood, *The Radicalism of the American Revolution* (Knopf, 1991), 109–124; and Jack P. Greene, *Pursuits of Happiness: The Social Development of Early Modern British Colonies and the Formation of American Culture* (UNC, 1988), 186–198.

22. See Paul C. Nagel, *The Lees of Virginia: Seven Generations of an American Family* (Oxford, 1990), esp. ch. 3.

23. *South Carolina Gazette*, May 31, 1770.

24. The classic study is Philip D. Curtin, *The Atlantic Slave Trade: A Census* (Wisconsin, 1969); the most current figures are from SlaveVoyages, www.slavevoyages.org; De la Fuente and Gross, *Becoming Free*, 77–79.

25. Useful high-level summaries are in Antoine Lilti, *L'Héritage des Lumières: Ambivalences de la modernité* (Seuil, 2019), 29; Siep Stuurman, *The Invention of Humanity: Equality and Cultural Difference in World History* (Harvard, 2017), ch. 6; Darrin M. McMahon, "Equality and the Horizon of Human Expectations," *Global Intellectual History* (2022). See also François-Xavier Guerra, *Modernidad e independencias: Ensayos sobre las revoluciones hispánicas* (MAPFRE, 1992), 85–102. On limits: Devin J. Vartija, *The Color of Equality: Race and Common Humanity in Enlightenment Thought* (Penn, 2021), and Daniel Gordon, *Citizens Without Sovereignty: Equality and Sociability in French Thought, 1670–1789* (Princeton, 1994).

26. Two exemplary studies along these lines are David A. Bell, *Lawyers and Citizens: The Making of a Political Elite in Old Regime France* (Oxford, 1994), and Steve Pincus, *1688: The First Modern Revolution* (Yale, 2009), 32–33; see also Gabriel Paquette, ed., *Enlightened Reform in Southern Europe and Its Atlantic Colonies, c. 1750–1830* (Routledge, 2016).

27. See Hill, *The World Turned Upside Down*; Alfred F. Young, "English Plebian Culture and Eighteenth-Century American Radicalism," in *The Origins of Anglo-American Radicalism*, eds. Margaret Jacob and James Jacob (Allen & Unwin, 1984): 185–212; Robert Darnton, *The Literary Underground of the Old Regime* (Harvard, 1982); Arlette Farge, *Subversive Words: Public Opinion in Eighteenth-Century France*, trans. Rosemary Morris (PSU, 1995); Wyger Velema, *Republicans: Essays on Eighteenth-Century Dutch Political Thought* (Brill, 2007), 43–49; Maarten Prak, *Citizens Without Nations: Urban Citizenship in Europe and the World, c. 1000–1789* (Cambridge, 2018), 296–298; David Brion Davis, *The Problem of Slavery in the Age of Revolution, 1770–1823* (Cornell, 1975), 43–48.

28. Mark A. Noll, *America's God: From Jonathan Edwards to Abraham Lincoln* (Oxford, 2002), 76–82; Rhys Isaac, *The Transformation of Virginia, 1740–1790* (UNC, 1982), 165–166.

29. David Biale et al., *Hasidism: A New History* (Princeton, 2018), 38–39; Ada Rapoport-Albert, "God and the Zaddik as the Two Focal Points of Hasidic

Worship," in *Essential Papers on Hasidism: Origins to Present*, ed. Gershon David Hundert (NYU, 1991), 315, 318.

30. Nathan O. Hatch, *The Sacred Cause of Liberty: Republican Thought and the Millennium in Revolutionary New England* (Yale, 1977), 44–54; Isaac, *Transformation*, chs. 8–9; Glenn Dynner, *Men of Silk: The Hasidic Conquest of Polish Jewish Society* (Oxford, 2006), ch. 2; Gershon David Hundert, *Jews in Poland-Lithuania in the Eighteenth Century: A Genealogy of Modernity* (California, 2004), 197–210; Biale et al., *Hasidism*, 85–98.

## CHAPTER 2: THE FIRST IMPERIAL CRISIS

1. John E. Ferling, *John Adams: A Life* (Oxford, 1992), 11–14; John Adams, "Autobiography," in *DAJA*, 3:257.

2. Locke, *Some Thoughts Concerning Education*, in *The Works of John Locke* (London: Rivington, 1824), 8:44, 61.

3. Page Smith, *John Adams*, 2 vols. (Doubleday, 1962), 1:12–23; Ferling, *John Adams*, 14–16.

4. Stephen Botein, "The Legal Profession in Colonial North America," in *Lawyers in Early Modern Europe and America*, ed. Wilfrid Prest (Holmes & Meier, 1981), 129–146, esp. 133–139.

5. Smith, *John Adams*, 1:37–38; Peter Charles Hoffer, *Law and People in Colonial America* (JHU, 1998), 63–67; *DAJA*, 1:56.

6. *DAJA*, 1:54, 58–59.

7. Ibid., 1:43–44, and Ferling, *John Adams*, 17–27; see also *LPJA*, 1:239–241; *DAJA*, 1:265, 218.

8. Fred Anderson, *The Crucible of War: The Seven Years' War and the Fate of Empire in British North America, 1754–1766* (Knopf, 2000).

9. John Adams to Abigail Smith, 4 October 1762, in *Adams Family Correspondence*, L. H. Butterfield et al., eds. (Belknap, 1963–), 1:2; Edith B. Gelles, *Abigail & John: Portrait of a Marriage* (Morrow, 2009), ch. 1; Smith, *John Adams*, 1:57–71.

10. [Daniel Dulany], *Considerations on the Propriety of Imposing Taxes in the British Colonies* (Annapolis: Jonas Green, 1765), 46–47. For context, see Brendan McConville, *The King's Three Faces: The Rise and Fall of Royal America, 1688–1776* (UNC, 2006); Eric Nelson, *The Royalist Revolution: Monarchy and the American Founding* (Harvard, 2014); Edmund S. Morgan and Helen M. Morgan, *The Stamp Act Crisis: Prologue to Revolution*, rev. ed. (Collier Books, 1963), ch. 6; Bernard Bailyn, *The Ideological Origins of the American Revolution* (Belknap, 1992); and Ned Blackhawk, *The Rediscovery of America: Native Peoples and the Unmaking of U.S. History* (Yale, 2023), 152–169.

11. Pauline Maier, *From Resistance to Revolution: Colonial Radicals and the Development of American Opposition to Britain, 1765–1776* (Knopf, 1972), ch. 4, esp. 78–87; Robert Middlekauff, *The Glorious Cause: The American Revolution, 1763–1789* (Oxford, 1982), 70–76; Mercy Otis Warren, *History of the Rise, Progress, and Termination of the American Revolution* (1805; Liberty Classics, 1988), 1:17–18. See also Dirk Hoerder, *Crowd Action in Revolutionary Massachusetts, 1765–1780* (Academic Press, 1977), 90–91; Jesse Lemisch, "Jack Tar in the Streets: New York's Merchant Seamen in the Politics of Revolutionary America," *WMQ* 25, no. 3 (1968); Pauline Maier, "The Charleston Mob and the Evolution of Popular Politics in Revolutionary South Carolina, 1765–1784," *Perspectives in American History* 4 (1970); and Richard Walsh, *Charleston's Sons of Liberty: A Study of the Artisans, 1763–1789* (South Carolina, 1959).

12. See Pauline Maier, *The Old Revolutionaries: Political Lives in the Age of Samuel Adams* (Knopf, 1980), 58–59; Gary B. Nash, *The Urban Crucible: Social Change, Political Consciousness, and the Origins of the American Revolution* (Harvard, 1979), 303, 296; Richard Alan Ryerson, *"The Revolution Is Now Begun": The Radical Committees of Philadelphia, 1765–1776* (Penn, 1978), 68–71; Stephen E. Patterson, *Political Parties in Revolutionary Massachusetts* (Wisconsin, 1973), ch. 3, esp. 63–64; Arthur M. Schlesinger Sr., *The Colonial Merchants and the American Revolution, 1763–1776* (1918; Ungar, 1957), 27; Carl Bridenbaugh, *Cities in Revolt: Urban Life in America, 1743–1776* (Capricorn Books, 1964), ch. 7; and Tom Cutterham, *Gentlemen Revolutionaries: Power and Justice in the New American Republic* (Princeton, 2017), 3.

13. On violence, see Joseph S. Tiedemann, *Reluctant Revolutionaries: New York City and the Road to Independence, 1763–1776* (Cornell, 1997), 62–74; Bernard Bailyn, *The Ordeal of Thomas Hutchinson* (Harvard, 1974); Morgan and Morgan, *Stamp Act Crisis*, 150–160.

14. William Bradford (Phila.) to New York Committee, 15 Feb 1766, Box 1, Lamb Papers, NYHS. For the burning, see Tiedemann, *Reluctant Revolutionaries*, 84.

15. Morgan and Morgan, *Stamp Act Crisis*, 94–96, 106–121; Maier, *From Resistance to Revolution*, 31–32; William Holt to William Palfrey, 10 Dec 1765, bMS Am 1704.3: Letters to William Palfrey, 1741–1781, Palfrey Family Papers, HLH; Newport *Mercury*, 24 Jun 1765, p. 3 ("disagreeable"); and discussion of epistolary rules in Nathan Perl-Rosenthal, "Corresponding Republics: Letter Writing and Patriot Organizing in the Atlantic Revolutions, Circa 1760–1792" (PhD diss., Columbia University, 2011), 36–39, and Toby L. Ditz, "Formative Ventures: Eighteenth-Century Commercial Letters and the Articulation of Experience," in *Epistolary Selves: Letters and Letter-Writers, 1600–1945*, ed. Rebecca Earle (Aldershot, 1999), 60–61.

16. On the genre, see Perl-Rosenthal, "Corresponding Republics," ch. 1. Committee of Baltimore to New York Committee, 8 Mar 1766; New York Committee to Sons of Liberty in Fairfield, 17 Mar 1766; New York Sons to Connecticut Sons, 20 Feb 1766, all in Box 1, Lamb Papers, NYHS.

17. Circular from Providence Sons of Liberty, 19 Mar 1766; New York Sons to Providence Sons, 2 Apr 1766; New York Sons to Boston Sons, 2 Apr 1766, all in Box 1, Lamb Papers, NYHS. But see Carl Bridenbaugh, *Silas Downer, Forgotten Patriot: His Life and Writings* (Rhode Island Bicentennial Foundation, 1974), 24–25, and Maier, *From Resistance to Revolution*, 94.

18. Roger J. Champagne, "The Sons of Liberty and the Aristocracy in New York Politics, 1765–1790" (PhD diss., University of Wisconsin, 1960), 116–117; Rosemary Niner Estes, "Charles Town's Sons of Liberty" (PhD diss., University of North Carolina, 2005), ch. 3; Ryerson, *Revolution Is Now Begun*, 26–27.

19. Ira Berlin, *Many Thousands Gone: The First Two Centuries of Slavery in North America* (Belknap, 1998), 369–371, 177–184; Robert G. Parkinson, *The Common Cause: Creating Race and Nation in the American Revolution* (OIEAHC, 2016), 19–25, 179–184.

20. Gerald Horne, *The Counter-Revolution of 1776: Slave Resistance and the Origins of the United States of America* (NYU, 2014), 239–241; Morgan and Morgan, *Stamp Act Crisis*, 37, 212; and for larger contexts, Wim Klooster, "Slave Revolts, Royal Justice, and a Ubiquitous Rumor in the Age of Revolutions," *WMQ* 71, no. 3 (2014).

21. Richard Price, *Maroon Societies: Rebel Slave Communities in the Americas* (Anchor, 1973), esp. 1–4; Shauna J. Sweeney, "Market Marronage: Fugitive Women and the Internal Marketing System in Jamaica, 1781–1834," *WMQ* 76, no. 2 (2019): 203–206; David Waldstreicher, *Runaway America: Benjamin Franklin, Slavery, and the American Revolution* (Hill & Wang, 2004), 10–25.

22. See Philip D. Morgan, *Slave Counterpoint: Black Culture in the Eighteenth-Century Chesapeake and Lowcountry* (OIEAHC, 1998), 238–244; Gary B. Nash, *Forging Freedom: The Formation of Philadelphia's Free Black Community, 1720–1840* (Harvard, 1988), 144–153, albeit with data from a slightly later period; Michael Jarvis, *In the Eye of All Trade: Bermuda, Bermudians, and the Maritime Atlantic World, 1680–1783* (OIEAHC, 2010), 100–109; Kevin Dawson, "The Cultural Geography of Enslaved Ship Pilots," in *The Black Urban Atlantic in the Age of the Slave Trade*, eds. Jorge Cañizares-Esguerra, Matt D. Childs, and James Sidbury (Penn, 2013), 163–184.

23. Lemisch, "Jack Tar," 391, 399–400; Benjamin Quarles, *The Negro in the American Revolution* (OIEAHC, 1961), 3–13.

24. Chernoh M. Sesay Jr., "The Revolutionary Black Roots of Slavery's Abolition in Massachusetts," *New England Quarterly* 87, no. 1 (2014): 111–125; Manisha Sinha, *The Slave's Cause: A History of Abolition* (Yale, 2016), 41–44; Isabelle Laskaris, "'Thousands Now Unhappy': Slave Petitions in Eighteenth-Century Connecticut," *Slavery & Abolition* 44, no. 1 (2023): 26–34.

25. *South Carolina Gazette*, 24 Sep 1772, 12 Nov 1772, and 31 May 1770.

26. See Hilary Beckles, "Black Females Slaves and White Households in Barbados," in *More Than Chattel: Black Women and Slavery in the Americas*, eds. David Barry Gaspar and Darlene Clark Hine (Indiana, 1996), 117–118, 122; Sweeney, "Market Marronage," 206; *South Carolina Gazette*, 24 Sep 1772; *South Carolina and American General Gazette*, 16 Jun 1775.

27. See Morgan, *Slave Counterpoint*, 250–253; Sweeney, "Market Marronage," 212; and the discussion of clothes in Karen Cook Bell, *Running from Bondage: Enslaved Women and Their Remarkable Fight for Freedom in Revolutionary America* (Cambridge, 2021), 53–54.

28. *South Carolina Gazette*, 24 Sep 1772; *Gazette of the State of South-Carolina*, 5 May 1777; *South Carolina Gazette*, 31 May 1774.

29. Robert J. Chaffin, "The Townshend Acts Crisis, 1767–1770," in *A Companion to the American Revolution*, eds. Jack P. Greene and J. R. Pole (Blackwell, 2000), 134–150.

30. Schlesinger, *Colonial Merchants*, 94–105.

31. See *Essex Gazette*, 22 Aug 1769; Ryerson, *Revolution Is Now Begun*, 27–29; Schlesinger, *Colonial Merchants*, 113–119; John W. Tyler, *Smugglers and Patriots: Boston Merchants and the Advent of the American Revolution* (Northeastern, 1987), 113; Charles McLean Andrews, *The Boston Merchants and the Non-Importation Movement* (John Wilson & Son, 1917), 206, 211; Perl-Rosenthal, "Corresponding Republics," 59–72.

32. Tyler, *Smugglers and Patriots*, ch. 3, esp. 109–110.

33. For Philadelphia, see *Pennsylvania Gazette*, 3 Aug 1769; for New York, see Tiedemann, *Reluctant Revolutionaries*, 155, and *Pennsylvania Gazette*, 23 Mar 1769; for Boston, see Andrews, *Boston Merchants*, 204–206; *Pennsylvania Gazette*, 19 Oct 1769; *The Merchants and All Others, Who Are Any Ways Concerned in, or Connected with Trade* (Boston, April 19, 1770).

34. James F. Shepherd and Gary M. Walton, *Shipping, Maritime Trade, and the Economic Development of Colonial North America* (Cambridge, 1972), 163–164; T. H. Breen, *The Marketplace of Revolution: How Consumer Politics Shaped American Independence* (Oxford, 2004); Schlesinger, *Colonial Merchants*, chs. 4–5.

35. Merrill Jensen, *The Founding of a Nation: A History of the American Revolution, 1763–1776* (Oxford, 1968), 325–327.

## CHAPTER 3: THE AMERICAN REVOLUTION

1. Maier, *From Resistance to Revolution*, chs. 7–8; Nathan R. Perl-Rosenthal, "The 'Divine Right of Republics': Hebraic Republicanism and the Debate over Kingless Government in Revolutionary America," *WMQ* 66, no. 3 (July 2009).

2. *DAJA*, 1:251, 253.

3. *LPJA*, 2:181, 194–196.

4. Smith, *John Adams*, 1:96–101; *LPJA*, 2:173–210.

5. *LPJA*, 2:197–202, quotation 198.

6. Ibid., 2:206–209, 182–183, 191.

7. *DAJA*, 3:286–287. Adams misremembered the year when he described the conversation: see Carl Ubbelohde, *The Vice-Admiralty Courts and the American Revolution* (UNC, 1960), 139–140, 145.

8. *DAJA*, 3:288.

9. See Hiller B. Zobel, *The Boston Massacre* (Norton, 1970), and the recent Serena R. Zabin, *The Boston Massacre: A Family History* (Houghton Mifflin Harcourt, 2020), and Eric Hinderaker, *Boston's Massacre* (Belknap, 2017).

10. Ferling, *John Adams*, 64–70; and Hinderaker, *Boston's Massacre*, 201–209, on how Adams threaded the needle.

11. Ferling, *John Adams*, 70–78; Smith, *John Adams*, 155–157.

12. Maier, *From Resistance to Revolution*, 225–226.

13. Benjamin L. Carp, *Defiance of the Patriots: The Boston Tea Party and the Making of America* (Yale, 2010), 79–80, 97–98; Benjamin W. Labaree, *The Boston Tea Party* (Oxford, 1964), 88–91; [Hampden], *The Alarm. Number II* (New York, October 9, 1773), 2.

14. Breen, *Marketplace of Revolution*, 244–247.

15. Carp, *Defiance of the Patriots*, 73–85.

16. This and next paragraph: Labaree, *Boston Tea Party*, 126–132, and Carp, *Defiance of the Patriots*, 97–98, 166–167.

17. David Ammerman, *In the Common Cause: American Response to the Coercive Acts of 1774* (Virginia, 1974), 5–12.

18. Samuel Adams to James Warren, 14 May 1774, in Samuel Adams, *The Writings of Samuel Adams*, ed. Henry Alonzo Cushing (Octagon Books, 1968), 3:112; Ammerman, *In the Common Cause*, 19–34.

19. Ammerman, *In the Common Cause*, 30–34; Jensen, *Founding of a Nation*, 474–479.

20. Hugh T. Lefler and William S. Powell, *Colonial North Carolina: A History* (Scribner's, 1973), 261–262; Cynthia A. Kierner, "The Edenton Ladies: Women, Tea, and Politics in Revolutionary North Carolina," in *North Carolina Women: Their Lives and Times*, ed. Michele Gillespie and Sally G. McMillen

(Georgia, 2014); and Richard Dillard, *The Historic Tea-Party of Edenton, October 25th, 1774* (Capital Printing Company, 1901).

21. Kierner, "The Edenton Ladies," 17–19, 21–24; Lefler and Powell, *Colonial North Carolina*, 225–228. See also T. H. Breen, *Tobacco Culture: The Mentality of the Great Tidewater Planters on the Eve of Revolution* (Princeton, 1985), 75–83; Carol Berkin, *Revolutionary Mothers: Women in the Struggle for America's Independence* (Knopf, 2005), ch. 2; Richard Bushman, *The Refinement of America: Persons, Houses, Cities* (Knopf, 1992), 120–127.

22. Benjamin H. Irvin, *Clothed in Robes of Sovereignty: The Continental Congress and the People Out of Doors* (Oxford, 2011), 39–44.

23. Jensen, *Founding of a Nation*, 491–492. See also the discussions in *JCC*, 1:25, and Paul Hubert Smith, ed., *Letters of Delegates to Congress, 1774–1789*, 26 vols. (Library of Congress, 1976), 1:30–31.

24. Smith, *Letters of Delegates*, 1:103–105; Middlekauff, *Glorious Cause*, 247–248; Jerrilyn Greene Marston, *King and Congress: The Transfer of Political Legitimacy, 1774–1776* (Princeton, 1987), 111–122; *JCC*, 1:63–73; Jack N. Rakove, *The Beginnings of National Politics: An Interpretive History of the Continental Congress* (Knopf, 1979), 58–59.

25. Jensen, *Founding of a Nation*, 510, 526–528; Michael A. McDonnell, *The Politics of War: Race, Class, and Conflict in Revolutionary Virginia* (OIEAHC, 2007), 35–40.

26. Samuel Johnson, *Taxation No Tyranny; an Answer to the Resolutions and Address of the American Congress* (Cadell, 1775), 85.

27. *London Gazetteer and New Daily Advertiser*, 16 Jan 1775.

28. See Mariët Westermann and Jan Steen, *The Amusements of Jan Steen: Comic Painting in the Seventeenth Century* (Waanders, 1997), 29, 159–176; Karen Harvey, *The Little Republic: Masculinity and Domestic Authority in Eighteenth-Century Britain* (Oxford, 2012), 34–41.

29. For identifications, see Kierner, "The Edenton Ladies," 18–19, and Dillard, *Historic Tea-Party*, 12–13.

30. Catherine Molineux, *Faces of Perfect Ebony: Encountering Atlantic Slavery in Imperial Britain* (Harvard, 2012), ch. 6.

31. Linda K. Kerber, *Women of the Republic: Intellect and Ideology in Revolutionary America* (OIEAHC, 1980), 74–83; Toby L. Ditz, "Masculine Republics and 'Female Politicians' in the Age of Revolution," *JER* 35, no. 2 (2015).

32. Abigail Adams to Mercy Otis Warren, 3 Feb 1775, *Adams Family Correspondence*, 1:183–184.

33. Jensen, *Founding of a Nation*, 568–587; David Hackett Fischer, *Paul Revere's Ride* (Oxford, 1994), esp. 184–201.

34. Jensen, *Founding of a Nation*, 594–597; McDonnell, *Politics of War*, 49–63; John Adams to Abigail Adams, 30 Apr 1775, *Adams Family Correspondence*, 1:190.

35. Don Higginbotham, *The War of American Independence: Military Attitudes, Policies, and Practice, 1763–1789* (Macmillan, 1971), 82–95; Jensen, *Founding of a Nation*, 608–611.

36. Alan Taylor, *The Internal Enemy: Slavery and War in Virginia, 1772–1832* (Norton, 2013), 22–23; Woody Holton, *Forced Founders: Indians, Debtors, Slaves, and the Making of the American Revolution in Virginia* (UNC, 1999), 146–152.

37. Cassandra Pybus, *Epic Journeys of Freedom: Runaway Slaves of the American Revolution and Their Global Quest for Liberty* (Beacon Press, 2006), 11–17; Cook Bell, *Running from Bondage*, 67–105, esp. 72–87; Taylor, *Internal Enemy*, 26–28; Judith L. Van Buskirk, *Standing in Their Own Light: African American Patriots in the American Revolution* (Oklahoma, 2017), 60–69.

38. Jasanoff, *Liberty's Exiles*, ch. 9.

39. Jack N. Rakove, *The Beginnings of National Politics: An Interpretive History of the Continental Congress* (Knopf, 1979), 76–85; Jensen, *Founding of a Nation*, 640–646.

40. This and next paragraph: Jensen, *Founding of a Nation*, chs. 23–24, esp. 607–608, 655–665; Paine, "Common Sense" (1776), in *Complete Writings of Thomas Paine*, 1:24, 21.

## CHAPTER 4: THE REVOLUTIONS IN THE ANDES

1. Teodoro de Croix (viceroy of Peru) to José de Gálvez, Marquess of Sonora, no. 567, 28 Feb 1787, Gobierno, Lima 674, AGI.

2. José Antonio del Busto Duthurburu, *José Gabriel Túpac Amaru antes de su rebelión* (Universidad Católica, 1981), 21–24, 53–54.

3. Enrique Mayer, *The Articulated Peasant: Household Economies in the Andes* (Westview Press, 2002), ch. 2; Steve Kosiba, "Cultivating Empire: Inca Intensive Agricultural Strategies," in *The Oxford Handbook of the Incas*, ed. Sonia Alconini and Alan Covey (Oxford, 2018), 231–241; Nigel Davies, *The Incas* (Colorado, 1995), ch. 5.

4. Kris E. Lane, *Potosí: The Silver City That Changed the World* (California, 2019), 33–42.

5. See Susan E. Ramírez, *Provincial Patriarchs: Land Tenure and the Economics of Power in Colonial Peru* (New Mexico, 1986), esp. 44–47, 100–105; James Lockhart, *Spanish Peru, 1532–1560: A Colonial Society* (Wisconsin, 1974), esp. 11–37.

6. John R. Fisher, *Bourbon Peru, 1750–1824* (Liverpool, 2003), 13, 22, 64; Kendall W. Brown, *Bourbons and Brandy: Imperial Reform in Eighteenth-Century Arequipa* (New Mexico, 1986), 190–196; and the survey in Allan J. Kuethe and Kenneth J. Andrien, *The Spanish Atlantic World in the Eighteenth Century: War and the Bourbon Reforms, 1713–1796* (Cambridge, 2014).

7. David T. Garrett, *Shadows of Empire: The Indian Nobility of Cusco, 1750–1825* (Cambridge, 2005), 213–214; John R. Fisher, *The Economic Aspects of Spanish Imperialism in America, 1492–1810* (Liverpool, 1997), 176–186; Timothy E. Anna, *The Fall of the Royal Government in Peru* (Nebraska, 1979), 6–16.

8. Alberto Flores Galindo, *In Search of an Inca: Identity and Utopia in the Andes*, trans. Carlos Aguirre, Charles F. Walker, and Willie Hiatt (Cambridge, 2010), 30–40, 68–79.

9. Charles F. Walker, *The Tupac Amaru Rebellion* (Belknap, 2014), 18–20, 25–27; Duthurburu, *Túpac Amaru*, 101–103.

10. Walker, *Tupac Amaru*, chs. 2 and 4.

11. Garrett, *Shadows of Empire*, ch. 3; Karen B. Graubart, *With Our Labor and Sweat: Indigenous Women and the Formation of Colonial Society in Peru, 1550–1700* (Stanford, 2007), ch. 5; David T. Garrett, "'In Spite of Her Sex': The Cacica and the Politics of the Pueblo in Late Colonial Cusco," *The Americas* 64, no. 4 (2008); Deborah A. Rosen, "Women and Property Across Colonial America: A Comparison of Legal Systems in New Mexico and New York," *WMQ* 60, no. 2 (2003): 358–359.

12. Leon G. Campbell, "Women and the Great Rebellion in Peru, 1780–1783," *The Americas* 42, no. 2 (1985): 184; Scarlett O'Phelan Godoy, *Rebellions and Revolts in Eighteenth Century Peru and Upper Peru* (Böhlau, 1985), 234–236; Auto of Cecilia Tupac Amaru, 7 Jun 1781, in *Mártires y heroines*, ed. F. A. Loayza (Lima, 1945), 195.

13. Micaela Bastidas (MB) to Túpac Amaru (TA), 10 Dec 1780, *CDBTA*, 4:23–24. Angela Pacuri to MB, 12 Dec 1780; Francisca Herrera and unknown to MB, 13 Dec 1780; MB proclamation, 13 Dec 1780; Diego Visa to MB, 13 Dec 1780, all in *CDBTA*, 4:27, 22, 27, 14–15, 31.

14. Tomás Guaca to MB, 15 Dec 1780; MB to Antonio de Chavez y Mendoza, 6 Feb 1781; MB to TA, 7 Dec 1780; MB to TA, 23 Nov 1780; MB to TA, n.d., all in *CDBTA*, 4:33, 17, 84–85, 81, 79–80. See also Jorge Cornejo Bouroncle, *Micaela Bastidas; la heroina máxima del Perú* (Cuzco, 1948).

15. "Confesión de Micaela Bastidas," 22 Apr 1781, *CDBTA*, 4:40–41.

16. *Edito a los moradores de Lampa*, 25 Nov 1780, *CDIP* t. 2, v. 2, 303.

17. Luis Durand Flórez, *Criollos en conflicto: Cuzco después de Túpac Amaru* (Universidad de Lima, 1985), 54–62. TA to Antonio and Gabriel Ugarte, 22 Nov 1780, *CDBTA*, 1:117; Ana María Lorandi and Cora Virginia Bunster,

*La pedagogía del miedo: los Borbones y el criollismo en el Cuzco, 1780–1790* (Instituto Francés de Estudios Andinos, 2013), 97–104.

18. Maria Dominga de Rivadeneyra to the Queen, 14 Nov 1797, in Gobierno, Cuzco 30, AGI (lineage); Quad.o 2o De los autos seguidos conc. dn Ant.o, f. 17, in Gobierno, Cuzco 30, AGI; Testimony of Don Bernardo Tayo, 8 Mar 1783, and Declaración of Padre Fray Sebastian, 8 May 1783, both in Croix to Gálvez , no. 567, 28 Feb 1787, Gobierno, Lima 674, AGI (tastes); Andrés Eichmann Oehrli, "Teatro breve y brevísimo en el sur andino," *Bulletin of the Comediantes* 65, no. 2 (2013).

19. We do not know the precise date of her entry into the convent, but no document I found refers to her being there before the late 1770s. On convent finances and their age structure, see Kathryn Burns, *Colonial Habits: Convents and the Spiritual Economy of Cuzco, Peru* (Duke, 1999), 119–121, 134–139, and Margaret Chowning, *Rebellious Nuns: The Troubled History of a Mexican Convent, 1752–1863* (Oxford, 2006), 42–44.

20. "Alboroto el Convento en el ano de 81, quando les feos [uncl] de la sublevacion acababan de entrar en aquella Ciudad": Benito de Mata Linares to Gálvez, no. 37, 9 Sep 1786, Gobierno, Cuzco 69, AGI.

21. Copia de la Declaracion que el Padre Fray Sebastian segueiros del orden de Sto Domingo hizo ante el senor Privosor de la ciudad del cuzco, 8 May 1783, in Copia de la carta que el Religioso Dominico Fr Manuel savala escribio…, in Gobierno, Lima 674, AGI. The translation given in the original source is "te estoy queriendo fuertam.te mi criadito, o hijito, y lo tengo en el centro de mi coraz.n." I am grateful to Professor Zoila Mendoza for her assistance with this text. Bruce Mannheim, *The Language of the Inka Since the European Invasion* (Texas, 1991), 126, finds most colonial-era texts in Quechua were written by those who acquired it "as a second or later language," which seems very unlikely in this instance.

22. There are no very precise numbers: some observers estimated five thousand within the city and forty thousand in the *amarista* camp. Even if that were a fourfold exaggeration of Túpac Amaru's forces, he still had a two-to-one advantage in manpower: Walker, *Tupac Amaru*, 120. Sergio Serulnikov, *Revolution in the Andes: The Age of Túpac Amaru* (Duke, 2013), 92–96, focused on the southern Andes, stresses the "unprecedented" violence of the movement.

23. 17 Nov 1781, *La rebelión de Túpac Amaru, CDIP*, 2:275. Lorandi and Bunster, *Pedagogía*, 102–103.

24. Walker, *Tupac Amaru*, chs. 6 and 7.

25. Campbell, "Women and the Great Rebellion," 168–170. Accusation of Fiscal, 4 May 1781, *CDBTA*, 4:59.

26. Walker, *Tupac Amaru*, ch. 12; Francisco A. Loayza, *Cuarenta años de cautiverio: Memorias del Inka Juan Bautista Túpac Amaru* (Editorial Domingo Miranda, 1941), 48–53. My thanks to Chuck Walker for this reference.

27. Petition of Nuns of Santa Catalina, 30 Nov 1786, Gobierno, Cuzco 69, AGI; Burns, *Colonial Habits*, 137, 139, 146–147; Lorandi and Bunster, *Pedagogía*, 138–139.

28. See Testimonio relativo al capitulo del Monasterio de Santa Catalina del Cuzco. Remetido por el Virrey, 20 de Dic 1792, Gobierno, Cuzco 69, AGI, esp. testimonies of Martin Mariano de Toledo, 8 Aug 1792, and Miguel de Chirinos and Josef Pérez, both 3 Aug 1792; Sub-Priora de Santa Catalina to Juan Manuel Moscoso, 13 Jun 1780, and Permiso que pide la Madre Trancito, *CDBTA*, 2:122, 123–124; and Recurso de fuerza interpuesto por Francisca del Transito y Valdés, 26 Apr 1781, RACE 2, legajo 1, cuaderno 7, Archivo General de la Nación, Lima.

29. See Quad.o 11.o de los autos, 1784, in Gobierno, Cuzco 31, AGI; Testimony of Don Bernardo Tayo, 8 Mar 1783, in Copia de la Sumaria que en Testimonio se halla en los Autos, in Gobierno, Lima 674, AGI; Bunster and Lorandi, *Pedagogía*, 138–139, 149.

30. Maria de la O and Francisca del Trancito to Moscoso, 12 May 1783, Colonial XXXII, 2, 26, AAC.

31. Lorandi and Bunster, *Pedagogía*, 140–141; Consulta regarding Mata Linares to Gálvez, no. 37, 9 Sep 1786 (epithet); Testimonies of Madre Maria de la O et al., n.d. [1783], in Quad.o. 2o de los autos seguidos conc.a dn Ant.o, Gobierno, Cuzco 30, AGI (theater).

32. See testimonies of Fray Sebastian Segueiros, Fray Andres Aragon, Fray Igancio Bargas, and Bernardo Tayo, 8 Mar 1783, all in Gobierno, Lima 674, AGI.

33. Art historians have attributed this work, without firm evidence, to the Native artist Tadeo Escalante, active in the early nineteenth century: José de Mesa and Teresa Gisbert, *Historia de la pintura cuzqueña*, new ed., 2 vols. (Fundación A.N. Wiese, 1982), 251–252; Ananda Cohen Suarez, *Heaven, Hell, and Everything in Between: Murals of the Colonial Andes* (Texas, 2016), 158; also Jorge A. Flores Ochoa et al., *Pintura mural en el sur andino* (Banco de Crédito del Perú, 1993). This was a major project and the convent was short of money in the early 1800s; an earlier date, during the 1780s, is more likely, and the subject matter points in that direction too.

34. Moscoso to Madre Barbara del Sacramento, n.d. [1783], Moscoso to Trancito, 2 Aug 1783, and Moscoso to Trancito, 9 Sep 1783, all in Mata Linares to Gálvez, no. 37, Gobierno, Cuzco 69, AGI; and Remis.n del Yltmo S.or Obpo a su Prov.or, [7?] Mar 1783, Copia de la Sumaria, Gobierno, Lima 674, AGI.

35. See Croix to Gálvez, no. 567, 28 Feb 1787, Gobierno, Lima 674, AGI; I follow the chronology (nuns' revolt, then troops) reported in Gobierno, Cuzco 30 and discussed in Lorandi and Bunster, *Pedagogía*, 145–146. See also Rivadeneyra to the Minister, 19 Dec 1787, in Testimonios no. 2, Gobierno, Cuzco 21, AGI; and El consejo pleno a 26 de May de 1788, Gobierno, Cuzco 69, AGI.

36. Lorandi and Bunster, *Pedagogía*, 158. For the delay in turning their attention to the criollos, see Durand Flórez, *Criollos en conflicto*, 91–137.

37. Charles F. Walker, *Smoldering Ashes: Cuzco and the Creation of Republican Peru, 1780–1840* (Duke, 1999), 58–59.

38. Lorandi and Bunster, *Pedagogía*, 158–165, 75.

39. Ibid., 215. See the discussion in Durand Flórez, *Criollos en conflicto*, 79–89, esp. 88.

40. Cecilia de S. Sebastian to Pérez and Mata Linares, 10 Jun 1786, in Mata Linares to Gov. Intendente, 9 Jul 1786, no. 33, Gobierno, Cuzco 69, AGI; Mata Linares to Croix, 19 Jan 1786, and Mata Linares to Gov Intendente, 9 Jul 1786, no. 33, both in Gobierno, Cuzco 69, AGI. In 1783 alone, Madre Maria appealed multiple times to the audiencia: Mata Linares to Gálvez, no. 37, Gobierno, Cuzco 69, AGI.

41. Croix to Gálvez, no. 567, 28 Feb 1787, Gobierno, Lima 674, AGI.

42. Rivadeneyra to [Viceroy?], 30 Jan 1787, Gobierno, Cuzco 69, AGI.

43. Nuns of Santa Catalina, petition, 30 Nov 1786, Gobierno, Cuzco 69, AGI.

44. Certificación, 1 Oct 1786, in Mata Linares to Gálvez, no. 48, 16 Jan 1787; Nuns of Santa Catalina, petition, 30 Nov 1786; and Mata Linares to Gálvez, no. 37, all in Gobierno, Cuzco 69, AGI.

45. See above, ch. 3, and Holger Hoock, *Scars of Independence: America's Violent Birth* (Crown, 2017), esp. 12–20.

## CHAPTER 5: THE NEWS OF WAR

1. Jonathan R. Dull, *A Diplomatic History of the American Revolution* (Yale, 1985), 60–61.

2. Ibid., 51–52.

3. Perl-Rosenthal, "Atlantic Cultures and the Age of Revolution," 685; Perl-Rosenthal, "Corresponding Republics," 30–35, 99–101, 123–124; Kenneth J. Banks, *Chasing Empire Across the Sea: Communications and the State in the French Atlantic, 1713–1763* (McGill-Queen's University Press, 2002), 156–164.

4. Brian Cowan, *The Social Life of Coffee: The Emergence of the British Coffeehouse* (Yale, 2005), 169–175, 132–145; Markman Ellis, *The Coffee-House:*

*A Cultural History* (Weidenfeld & Nicolson, 2004), ch. 11; Johann Wilhelm von Archenholz, *A Picture of England* (London: Edward Jeffery, 1789), 106–107, in *Eighteenth-Century Coffee-House Culture*, ed. Markman Ellis (Pickering & Chatto, 2006), 2:372–373.

5. See Slauter, "News and Diplomacy"; *A Sunday Ramble; or, Modern Sabbath-Day Journey; in and About the Cities of London and Westminster*, 2nd ed. (London, 1776), 30–31, in *Eighteenth-Century Coffee-House Culture*, 2:362–363; Coffee-man, *The Case of the Coffee-Men* (London, [1728?]), 5–7, in *Eighteenth-Century Coffee-House Culture*, 2:95–97.

6. Slauter, "News and Diplomacy," 199–201; Will Slauter, "Forward Looking Statements: News and Speculation in the Age of the American Revolution," *JMH* 81, no. 4 (2009).

7. Dull, *Diplomatic History*, 66–69; Jeremy Black, *Crisis of Empire: Britain and America in the Eighteenth Century* (Bloomsbury, 2011), 123–124. News of the Túpac Amaru revolt was received in a similar fashion: Sinclair Thomson, "Sovereignty Disavowed: The Tupac Amaru Revolution in the Atlantic World," *Atlantic Studies* 13, no. 3 (2016): 414–418.

8. Raynal, *A Philosophical and Political History of the Settlements and Trade . . . in the East and West Indies*, trans. J. Justamond (Dublin: Exshaw, 1776), 3:165ff.; Sankar Muthu, *Enlightenment Against Empire* (Princeton, 2003), 87–97; see also Anatole Feugère, *Bibliographie critique de l'abbé Raynal* (Imprimerie Ouvrière, 1922), and Anatole Feugère, *Un Précurseur de la Révolution française: L'abbé Raynal (1713–1796)* (Imprimerie Ouvrière, 1922), esp. 259–264.

9. See, e.g., Henri Doniol, *Histoire de la participation de la France à l'établissement des États-Unis d'Amérique* (Imprimerie Nationale, 1886), 1:10–11, 633–636; Franco Venturi, *The End of the Old Regime in Europe, 1776–1789*, trans. R. Burr Litchfield (Princeton, 1991), 1:375–379.

10. William Murchison, *The Cost of Liberty: The Life of John Dickinson* (Intercollegiate Studies Institute, 2014), 43; Luther Samuel Livingston, ed., *Franklin and His Press at Passy* (Grolier Club, 1914); Durand Echeverria, *Mirage in the West: A History of the French Image of American Society to 1815* (Princeton, 1957), 25–30, 36–37; Bernard Bailyn, *The Ideological Origins of the American Revolution* (Belknap, 1992), 215–216.

11. For examples, see Durand Echeverria and Everett C. Wilkie, *The French Image of America: A Chronological and Subject Bibliography of French Books Printed Before 1816 Relating to the British North American Colonies and the United States*, 2 vols. (Scarecrow Press, 1994), 1:329–330, 345, 367–368. [Regnier], *Recueil des lois constitutives* (1778), quoted in Echeverria, *Mirage in the West*, 72.

12. See Dull, *Diplomatic History*, ch. 8.

13. Stéphanie Whitlock, "La culture du commerce: la promenade et le Jardin royal de Bordeaux au XVIIIe siècle," *Annales du Midi* 118, no. 254 (2006): 221; Daniel Roche, *The People of Paris: An Essay in Popular Culture in the 18th Century*, trans. Marie Evans (California, 1987), 33 (quotation); and Arlette Farge, *Vivre dans la rue à Paris au XVIIIe siècle* (Gallimard, 1979), 124–125.

14. Charles Higounet, *Histoire de Bordeaux* (Privat, 1980), 177–182; F. G. Pariset, ed., *Bordeaux aux XVIIIe siècle* (Fédération Historique du Sud-Ouest, 1968), 325–327; and (for Paris) Roche, *People*, 22–26, and Vincent Milliot, *"L'admirable police": Tenir Paris au siècle des lumières* (Champ Vallon, 2016), 224–232.

15. Pariset, *Bordeaux aux XVIIIe*, 359–363.

16. Plainte et informations of Jeanne Faucon et al., 2 Jan 1780, 12B 364, ADG.

17. Procès verbal concerning Jean Dussol, 12 May 1779, 12B 360, ADG.

18. Procès verbal concerning François Pelusset, 12 Mar 1779, Case against Pierre Sicot, colporteur, 12B 360, ADG.

19. Pariset, *Bordeaux aux XVIIIe*, 287–301, esp. 301; case in 12B 366, ADG.

20. Jean de Maupassant, *Un grand armateur de Bordeaux, Abraham Gradis (1699?–1780)* (Feret, 1917), 139–141.

21. Dull, *Diplomatic History*, 57–61; Doniol, *Histoire*, 1:265–279.

22. Smith, *John Adams*, 1:320–322, 355.

23. Higounet, *Histoire de Bordeaux*, 203–204.

24. *DAJA*, 2:292–293; 4:33.

25. J. H. Sheppard, *The Life of Samuel Tucker* (A. Mudge and Son, 1868), 282; John Adams quoted in Smith, *John Adams*, 1:365–367.

26. Smith, *John Adams*, 1:368–369.

27. Dull, *Diplomatic History*, 85–88; Smith, *John Adams*, 1:375–383.

28. Arthur Lee, *An Essay in Vindication of the Continental Colonies* (London: Becket, 1764), 37; Louis W. Potts, *Arthur Lee: A Virtuous Revolutionary* (LSU, 1981), 14–15; Edmund S. Morgan, *Benjamin Franklin* (Yale, 2002), 245–251; George L. Clark, *Silas Deane, a Connecticut Leader in the American Revolution* (Putnam's Sons, 1913), 3, 10–11.

29. David McCullough, *John Adams* (Simon & Schuster, 2001), 201–206.

30. Ibid., 197–200.

31. *DAJA*, 4:48, 82; 2:298–299, 302, 314, 309.

32. Ibid., 2:300; 4:59; 2:309–310; 4:130–132.

## CHAPTER 6: THE TOP-DOWN REVOLUTIONS

1. For a discussion of the rebellion in neighboring Brabant, which had a similar pattern, see Janet L. Polasky, *Revolution in Brussels, 1787–1793* (University Press of New England, 1987).

2. Jonathan Israel, *The Dutch Republic: Its Rise, Greatness, and Fall, 1477–1806* (Oxford, 1995), 199–203, 276–306.

3. Ibid., esp. 300–306.

4. Ibid., 702–704, 1016–1017.

5. Ibid., 803–805, 809–815.

6. Ibid., 1006–1011, 1079–1087; N. C. F. van Sas, "The Patriot Revolution: New Perspectives," in *The Dutch Republic in the Eighteenth Century: Decline, Enlightenment, and Revolution*, eds. Margaret C. Jacob and Wijnand W. Mijnhardt (Cornell, 1992), 91–95, 101–103.

7. Israel, *Dutch Republic*, 1080–1084.

8. Ibid., 1095–1097.

9. Murk de Jong Hendriksz, *Joan Derk van der Capellen* (J. B. Wolters, 1921), 5–11, 15–17, 203, 342–371; C. H. E. de Wit, *De nederlandse revolutie van de achttiende eeuw 1780–1787. Oligarchie en proletariaat* (Lindelauf, 1974), 42; Jan Willem Schulte Nordholt, *The Dutch Republic and American Independence*, trans. Herbert H. Rowen (UNC, 1982), 25–30.

10. Joan Derk van der Capellen, *Aan het volk van Nederland* (Ostend, 1781), 22–23.

11. Ibid., 75. For a thorough discussion see De Jong Hendriksz, *Van der Capellen*, 417–440.

12. See Schulte Nordholt, *Dutch Republic*, 214–246, esp. 214–217; Simon Schama, *Patriots and Liberators: Revolution in the Netherlands, 1780–1813* (Knopf, 1977), 82–83; Wayne Ph. Te Brake, *Regents and Rebels: The Revolutionary World of an Eighteenth-Century Dutch City* (Blackwell, 1989), 51; A. van Hulzen, *Utrecht in de patriottentijd* (Europese Bibliotheek, 1966), 53.

13. See especially S. R. E. Klein, *Patriots republikanisme: Politieke cultuur in Nederland (1766–1787)* (Amsterdam University Press, 1995), 167–176; Wyger Velema, *Republicans: Essays on Eighteenth-Century Dutch Political Thought* (Brill, 2007), 149–150; Schama, *Patriots and Liberators*, 84.

14. Israel, *Dutch Republic*, 121; Te Brake, *Regents and Rebels*, 119–120, 81–82; Hulzen, *Utrecht in de patriottentijd*, 56–61; J. L. Price, *Culture and Society in the Dutch Republic During the 17th Century* (Batsford, 1974), 80.

15. "Plan van correspondentie zo als hetzelve in den bijeen komst ond. 16 Aug 1783 is voorgedragen," 561: Stukken betreffende de vergaderingen der Regenten, Familiearchief Van der Capellen, Gelders Archief, Arnhem.

16. H. T. Colenbrander, "Aanteekeningen Betreffende de Vergaderingen van Vaderlandsche Regenten te Amsterdam 1783–1787," in *Bijdragen en Mededelingen van het Historisch Genootschap te Utrecht* (1899), 135.

17. Israel, *Dutch Republic*, 1105; Te Brake, *Regents and Rebels*, 148–155.

18. N. C. F. van Sas, *De metamorfose van Nederland: Van oude orde naar moderniteit, 1750–1900* (Amsterdam University Press, 2004), 179; H. T. Colenbrander, *De patriottentijd: hoofdzakelijk naar buitenlandsche bescheiden*, 3 vols. (Nijhoff, 1897), 2:366–367; Jeremy D. Popkin, "Dutch Patriots, French Journalists, and Declarations of Rights: The Leidse Ontwerp of 1785 and Its Diffusion in France," *Historical Journal* 38, no. 3 (September 1995): 555. On the *Leidse ontwerp*, see Wit, *De nederlandse revolutie*, 65–66, and Schama, *Patriots and Liberators*, 95; a contrasting view is in Klein, *Patriots republikanisme*, 252.

19. "Tekst van de welkomstwoort door D. v.d. Bos, sergeant bij het exercitiegenootschap 'Pro Patria et Libertate' te Utrecht, gericht tot vdC bij diens bezoek aldaar op 19 juli 1783," 291, Collectie J. D. Van der Capellen (1.10.18), Nationaal Archief, The Hague; De Jong Hendriksz, *Van der Capellen*, 664–679; G. T. Hartong, "Joan Derk, bejubeld en beschimpt," in *De wekker van de nederlandse natie*, eds. E. A. van Dijk et al. (Waanders, 1984), 63–71.

20. Leiden *schutterij* to R. J. van der Capellen, 10 Jun 1786, and Delft *schutterij* to same, 13 Jun 1786, and other letters in 496: Van Patriotische Genootschappen, 1784–86, Familiearchief Van der Capellen. See also Perl-Rosenthal, "Corresponding Republics," 195–197. On Paape: Peter Altena and Mireille Oostindie, eds., *Gerrit Paape. De Bataafsche Republiek* (Vantilt, 1998), and Israel, *Dutch Republic*, 1109–1110.

21. This and subsequent paragraph. On Utrecht: Schama, *Patriots and Liberators*, 88–92; R. E. de Bruin, *Revolutie in Utrecht: studenten, burgers en regenten in de Patriottentijd, 1780–1787* (Impress, 1987), 34–36 and ch. 7; Palmer, *Age*, 1:334–35. On Deventer: Te Brake, *Regents and Rebels*, 82. On Rotterdam: Colenbrander, *Patriottentijd*, 2:67–71; Schama, *Patriots and Liberators*, 87–88.

22. Schama, *Patriots and Liberators*, 128–35; W. A. Knoops and F. C. Meijer, *Goejanverwellesluis: de aanhouding van de prinses van Oranje op 28 juni 1787 door het vrijkorps van Gouda* (De Bataafsche Leeuw, 1987), 36–41.

23. John Adams to John Jay, 9 Oct 1787, in *PJA*, 19:181.

24. Merrill Jensen, *The New Nation: A History of the United States During the Confederation, 1781–1789* (Knopf, 1950), 187–193; Terry Bouton, *Taming Democracy: The People, the Founders, and the Troubled Ending of the American Revolution* (Oxford, 2007), 89–94.

25. Jensen, *New Nation*, 292–326; Leonard L. Richards, *Shays's Rebellion: The American Revolution's Final Battle* (Penn, 2002), 4–42.

26. Jack N. Rakove, *The Beginnings of National Politics: An Interpretive History of the Continental Congress* (Knopf, 1979), 170–174, 179–182.

27. "Editorial Note," in *Papers of James Madison: Congressional Series*, eds. William T. Hutchinson et al. (Chicago and Virginia, 1962–1991), 9:115–118; "Address of the Annapolis Convention," in *The Papers of Alexander Hamilton*, eds. Harold C. Syrett et al. (Columbia, 1961–1987), 3:689.

28. Financial profiles of the delegates: Forrest McDonald, *We the People: The Economic Origins of the Constitution* (Chicago, 1958), 38–92; mobilization of the elite: Cutterham, *Gentlemen Revolutionaries*, 133–142.

29. Charles A. Beard, *An Economic Interpretation of the Constitution of the United States* (Macmillan, 1913), 73–151, esp. 149–151; McDonald, *We the People*, 93–110, esp. 110.

30. Katlyn Carter, *Democracy in Darkness: Secrecy and Transparency in the Age of Revolutions* (Yale, 2023), 75–91; Catherine Drinker Bowen, *Miracle at Philadelphia: The Story of the Constitutional Convention* (Little Brown, 1966), 113–114, 123–124.

31. Jackson Turner Main, *The Upper House in Revolutionary America, 1763–1788* (Wisconsin, 1967), 219–224; Eric Nelson, *The Royalist Revolution: Monarchy and the American Founding* (Harvard, 2014), 184–203, esp. 187; David Waldstreicher, *Slavery's Constitution: From Revolution to Ratification* (Hill & Wang, 2009), 101–105.

32. George Washington to the president of Congress, 17 Sep 1787, in *Papers of George Washington: Confederation Series*, eds. W. W. Abbot et al. (Virginia, 1987–), 5:330.

33. Willi Paul Adams, *The First American Constitutions: Republican Ideology and the Making of the State Constitutions in the Revolutionary Era* (OIEAHC, 1980), 85–90; Pauline Maier, *Ratification: The People Debate the Constitution, 1787–1788* (Simon & Schuster, 2010), 100; [Findley], "Letter by an Officer of the Late Continental Army," *Philadelphia Independent Gazette*, 6 Nov 1787, in *The Complete Anti-Federalist*, ed. Herbert J. Storing (Chicago, 1981), 3:95.

34. Maier, *Ratification*, 92–95.

35. Middlekauff, *Glorious Cause*, 681–683.

36. Thomas Jefferson to John Adams, 28 Sep 1787, and John Adams to Thomas Jefferson, 9 Oct 1787, *PJA*, 19:170–171, 182–183.

## CHAPTER 7: THE REVOLUTION BEGINS IN PARIS

1. On the defeat and the flight to France, see Colenbrander, *Patriottentijd*, vol. 3; Theo van der Zee, J. G. M. M. Rosendaal, and Peter Thissen, *1787: De Nederlandse revolutie?* (De Bataafsche Leeuw, 1988); J. G. M. M. Rosendaal,

*Bataven! Nederlandse vluchtelingen in Frankrijk 1787–1795* (Vantilt, 2003), 161–162.

2. Rules for proprietors in Victor Champier and G.-Roger Sandoz, *Le Palais-Royal d'après des documents inédits (1629–1900)* (Société de Propagation des Livres d'Art, 1900), 1:438; "Vue Perspective du Palais Royal du côté du Jardin," colored engraving, ca. 1760, BNF. See also Jan Synowiecki, *Paris en ses jardins. Nature et culture urbaine au XVIIIe siècle* (Champ Vallon, 2021), chs. 7 and 8.

3. *Observations sur la destruction de la promenade* (1781), 31–33; Louis-Sébastien Mercier, *Tableau de Paris, nouvelle édition* (1782–1788), 10:229–230, 237–238; "Les Trente deux filles, dans l'Allée des soupirs," ca. 1785–1788, BNF. But see also Synowiecki, *Paris en ses jardins*, 331–339.

4. This plan aroused controversy: *Observations sur la destruction de la promenade* (1781); Champier and Sandoz, *Palais-Royal*, 1:416–422; Darrin M. McMahon, "The Birthplace of the Revolution: Public Space and Political Community in the Palais-Royal of Louis-Philippe-Joseph d'Orléans, 1781–1789," *French History* 10, no. 1 (1996): 7–16.

5. Robert M. Isherwood, *Farce and Fantasy: Popular Entertainment in Eighteenth-Century Paris* (Oxford, 1986), 217–245; F. M. Mayeur de St. Paul, *Tableau du nouveau palais-royal* (Paris: Maradin, 1788), 2:107–113, 1:109–111; Champier and Sandoz, *Palais-Royal*, 1:436–438; "Mlle La Pierre, jeune géante," etching, ca. 1780s, Musée Carnavalet, Paris; *Almanach du Palais Royal pour l'année 1785* (Paris: Royez, 1786), 69; Mercier, *Tableau*, 10:239; Garrioch, *Making*, 99–101.

6. Mercier, *Tableau*, 1:136–138; McMahon, "Birthplace," 19–24; Sarah C. Maza, *Private Lives and Public Affairs: The Causes Célèbres of Prerevolutionary France* (California, 1993), 182–187; John Hardman, *Marie Antoinette: The Making of a French Queen* (Yale, 2019), 97–121.

7. Dull, *Diplomatic History*, 61, 119–120, 151; William Doyle, *Origins of the French Revolution* (Oxford, 1980), 44–52.

8. Jean Egret, *La pré-révolution française, 1787–1788* (PUF, 1962), 69–80; Vivian R. Gruder, *The Notables and the Nation: The Political Schooling of the French, 1787–1788* (Harvard, 2007), 29; John Hardman, *Overture to Revolution: The 1787 Assembly of Notables and the Crisis of France's Old Regime* (Oxford, 2010), 272–276.

9. Egret, *La pré-révolution*, 306–337; Gilbert Shapiro et al., *Revolutionary Demands: A Content Analysis of the Cahiers de Doléances of 1789* (Stanford, 1998), 99–113; Beatrice Fry Hyslop, *A Guide to the General Cahiers of 1789 with the Texts of Unedited Cahiers* (Columbia, 1936); Esther Benbassa, *The Jews of France: A History from Antiquity to the Present* (Princeton, 1999), 80.

10. Timothy Tackett, *Becoming a Revolutionary: The Deputies of the French National Assembly and the Emergence of a Revolutionary Culture (1789–1790)* (Princeton, 1996), chs. 4 and 5, esp. 152–153; Doyle, *Origins*, 168–177; Georges Lefebvre, *The Coming of the French Revolution*, trans. R. R. Palmer (Princeton, 1967), 78–85.

11. Mona Ozouf, "Liberty" and "Regeneration," in *A Critical Dictionary of the French Revolution*, eds. François Furet and Mona Ozouf, trans. Arthur Goldhammer (Belknap, 1989), 716–727, 781–791; Lefebvre, *Coming*, part 5.

12. Marcel Reinhard, *Paris pendant la Révolution* (Centre de Documentation Universitaire, 1966), 164–173; Albert Mathiez, *La révolution française* (Colin, 1922), 1:49–59.

13. "Soirée du 30 Juin 1789. Dédiée à l'assemblée du Palais Royal," engraving, 1789, BNF; Marcel Rouff, "Le peuple ouvrier de Paris aux journées du 30 juin et du 30 août 1789," *La Révolution française* 66 (July–September 1912): 430–447.

14. "Événement du 30 juin 1789 entre 7 & 8 heures du soir," engraving, 1789, BNF. See also "Motions du Palais Royal le 12 j.et 1789," engraving, 1789, BNF, a depiction of a later gathering in the *jardin*, discussed in Paul G. Spagnoli, "The Revolution Begins: Lambesc's Charge, 12 July 1789," *FHS* 17, no. 2 (1991): 466–497.

15. Raymonde Monnier, *Le faubourg Saint-Antoine, 1789–1815* (Société des Études Robespierristes, 1981), 25, 35–41, 111; Jacques L. Godechot, *The Taking of the Bastille, July 14th, 1789*, trans. Jean Stewart (Scribner, 1970), 90–91.

16. Godechot, *Taking*, 116–117; Reinhard, *Paris pendant la Révolution*, 140–152.

17. Reinhard, *Paris pendant la Révolution*, 173; Godechot, *Taking*, 221–222; George Rudé, *The Crowd in the French Revolution* (Oxford, 1959), 34–39; Julie Hardwick, *Sex in an Old Regime City: Young Workers and Intimacy in France, 1660–1789* (Oxford, 2020), 35–38.

18. Garrioch, *Making*, 76–78, 100–101, 261; Michael Sonenscher, *Work and Wages: Natural Law, Politics, and the Eighteenth-Century French Trades* (Cambridge, 1989), 82–86, 330.

19. This and next paragraph: Rudé, *Crowd in the French Revolution*, 50–54; Godechot, *Taking*, 214–216.

20. Hans-Jürgen Lüsebrink and Rolf Reichardt, *The Bastille: A History of a Symbol of Despotism and Freedom* (Duke, 1997), 6–45.

21. Rolf Reichardt, *L'imagerie révolutionnaire de la Bastille: Collections du Musée Carnavalet* (Paris Musées, 2009); Héloïse Bocher, *Démolir la Bastille: L'édification d'un lieu de mémoire* (Vendémiaire, 2012), esp. 127–136; Rolf

Reichardt and Hubertus Kohle, *Visualising the Revolution: Politics and Pictorial Arts in Late Eighteenth-Century France* (Reaktion, 2008), ch. 2.

22. See, e.g., "Prise de la Bastille, le 14 juillet 1789: Par les citoyens et les cidevant Gardes françaises," colored print, 1789, BNF; and "Prise de la Bastille: cette forteresse qui avoit scu resister au Grand Condé fut attaquée le 14 juillet 1789," colored print, 1789, BNF; Reichardt, *L'imagerie*, 66–77.

23. "La Prise de la Bastille: Couplets dédiés à la nation par M. Déduit," colored print, 1789; "Prise de la Bastille en 1789: Cette forteresse devant laquelle avoit échoué le courage du grand Condé," etching, 1789; "Le Siege de la Bastille prise par la bourgeoisie et aux braves grenadiers des gardes francoises," print, 1789; Charles Thévenin, "Prise de la Bastille, le 14 juillet 1789," etching, 1790, all in BNF; Arlette Farge and Jacques Revel, *The Vanishing Children of Paris: Rumor and Politics Before the French Revolution*, trans. Claudia Miéville (Harvard, 1991), 46–50.

24. Prieur and Berthaud, "Prise de la Bastille: Le 14 juillet 1789," etching, 1791, BNF.

25. E.g., John Wells, "The Taking of the Bastile on the 14 of July 1789," London, 1789; Reichardt, *L'imagerie*, 29. See also Prieur and Berthault, "Paris gardé par le people la nuit du 12 au 13 Juillet 1789," etching, [1789?], Portefeuille 219, p. 135, Cabinet des Estampes, Bibliothèque de l'Arsenal, Paris, for another view of popular dominion in mid-July.

26. François Lanthenas to Henri Bancal, 13 Jul 1789, NAF 9534, BNF; Lüsebrink and Reichardt, *Bastille*, ch. 1; François Ravaisson, ed., *Archives de la Bastille; documents inédits recueillis et publiés* (Durand, 1866), 1:i–iii.

27. Godechot, *Taking*, 236–244; "Prise de la Bastille, le 14 juillet 1789: Par les citoyens et les cidevant Gardes françaises."

28. Adolphe Thiers, *Histoire de la Révolution française*, 13th ed. (Paris: Furne, 1865), 1:87, 102–103.

29. Georges Lefebvre, *The Great Fear of 1789: Rural Panic in Revolutionary France*, trans. Joan White (Pantheon, 1973), esp. 143–168.

30. Rafe Blaufarb, *The Great Demarcation: The French Revolution and the Invention of Modern Property* (Oxford, 2016), 48–73; Fitzsimmons, *Night the Old Regime Ended*, 12–28.

31. Alphonse Aulard, *Histoire politique de la Révolution française* (Colin, 1901), 39–45; Marcel Gauchet, *La Révolution des droits de l'homme* (Gallimard, 1989), part 1, esp. 70–87.

32. This and the next paragraph: Rudé, *Crowd in the French Revolution*, 73–79.

33. Aulard, *Histoire politique*, 58–59.

## CHAPTER 8: THE POLITICS OF CROWDS AND CLUBS

1. François Lanthenas to Henri Bancal, 13 Jul 1789 and 17 Jul 1789, NAF 9534, BNF.

2. See the classic interpretation of Richard Cobb, *The Police and the People: French Popular Protest, 1789–1820* (Oxford, 1970), xiv–xv, 196–199.

3. Tackett, *Becoming*, 138–146; Michael L. Kennedy, *The Jacobin Clubs in the French Revolution: The First Years* (Princeton, 1982), 3–4.

4. Micah Alpaugh, *Friends of Freedom: The Rise of Social Movements in the Age of Atlantic Revolutions* (Cambridge, 2021), 1–6, 225–231.

5. See Leigh Ann Whaley, *Radicals: Politics and Republicanism in the French Revolution* (Sutton, 2000), 1–17; Tackett, *Becoming*, 35–47; Peter McPhee, *Robespierre: A Revolutionary Life* (Yale, 2012), chs. 3–4; Kennedy, *Jacobin Clubs*, 74–75; Marisa Linton, *Choosing Terror: Virtue, Friendship, and Authenticity in the French Revolution* (Oxford, 2013), 75–76.

6. Charles Le Guin, "Roland de la Platière: A Public Servant in the Eighteenth Century," *Transactions of the American Philosophical Society* 56, no. 6 (1966): 14–61, esp. 53–61; Siân Reynolds, *Marriage and Revolution: Monsieur and Madame Roland* (Oxford, 2012), 12–21, 32–38; Eloise Ellery, *Brissot de Warville: A Study in the History of the French Revolution* (1915; Burt Franklin, 1970), 53–58; Robert Darnton, "The Grub Street Style of Revolution: J.-P. Brissot, Police Spy," *JMH* 40, no. 3 (1968): 302–327; and appendices to Claude Perroud, ed., *Lettres de madame Roland: 1780–1793*, 2 vols. (Imprimerie nationale, 1900–1902), 549–793.

7. Kennedy, *Jacobin Clubs*, 36; Alphonse Aulard, ed., *La société des Jacobins. Recueil de documents pour l'histoire du club des Jacobins de Paris* (Jouaust, 1889), 1:lxxvii–lxxix; Alpaugh, *Friends*, 235–239.

8. Lynn A. Hunt, *Revolution and Urban Politics in Provincial France: Troyes and Reims, 1786–1790* (Stanford, 1978), 113–116, 142–146; Maurice Genty, "Les élections Parisiennes de 1789 à 1792. Étude socio-professionnelle des élus locaux," in *Paris et la Révolution*, ed. Michel Vovelle (Publications de la Sorbonne, 1988), 59–68.

9. Isabelle Bourdin, *Les sociétés populaires à Paris pendant la révolution* (Librairie du Recueil Sirey, 1937), 132–153, 161–163.

10. Ibid., 174–177; Rachel Hammersley, *French Revolutionaries and English Republicans: The Cordeliers Club, 1790–1794* (Boydell Press, 2005), 12–22; Albert Mathiez, *Le Club des Cordeliers pendant la crise de Varennes, et le massacre du Champ de Mars* (Champion, 1910), esp. 1–13.

11. David Andress, *The Terror: The Merciless War for Freedom in Revolutionary France* (FSG, 2005), 45–47; Bourdin, *Sociétés populaires*, 161.

12. Ellery, *Brissot*, 11.

13. Melvin Edelstein, *The French Revolution and the Birth of Electoral Democracy* (Ashgate, 2014), 44, 76–81; Aulard, *Histoire politique*, 62–80; Hunt, *Politics, Culture, and Class*, 156–176; Perl-Rosenthal, "Corresponding Republics," 239–240.

14. Maurice Wahl, *Les Premières années de la Révolution à Lyon (1788–1792)* (Colin, 1894), 177–192.

15. Bosc claims this in his "Memoire pour servir," though no trace appears in Aulard, ed., *Société des Jacobins*; see also Kennedy, *Jacobin Clubs*, 36–37; Perl-Rosenthal, "Corresponding Republics," 243–253. On the newspaper, see Ellery, *Brissot*, 59–64, 113–120; Claude Perroud, ed., *J.-P. Brissot: Mémoires (1754–1793)* (Picard, 1911); Slauter, "News and Diplomacy," 114–118, 122–134.

16. Ted W. Margadant, *Urban Rivalries in the French Revolution* (Princeton, 1992), 220–256; Anthony Crubaugh, *Balancing the Scales of Justice: Local Courts and Rural Society in Southwest France* (PSU, 2001), 133–142; John McManners, *The French Revolution and the Church* (Harper & Row, 1970), 24–45.

17. Timothy Tackett, *When the King Took Flight* (Harvard, 2003), 41–42, 71–73; Mona Ozouf, *Varennes: La mort de la royauté, 21 juin 1791* (Gallimard, 2005), 17–46, 84–104.

18. Ran Halévi, "Feuillants," in *Dictionnaire critique de la Révolution française*, eds. François Furet and Mona Ozouf (Flammarion, 1988), 366–367; Kennedy, *Jacobin Clubs*, 284–285; Patrice L. R. Higonnet, *Goodness Beyond Virtue: Jacobins During the French Revolution* (Harvard, 1998), 30–31; Ozouf, *Varennes*, 272–276; Aulard, *Histoire politique*, 154–158.

19. Ozouf, *Varennes*, 274–278; Gérard Maintenant, "Les Jacobins à l'épreuve. La scission des Feuillants, été 1791," *Cahiers de l'Institut Maurice Thorez* 13, no. 32–33 (1979): 77–85, 107; Georges Michon, *Essai sur l'histoire du parti feuillant; Adrien Duport* (Payot, 1924), ch. 12.

20. J.-M. Roland to L.-A. Champagneux, 21 [Jul 1791], NAF 6241, BNF; Mme Roland to Bancal, 20 Jul 1791, and Mme Roland to Bancal, 17–18 Jul 1791, in *Lettres de madame Roland*, 2:340–343, 333–334; Gilbert Romme to Bosc, 23 Jul [1791] and 2 Aug 1791, and Dubreul to Bosc, 6 Aug 1791, all MS 1009: Correspondance, Papiers Bosc, BHVP. For a fuller discussion of the Roland circle's role in keeping the Jacobin network together after Varennes, see Perl-Rosenthal, "Corresponding Republics," 266–273.

21. Maintenant, "Les Jacobins à l'épreuve," 78–79. See also Christine Peyrard, *Les Jacobins de l'Ouest: Sociabilité révolutionnaire et formes de politisation dans le Maine et la Basse-Normandie* (Publications de la Sorbonne, 1996), 95–97; Paul R. Hanson, *Provincial Politics in the French Revolution: Caen and Limoges, 1789–1794* (LSU, 1989), 49; and Deliberations of the Société des

Amis de la Constitution de Lyon (Section de la Croix-Rousse), 24 Jul, 1 Aug, and 17 Aug 1791, 34 L 3, ADR, for examples of provincial club splits.

22. Wahl, *Premières années*, 400; Roland to Champagneux, 24 Jul 1791 and 4 Aug 1791, NAF 6241, BNF; Le Guin, "Roland de la Platière: A Public Servant in the Eighteenth Century," 66–67; Perroud, ed., *Lettres de madame Roland*, appendix N.

23. W. D. Edmonds, *Jacobinism and the Revolt of Lyon, 1789–1793* (Oxford, 1990), 97–103; Frères Richard to Lanthenas, 22 Aug 1791 and 25 Aug 1791, both NAF 9534, BNF; Mme Roland to Champagneux, 31 Jul 1791 in Perroud, ed., *Lettres de madame Roland*, 2:356; Aulard, *Société des Jacobins*, 3:104.

24. Maintenant, "Les Jacobins à l'épreuve," 95–97; Kennedy, *Jacobin Clubs*, ch. 15.

25. Ellery, *Brissot*, ch. 9, esp. 216–229.

26. C. J. Mitchell, *The French Legislative Assembly of 1791* (Brill, 1988), 44–60; Ellery, *Brissot*, 227–229.

27. Le Guin, "Roland de la Platière," 75–80; and the excellent discussions in Gary Kates, *The Cercle Social, the Girondins, and the French Revolution* (Princeton, 1985), 190–193, 249–270.

28. Linton, *Choosing Terror*, 107–111, 116–120; Andress, *Terror*, 66–70; Ellery, *Brissot*, 232–257.

29. Marisa Linton, "Fatal Friendships: The Politics of Jacobin Friendship," *FHS* 31, no. 1 (2008): 61–75; Linton, *Choosing Terror*, 141–142; Perl-Rosenthal, "Corresponding Republics," 308–312.

30. Morris Slavin, *The French Revolution in Miniature: Section Droits-de-l'homme, 1789–1795* (Princeton, 1984), 82–96.

31. Charles J. Esdaile, *The Wars of the French Revolution, 1792–1801* (Routledge, 2019), 74–78; Michel Biard and Marisa Linton, *Terror: The French Revolution and Its Demons* (Polity, 2021); M. J. Sydenham, *The Girondins* (Athlone, 1961), 115–118.

32. Aulard, *Histoire politique*, 215–272.

33. Alison Patrick, *The Men of the First French Republic: Political Alignments in the National Convention of 1792* (JHU, 1972), 139–195, for an exhaustive discussion of the elections; Aulard, *Histoire politique*, 272–273.

34. Sydenham, *Girondins*, 123–140. Though I use the term Girondin, I am skeptical of the efforts to define it as a group with a precise membership. As Albert Soboul put it, "Girondins et Montagnards n'ayant jamais constitué de partis organisés et disciplinés": "Introduction" in *Girondins et Montagnards: Actes du colloque, Sorbonne, 14 décembre 1975*, ed. Albert Soboul (Société des Études Robespierristes, 1980), 20.

35. Albert Soboul, *Les Sans-culottes parisiens en l'an II; mouvement populaire et gouvernement révolutionnaire, 2 Juin 1793–9 Thermidor An II*

(Clavreuil, 1958), 36–42; and the contrasting interpretations in Biard and Linton, *Terror*, 105–108, and Sydenham, *Girondins*, 173–179.

36. Roussillon to Comité Révolutionnaire, 31 May 1793, and Leclerc to Comité Révolutionnaire, 1 Jun 1793, both in Direction des Postes, BB/3/80, ANP. On the importance of seized letters in revolutionary justice, see Carla Hesse, "La preuve par la lettre: pratiques juridiques au tribunal révolutionnaire de Paris (1793–1794)," *Annales. Histoire, Sciences Sociales* 51 no. 3 (1996): 632–639.

37. Reynolds, *Marriage and Revolution*, 266–268; Da Sylva, *De Rousseau à Hugo*, chs. 6–8.

38. R. R. Palmer, *Twelve Who Ruled: The Year of the Terror in the French Revolution* (Princeton, 1941), 78–92 and 226–242; Andress, *Terror*, 213–222; and Soboul, *Les Sans-culottes*, 241–329, 932–951.

39. Andress, *Terror*, 95–107; René Bittard des Portes, *Contre la terreur: l'insurrection de Lyon en 1793* (Paris: Emile-Paul, 1906), esp. 209–233, 554–571; Jean-Clément Martin, *La guerre de Vendée, 1793–1800* (Seuil, 2014), xx.

40. Palmer, *Twelve Who Ruled*, 3–5; Biard and Linton, *Terror*, 85–87; Carter, *Democracy in Darkness*, 162–164.

41. Andress, *Terror*, 333–344; Colin Jones, *The Fall of Robespierre: 24 Hours in Revolutionary Paris* (Oxford, 2021).

## CHAPTER 9: THE ASSAULT ON SLAVERY

1. David Geggus, "Major Port Towns of St. Domingue," in *Atlantic Port Cities: Economy, Culture, and Society in the Atlantic World, 1650-1850*, eds. Franklin W. Knight and Peggy K. Liss (Tennessee, 1991), 88–93; Banks, *Chasing Empire*, 76–78; John Garrigus, *Before Haiti: Race and Citizenship in French Saint-Domingue* (Palgrave Macmillan, 2010), 23, 26–32; Manuel Covo, *Entrepôt of Revolutions: Saint-Domingue, Commercial Sovereignty, and the French-American Alliance* (Oxford, 2022), 50–62.

2. Stewart R. King, *Blue Coat or Powdered Wig: Free People of Color in Pre-Revolutionary Saint Domingue* (Georgia, 2001), 42–46, 118–120, 207–214; Garrigus, *Before Haiti*, 83–108, esp. 83–87; Rogers, "Les libres," 80–114, 164, 592.

3. John D. Garrigus, "Vincent Ogé 'jeune' (1757–91): Social Class and Free Colored Mobilization on the Eve of the Haitian Revolution," *Americas* 68, no. 1 (2011): 57–61; Charles Frostin, *Les révoltes blanches à Saint-Domingue aux XVIIe et XVIIIe siècles* (PUR, 2008), 229–241; Laurent Dubois, *Avengers of the New World: The Story of the Haitian Revolution* (Belknap, 2004), 87–89.

4. Dubois, *Avengers*, 100–109; Carolyn E. Fick, *The Making of Haiti: The Saint Domingue Revolution from Below* (Tennessee, 1990), 100; Sudhir

Hazareesingh, *Black Spartacus: The Epic Life of Toussaint Louverture* (FSG, 2020), ch. 1, esp. 32–33.

5. Paul Cheney, *Cul de Sac: Patrimony, Capitalism, and Slavery in French Saint-Domingue* (Chicago, 2017), ch. 3, esp. 82–86.

6. Fick, *Making*, 100–105; Dubois, *Avengers*, 119.

7. Dubois, *Avengers*, 119–125, 147–151; Thomas Madiou, *Histoire d'Haiti* (Courtois, 1847–1848), 1:104–115.

8. Madiou, *Histoire*, 1:104–105, 116–117; Dubois, *Avengers*, 142–147.

9. Madiou, *Histoire*, 1:116–122; Dubois, *Avengers*, 147–148; Fick, *Making*, 159–160; Hazareesingh, *Black Spartacus*, 56–58; David Geggus, "The 'Volte-Face' of Toussaint Louverture," in *Haitian Revolutionary Studies* (Indiana, 2002), ch. 8.

10. Madiou, *Histoire*, 1:134–143; Jeremy D. Popkin, *You Are All Free: The Haitian Revolution and the Abolition of Slavery* (Cambridge, 2010), ch. 8; and (for Guadeloupe) Laurent Dubois, *A Colony of Citizens: Revolution & Slave Emancipation in the French Caribbean, 1787–1804* (OIEAHC, 2004), esp. 155–168.

11. Pierre-Gabriel Berthault and J. F. J. Swebach, "Incendie du Cap Français," engraving, 1802, BNF; "Incendie du Cap. Révolte générale des Nègres. Massacre des Blancs," engraving, ca. 1820, JCB.

12. J. L. Boquet, "Passage des 11 jours du pillage de la ville du Cap Français," engraving, ca. 1795, JCB.

13. Ibid.

14. Marraine: Jean Dueloz (Baltimore) to Marie Bunel, 21 Apr 1806, folder 8, BHSP; tante and tantine: Louis-Ambrose Grandjean to Marie Bunel, 19 Sep 1804, folder 6, BHSP. See David Geggus, "The Slaves and Free People of Color of Cap Français," in *The Black Urban Atlantic in the Age of the Slave Trade*, eds. Jorge Cañizares-Esguerra, Matt D. Childs, and James Sidbury (Penn, 2013), 292n20; Philippe R. Girard, "Trading Races: Joseph and Marie Bunel, a Diplomat and a Merchant in Revolutionary Saint-Domingue and Philadelphia," *JER* 30, no. 3 (2010): 355.

15. *Poulson's American Daily Advertiser* (Philadelphia), 22 Mar 1802; *Norwich Courier* (Connecticut), 31 Mar 1802 (erroneously claiming Bunel owned "300 Negroes"); *Affiches Americaines*, 12 Jul 1786. House: Courville (Philadelphia) to Marie Bunel, 15 Sep 1808, folder 10, BHSP; Grandjean to Marie Bunel, 18 Sep 1804, folder 6, BHSP; Rogers, "Les libres," 107; and Geggus, "Slaves and Free People of Color," 104.

16. A. Clervaux to Marie Bunel, 6 pluviôse 6 [25 Jan 1798], folder 1; Charles Bitters receipt for "large Red fox Muff," 8 Jun 1808, folder 10; Grandjean

to Marie Bunel, 19 Sep 1804, folder 6, all in BHSP. In 1801 she paid the fairly princely sum of 25 *portuguaises* for three sashes for brigadier generals: for value, see John J. McCusker, *Money and Exchange in Europe and America, 1600–1775: A Handbook* (UNC, 1978), 280–281. On the role of traders in the Haitian Revolution, see Covo, *Entrepôt of Revolutions*, esp. 10–11.

17. Geggus, "Slaves and Free People of Color," 104; Carrie Glenn, "The Revolutionary Atlantic of Elizabeth Beauveau and Marie Rose Poumaroux: Commerce, Vulnerability, and U.S. Connections to the French Atlantic, 1780–1860" (PhD diss., University of Delaware, 2020), 18–19, 98–99; Dominique Rogers, "Les libres de couleur dans la capitale de Saint-Domingue: Fortune, mentalités, et intégrations à la fin de l'ancien régime (1776–1789)" (PhD diss., Université Michel de Montaigne, 1999), 216–220, 515–521; Receipts for Orphise Bunel's education, folder 1, BHSP.

18. [Jacques Périès], "La révolution de Saint-Domingue," f.20, MS 38074, BLL; Geggus, "Slaves and Free People of Color," 114–116; Garrigus, *Before Haiti*, ch. 7; Nash, *Forging Freedom*, 144–158.

19. "Révolution de Saint-Domingue," f.19, MS 38074, BLL; Joseph Bunel to Mussy, 30 Aug 1795, and Joseph Bunel to Tribunal de Commerce du Cap, 18 prairial 7 [6 Jun 1799], both in folder 1, BHSP; Joseph Bunel to Mr. Mussy's creditors, 25 Nov 1797, Stephen Girard Papers, APS.

20. Richard Merick to Joseph Bunel, 7 Apr 1807, folder 9, BHSP; Jarrette, Secrétaire to Christophe, to Joseph Bunel, 7 Jan 1802, folder 4, BHSP.

21. Joseph Bunel to Marie Bunel, 10 Sep 1808, folder 10, BHSP; "Révolution de Saint-Domingue," f.20, MS 38074, BLL; Morgan, *Slave Counterpoint*, 398–412; Jennifer L. Morgan, *Laboring Women: Reproduction and Gender in New World Slavery* (Penn, 2004), ch. 4; Garrigus, *Before Haiti*, chs. 2 and 6.

22. Joseph Bunel to Marie Bunel, 15 Aug 1804, folder 6, and Joseph Bunel to Marie Bunel, 25 Apr 1809, folder 11, both in BHSP.

23. Henry Christophe to Joseph Bunel, 3 Feb 1802, folder 4, BHSP; "Révolution de Saint-Domingue," f.21, f.112, MS 38074, BLL.

24. Joseph Bunel to Stephen Girard, 10 Sep 1798, Girard Papers, APS; "Révolution de Saint-Domingue," f.18, f.9, MS 38074, BLL.

25. Marie Bunel to Maurin, 27 frimaire 11 [18 Dec 1802], folder 14, BHSP; N. A. T. Hall, "Maritime Maroons: 'Grand Marronage' from the Danish West Indies," *WMQ* 42, no. 4 (October 1985): 476–498.

26. Fick, *Making*, 185–191; Popkin, *You Are All Free*, esp. 2–9 and 329–345. In general: C. L. R. James, *The Black Jacobins: Toussaint L'Ouverture and the San Domingo Revolution* (Vintage, 1963); Dubois, *Avengers*; David Patrick Geggus, *Slavery, War, and Revolution: The British Occupation of Saint Domingue,*

*1793–1798* (Clarendon, 1982); David Barry Gaspar and David Patrick Geggus, *A Turbulent Time: The French Revolution and the Greater Caribbean* (Indiana, 1997).

27. Hazareesingh, *Black Spartacus*, 31–32, 51, 86–87, 94–96, 36–37.

28. See also discussion in Perl-Rosenthal, "Atlantic Cultures," 689–694, and works cited therein, esp. Stewart King, "Toussaint L'Ouverture Before 1791: Free Planter and Slave-Holder," *Journal of Haitian Studies* 3/4 (1997), 66–71. It is interesting to compare Louverture's methods of military recruitment to those of Victor Hugues in Guadeloupe, for which see Dubois, *Colony of Citizens*, 227–248.

29. Jonathan Gibson, "Significant Space in Manuscript Letters," *Seventeenth Century* 12, no. 1 (1997): 1–9, and Giora Sternberg, "Epistolary Ceremonial: Corresponding Status at the Time of Louis XIV," *Past and Present*, no. 204 (August 2009): 66–74.

30. See Gerard M. Laurent, *Toussaint Louverture à travers sa correspondance (1794–1798)* (Madrid, 1953). This paragraph and the next: Perl-Rosenthal, "Atlantic Cultures," 690–692; Bell, *Men on Horseback*, 142–146; Deborah Jenson, "Toussaint Louverture, Spin Doctor? Launching the Haitian Revolution in the French Media," in *Tree of Liberty: Cultural Legacies of the Haitian Revolution in the Atlantic*, ed. Doris L. Garraway (Virginia, 2008), 49–60.

31. Toussaint Louverture to Dieudonné, 12 Feb 1796, in Laurent, *Toussaint Louverture*, 327–329.

32. Dubois, *Avengers*, 198–199.

33. Ibid., 205; Hazareesingh, *Black Spartacus*, 109–117, 145–150.

34. See Julia Gaffield, *Haitian Connections in the Atlantic World: Recognition After Revolution* (UNC, 2015).

35. Toussaint Louverture to John Adams, 6 Nov 1798, in "Letters of Toussaint Louverture and of Edward Stevens, 1798–1800," *AHR* 16, no. 1 (1910): 66 and 81–82. See Gordon S. Brown, *Toussaint's Clause: The Founding Fathers and the Haitian Revolution* (University of Mississippi Press, 2005), and Ronald Angelo Johnson, *Diplomacy in Black and White: John Adams, Toussaint Louverture, and Their Atlantic World Alliance* (Georgia, 2014).

36. Johnson, *Diplomacy in Black and White*, 13–36; Brown, *Toussaint's Clause*, 136–137; Girard, "Trading Races," 363–365.

37. Hazareesingh, *Black Spartacus*, ch. 9.

38. This and next paragraph: Johnhenry Gonzalez, *Maroon Nation: A History of Revolutionary Haiti* (Yale, 2019), 67–69; Hazareesingh, *Black Spartacus*, 239–251, esp. 243, and 262. A somewhat similar story unfolded on Guadeloupe: Dubois, *Colony of Citizens*, 308–314.

39. Dubois, *Colony of Citizens*, 278.

## CHAPTER 10: RUINS AND RECONSTRUCTION

1. Document of 25 Jan 1794 in Sobre las causas seguidas . . . sobre la propiedad de la mina de Ocontaya, Legajo 16, Audiencia, Causas Civiles, ARC; Cecilia de San Sebastian to Bishop, 3 Jan 1795, Trancito to Bishop, ca. 23 May 1796, Rivadeneyra to Bishop, ca. 7 Nov 1796, all in Autos seguidos por la priora de Santa Catalina Cecilia de SS contra la Madre Maria de la Concepción Rivadeneyra, 1795, Colonial XIV, 3, 47, AAC.

2. Rivadeneyra to Bishop, ca. 7 Nov 1796, Annotations of 23 May 1796 and 7 Nov 1796; *decisión* of 18 May 1797, all in Autos seguidos por la priora, AAC.

3. Prioress of Santa Teresa to [Bishop?], 3 Jan 1795, in ibid.

4. Maria Dominga de Rivadeneyra to Queen, 14 Nov 1797, and Maria de la Concepción Rivadeneyra and Martina de San Miguel de Rivadeneyra to Queen, Cuzco, 10 Mar 1797, both in Gobierno, Cuzco 30, AGI.

5. David A. Bell, *Napoleon: A Concise Biography* (Oxford, 2015), 15–24.

6. Alan I. Forrest, *Conscripts and Deserters: The Army and French Society During the Revolution and Empire* (Oxford, 1989), 35–40; Jean-Clément Martin, *La Vendée et la France* (Seuil, 1987); the controversial Reynald Secher, *Le génocide franco-français: La Vendée-Vengé* (PUF, 1986), esp. 137–185; David A. Bell, *The First Total War: Napoleon's Europe and the Birth of Warfare as We Know It* (Houghton Mifflin, 2007), 270–291.

7. George A. King, "The French Spoliation Claims," *American Journal of International Law* 6, no. 2 (1912): 359–360; Anthony McFarlane, *Colombia Before Independence: Economy, Society, and Politics Under Bourbon Rule* (Cambridge, 1993), 298–299.

8. Anthony McFarlane, *War and Independence in Spanish America* (Routledge, 2014), 85–217; J. C. A. Stagg, *The War of 1812: Conflict for a Continent* (Cambridge, 2012), 128–130.

9. See Elizabeth Blackmar, *Manhattan for Rent, 1785–1850* (Cornell, 1991), ch. 4.

10. *Esto es peor, Tanto y mas, Que hai que hacer mas?*, all in Francisco Goya, *The Disasters of War*, 1810–1820. See also *Grande hazana! Con muertos* for decapitated figures.

11. For discussions see Charles J. Esdaile, *The Peninsular War: A New History* (Allen Lane, 2002); Charles J. Esdaile, *Women in the Peninsular War* (Oklahoma, 2014).

12. Examples include Stuart B. Schwartz, *Sea of Storms: A History of Hurricanes in the Greater Caribbean from Columbus to Katrina* (Princeton,

2015); Charles F. Walker, *Shaky Colonialism: The 1746 Earthquake-Tsunami in Lima, Peru, and Its Long Aftermath* (Duke, 2008); Mark Molesky, *This Gulf of Fire: The Destruction of Lisbon, or Apocalypse in the Age of Science and Reason* (Knopf, 2015); Benjamin L. Carp, *The Great New York Fire of 1776: A Lost Story of the American Revolution* (Yale, 2023).

13. See, e.g., Charles F. Walker, "The Upper Classes and Their Upper Stories: Architecture and the Aftermath of the Lima Earthquake of 1746," *Hispanic American Historical Review* 83, no. 1 (2003): 53–82.

14. Thomas Paine, "Appendix to Common Sense" (1776), in *Complete Writings of Thomas Paine*, 1:45.

15. See Sarah-Jayne Blakemore, *Inventing Ourselves: The Secret Life of the Teenage Brain* (PublicAffairs, 2018), and Frances E. Jensen with Amy Ellis Nutt, *The Teenage Brain* (HarperCollins, 2015).

16. Michael W. Flinn, *The European Demographic System, 1500–1820* (JHU, 1981), 27–30; Hardwick, *Sex in an Old Regime City*, 36–37.

17. C. H. Vincent, "Plan de l'état actuel de la ville du Cap servant à indiquer les progrès de ses reconstructions," manuscript map, ca. 1800, BNF.

18. Popkin, *You Are All Free*, 391.

19. C. F. Volney, *Les ruines, ou Méditation sur les révolutions des empires* (Paris: Desenne, 1791), 3.

20. Caspar David Friedrich, *After the Storm*, 1817, oil on canvas, Statens Museum for Kunst, Copenhagen. See also the famous scene at the end of *Atala*: F.-R. de Chateaubriand, *Atala-René* (Pocket, 2009), 91–94.

21. Caspar David Friedrich, *Grabmale alter Helden*, 1812, oil on canvas, Hamburger Kunsthalle, Hamburg.

22. *Decreto* of Viceroy Francisco Gil, Lima, 22 Dec 1792, in El consejo pleno a 26 de Mayo de 1788, Gobierno, Cuzco 69, AGI; Recurso de las madres de Santa Catalina de Sena en esta ciudad, Legajo 152 #42, Audiencia, Asuntos Administrativos, ARC; Trancito to Bishop, ca. 23 May 1796, in Autos seguidos por la priora, Colonial XIV, 3, 47, AAC.

23. Burns, *Colonial Habits*, 134.

24. Doña Josefa Sotomayor to *provisor*, 28 Apr 1791, Colonial, Pareceres, LXXIV, 1, 6, AAC.

25. Doña Manuela Gonsales to *provisor*, n.d. [1791], ibid.

## CHAPTER 11: THE LIMITS OF REPUBLICANISM

1. Stanley Elkins and Eric McKitrick, *The Age of Federalism* (Oxford, 1993), 33.

2. Ron Chernow, *Alexander Hamilton* (Penguin Press, 2004), 22–26, 41–51, 89–101, 129–132.

3. Elkins and McKitrick, *Age of Federalism*, 123, 260–261; Chernow, *Hamilton*, 374–378.

4. Sean Wilentz, *The Rise of American Democracy: Jefferson to Lincoln* (Norton, 2005), 42–49.

5. See Jessica C. Roney, *Governed by a Spirit of Opposition: The Origins of American Political Practice in Colonial Philadelphia* (JHU, 2014), ch. 4; Steven C. Bullock, *Revolutionary Brotherhood: Freemasonry and the Transformation of the American Social Order, 1730–1840* (UNC, 1996), ch. 2.

6. "A Calm Observer" to "Federal Members," 9 Feb 1795, in *The Democratic-Republican Societies, 1790–1800: A Documentary Sourcebook of Constitutions, Declarations, Addresses, Resolutions, and Toasts*, ed. Philip S. Foner (Greenwood Press, 1976), 210.

7. Foner, *Democratic-Republican Societies*, 64–65, 151–153, 282–283.

8. Albrecht Koschnik, "The Democratic Societies of Philadelphia and the Limits of the American Public Sphere, circa 1793–1795," *WMQ* 58, no. 3 (2001): 620. This accords with the account in Alfred F. Young, *The Democratic Republicans of New York: The Origins, 1763–1797* (OIEAHC, 1967), 394–395. See Eugene P. Link, *Democratic-Republican Societies, 1790–1800* (Columbia, 1942), 93, 72. Address to "Fellow Freemen," 26 Jan 1795, in Foner, *Democratic-Republican Societies*, 194–195.

9. Link, *Democratic-Republican Societies*, 98–99; Kenneth Owen, *Political Community in Revolutionary Pennsylvania, 1774–1800* (Oxford, 2018), 133–134.

10. Foner, *Democratic-Republican Societies*, 141, 119–121, 152–153; *Annals of Congress*, House of Representatives, 3rd Cong., 2nd Sess., 900.

11. Address to the Republican Citizens of the US, 28 May 1794, in Foner, *Democratic-Republican Societies*, 174, and similar language on 66 and 282; Link, *Democratic-Republican Societies*, 97.

12. Democratic Society of Pennsylvania, "Address," Mar 1794, and Constitution of the Political Society of Mount Prospect, 26 Mar 1794, in Foner, *Democratic-Republican Societies*, 73, 141–142; Link, *Democratic-Republican Societies*, 112–114, 117–118, 120–121; Sean Wilentz, *Chants Democratic: New York City & the Rise of the American Working Class, 1788–1850* (Oxford, 1984), 74–75.

13. Foner, *Democratic-Republican Societies*, 66–67.

14. David Waldstreicher, *In the Midst of Perpetual Fetes: The Making of American Nationalism, 1776–1820* (UNC, 1997), 134–139; Link, *Democratic-Republican Societies*, 150–151.

15. Elkins and McKitrick, *Age of Federalism*, 462–463.

16. Thomas P. Slaughter, *The Whiskey Rebellion: Frontier Epilogue to the American Revolution* (Oxford, 1986), 149–157.

17. Link, *Democratic-Republican Societies*, 145–147.

18. Democratic Society of Pennsylvania, Minutes, 31 Jul and 4 Sep 1794; Republican Society of Newark, Resolutions, 22 Sep 1794; Democratic Society of New York, Resolutions, 20 Aug 1794, in Foner, *Democratic-Republican Societies*, 88, 90–91, 147–148, 183–184.

19. Elkins and McKitrick, *Age of Federalism*, 480–483; Slaughter, *Whiskey Rebellion*, 215–221.

20. George Washington, *The Papers of George Washington: Presidential Series*, eds. W. W. Abbot and Dorothy Twohig (Virginia, 1983–), 17:181.

21. "Self-Created Societies," *Columbian Centinel* (Boston), 13 Dec 1794; *Gazette of the United States* (Philadelphia), 23 Mar 1795; *Annals of Congress*, House of Representatives, 3rd Cong., 2nd Sess., 906.

22. See *Annals of Congress*, House of Representatives, 3rd Cong., 2nd Sess., 899–947.

23. Alexis de Tocqueville, *Democracy in America*, vol. 1 (Vintage, 1990), ch. 12; *Annals of Congress*, House of Representatives, 3rd Cong., 2nd Sess., 899–900.

24. *Annals of Congress*, House of Representatives, 3rd Cong., 2nd Sess., 912, 920, 901; "An Observer," *Gazette of the United States*, 5 Aug 1800, and Address to "Fellow Freemen," 26 Jan 1795, in Foner, *Democratic-Republican Societies*, 113, 194.

25. *South-Carolina State-Gazette* (Charleston), 19 Dec 1794; Address to "Fellow Freemen," 26 Jan 1795, in Foner, *Democratic-Republican Societies*, 194.

26. See, e.g., French Commissioners to Commissioner of Foreign Relations, 16 fructidor 2 [2 Sep 1794] and 15 vendémiaire 3 [6 Oct 1794], in *Correspondence of the French Ministers to the United States*, ed. Frederick Jackson Turner (Annual Report of the American Historical Association, 1903), 402–406 and 432–436.

27. Aulard, *Histoire politique*, 504–507, 523–524, 529–530.

28. Edelstein, *French Revolution and the Birth*, 305–306; Malcolm Crook, *Elections in the French Revolution: An Apprenticeship in Democracy, 1789–1799* (Cambridge, 1996), 118–119.

29. See Isser Woloch, *Jacobin Legacy: The Democratic Movement Under the Directory* (Princeton, 1970), 287–310; Pierre Serna, *La République des girouettes: 1789–1815 . . . et au-delà: une anomalie politique, la France de l'extrême centre* (Champ Vallon, 2005).

30. Albert Sorel, *L'Europe et la révolution française* (Plon, Nourrit et Cie, 1885), esp. 5:1–30.

31. See Pierre Serna, ed., *Républiques soeurs: Le Directoire et la révolution atlantique* (PUR, 2009); Jacques Godechot, *La grande nation: L'expansion révolutionnaire de la France dans le monde de 1789 à 1799* (Aubier, 1956), 211–229;

Matthieu Ferradou, "'Aux États-Unis de France et d'Irlande': Circulations révolutionnaires entre France et Irlande à l'époque de la République atlantique" (PhD diss., Paris 1, 2019).

32. Giovanni Assereto, *La Repubblica ligure: Lotte politiche e problemi finanziari (1797–1799)* (Einaudi, 1975), 73, 83–89; Franco Venturi, *Settecento riformatore* (Einaudi, 1969), 271, 215–227, 237, 231, 255–256.

33. Venturi, *Settecento riformatore*, chs. 6–7; Vito Vitale, "Onofrio Scassi e la vita genovese del suo tempo (1768–1836)," *Atti della Società ligure di storia patria* 59 (1932): 16–17.

34. Vitale, "Onofrio Scassi," 34–37; G. Bigoni, "La caduta della Repubblica di Genova nel 1797," *Giornale ligustico di archeologia, storia e belle arti* 2, n.s. (1897): 263–284.

35. Vitale, "Onofrio Scassi," 35–40; Leo Morabito, *Il giornalismo giacobino genovese, 1797–1799* (Associazione Piemontese dei Bibliotecari, 1973), 63–84, esp. 64–68; *Gazzetta nazionale genovese*, no. 1, 17 Jun 1797.

36. *Gazzetta nazionale genovese*, no. 3, 1 Jul 1797, and no. 4, 8 Jul 1797.

37. Antonino Ronco, *Storia della Repubblica Ligure, 1797–1799* (SAGEP, 1988), 177, 185–186.

38. Ibid., 193–198, 208–209, 215–219.

39. Ibid., 221–226, 236–237; Assereto, *La Repubblica ligure*, 93–95.

40. Giulio Giacchero, *Economia e società del Settecento genovese* (SAGEP, 1973), 201–218, 180, 297, 309–315.

41. Ibid., 335–351.

42. Ibid., 383, 403–404; 31: Corrispondenza del cittadino Olivieri, no. 513 (1801), ASG; Mazzo 4, 177: Direttorio Esecutivo, 1 (1798), ASG.

43. *Gazzetta nazionale genovese*, no. 5, 15 Jul 1797.

44. See Simon P. Newman, *Parades and the Politics of the Street: Festive Culture in the Early American Republic* (Penn, 1997); Wilentz, *Chants Democratic*, 87–94; Frans Grijzenhout, *Feesten voor het Vaderland: patriotse en Bataafse feesten 1780–1806* (Waanders, 1989).

45. For the French model, see Mona Ozouf, *La fête révolutionnaire, 1789–1799* (Gallimard, 1976), esp. 150–158. Giacchero, *Economia e società*, 390; *Gazzetta nazionale genovese*, no. 5, 15 Jul 1797, 37–39.

46. Police Committee to Directory, 22 Feb 1798, Mazzo 4, 177: Direttorio Esecutivo, 1 (1798), ASG; for a similar story in Piedmont, see Giorgio Vaccarino, *I giacobini piemontesi (1794–1814)*, 2 vols. (Ministero per i beni culturali e ambientali, 1989), 85–113.

47. 19 and 30 Jan and 11 Feb 1798, Mazzo 4, 177: Direttorio Esecutivo, 1 (1798); Minister of Police to Directory, 3 Mar 1798, Mazzo 3, 178: Direttorio Esecutivo, 2 (1798), all ASG.

48. Giacchero, *Economia e società*, 184–186; Lefebvre, *Coming of the French Revolution*, 198.

49. 15 Feb and 6 Feb 1798, Mazzo 4, 177: Direttorio Esecutivo, 1 (1798); Dossier, Dec 1798, 32: Ruzza ministro Esteri e Giustizia, all ASG.

50. Calogero Farinella, "Il 'genio della libertà': Società e politica a Genova dalla Repubblica Ligure alla fine dell'impero napoleonico," *Atti della Società ligure di storia patria* n.s. 44 (2004): 140–144, 162–164.

51. 13 Feb and 18 Mar 1798, Mazzo 4, 177: Direttorio Esecutivo, 2 (1798); 21 Jun 1798, 180: Direttorio Esecutivo, 4 (1798); 11 Mar and 2 Jun 1798, Mazzo 3, 178: Direttorio Esecutivo, 2 (1798), all ASG.

52. Police Committee to Directory, 22 Feb 1798, Mazzo 4, 177: Direttorio Esecutivo, 1 (1798), ASG.

53. Aulard, *Histoire politique*, 690–700; Antonino Ronco, *Genova tra Massena e Bonaparte: Storia della Repubblica Ligure—il 1800* (SAGEP, 1988), 29, 191–230.

54. Assereto, *La Repubblica ligure*, 159–198.

55. Palmer, *Age*, 2:346–353.

56. Vaccarino, *I giacobini piemontesi*, 1:37–52; H. T. Colenbrander, *De Bataafsche republiek* (Meulenhoff, 1908), 254–262; Palmer, *Age*, 2:318.

## CHAPTER 12: THE NEW SOCIAL ORDER EMERGES

1. I rely primarily on Douglas R. Egerton, *Gabriel's Rebellion: The Virginia Slave Conspiracies of 1800 and 1802* (UNC, 1993), 21–29, but see also Michael L. Nicholls, *Whispers of Rebellion: Narrating Gabriel's Conspiracy* (Virginia, 2012), ch. 2.

2. Egerton, *Gabriel's Rebellion*, 34–49, 51, 57, 76–79; Julius S. Scott, "The Common Wind: Currents of Afro-American Communication in the Age of the Haitian Revolution" (PhD diss., Duke University, 1986), 292–293.

3. Dell Upton, *Another City: Urban Life and Urban Spaces in the New American Republic* (Yale, 2008), 118; Nicholas Papayanis, *Planning Paris Before Haussmann* (JHU, 2004), ch. 1, esp. 17–19.

4. Adam Costanzo, *George Washington's Washington: Visions for the National Capital in the Early American Republic* (Georgia, 2018), 19–26; W. B. Bryan, *A History of the National Capital from Its Foundation Through the Period of the Adoption of the Organic Act* (Macmillan, 1914), 1:147–153.

5. Bryan, *History*, ch. 2; Constance McLaughlin Green, *Washington* (Princeton, 1962), 1:19–22, 52–53.

6. James Sterling Young, *The Washington Community, 1800–1828* (Columbia, 1966), 41–44, 66–69; Green, *Washington*, 1:21.

7. Young, *Washington Community*, 47–48, 71, 74; Margaret Bayard Smith, *The First Forty Years of Washington Society*, ed. Gaillard Hunt (Scribner's, 1906), 27; Barbara Boyle Torrey and Clara Myrick Green, "Free Black People of Washington County, D.C.: George Pointer and His Descendants," *Washington History* 28, no. 1 (2016): 23; Letitia W. Brown, "Residence Patterns of Negroes in the District of Columbia, 1800–1860," *Records of the Columbia Historical Society* 69/70 (1969): 74–75, 69 (map).

8. Richard Hofstadter, *The Idea of a Party System: The Rise of Legitimate Opposition in the United States* (California, 1969), 9–16.

9. Noble E. Cunningham, *The Jeffersonian Republicans: The Formation of Party Organization, 1789–1801* (OIEAHC, 1957), 33–36, 41–45; George Daniel Luetscher, "Early Political Machinery in the United States" (PhD diss., University of Pennsylvania, 1903), 72–94.

10. Cunningham, *Jeffersonian Republicans*, 104–105, 110–113; Jeffrey L. Pasley, "'A Journeyman, Either in Law or Politics': John Beckley and the Social Origins of Political Campaigning," *JER* 16, no. 4 (1996): 553–554.

11. Andrew W. Robertson, "Voting Rights and Voting Acts: Electioneering Ritual, 1790–1820," in *Beyond the Founders: New Approaches to the Political History of the Early American Republic*, eds. Jeffrey L. Pasley, Andrew W. Robertson, and David Waldstreicher (UNC, 2004), 73–74; Wilentz, *Chants Democratic*, 71–73; Cunningham, *Jeffersonian Republicans*, 180–181.

12. Alexander DeConde, *The Quasi-War: The Politics and Diplomacy of the Undeclared War with France, 1797–1801* (Scribner's, 1966); Wilentz, *Rise*, 90–98.

13. See Mapheus Smith and Marian L. Brockway, "Some Political Characteristics of American Congressmen, 1800–1919," *Southwestern Social Science Quarterly* 22, no. 3 (1941): 212; James Traub, *John Quincy Adams: Militant Spirit* (Basic, 2016), 120, 157.

14. Jonathan Roberts, "Notes and Documents: Memoirs of a Senator from Pennsylvania: Jonathan Roberts, 1771–1854," *Pennsylvania Magazine of History and Biography* 62, no. 1 (1938): 83–84; John Quincy Adams, Diary 11, 26 Sep 1786, *The Diaries of John Quincy Adams: A Digital Collection*, Massachusetts Historical Society, accessed January 2021, www.masshist.org/jqadiaries/php/.

15. Cynthia D. Earman, "A Census of Early Boardinghouses," *Washington History* 12, no. 1 (2000), and Wendy Gamber, *The Boardinghouse in Nineteenth-Century America* (JHU, 2007), 3, 11–24. Young, *Washington Community*, 76–77; John Ball Osborne, "The Removal of the Government to Washington," *Records of the Columbia Historical Society* 3 (1900): 159; Smith, *First Forty Years*, 12, 52–53.

16. A. I. Mudd, "Early Theatres in Washington City," *Records of the Columbia Historical Society* 5 (1902): 71; Young, *Washington Community*, 47; Brown, "Residence Patterns," 77; John Quincy Adams, *Memoirs of John Quincy Adams, Comprising Portions of His Diary from 1795 to 1848*, ed. C. F. Adams (Lippincott, 1874), 1:272; Green, *Washington*, 1:37–38, 45.

17. Young, *Washington Community*, 45; Smith, *First Forty Years*, 59, 30 and 46; David S. Shields and Fredrika J. Teute, "The Republican Court and the Historiography of a Women's Domain in the Public Sphere," *JER* 35, no. 2 (2015): 169–183.

18. Wilentz, *Chants Democratic*, ch. 1, esp. 48–52; Stuart M. Blumin, *The Emergence of the Middle Class: Social Experience in the American City, 1760–1900* (Cambridge, 1989), ch. 3, esp. 70–73; Betsy Blackmar, "Re-walking the 'Walking City': Housing and Property Relations in New York City, 1780–1840," *Radical History Review* 1979, no. 21 (1979), 131–148; Tyler Anbinder, *Five Points: The 19th-Century New York City Neighborhood That Invented Tap Dance, Stole Elections, and Became the World's Most Notorious Slum* (Free Press, 2001), 16–27.

19. Durand Flórez, *Criollos en conflicto*, 177.

20. John Leddy Phelan, *The People and the King: The Comunero Revolution in Colombia, 1781* (Wisconsin, 1978), 39–46, 131–155, 212–220; McFarlane, *Colombia*, 264–271.

21. Thomson, "Sovereignty Disavowed," 418–424.

22. Walker, *Smoldering Ashes*, 126; J. M. Valega, *República del Perú* (D. Miranda, 1829–1833), 2:14–15; José de San Martín to José Ignacio Zenteno, Jan 25 and Feb 26, 1821, in *Asuntos Militarios, CDIP*, ed. Félix Denegri Luna, 2:226, 255; Alberto Flores Galindo, *Buscando un Inca: Identidad y utopia en los Andes* (Editorial Horizonte, 1994), 148–53, 174; Carlos Ponce Sanginés, *El conato revolucionario de 1805* (Casa Municipal de la Cultura Franz Tamayo, 1976), 47–48.

23. McFarlane, *Colombia*, 298–299; John R. Fisher, *Commercial Relations Between Spain and Spanish America in the Era of Free Trade, 1778–1796* (Liverpool, 1985), 47–51; Susan M. Socolow, *The Merchants of Buenos Aires, 1778–1810: Family and Commerce* (Cambridge, 1978), 162–164; Jeremy Adelman, *Republic of Capital: Buenos Aires and the Legal Transformation of the Atlantic World* (Stanford, 1999), 40–43; Mariano M. Schlez, "El comercio de un monopolista. Volumen, contenido y sentido de la circulación, según un estudio de caso (Río de la Plata, 1770–1820)," *Anuario de Estudios Americanos* 73, no. 1 (2016): 168–173.

24. Tulio Halperín Donghi, *Revolución y guerra: Formación de una élite dirigente en la Argentina criolla* (Siglo Veintiuno, 1972), 64; Belgrano, "Autobiografía," in Bartolomé Mitre, *Historia de Belgrano y de la independencia*

*argentina* (Buenos Aires: Félix Lajouane, 1887), 1:429–432; Cristina Soriano, *Tides of Revolution: Information, Insurgencies, and the Crisis of Colonial Rule in Venezuela* (New Mexico, 2018).

25. Luis Durand Flórez, *El proceso de independencia en el sur andino: Cuzco y La Paz, 1805* (Universidad de Lima, 1993), bk. 2, esp. 344–345 and 380–381; Flores Galindo, *Buscando*, ch. 6; and (for New Granada) Aline Helg, "The Limits of Equality: Free People of Colour and Slaves During the First Independence of Cartagena, Colombia, 1810–15," *Slavery & Abolition* 20, no. 2 (1999): 21.

26. Interrogation of Manuel Ubalde in Ponce Sanginés, *El conato*, 66–69, 72; see also Flores Galindo, *Buscando*, 136–137.

27. Ponce Sanginés, *El conato*, 51–52, and Flores Galindo, *Buscando*, 145–147. On mining: John R. Fisher, *Silver Mines and Silver Miners in Colonial Peru, 1776–1824* (Liverpool, 1977); Kris E. Lane, *Potosí: The Silver City That Changed the World* (California, 2019), 69–74.

28. Ponce Sanginés, *El conato*, 41–42, 44.

29. Ibid., 47, 78–79, 62–65.

30. Ibid., 47, 77–79.

31. Ibid., 79. He set his visions firmly in the spaces of power in his urban milieu, especially cathedrals and churches: see Ibid., 78, 65.

32. Guillermo Ugarte Chamorro, ed., *El teatro en la independencia*, *CDIP*, 1:53, and Salomón Lerner Febres and Ricardo Silva-Santisteban, eds., *Antología general del teatro peruano* (Universidad Católica, 2000), 3:xxii. For more on the form in general: George Tyler Northup, *Ten Spanish Farces of the 16th, 17th and 18th Centuries* (Heath & Co., 1922), vi–xxiv; and Eugenio Asensio, *Itinerario del Entremés: desde Lope de Rueda a Quiñones de Benavente* (Editorial Gredos, 1971), ch. 1. For Peru: Andrés Eichmann Oehrli, "Teatro breve y brevísimo en el sur andino," *Bulletin of the Comediantes* 65, no. 2 (2013): 57–67, and Irving A. Leonard, "El teatro en Lima, 1790–1793," *Hispanic Review* 8, no. 2 (1940): 93–112; Ugarte Chamorro, *El teatro en la independencia*, 1:244–246, 249.

33. Ponce Sanginés, *El conato*, 62–63, 33–34.

34. Ibid., 254–255; Flores Galindo, *Buscando*, 145–146, 168–169.

## CHAPTER 13: THE HAITIAN STATE

1. Madiou, *Histoire d'Haiti*, vols. 3 and 4, and Leslie Péan, *Aux origines de l'Etat marron en Haïti: 1804–1860* (Editions de l'Université d'Etat d'Haiti, 2009).

2. This and next paragraph: Hazareesingh, *Black Spartacus*, 224–227, 298–302. On the Leclerc expedition: Claude Bonaparte Auguste and Marcel Bonaparte Auguste, *L'expédition Leclerc, 1801–1803* (H. Deschamps, 1985);

Henri Mézière, *Le général Leclerc (1772–1802) et l'expédition de Saint-Domingue* (Tallandier, 1990), part 2; Philippe R. Girard, *The Slaves Who Defeated Napoleon: Toussaint Louverture and the Haitian War of Independence, 1801–1804* (Alabama, 2011).

3. Dubois, *Avengers*, 251; Vergniaud Leconte, *Henri Christophe dans l'histoire d'Haiti* (Editions Berger-Levrault, 1931), 61–62; Henry Christophe to Joseph Bunel, 3 Feb 1802 (copy minuted "certifie conforme a loriginne J Bunel"), folder 4, BHSP; Madiou, *Histoire d'Haiti*, 2:188–199.

4. Hazareesingh, *Black Spartacus*, 314–318; Dubois, *Avengers*, 255–257.

5. Auguste and Auguste, *L'expédition Leclerc*, ch. 8, esp. 170–171. The chronology is ambiguous: Gellibert to Leclerc, 24 Mar 1802, GR B7 13, SHD, indicates both were arrested, but Marie Bunel to [Daure], 21 brumaire 11 [12 Nov 1802], SHD, says she has been in jail for only twelve days. Girard, "Trading Races," 369, follows the chronology implied by Daure's letter. Femme Bunel to Rochambeau, 2 frimaire 11 [23 Nov 1802], Box 14, f. 1363, Rochambeau Papers, University of Florida (conditions); Marie Bunel to Morin, 2 messidor 10 [21 Jun 1802], folder 4, BHSP (loan). Rochambeau an "expert in atrocity": Dubois, *Avengers*, 293; Madiou, *Histoire d'Haiti*, 3:15.

6. Femme Bunel to Rochambeau, 2 frimaire 11 [23 Nov 1802]. Emphasis mine.

7. Cairon, *déclaration*, 20 Oct 1812, and Coniquot to Marie Bunel, 30 frimaire 11 [21 Dec 1802], both folder 4, BHSP.

8. Cairon, *déclaration*, 20 Oct 1812, folder 4, and Duroc to Marie Bunel (?), 18 Apr 1812, folder 13, BHSP.

9. Cairon, *déclaration*, 20 Oct 1812, folder 4, BHSP; *Philadelphia Gazette*, 17 May 1800; *Daily Advertiser* (New York), 6 Apr 1802; *Aurora* (Philadelphia), 28 Oct 1803; "Tremel v Bunel, List of witnesses," folder 4, and "Madame Marie Jeanne La Bordelaise will declare," folder 14, both BHSP. See the similar story in Rebecca J. Scott, "Paper Thin: Freedom and Re-enslavement in the Diaspora of the Haitian Revolution," *Law and History Review* 29, no. 4 (2011): 1065–1071.

10. See "Kingston Jamaica 1802" and "Tremel v Bunel, List of witnesses," both folder 4, BHSP; Mme Bunel to Boyer, 24 Mar 1803, folder 5, BHSP; Furstenberg, *When the United States Spoke French*, 78–80 and ch. 2.

11. Madiou, *Histoire d'Haiti*, 3:40, 43. For this and next paragraph, see also Auguste and Auguste, *L'expédition Leclerc*, ch. 9, and Girard, *Slaves*, chs. 11–15.

12. Madiou, *Histoire d'Haiti*, 3:76–78, 84–99.

13. Deborah Jenson, "Dessalines's American Proclamations of the Haitian Independence," *Journal of Haitian Studies* 15, no. 1/2 (2009): 82–85; David Geggus, "La declaración de independencia de Haití," in *Las declaraciones de*

*Independencia*, eds. Alfredo Ávila, Jordana Dym, and Erika Pani (Colegio de México, 2013), 129–130; "Appendix: The Haitian Declaration of Independence," in *The Haitian Declaration of Independence: Creation, Context, and Legacy*, ed. Julia Gaffield (Virginia, 2016), 246; and Madiou, *Histoire d'Haiti*, 3:169–175.

14. Gellibert's mission: Gellibert to Leclerc, 24 Mar 1802; seizure of the funds: Liot to Leclerc, 28 ventôse 10 [19 Mar 1802], and Pichon to Liot, 16 messidor 10 [5 Jul 1802]; deposit of the funds: Liot to Daure, 9 fructidor 10 [27 Aug 1802], and *acte* of Chancellery in Philadelphia, 24 messidor 10 [13 Jul 1802], all in GR B7 13, SHD. See also Gellibert to Joseph Bunel, 18 Jan 1802, folder 4, BHSP; Rogers, "Les libres," 445.

15. Joseph Bunel to Marie Bunel, 15 Aug 1804, folder 6; Inventaire des objets appartenants a Mme Bunel, sur son habitation, folder 14; Receipts, Sep 1808–Jan 1809, and Account of souliers to Mme Bunel, 11 Jul 1809, folder 11; Receipts, folder 8; Courville to Marie Bunel, 15 Sep 1808, folder 10, all in BHSP.

16. John Northrop to Marie Bunel, 10 Nov 1807, folder 6, and "Recd August 30th 1808 of Maddam Boenall . . . by Jon.n Scholfield," folder 10, both BHSP.

17. Johnson, *Diplomacy in Black and White*, 79; Grandjean to Marie Bunel, 18 Sep 1804, and Joseph Bunel to Marie Bunel, 7 Sep 1804, both folder 6, BHSP; Gonzalez, *Maroon Nation*, 66–70, 85–88; Hazareesingh, *Black Spartacus*, 276–280; Pompée Valentin Vastey, *Essai sur les causes de la révolution et des guerres civiles d'Hayti* (Sans-Souci: Imprimerie royale, 1819), 178.

18. Veuve Bellony to Marie Bunel, 8 Apr 1804; [unknown] (Cap) to Marie Bunel, 12 Apr 1804; Joseph Bunel to Marie Bunel, 7 Sep 1804, all folder 6, BHSP. See also Mme Dessalines to Marie Bunel, 12 Nov[?] 1804, Henry P. Slaughter Collection, box 37, folder 64, Robert W. Woodruff Library, Atlanta University Center, Atlanta. Thanks to Julia Gaffield for sharing this source.

19. See Rebecca J. Scott, *Degrees of Freedom: Louisiana and Cuba After Slavery* (Harvard, 2005), and Rebecca J. Scott and Michael Zeuske, "Property in Writing, Property on the Ground: Pigs, Horses, Land, and Citizenship in the Aftermath of Slavery, Cuba, 1880–1909," *Comparative Studies in Society and History* 44, no. 4 (2002): 672.

20. House #893, DPPC G1 496, ANOM, Aix-en-Provence and De Grieu, "Plan de la ville de Cap," 1 vend 11, Fonds Rochambeau, 135 AP 4, ANP. Thanks to Carrie Glenn for sharing this source. See also Grandjean to Joseph Bunel, Oct 1804, folder 6, BHSP.

21. Exaggerated estimates appeared in *Poulson's American Daily Advertiser*, 22 Mar 1802, and *Norwich Courier*, 31 Mar 1802.

22. Gonzalez, *Maroon Nation*, 93–96; Cheney, *Cul de Sac*, 185–187. Grandjean to Marie Bunel, 18 Sep 1804, folder 6, BHSP. On the economic status of free people of color, see Garrigus, *Before Haiti*, esp. 175–177.

23. Folder 14, BHSP.

24. [Jacques Périès,] "La révolution de Saint-Domingue," f.20, MS 38074, BLL; Raymond Gaudriault and Thérèse Gaudriault, *Filigranes et autres caractéristiques des papiers fabriqués en France aux XVIIe et XVIIIe siècles* (CNRS Editions, 1995), 255; some slips have the "C RADWAY 18xx" watermark, probably from the Radway mill in Gloucestershire: Thomas L. Gravell and George Miller, *A Catalogue of Foreign Watermarks Found on Paper Used in America, 1700–1835* (Garland, 1983), 167 (image 590) and 236.

25. Garrigus, *Before Haiti*, 4–8; Furstenberg, *When the United States Spoke French*, ch. 2; James Alexander Dun, *Dangerous Neighbors: Making the Haitian Revolution in Early America* (Penn, 2016), 137–142.

26. Merchant gifts: see Joseph Bunel to Marie Bunel, 1 Apr 1808, folder 10, BHSP. Grandjean to Marie Bunel, 18 Sep 1804, folder 6; Mme Grandjean to Marie Bunel, 16 Jun 1810, folder 12; and Bond to Marie Bunel, 28 Sep 1807, folder 9, all BHSP.

27. Leconte, *Henri Christophe*, 4; Marie-Louise Christophe to Marie Bunel, 3 Sep 1810, folder 12, BHSP; Marie-Louise Christophe to Marie Bunel, 18 Feb 1809, Henry P. Slaughter Collection, Box 37, folder 62, Robert W. Woodruff Library, Atlanta University Center, Atlanta. My thanks to Julia Gaffield for sharing this source. See also Rogers, "Les libres," 458–461.

28. Henry Christophe to Joseph Bunel, 6 Nov 1804, folder 6, BHSP; (earlier) Louis-André Pichon to James Madison, 17 floréal 12 [7 May 1804], in *The Papers of James Madison: Secretary of State Series*, eds. Robert J. Brugger et al. (Virginia, 1986–), 7:186.

29. Leconte, *Henri Christophe*, 202–204, 212–213; Paul Clammer, *Black Crown: Henry Christophe, the Haitian Revolution, and the Caribbean's Forgotten Kingdom* (Hurst, 2023), 152–157, 205. Arrival: Will of Joseph Bunel, 28 Jan 1807, and Simon to Marie Bunel, 11 Aug 1807, both folder 9, BHSP.

30. Simon to Marie Bunel, 11 Aug 1807, folder 9, BHSP.

31. Henry Christophe to General Raphael, 13 Apr 1805, and Christophe to Commandant fidèle, 16 Apr 1805, both in "Henri Christophe, Copie des Lettres 1805 [& 1806]," FOL. F1924 HEN, Foreign, Commonwealth & Development Office Historical Collection, Foyle Special Collections, King's College, London; Leconte, *Henri Christophe*, 212–213, 321–322; and Gonzalez, *Maroon Nation*, 107–108.

32. Joseph Bunel to Marie Bunel, 3 Nov 1808, and 10 Sep 1808, both folder 10, BHSP.

33. *Federal Gazette and Baltimore Advertiser*, 7 Dec 1809; Robert Cooke to Marie Bunel, 31 Jul 1810, folder 12, BHSP, possibly about the same ship.

34. "taste": Grandjean to Marie Bunel, 19 Sep 1804, folder 6, BHSP. Joseph Bunel seems to have fallen out of favor with Christophe in 1812, but tellingly this disgrace does not seem to have touched Marie Bunel: Clammer, *Black Crown*, 204–205.

## CHAPTER 14: A CULTURAL TRANSFORMATION

1. A. W. Thayer and Elliot Forbes, *Thayer's Life of Beethoven* (Princeton, 1967), 348–349, 330; Scott Burnham, *Beethoven Hero* (Princeton, 1995), xvi–xix, 143–145.

2. The entire section I discuss here begins at the end of the section marked *Maggiore*, about measure 69, and ends about measure 153.

3. Wilhelm Furtwängler, *Concerning Music* (Boosey & Hawkes, 1953), 31; Harvey Sachs, *The Ninth: Beethoven and the World in 1824* (Random House, 2010), 124; Charles Rosen, *The Romantic Generation* (Harvard, 1995), 77–87; see also the idea of "collective coming together": Reinhold Brinkmann, "In the Time of the Eroica," in *Beethoven and His World*, eds. Scott Burnham and Michael P. Steinberg (Princeton, 2000), 21.

4. Thayer and Forbes, *Life of Beethoven*, 134, 154–159, 324–339.

5. Colin Jones, *Paris: Biography of a City* (Allen Lane, 2004), 324; Roy Porter, *London, A Social History* (Harvard, 1995), 131–132; Nicholas Daly, *The Demographic Imagination and the Nineteenth-Century City: Paris, London, New York* (Cambridge, 2015), 2–4.

6. Jones, *Paris*, 334–338; Allan Potofsky, *Constructing Paris in the Age of Revolution* (Palgrave Macmillan, 2009), 34–40, 256–259.

7. Christine Stansell, *City of Women: Sex and Class in New York, 1789-1860* (Knopf, 1986), 41–42; Papayanis, *Planning Paris*, 66; Gareth Stedman Jones, *Outcast London: A Study in the Relationship Between Classes in Victorian Society* (Clarendon, 1971), 159–164.

8. Joseph Guinness Broodbank, *History of the Port of London* (D. O'Connor, 1921), 80–83, 88–91; Stedman Jones, *Outcast London*, 164, 170–179.

9. James Fenimore Cooper, *Afloat and Ashore: A Sea Tale* (J. G. Gregory, 1864), 148; Charles Dickens, *American Notes*, quoted in Anbinder, *Five Points*, 33.

10. Richard D. E. Burton, *The Flaneur and His City: Patterns of Daily Life in Paris, 1815-1851* (University of Durham, 1994), 25–28; Stuart M. Blumin, *The Emergence of the Middle Class: Social Experience in the American City, 1760–1900* (Cambridge, 1989), 145–146.

11. Seth Koven, *Slumming: Sexual and Social Politics in Victorian London* (Princeton, 2004), 5; T. A. Critchley and P. D. James, *The Maul and the Pear Tree: The Radcliffe Highway Murders, 1811* (Mysterious Press, 1986).

12. Thomas De Quincey, "On Murder Considered as One of the Fine Arts," in *Miscellaneous Essays* (Boston: Ticknor, Reed, and Fields, 1851), 19, 25–26, 53–54.

13. See Richard Sennett, *Flesh and Stone: The Body and the City in Western Civilization* (Norton, 1994), 260–270, 322.

14. Émile Zola, *Le Ventre de Paris* (Paris, 1873); Papayanis, *Planning Paris*, ch. 2.

15. Burton, *Flaneur and His City*; Maria Isabel Vila-Cabanes, *The Flaneur in Nineteenth-Century British Literary Culture* (Cambridge Scholars Publishing, 2018), 21–22; Elizabeth Wilson, *The Contradictions of Culture: Cities, Culture, Women* (Sage, 2001), 75–76.

16. Vincent Milliot, *Les "Cris de Paris," ou, Le peuple travesti: Les représentations des petits métiers parisiens (XVIe-XVIIIe siècles)* (Publications de la Sorbonne, 1995); Louis-Sébastien Mercier, *Tableau de Paris* (Amsterdam, 1782); John Brewer, *The Pleasures of the Imagination: English Culture in the Eighteenth Century* (HarperCollins, 1997), 31–55.

17. Marie-Louise Pailleron, "Les aventures de M. de Jouy de l'Académie française," *La Revue hebdomadaire* 28, no. 2 (1919): 442–447; Etienne de Jouy, *L'Hermite de la Chaussée-d'Antin, ou Observations sur les moeurs et les usages Parisiens au commencement du XIXe siècle*, 5 vols. (Paris: Pillet, 1813), 1:4, 6.

18. Jouy, *Hermite*, 1:7–9.

19. Lawrence M. Bryant, *The King and the City in the Parisian Royal Entry Ceremony: Politics, Ritual, and Art in the Renaissance* (Droz, 1986), ch. 3, esp. 67; George Rudé, *The Crowd in History: A Study of Popular Disturbances in France and England, 1730–1848* (Wiley, 1964); Ozouf, *La fête*, 60–62; Newman, *Parades*.

20. Moritz Gleich, "Liquid Crowds: Regulatory Discourse and the Architecture of People Flows in the Nineteenth Century," *Grey Room*, no. 67 (2017): 49–51; Mary P. Ryan, *Civic Wars: Democracy and Public Life in the American City During the Nineteenth Century* (California, 1997), esp. 55–57; Sergio Luzzatto, *Mémoire de la Terreur: Vieux montagnards et jeunes républicains au XIXe siècle* (Presses universitaires de Lyon, 1991), 158–174.

21. E. P. Thompson, "The Moral Economy of the English Crowd in the Eighteenth Century," *Past and Present* 50 (1971); George Rudé, *Paris and London in the Eighteenth Century: Studies in Popular Protest* (Viking, 1971), 21 (crowds included members of different groups from the lower orders); Israel, *Dutch Republic*, 1067–1070; Olwen H. Hufton, *Women and the Limits of Citizenship in the French Revolution* (Toronto, 1992), 7–18.

22. Richard D. Altick, *The Shows of London* (Belknap, 1978), 235–248; Burton, *Flaneur*, 33–35.

23. Jouy, *Hermite*, 2:234; Frederic William John Hemmings, *The Theatre Industry in Nineteenth-Century France* (Cambridge, 1993), 122–128.

24. Vanessa R. Schwartz, *Spectacular Realities: Early Mass Culture in Fin-de-Siècle Paris* (California, 1998), 19.

25. Jouy, *Hermite*, 4:247; Burton, *Flaneur*, 7–9; David Kuchta, *The Three-Piece Suit and Modern Masculinity: England, 1550–1850* (California, 2002), 162–164; Michael Zakim, *Ready-Made Democracy: A History of Men's Dress in the American Republic, 1760–1860* (Chicago, 2003), 41–46; Anne Hollander, *Sex and Suits: The Evolution of Modern Dress* (Bloomsbury, 2016), 65–74. This process may have already begun on the Paris boulevards in the late eighteenth century, but it remained very "limited" before the nineteenth century: see William H. Sewell Jr., *Capitalism and the Emergence of Civic Equality in Eighteenth-Century France* (Chicago, 2021), 137–147.

26. Jouy, *Hermite*, 4:282.

27. *Pirkei toldot* in Menachem Mendel of Rimanov, *Sefer menahem tziyon ha-mevoar* (Mechon or la-yesharim, 2020), 4; David Sorkin, *The Transformation of German Jewry, 1780–1840* (Oxford, 1987), ch. 1.

28. Menachem Mendel of Rimanov, *Sefer menahem tziyon*, 110.

29. Menachem Mendel of Rimanov, *Igeret kodesh* to Haim of Sanz [?], parshat Tetzaveh 5572 [Feb 1812], in *Sefer divrei menachem*, ed. Avraham Yitzchak Goldberger (Hanoe Ve-hanetzach Printing, 2008), 17–18.

30. Thomas W. Laqueur, *The Work of the Dead: A Cultural History of Mortal Remains* (Princeton, 2015), 215–238.

31. Anne L. Poulet, *Jean-Antoine Houdon: Sculptor of the Enlightenment* (National Gallery of Art, 2003), 127–128; Brongniart to Brongniart père, 7 May 1793, Fonds Alexandre Brongniart, AP suppl. 668 AP, ANP (thanks to Dena Goodman for sharing this source); [Bosc,] "Journal," f. 48, MS 1007, Papiers Bosc, BHVP; Laqueur, *Work of the Dead*, 260–261; "Ordonnance concernant les décès et Sépultures," 14 messidor 12 [3 Jul 1804], item 2649, VD4: Pieces imprimées et documents officielles, an VII–1859, Archives de Paris, Paris.

32. Laqueur, *Work of the Dead*, 261–262; Roger père et fils, *Le Champ du repos, ou, le Cimitière Mont-Louis, dit du Père delachaise, ouvrage orné de planches* (Paris: Lebègue, 1816).

33. Laqueur, *Work of the Dead*, 303–304, 306–307; Jouy, *Hermite*, 1:163–164.

34. Réglement général, Cimetières de la Ville de Paris, Préfecture de la Seine, 10 Apr 1827, item 2885, and Arrêt du Préfet de la Seine, 15 ventôse 13 [6 Mar 1802], item 2876, both in VD4, Archives de Paris, Paris.

35. Antoine Caillot, *Voyage pittoresque et sentimental au champ du repos sous Montmartre, et à la maison de campagne du Père Lachaise, à Montlouis* (Paris: Hénée, 1808).

36. Clémence Robert, *Les Amants du Père-Lachaise* (Paris: C. Vanier, 1869), 26; Daly, *Demographic Imagination*, 47–48.

37. Emmanuel Fureix, "Un rituel d'opposition sous la Restauration: Les funérailles libérales à Paris (1820–1830)," *Genèses* 46, no. 1 (2002): 78–83; Order of Préfet, 8 Jun 1820, Documents divers relatifs aux . . . cimetières, Ms NA 479, f.395, BHVP.

38. Laqueur, *Work of the Dead*, 265.

## CHAPTER 15: THE WORLDS NAPOLEON MADE

1. For a similar approach to the "inter-leaving" of empire and revolution, see Jeremy Adelman, "An Age of Imperial Revolutions," *AHR* 113, no. 2 (April 2008), esp. 319, 337.

2. Christine Desan, *The Family on Trial in Revolutionary France* (California, 2004), 284–305, esp. 285, 297, 304; Thierry Lentz and Pierre Branda, *Napoléon, l'esclavage et les colonies* (Fayard, 2006), 103–131; Blaufarb, *The Great Demarcation*, 196–200.

3. Edelstein, *French Revolution and the Birth*, 329–330; Josiane Bourguet-Rouveyre, "La survivance d'un système électoral sous le Consulat et l'Empire," *AHRF* 346 (October–December 2006): 17–29, insists on the real and practical existence of the electoral system; (on falsification) Claude Langlois, "Le plébiscite de l'an VIII, ou le coup d'État du 18 pluviôse an VIII," part 1, *AHRF* 207 (January–March 1972): 43–48.

4. William Beik, *Absolutism and Society in Seventeenth-Century France: State Power and Provincial Aristocracy in Languedoc* (Cambridge, 1985), 14, 304–316; David A. Bell, *The Cult of the Nation in France: Inventing Nationalism, 1680–1800* (Harvard, 2001), esp. 199–201, on the ideological dimension; Michel Biard, *Missionnaires de la République. Les Représentants du peuple en mission (1793–1795)* (Éditions du CTHS, 2002), esp. 234–248; Aulard, *Histoire politique*, 605–608.

5. Fitzsimmons, *Night the Old Regime Ended*, 17–23, 195–204, 216–217; Crook, *Elections*, 84–88, 98–101, emphasizes how little the franchise expanded in 1792; on the formation of *départements*, see Ted Margadant, *Urban Rivalries in the French Revolution* (Princeton, 1992), 84–110, esp. 102–106.

6. Jean Tulard and Marie-José Tulard, *Napoléon et 40 millions de sujets* (Tallandier, 2014), 97–105; Edward A. Whitcomb, "Napoleon's Prefects," *AHR* 79, no. 4 (1974): 1100.

7. Whitcomb, "Napoleon's Prefects," 1091–1093, 1095–1098; Serna, *République des girouettes*, 477–503.

8. Tulard, *Napoléon*, 103–106; Michael Broers, *The Napoleonic Empire in Italy, 1796–1814: Cultural Imperialism in a European Context?* (Palgrave Macmillan, 2005), 118–122, 207–212.

9. Woloch, *New Regime*, 164–169; C. C. Gillispie, *Science and Polity in France: The Revolutionary and Napoleonic Years* (Princeton, 2004), 521–529.

10. Tamar Herzog, *A Short History of European Law: The Last Two and a Half Millennia* (Harvard, 2018), ch. 12; Woloch, *New Regime*, 339–344; Edelstein, *French Revolution and the Birth*, 328–331; François-René de Chateaubriand, *Mémoires d'outre-tombe* (Paris: Penaud frères, 1849–1850), 7:115.

11. Aulard, *Histoire politique*, 735–738; Burdette C. Poland, *French Protestantism and the French Revolution: A Study in Church and State, Thought and Religion, 1618–1815* (Princeton, 1957), 264–267; Simon Schwarzfuchs, *Napoleon, the Jews, and the Sanhedrin* (Routledge, 1979), 41–43; Jay R. Berkovitz, *Rites and Passages: The Beginnings of Modern Jewish Culture in France, 1650–1860* (Penn, 2004), 138–139.

12. Forrest, *Conscripts and Deserters*, esp. 35–39, 188–197, 208–213, 219; Jean-Paul Bertaud, *La révolution armée: Les soldats-citoyens et la Révolution française* (Laffont, 1979); Harold D. Blanton, "Conscription in France During the Era of Napoleon," in *Conscription in the Napoleonic Era: A Revolution in Military Affairs?*, eds. Donald Stoker, Frederick C. Schneid, and Harold D. Blanton (Routledge, 2008), 6–23, esp. 9–12.

13. Woloch, *New Regime*, 381–407, 418–421; Bell, *First Total War*, 244–247.

14. Owen Connelly, *The Wars of the French Revolution and Napoleon, 1792–1815* (Routledge, 2006), 143–168; Alexander I. Grab, *Napoleon and the Transformation of Europe* (Palgrave Macmillan, 2003), 9–18.

15. This and next paragraph: R. F. Delderfield, *Napoleon's Marshals* (Methuen, 1909), xviii; Broers, *Napoleonic Empire in Italy*, 118–121, 256–268; Michael Broers, *Napoleonic Imperialism and the Savoyard Monarchy, 1773–1821* (Edwin Mellen Press, 1997), 283–311; Grab, *Napoleon and the Transformation*, esp. 26–29, 99–103; Alexander Grab, "State, Society and Tax Policy in Napoleonic Europe," in *Napoleon and Europe*, ed. Philip G. Dwyer (Routledge, 2014), 177–186.

16. Dynner, *Men of Silk*, 21; Hundert, *Jews in Poland-Lithuania in the Eighteenth Century.*

17. Biale et al., *Hasidism*, 38–39; Immanuel Etkes, *The Besht: Magician, Mystic, and Leader* (Brandeis, 2004), 115–116, 129–131.

18. Rapoport-Albert, "God and the Zaddik," in *Essential Papers*, 318, 315; Yaakov Yosef ha-Kohen, *Sefer toldot yaakov yosef* (Or ha-hayyim, 2007–2008), 1:358.

19. Biale et al., *Hasidism*, 245–249; Simon Dubnov, *Toldot ha-hasidut* (Dvir, 1930–1932), 1: 114–125; Hundert, *Jews in Poland-Lithuania*, 195–202.

20. Biale et al., *Hasidism*, 259; Marcin Wodziński and Waldemar Spallek, *Historical Atlas of Hasidism* (Princeton, 2018), 39–40; Shneur Zalman of Liadi, *Sefer likkutei amarim tanya* (Peer mikdoshim, 2013–2014), 2; Dynner, *Men of Silk*, 251; Kalonymus Kalman Epstein, *Sefer maor va-shemesh* (Or ha-hayyim, 2015–2016), 29.

21. David Assaf, *The Regal Way: The Life and Times of Rabbi Israel of Ruzhin* (Stanford, 2002), ch. 13; Biale et al., *Hasidism*, 230–232; Epstein, *Sefer maor va-shemesh*, 39.

22. Dynner, *Men of Silk*, 34.

23. See Assaf, *Regal Way*; Immanuel Etkes, *Rabbi Shneur Zalman of Liady: The Origins of Chabad Hasidism* (Brandeis, 2015), 41–49, 54–63; Biale et al., *Hasidism*, 304–307, 127.

24. Rapaport-Albert, "God and the Zaddik," in *Essential Papers*, 321.

25. See Dubnov, *Toldot ha-hasidut*, 2:319, for the opposite view of the Rimanov rebbe.

26. Menachem Mendel of Rimanov, *Sefer menahem tziyon ha-mevoar*, 74.

27. Ibid., 95, 72.

28. Ibid., 104–105; Exodus 16:15.

29. Naftali Loewenthal, *Communicating the Infinite: The Emergence of the Habad School* (Chicago, 1990), 43–51; Simcha Bunim's attention to the "horizontal" influences among his hasidim dovetails with an unusually critical view of the tzaddik. "He always hates himself," he wrote in one discourse, "and finds fault with himself." He criticized the founding fathers of Judaism, including Jacob, Moses, and Joseph: see Simcha Bunim of Peschicha, *Sefer kol simcha* (Nofet tzufim, 1996–1997), 34, 39–40, 56; Zvi Meir Rabinowitz, *Rabi simha bunam mi-peshishah: hayav ve-torato* (Tevunah, 1944), 77–78.

30. [Dovber Shneuri, Letter 8], Tishri 5574 [Sep-Oct 1813], *Igrot kodesh* (Kehot, 1987), 237–238; Etkes, *Rabbi Shneur Zalman*, 264–266; stories in Barukh Mevorakh, *Napoleon u-tekufato: Reshumot ve-eduyot ivriyot shel bene ha-dor* (Mosad Byalik, 1968), 184–185, and David Assaf, "When the Rabbis 'Met' Napoleon," *Tradition* 54, no. 2 (Spring 2022): 59–63.

31. Bell, *First Total War*, 256–262; Connelly, *Wars of the French Revolution*, 199–217.

32. Michael Broers, *Europe Under Napoleon 1799–1815* (Arnold, 1996), 248; Connolly, *Wars of the French Revolution*, 226–229.

33. Adam Zamoyski, *Rites of Peace: The Fall of Napoleon and the Congress of Vienna* (HarperCollins, 2007), 186–203; Munro Price, *Napoleon: The End of Glory* (Oxford, 2014).

34. Malcolm Crook, "'Ma volonté est celle du peuple': Voting in the Plebiscite and Parliamentary Elections During Napoléon's Hundred Days, April–May 1815," *FHS* 32, no. 4 (2009): 628–629.

35. Broers, *Europe Under Napoleon*, 202–203; Schama, *Patriots and Liberators*, ch. 13.

36. On the complex structure of the Dutch Republic's government, see supra, 128–130.

37. Jeroen Koch, *Koning Willem I: 1772–1843* (Boom, 2013), 44–47, 88–133; Knoops and Meijer, *Goejanverwellesluis*; Palmer, *Age*, 2:178–188.

38. Koch, *Willem I*, 46–47.

39. See Israel, *Dutch Republic*, 276–280; Harold Nicolson, *The Congress of Vienna: A Study in Allied Unity, 1812–1822* (Harcourt, 1946), 100.

40. Nicolson, *Congress of Vienna*, 206–207; P. J. Blok, *Geschiedenis van het Nederlandsche volk*, 3rd ed. (1892; A. W. Sijthoff, 1923–1926), 4:200–206; Henri Pirenne, *Histoire de Belgique* (Lamertin, 1900–1926), 6:76–80.

41. Blok, *Geschiedenis*, 4:163–164, 235–237, 265.

42. Koch, *Willem I*, 334–336.

43. Ibid., 288–289.

44. Ibid., 289–294, 302–303.

45. Ibid., 334–335, 372.

46. Ibid., 373–377.

47. Joris Oddens, *Op veler verzoek: Inclusieve politiek in Nederland (1780–1860)* (Boom, 2023), 195–204.

48. Blok, *Geschiedenis*, 4:228–230, 261; De Loen to Van Maanen, 8 May 1822, and Keverberg to Van Maanen, 24 Jul 1816, both in *Gedenkstukken der algemeene geschiedenis van Nederland van 1795 tot 1840*, ed. H. T. Colenbrander, 10 vols. (Nijhoff, 1905), 8(2): 575, 371.

49. Blok, *Geschiedenis*, 4:231, 254, 259; Stefaan Martel, *The Intellectual Origins of the Belgian Revolution* (Palgrave, 2018), 67–81, 191–220.

50. Velema, *Republicans*, 210–213, sees Dutch republicanism as "exhausted"; see also Remieg Aerts, "The Demise of Dutch Republicanism in the Nineteenth Century," in *Discourses of Decline: Essays on Republicanism in Honor of Wyger R.E. Velema*, eds. Joris Oddens, Mart Rutjes, and Arthur Weststeijn (Brill, 2022), 139–143. A. de Hodancourt to King William, 13 Jan 1816, in *Gedenkstukken*, 8(2):17.

51. *Sefer eser orot* (1907), 74, quoted in Zvi Meir Rabinovitz, *Ha-maggid mi-koznitz: hayyav ve-torotav* (Tevuna, 1946–1947), 100.

## CHAPTER 16: THE JOURNEYS OF LOUIS-AUGUSTIN BOSC

1. See Luzzatto, *Mémoire de la Terreur*, 101–112.

2. Da Sylva, *De Rousseau à Hugo*, 53–54; letters of 2 vendémiaire 4 [24 Sep 1795] and 19 vendémiaire 4 [11 Oct 1795] to L. A. G. Bosc, both in MS 1008: Papiers personnels, Papiers Bosc, BHVP; Bosc to Henri-Albert Gosse in Eudora Roland to Henri-Albert Gosse, 18 pluviôse 3 [6 Feb 1795], Ms. Fr. 2637, Papiers Gosse, BDG.

3. This and next paragraph: Perroud, ed., *Lettres de madame Roland*, 2:683–685; [Bosc,] "Notes sur ma vie"; François de Neufchâteau to Bosc, 15 frimaire 7 [5 Dec 1798], and Charles Delacroix to Bosc, 13 prairial 5 [1 Jun 1797], both in MS 1008, Papiers Bosc, BHVP.

4. On this controversy, see DeConde, *The Quasi-War.* Probably Wilmington, North Carolina, though Bosc's official commission and other documents are not clear on the exact location.

5. See Phillip R. Sloan, "The Buffon-Linnaeus Controversy," *Isis* 67, no. 3 (1976); Lisbet Koerner, *Linnaeus: Nature and Nation* (Harvard, 1999), 28–29.

6. Frans Antonie Stafleu, *Linnaeus and the Linnaeans: The Spreading of Their Ideas in Systematic Botany, 1735–1789* (Oosthoek, 1971), 289; Jean-Luc Chappey, *Des naturalistes en Révolution: Les procès-verbaux de la Société d'histoire naturelle de Paris (1790–1798)* (CTHS, 2009), 39–40; Gillispie, *Science and Polity*, 167–171.

7. For a slightly overstated version of this argument, see Stafleu, *Linnaeus*, 303.

8. "Agrostographie carolinienne," Ms 875, and Louis-Guillaume Bosc to Alexandre Brongniart, Charleston, 7 fructidor 5 [24 Aug 1797], Ms 2354, both in MNHN; Victoria Johnson, *American Eden: David Hosack, Botany, and Medicine in the Garden of the Early Republic* (Liveright, 2018), 130–131; Albert E. Sanders and William D. Anderson, *Natural History Investigations in South Carolina: From Colonial Times to the Present* (South Carolina, 1999), 31–32.

9. Marcel Dorigny and Bernard Gainot, *La société des amis des noirs 1788–1799: Contribution a l'histoire de l'abolition de l'esclavage* (Editions UNESCO, 1998), 32–39; [Bosc,] "Journal," ff. 73 and 89, MS 1007, Papiers Bosc, BHVP.

10. "Notice biographique sur . . . Bosc . . . , lue à . . . la société [royale et centrale d'Agriculture], le 28 avril 1829, par . . . Silvestre," 12–13, in MS 1008, Papiers Bosc, BHVP.

11. Howard G. Brown, *Ending the French Revolution: Violence, Justice, and Repression from the Terror to Napoleon* (Virginia, 2006), 23–46; Lynn Hunt, David Lansky, and Paul Hanson, "The Failure of the Liberal Republic in France, 1795–1799: The Road to Brumaire," *JMH* 51, no. 4 (1979): 741–743; Woloch,

*Jacobin Legacy*, 347–359; Albert Meynier, *Les coups d'État du Directoire* (PUF, 1927) 2: 223-230.

12. "Notes sur des époques intéressantes," in MS 1008, Papiers Bosc, BHVP and "Notes sur ma vie," f. 47, MS 1007, Papiers Bosc, BHVP.

13. "Notice biographique sur . . . Bosc" and "Académie . . . des Sciences . . . Discours de M. Duméril . . . prononcé aux funérailles de M. Bosc, 1828," in MS 1008, Papiers Bosc, BHVP.

14. See Gillispie, *Science and Polity*, 610–611.

15. "Notice biographique sur . . . Bosc" and "Notes sur des époques intéressantes," in MS 1008, Papiers Bosc, BHVP.

16. Bosc, "Notes sur ma vie," f. 51, 54. His interests before this time had often focused on fauna: Lafarge to Bosc, 2 complémentaire 10 [19 Sep 1802], MS 1009, BHVP (collections of insects); Bosc to Alexandre Brongniart, 7 fructidor 5 [24 Aug 1797], Ms 2354, MNHN (sending birds and amphibians); "Araignées de la forêt de Montmorency," MS 872, MNHN (spiders).

17. Bosc, "Notes sur ma vie," f. 53, 54.

18. Richard W. Burkhardt Jr., *The Spirit of System: Lamarck and Evolutionary Biology* (Harvard, 1977), 143–185, esp. 181–185.

19. See Da Sylva, *De Rousseau à Hugo*, 30; Cuvier's eulogy for Bosc in MS 1007, Papiers Bosc, BHVP; Dorinda Outram, *Georges Cuvier: Vocation, Science, and Authority in Post-Revolutionary France* (Manchester University Press, 1984), 172.

20. See Appointment as Inspecteur des pépinières, effective 1 Jan 1815, MS 1008, Papiers Bosc, BHVP; Bosc to Picot de la Peyrouse, 6 Apr 1816, Ms 1990, MNHN.

21. Darcy Grimaldo Grigsby, *Extremities: Painting Empire in Post-Revolutionary France* (Yale, 2002), 169–176; Jenna Nigro, "Settler Colonialism in West Africa?: The Colonial Philanthropic Society in Senegambia, 1814–1818," *Journal of the Western Society for French History* 45 (2017); L. A. G. Bosc et al., *Mémoire au Conseil d'État pour la Société coloniale philanthropique de la Sénégambie* (1817), 1–3, 13, 16–17, 63; "Notice biographique sur . . . Bosc," 18 in MS 1008, Papiers Bosc, BHVP.

22. Bosc et al., *Mémoire*, 12, 33.

23. Ibid., 20, 29–31.

24. Ibid., 32.

25. Nigro, "Settler Colonialism," 74–75; Jonathan Miles, *The Wreck of the Medusa: The Most Famous Sea Disaster of the Nineteenth Century* (Grove Press, 2007), esp. 74–111.

26. "Notice biographique sur . . . Bosc," 18–20; Bosc, "Notes sur ma vie," 56–57.

27. "Académie des Sciences . . . Discours de M. Duméril . . . prononcé aux funérailles de M. Bosc, 1828," in MS 1008, Papiers Bosc, BHVP.

28. Outram, *Georges Cuvier*, 171–172.

29. On the ideal of science as sociable and embedded in family life in eighteenth-century France, see the excellent Meghan K. Roberts, *Sentimental Savants: Philosophical Families in Enlightenment France* (Chicago, 2016), 4–6, 31–39; Outram, *Georges Cuvier*, 171–176.

30. See notes on Bosc family by Mlle Soubeiran, ca. early twentieth century, in MS 1008, Papiers Bosc, BHVP.

31. Jean-Baptiste Van Mons, "Essai pomologique," *Annales generales de sciences physiques* (Brussels: Weissenbruch, 1819), 2:65–67; André Leroy, *Dictionnaire de pomologie: Contenant l'histoire, la description, la figure des fruits anciens et des fruits modernes le plus généralement connus et cultivés* (Angers and Paris: Chez l'auteur et al., 1867–1879), 1:320–322.

32. "Détails de l'ouverture du corps de M. Bosc," MS 1008, Papiers Bosc, BHVP.

## CHAPTER 17: THE REVOLUTIONS CURTAILED

1. Noble E. Cunningham, *The Jeffersonian Republicans in Power: Party Operations, 1801–1809* (OIEAHC, 1963), 128–140, 150–155; "sophisticated": Wilentz, *Rise*, 121.

2. Wilentz, *Rise*, 117–125. Van Gosse, *The First Reconstruction: Black Politics in America from the Revolution to the Civil War* (UNC, 2021), esp. 14–19, shows that there was a Black electorate in northern states during the antebellum period; its numbers, however, were small as a share of the Republican coalition.

3. David Waldstreicher, "Federalism, the Styles of Politics, and the Politics of Style" and Andrew Siegel, "'Steady Habits' Under Siege: The Defense of Federalism in Jeffersonian Connecticut," in *Federalism Reconsidered*, eds. Doron Ben-Atar and Barbara B. Oberg (Virginia, 1998), 113, 214–216.

4. Francis D. Cogliano, *Emperor of Liberty: Thomas Jefferson's Foreign Policy* (Yale, 2014), 236–242; Wilentz, *Rise*, 131–133.

5. For surveys, see Daniel Walker Howe, *What Hath God Wrought: The Transformation of America, 1815–1848* (Oxford, 2007); Wilentz, *Rise*; Taylor, *American Republics*.

6. Sarah L. H. Gronningsater, "James Tallmadge Jr. and the Personal Politics of Antislavery," in *A Fire Bell in the Past: The Missouri Crisis at 200*, vol. 1: *Western Slavery, National Impasse*, eds. Jeffrey L. Pasley and John Craig Hammond (Missouri, 2021), 253–284, esp. 257–262.

7. William Pinkney, *Speech of William Pinkney, Esq. in the House of Delegates of Maryland, at Their Session in November, 1789* (Philadelphia: Cruikshank, 1790), 15, 17, quoted in Glover Moore, *The Missouri Controversy, 1819–1821* (Kentucky, 1953), 99; Robert Elder, *Calhoun: American Heretic* (Basic, 2021), 29; Wilentz, *Rise*, 145–146.

8. John R. Van Atta, *Wolf by the Ears: The Missouri Crisis, 1819–1821* (JHU, 2015), 53–54; Wilentz, *Rise*, 219–227.

9. Clay, "Speech on the Admission of Maine," 30 Dec 1819, in *The Papers of Henry Clay: The Rising Statesman, 1815–1820*, eds. James F. Hopkins and Mary W. M. Hargreaves (Kentucky, 1961–2014), 2:741.

10. Moore, *Missouri Controversy*, 66–83.

11. Rufus King to C. Gore, 17 Feb 1820, in *The Life and Correspondence of Rufus King*, ed. Charles R. King (Putnam, 1894–1900), 6:277; Sinha, *Slave's Cause*, 94–96; *New York Daily Advertiser*, 19–20 Feb 1820, quoted in Van Atta, *Wolf by the Ears*, 77.

12. Adams, *Memoirs of John Quincy Adams*, 5:10; Henry Clay, "Speech on the Missouri Bill," 8 Feb 1820, in *Papers of Henry Clay*, 2:777.

13. Speech of John Taylor, 27 Jan 1820, *Annals of Congress*, House of Representatives, 16th Cong., 1st Sess., 966; Abner Lacock to James Monroe, 30 Jan 1820, James Monroe Papers, LOC; Moore, *Missouri Controversy*, 94; Henry Clay to Adam Beatty, 22 Jan 1820, in *Papers of Henry Clay*, 2:766, also quoted in Robert V. Remini, *Henry Clay: Statesman for the Union* (Norton, 1991), 181.

14. Moore, *Missouri Controversy*, 93; James Barbour to James Madison, 10 Feb 1820, in *The Papers of James Madison: Retirement Series*, eds. David B. Mattern et al. (Virginia, 2009–), 2:8, also discussed in Van Atta, *Wolf by the Ears*, 97; see also James Monroe to James Madison, 19 Feb 1820, in *Papers of James Madison: Retirement*, 2:14–15.

15. Wilentz, *Rise*, 166–168, 374–389.

16. Donald Ratcliffe, "The Surprising Politics of the Missouri Compromise: Antislavery Doughfaces, Maine, and the Myth of Sectional Balance," in *Fire Bell in the Past*, 229, 243.

17. Wilentz, *Rise*, 233–236.

18. Speech of Charles Kinsey, Mar 1820, *Annals of Congress*, House of Representatives, 16th Cong., 1st Sess., 1578, 1582–83; Speech of John Holmes (Mass.), 27 Jan 1820, *Annals of Congress*, House of Representatives, 16th Cong., 1st Sess., 989.

19. Adams, *Memoirs of John Quincy Adams*, 5:11; David Waldstreicher, "John Quincy Adams, the Missouri Crisis, and the Long Politics of Slavery," in *Fire Bell in the Past*, 356–359.

20. Wilentz, *Rise*, 240, who follows Moore, *Missouri Controversy*, 111.

21. Leconte, *Henri Christophe*, 202–209.

22. *Procès Verbal des Séances du Conseil Général de la Nation* (Cap-Henry: Roux, 1814), 19; F. Darfour, *L'Avertisseur Haytien, journal politique, commercial et littéraire*, no. 13 (1818) and no. 18 (1819).

23. Leconte, *Henri Christophe*, 198, 221–235; Clammer, *Black Crown*, 200–208.

24. Christophe, Proclamation of 1 Jan 1819, in Madiou, *Histoire d'Haiti*, 6:38; Leconte, *Henri Christophe*, 377–379; Péan, *Aux origines*, 122.

25. W. W. Harvey, *Sketches of Hayti; from the Expulsion of the French, to the Death of Christophe* (London: Seeley and Son, 1827), 171–178; Code Henry, Loi Militaire, Articles 1 and 5.

26. See *Procès Verbal des Séances du Conseil Général de la Nation*, 19; Lebrun et al. to Boyer, 19 Oct 1820, in Madiou, *Histoire d'Haiti*, 6:137; Leconte, *Henri Christophe*, 300.

27. Code Henry, Loi Militaire, Articles 271 and 296.

28. Doris L. Garraway, "Empire of Freedom, Kingdom of Civilization: Henry Christophe, the Baron de Vastey, and the Paradoxes of Universalism in Postrevolutionary Haiti," *Small Axe* 16, no. 339 (2012): 8, characterizes both Christophe's State and Pétion's Republic as "authoritarian" revolutionary governments. See also Chelsea Stieber, *Haiti's Paper War: Post-Independence Writing, Civil War, and the Making of the Republic, 1804–1954* (NYU, 2020), 68; Gonzalez, *Maroon Nation*, 106–108, 121–123; Hazareesingh, *Black Spartacus*, 276–279; and Harvey, *Sketches of Hayti*, 266–267.

29. Stieber, *Haiti's Paper War*, 65–69, 93, 102–106; Leconte, *Henri Christophe*, 326–327.

30. Leconte, *Henri Christophe*, 422–425; Madiou, *Histoire d'Haiti*, 6:129–143.

31. Gonzalez, *Maroon Nation*, 84–86.

32. See Péan, *Aux origines*, 108, 149–151.

33. This and next paragraph: Alex Dupuy, *Rethinking the Haitian Revolution: Slavery, Independence, and the Struggle for Recognition* (Rowman & Littlefield, 2019), 102; Laurent Dubois, *Haiti: The Aftershocks of History* (Metropolitan, 2012), 93–104, 119–127.

## CHAPTER 18: THE CONSTITUTIONS PROMULGATED

1. Admision a práctica de leyes de Don Gabriel de Ugarte en este real audiencia, 6 Nov 1804, Legajo 164, #49, Asuntos Administrativos, Audiencia, AAC; Durand Flórez, *El proceso de independencia*, 243, 253–254; Jorge Cornejo Bouroncle, *Pumacahua, la revolución del Cuzco de 1814* (Rozas, 1956), 140–142.

2. Manuel Jesús Aparicio Vega, *El clero patriota en 1814* (Cervesur, 2001), 85; Walker, *Smoldering Ashes*, 59–61; Fisher, *Bourbon Peru*, 41–44; John R. Fisher, *Government and Society in Colonial Peru: The Intendant System 1784–1814* (University of London, 1970); Anna, *Fall*, 36–37; Manuel Vidaurre, "Plan del Perú y otros escritos," in Alberto Tauro, ed., *Los ideólogos, CDIP*, 5:22–26.

3. Nicolás Sánchez-Albornoz, "The Population of Colonial Spanish America," in *The Cambridge History of Latin America*, ed. Leslie Bethell (Cambridge, 1984), 34.

4. Ibid., 34–36; Aline Helg, *Liberty and Equality in Caribbean Colombia, 1770–1835* (UNC, 2004), 46–48.

5. Jean René Aymes, ed., *España y la Revolución Francesa* (Editorial Crítica, 1989); Anna, *Fall*, 11–12.

6. On this topic, see esp. Ada Ferrer, *Freedom's Mirror: Cuba and Haiti in the Age of Revolution* (Cambridge, 2014); Ernesto Bassi, *An Aqueous Territory: Sailor Geographies and New Granada's Transimperial Greater Caribbean World* (Duke, 2016), chs. 4–6; Soriano, *Tides of Revolution*, chs. 2–3; Cristina Gómez Álvarez, *La circulación de las ideas. Bibliotecas particulares en una época revolucionaria. Nueva España, 1750–1819* (Trama Editorial, 2019); Claudia Rosas, *Del trono a la guillotina: El impacto de la Revolución Francesa en el Perú* (IFEA, 2006), esp. 53–91.

7. Gabriel di Meglio, *¡Viva el bajo pueblo!: La plebe urbana de Buenos Aires y la política entre la revolución de Mayo y el rosismo (1810–1829)* (Prometeo, 2006), 72–83.

8. Connelly, *Wars of the French Revolution*, 144–145; and on the Portuguese, Kirsten Schultz, *Tropical Versailles: Empire, Monarchy, and the Portuguese Royal Court in Rio de Janeiro, 1808–1821* (Routledge, 2001).

9. Connelly, *Wars of the French Revolution*, 146; José Maria Portillo Valdés, *Crisis atlántica: Autonomía e independencia en la crisis de la monarquía hispana* (Marcial Pons, 2006), 53–57; Jeremy Adelman, *Sovereignty and Revolution in the Iberian Atlantic* (Princeton, 2006), 2–9.

10. Connelly, *Wars of the French Revolution*, 146–148; José María Portillo Valdés, *Revolución de nación: Orígenes de la cultura constitucional en España, 1780–1812* (Centro de Estudios Políticos y Constitucionales, 2000), 183–187; Adelman, *Sovereignty and Revolution*, 179; Timothy Anna, *Spain and the Loss of America* (Nebraska, 1983), esp. ch. 2.

11. McFarlane, *War and Independence*, 44–50.

12. Anna, *Spain and the Loss of America*, 59–75; Portillo Valdés, *Crisis atlántica*, 135–138, 154–156.

13. McFarlane, *War and Independence*, 51–53.

14. Brian R. Hamnett, *The End of Iberian Rule on the American Continent, 1770–1830* (Cambridge, 2017), ch. 6; Joaquín Varela Suanzes-Carpegna, "Las Cortes de Cádiz y la Constitución de 1812," *Corts: Anuario de derecho parlamentario* 26 (2012): 200–201; Anna, *Spain and the Loss of America*, 71–82.

15. John Preston Moore, *The Cabildo in Peru Under the Hapsburgs: A Study in the Origins and Powers of the Town Council in the Viceroyalty of Peru, 1530–1700* (Duke, 1954), 197–222; Anna, *Fall*, 82–83.

16. Tamar Herzog, *Defining Nations: Immigrants and Citizens in Early Modern Spain and Spanish America* (Yale, 2003), 157–158, 162–163.

17. Jairo Gutiérrez Ramos, "La Constitución de Cádiz y la Nueva Granada durante la primera República," *Nuevas Lecturas de Historia* 31 (2022): 157–158.

18. *Constitución política de la Monarquía española* (Cádiz: Imprenta Real, 1812), 53–55; Ulrike Bock, "A Transatlantic Constitution in a Local Context: Symbolic Acts of Mediation and Revolutionary Practice in the Context of the Constitution of 1812 in Yucatán," in *Transatlantic Revolutionary Cultures, 1789–1861*, eds. Charlotte A. Lerg and Heléna Tóth (Brill, 2017), 61–64; Valentín Paniagua Corazao, *Los Orígenes del Gobierno Representativo en el Perú: Las Elecciones (1809–1826)* (Universidad Católica, 2021), 126–139.

19. Patricia Seed, *Ceremonies of Possession in Europe's Conquest of the New World, 1492–1640* (Cambridge, 1995), 69–72; Pablo Ortemberg, *Rituels du pouvoir à Lima: De la Monarchie à la République (1735–1828)* (EHESS, 2012), 52–53, 59–61.

20. Heraclio Bonilla, "La Constitución de 1812 y el Perú del Virrey Abascal," in *La Constitución de 1812 en Hispanoamérica y España*, ed. Heraclio Bonilla (Universidad Nacional de Colombia, 2012), 148; Ortemberg, *Rituels du pouvoir*, 155–156; "La Real Audiencia informa lo conveniente sobre la insurreccion," dated April 1815, in *Conspiraciones y rebeliones en el siglo XIX, CDIP*, ed. Horacio Villanueva Urteaga, 7:166. Date is incorrectly transcribed as 1813.

21. "Notas del ayuntamiento del Cuzco al Virrey de Lima," 26 Feb 1813, and "Memorial de 1812," dated 14 Dec 1815, both in *Conspiraciones y rebeliones, CDIP*, 6:183, 193.

22. Ortemberg, *Rituels du pouvoir*, 71–73; Manuel Pardo, "Memoria exacta e imparcial de la insurreccion que ha experimentado la provincia y capital del Cuzco," in *Conspiraciones y rebeliones, CDIP*, 6:259.

23. Pardo, "Memoria exacta"; Oficio de Pumaccahua al Virrey, 26 Apr 1813, in *Conspiraciones y rebeliones, CDIP*, 6:202–204.

24. Víctor Peralta Ruiz, *La independencia y la cultura política peruana (1808–1821)* (Instituto de Estudios Peruanos, 2010), 243–246. The Río de la Plata, though it did not accept the Constitution, also experienced a flowering of electoral politics: see Marcela Ternavasio, *La revolución del voto: Política y elecciones en Buenos Aires, 1810–1852* (Siglo Veintiuno, 2002), 43–51, and

Geneviève Verdo, *L'indépendance argentine entre cités et nation (1808–1821)* (Editions de la Sorbonne, 2006), 77–80, 225–238.

25. Jaime E. Rodríguez O., *"We Are Now the True Spaniards": Sovereignty, Revolution, Independence, and the Emergence of the Federal Republic of Mexico* (Stanford, 2012), 169–172, 175–177, 180; Virginia Guedea, "The First Popular Elections in Mexico City, 1812–1813," in *The Origins of Mexican National Politics, 1808–1847*, ed. Jaime E. Rodríguez O. (California, 1997), 45–47; Antonio Annino, "Pratiche creole e liberalismo nella crisi dello spazio urbano coloniale. Il 29 novembre 1812 a Città del Messico," *Quaderni storici* 23, no. 69 (3) (Dec 1988): 748–753.

26. Michael L. Conniff, "Guayaquil Through Independence: Urban Development in a Colonial System," *Americas* 33, no. 3 (1977): 406; Jaime E. Rodríguez O., "La antigua provincia de Guayaquil durante la época de la independencia, 1809–1820," in *Revolución, independencia y las nuevas naciones de América*, ed. Jaime E. Rodríguez O. (MAFPRE, 2005), 538–540; Ana Luz Borrero Vega, "El legado de Cádiz: Ciudadanía y cultura política en la Gobernación de Cuenca, 1812–1814," *Procesos: revista ecuatoriana de historia* 39 (January–June 2014): 23.

27. *Constitución política de la Monarquía española*, 39, art. 313, and 4, arts. 18–22; Anna, *Fall*, 83–84, has a good analysis of the complex situation of groups with respect to the vote.

28. Oficio de Pumaccahua al Virrey, 26 Apr 1813; Testimony of Prevendado Dn Francisco Carrascón; Libro de Actas del Cabildo, all in *Conspiraciones y rebeliones, CDIP*, 6:203, 151–152, 28–30.

29. *Conspiraciones y rebeliones, CDIP*, 6:150; see figures for Lima in Anna, *Fall*, 84.

30. Libro de Actas del Cabildo, in *Conspiraciones y rebeliones, CDIP*, 6:39–40, 46–56; Oficio de Pumaccahua al Virrey, 26 Apr 1813, in ibid., 6:203; Manuel Pardo, "Memoria exacta," in ibid., 6:259; "La Real Audiencia informa lo conveniente sobre la insurreccion," in ibid., 7:167.

31. Oficio de Pumaccahua al Virrey, 26 Apr 1813, in *Conspiraciones y rebeliones, CDIP*, 6:202.

32. Broers, *Europe Under Napoleon*, 246–248; Anna, *Fall*, 92, 103–104; Adelman, *Sovereignty and Revolution*, 268–273; Cornejo Bouroncle, *Pumacahua*; Walker, *Smoldering Ashes*, 97–105.

33. Merle E. Simmons, *La revolución norteamericana en la independencia de hispanoamérica* (MAPFRE, 1992), 211–217, 221.

34. Palmer, *Age*, 1:263–282; Simmons, *La revolución*, 138–139, 160–165, 173, 176. For the opposite view, see Jaime E. Rodríguez O., "Sobre la supuesta influencia de la independencia de los Estados Unidos en las independencias hispanoamericanas," *Revista de Indias* 70, no. 250 (2010): 702–704.

35. Jack Fruchtman Jr., *Thomas Paine: Apostle of Freedom* (Four Walls Eight Windows, 1994), esp. 415–431.

36. Pedro Grases and Alberto Harkness, *Manuel García de Sena y la independencia de Hispanoamérica* (Caracas, 1953); Merle E. Simmons, *U.S. Political Ideas in Spanish America Before 1830: A Bibliographic Study* (Indiana, 1977), 2, 38, 47–48; Simmons, *La revolución*, 233–235.

37. Simmons, *U.S. Political Ideas*, 35–36, 47–49; Eric Foner, *Tom Paine and Revolutionary America* (Oxford, 2005), ch. 4; A. O. Aldridge, *Thomas Paine's American Ideology* (Delaware, 1984), 223–253; Thomas Paine to George Washington, 30 Jul 1796, in *Complete Writings of Thomas Paine*, 2:693.

38. Vidaurre, "Plan del Perú y otros escritos," *Los ideólogos, CDIP*, 5:53, 93, 372–373, 389–396, 454.

39. Vidaurre, "Bases de la Constitucion politica de la Republica peruana," 17 Dec 1822, in *Primer Congreso Constituyente, CDIP*, eds. Gustavo Pons Muzzo and Alberto Tauro, 3:126; John Lynch, *The Spanish-American Revolutions, 1808–1826* (Norton, 1973), 245; Edgardo Pérez Morales, *No Limits to Their Sway: Cartagena's Privateers and the Masterless Caribbean in the Age of Revolutions* (Vanderbilt University Press, 2018), 59–61.

## CHAPTER 19: THE NATION UNDER ARMS

1. This summary draws on Elliott, *Empires of the Atlantic*; McFarlane, *War and Independence*; Lynch, *Spanish-American Revolutions.*

2. See Juan Marchena Fernández, *Ejército y milicias en el mundo colonial americano* (MAFPRE, 1992), esp. 204.

3. Alejandro Martin Rabinovich, *La société guerrière: Pratiques, discours et valeurs militaires dans le Rio de la Plata, 1806–1852* (PUR, 2017), 45–69; Clément Thibaud, *Républiques en armes: Les armées de Bolivar dans les guerres d'indépendance du Venezuela et de la Colombie* (PUR, 2006), 335.

4. Juan Luis Ossa Santa Cruz, "The Army of the Andes: Chilean and Rioplatense Politics in an Age of Military Organisation, 1814–1817," *Journal of Latin American Studies* 46, no. 1 (February 2014): 36; Di Meglio, *¡Viva el bajo pueblo!*, 145–150; Thibaud, *Républiques en armes*, 55–64.

5. Marcela Echeverri, *Indian and Slave Royalists in the Age of Revolution: Reform, Revolution, and Royalism in the Northern Andes, 1780–1825* (Cambridge, 2016), 128–132, 159–168.

6. Ben Vinson III, *Bearing Arms for His Majesty: The Free-Colored Militia in Colonial Mexico* (Stanford, 2002); Ben Vinson III and Matthew Restall, "Black Soldiers, Native Soldiers: Meanings of Military Service in the Spanish American Colonies," in *Beyond Black and Red: African-Native Relations in Colonial Latin America*, ed. Matthew Restall (New Mexico, 2005), 15–52;

Allan Kuethe, "The Status of the Free Pardo in the Disciplined Militia of New Granada," *Journal of Negro History* 56, no. 2 (April 1971): 105–117.

7. Thibaud, *Républiques en armes*, 345–347; Peter Blanchard, *Under the Flags of Freedom: Slave Soldiers and the Wars of Independence in Spanish South America* (University of Pittsburgh Press, 2008), 16.

8. On this point, see Thibaud, *Républiques en armes*, 284–285, 336–347. Thibaud is of course not overly rosy about the possibility of socialization in the army.

9. Ibid., 33.

10. Bell, *Men on Horseback*, 8–15.

11. John Lynch, *Simón Bolívar: A Life* (Yale, 2007), 13; Beatriz Bragoni, *San Martín, una biografía política del Libertador* (Edhasa, 2022), ch. 1.

12. Yesenia Barragan, *Freedom's Captives: Slavery and Gradual Emancipation on the Colombian Black Pacific* (Cambridge, 2021), 111–118 (quotation 113); George Reid Andrews, *The Afro-Argentines of Buenos Aires, 1800–1900* (Wisconsin, 1980), 47–49.

13. See the useful table in Barragan, *Freedom's Captives*, 137; Sinha, *Slave's Cause*, 72–85; Davis, *Problem of Slavery*, ch. 6.

14. Paul J. Polgar, *Standard-Bearers of Equality: America's First Abolition Movement* (UNC, 2019), 124; *Gazeta de Colombia*, 9 Sep 1821, quoted in Barragan, *Freedom's Captives*, 146.

15. Lynch, *Spanish-American Revolutions*, 127–142; Gustavo Pons Muzzo, ed., *La expedición libertadora*, *CDIP*, 1:381–411, esp. 409; Anna, *Fall*, 160–191.

16. Christine Hünefeldt, *Paying the Price of Freedom: Family and Labor Among Lima's Slaves, 1800–1854* (California, 1994), 9; Lynch, *Spanish-American Revolutions*, 157–158; Echeverri, *Indian and Slave Royalists*.

17. Decrees of 28 Aug 1821, 4 Aug 1821, and 12 Aug 1821, all in *Obra gubernativa y epistolario de San Martín*, *CDIP*, ed. José A. de la Puente Candamo, 1:350–352, 340.

18. Petitions of 20 Jul 1821 in *Obra gubernativa y epistolario*, *CDIP*, 2:389–390.

19. *Colección de leyes, decretos y ordenes publicadas en el Perú desde su independencia en el año de 1821, hasta 31 de diciembre de 1830*, tomo I (Lima: Imprenta de José Mastas, 1831), 16; Carlos Aguirre, *Agentes de su propia libertad: los esclavos de Lima y la desintegración de la esclavitud: 1821–1854* (Universidad Católica, 1993), 186–189.

20. Aguirre, *Agentes de su propia libertad*.

21. See decrees of 21, 23, and 24 Nov 1821 in *Obra gubernativa y epistolario*, *CDIP*, 1:341–343; and the parallel projects in Christopher L. Brown and Philip Morgan, eds., *Arming Slaves: From Classical Times to the Modern Age* (Yale, 2006), 180–208.

22. Peter Blanchard, *Slavery and Abolition in Early Republican Peru* (SR Books, 1992), 9–15, 189–200, 206–207.

## CONCLUSION

1. Thibaud, "Pour une histoire polycentrique," 151–170.
2. Palmer, *Age*, 2:4, 572–573; Hobsbawm, *Age*, 79–80.
3. See the excellent discussion of class as an analytic lens for revolutionary politics in Michael A. McDonnell, "Class War? Class Struggles During the American Revolution in Virginia," *WMQ* 63, no. 2 (2006): 308–313 and works cited therein.
4. Exemplary work in this vein includes Mathiez, *La révolution française*; Soboul, *Les Sans-culottes parisiens*; Wit, *De nederlandse revolutie van de achttiende eeuw*; Carl L. Becker, *The History of Political Parties in the Province of New York, 1760–1776* (Bulletin of the University of Wisconsin History Series, vol. 2, 1909); Schlesinger, *Colonial Merchants*. A classic critique of this tradition in the French context is François Furet, *Penser la Révolution française* (Gallimard, 1978). Like Oddens, *Op veler verzoek*, 10–11, I am interested in how political mobilizations become "inclusive."
5. Eudora Roland Champagneux to Mme Gosse, 11 pluviôse [8] [31 Jan 1800] and 18 pluviôse 3 [6 Feb 1795], both in Papiers Gosse, BDG; Paul Feuga, *Luc-Antoine Champagneux ou le destin d'un Rolandin fidèle* (Editions Lyonnaises d'Art et d'Histoire, 1991), 51–88, esp. 86–88; Luc-Antoine Champagneux, "Preliminary Discourse," in *The Works (Never Before Published) of Jeanne-Marie Phlipon Roland* (London: J. Johnson, 1800), lvii–lviii.
6. Léon Champagneux to H.-A. Gosse, 16 messidor 6 [4 Jul 1798] and 28 Oct 1797, both in Papiers Gosse, BDG; Feuga, *Champagneux*, 140–141, 144–145.
7. Bosc and Eudora Roland Champagneux to H.-A. Gosse, 18 pluviôse 3 [6 Feb 1795], and Mme Gosse to Eudora Roland Champagneux, Jan 1797, all in Papiers Gosse, BDG; Perroud, ed., *Lettres de Mme Roland*, 2: appendix L; Armand Praviel, *Mademoiselle Roland: Variété inédite* (Fayard, 1932), 362–376.
8. Eudora's mind has been consistently underrated. Bosc himself wrote that "il n'y a pas à esperer qu'elle vaille sa mere, mais elle ne sera cependant pas sans intérêt" : Bosc to H.-A. Gosse in Eudora Roland Champagneux to Gosse, 18 pluviôse 3 [6 Feb 1795], Papiers Gosse, BDG. There is good evidence that Eudora was an active intellectual presence: see, for instance, discussions of assembling a library at the Clos in Léon Champagneux to H.-A. Gosse, 15 frimaire 7 [5 Dec 1798]; Eudora Roland Champagneux to H.-A. Gosse, 16 brumaire [4] [7 Nov 1795]; Eudora Roland Champagneux to Mme Gosse, 14 Aug 1821, all in Papiers Gosse, BDG.

9. Author's visit to Clos de la Platière, 12 Oct 2021; Léon Champagneux to H.-A. Gosse, 6 fructidor 6 [23 Aug 1798], Papiers Gosse, BDG; Perroud, ed., *Lettres de Mme Roland*, 2:706–708.

10. Author's visit to Clos de la Platière, 12 Oct 2021; interviews with François Fierens at Clos de la Platière, 12 Oct 2021, and by phone, 6 Apr 2022; see also Feuga, *Champagneux*, 144. Chaley participated in the repression of the Revolt of the Canuts in Lyon in 1834: "Joseph Chaley," *Revue du Lyonnais*, 23 (1861): 74–75; image similar to *Portrait tissé à l'effigie de Napoléon Bonaparte, en profil de médaille*, lampas, 1802, Musée national des châteaux de Malmaison et Bois-Préau, Rueil-Malmaison, France.

# INDEX

INDEX

# INDEX

# INDEX